INTERVENTIONS FOR CHILDREN OF DIVORCE

Recent titles in the

WILEY SERIES ON PERSONALITY PROCESSES

IRVING B. WEINER, *Editor*
University of South Florida

Interventions for Children of Divorce

Custody, Access, and Psychotherapy

Second Edition

William F. Hodges

A WILEY-INTERSCIENCE PUBLICATION

JOHN WILEY & SONS, INC.

New York • Chichester • Brisbane • Toronto • Singapore

Library of Congress Cataloging-in-Publication Data

Hodges, William F.
    Interventions for children of divorce custody, access, and
psychotherapy / William F. Hodges. — 2nd ed.
        p.   cm.—(Wiley series on personality processes)
    Includes bibliographical references and indexes.
    ISBN 0-471-52255-4
    1. Children of divorced parents—Mental health.   2. Custody of
children.   3. Custody of children—Psychological aspects.   4. Child
psychotherapy.   5. Divorce therapy.   I. Title.   II. Series.
    [DNLM: 1. Child Psychology.   2. Divorce.   3. Parent-Child
Relations.   4. Psychotherapy—in infancy & childhood.   WS 105.5.F2
H689i]
RJ507.D59H63   1991
306.5′9—dc20
DNLM/DLC
for Library of Congress   91-746

Series Preface

This series of books is addressed to behavioral scientists interested in the nature of human personality. Its scope should prove pertinent to personality theorists and researchers as well as to clinicians concerned with applying an understanding of personality processes to the amelioration of emotional difficulties in living. To this end, the series provides a scholarly integration of theoretical formulations, empirical data, and practical recommendations.

Six major aspects of studying and learning about human personality can be designated: personality theory, personality structure and dynamics, personality development, personality assessment, personality change, and personality adjustment. In exploring these aspects of personality, the books in the series discuss a number of distinct but related subject areas: the nature and implications of various theories of personality; personality characteristics that account for consistencies and variations in human behavior; the emergence of personality processes in children and adolescents; the use of interviewing and testing procedures to evaluate individual differences in personality; efforts to modify personality styles through psychotherapy, counseling, behavior therapy, and other methods of influence; and patterns of abnormal personality functioning that impair individual competence.

IRVING B. WEINER

University of South Florida
Tampa, Florida

Preface

A second edition is exciting for me for three reasons. It permits (1) the fine tuning of interpretations of clinical experience and research; (2) the rewording of recommendations that feedback led me to believe were being misunderstood, and (3) the integration of new literature with the state of knowledge. This edition includes 202 new references, almost all published in the last 5 years. That brings the total number of references to 600, 34% added since the last addition.

Major changes in the state of knowledge have occurred in the following areas:

- Long-term effects of divorce on children
- Visitation and parent access
- Grandparent custody
- Mediation
- Father custody
- Conflict and parent access
- Homosexual parenting
- Contraindications for joint custody
- Dynamics for remarried families
- Allegations of sexual abuse in custody evaluations
- Effects of parentification or role reversal between parent and child.

This book continues to try to provide mental health professionals, lawyers, and judges with up-to-date principles for working with children of divorce. The approach is to place the research and clinical findings in a theoretical context and use that context to propose interventions for custody, access, and therapeutic interventions.

The text presents an integrated theory of development. The focus is a cognitive/dynamic one, guided by Piaget's cognitive concepts and the object relations theory concerning separation and individuation. These theoretical concepts are briefly summarized in Chapter 1 and guide the discussion of custody, access patterns, and interventions. The recommended orientation is always to determine how children make sense of the world, based on their cognitive abilities and attachments at different developmental stages. The child's ability to organize information about parental divorce and the subsequent stresses is strongly influenced by the context in which the divorce occurs. That context is defined, in part, by the parents' psychological functioning, stress, and attachment to the child; economics; conflict; and the help that the child receives.

The development of these conceptualizations is based on the research literature, my own clinical experience, and the clinical experience of those clients and professionals who have contributed to my understanding of children of divorce. I have tried to identify where I have confidence in the recommendations and where there is less evidence to support a point of view.

The reader might be tempted to skip over the first three chapters, which would seem to be less clinically oriented; however, I urge the reader to spend time with these sections. Intervention is likely to be more effective if the reader is informed about the research and theory on the effect of specific stressors on and characteristics of the child and family.

The book includes many implications for clinical interventions, which are set off in italic. The reader will find the justification for each summary or implication statement in the preceding section.

After a brief introduction of theory and terminology, Chapters 2 and 3 review in detail the literature and clinical experience on the relationship between developmental stages and adjustment to parental divorce. There are many new studies on the long-term effects of divorce on child development, and there is a converging literature on the effects of economics and parental conflict.

Chapters 4, 5, 6, and 7 on mediation, custody evaluations, and visitation (or preferably, parent access) may seem unusual in a book on intervention. The word "intervention" tends to generate pictures of psychotherapy. It is important for intervention to know the effects of all of these divorce-related decisions that affect the child's life. Even more central is the belief that if mediation, custody, and parent access are done well, they *are* interventions from which the child is likely to benefit.

Chapter 4 makes the case that mediation would seem to benefit families. Surprisingly, given the extensive literature that parents feel better and money is saved by mediation, no study yet demonstrates that children are better adjusted when the divorce is handled through mediation than through more adversarial approaches. Chapters 5 and 6 are not meant to be a definitive summary on how to do custody evaluations, but are designed to organize essential information and issues for the custody evaluator.

Access and visitation are likely to be major issues for parents consulting a mental health professional concerning postdivorce problems. Both parents and children act out the anger and hurt around such transition times. The most controversial recommendations are those regarding parent access for very young children. The data are still not available, but an increasing number of clinicians have expressed concern for the stability of the lives of very young children.

Research on single parenting and remarriage form a separate literature from that of divorce. When clinicians are working with families of divorce, issues of single parenting (Chapter 8) and remarriage (Chapter 9) are major and to some degree independent of the issues of divorce.

Chapter 10 reviews school-based programs, which tend to be group oriented, as well as other group approaches. New research literature on the effectiveness of school-based approaches is reviewed.

Chapter 11 on parent consultation is unique. The chapter provides a model of consultation that defines the child as client and the parent(s) as collaborator(s). The strategy can reduce defenses on the part of the parent and can increase the power of interventions.

Chapter 12 presents a model for working individually with children of divorce, using the information of the prior chapters as a base for defining the interventions needed. The treatment of choice is often family therapy, which can be a very powerful intervention for dysfunctional families. Family therapy is discussed in Chapter 13.

The final chapter reviews what is currently known and where the research is needed to facilitate the courts, lawyers, and clinicians supporting the family. Few of these issues have changed since the last edition.

I would like to express my appreciation to clients, both children and adults, who have helped me to understand their experience of divorce and how I might be helpful. Dr. Lanning Schiller, a clinical psychologist in Boulder, Colorado, gave me excellent additions to the chapters on custody and visitation. My deep appreciation goes to Linda Hodges, my wife, for her support, encouragement, and editorial assistance. I also am deeply appreciative of Peter Vik, an emerging scholar in child clinical psychology, for his editing and helpful comments on the manuscript.

I would like to thank Stuart L. Kaplan and *Family Process* for the use of two figures from "Structural Family Therapy for Children of Divorce: Case Reports."

WILLIAM F. HODGES

Boulder, Colorado
July 1991

Contents

CHAPTER 1

Introduction

Today, 40 percent of children in the United States will spend part of their childhoods living with one parent because of divorce (Glick, 1988). U.S. divorce rates increased startlingly from 1967 to their peak in 1981. Since that time, at least through 1987, the decline has been minimal (National Center for Health Statistics, 1990). In 1987, an estimated 1,038,000 U.S. children experienced the divorce of their parents, the smallest number since 1973. The mean duration of first marriages ending in divorce in 1987 was 10.8 years, only slightly changed from the 10.0-year average in 1970. The average number of children per divorce decree was .89, the smallest ratio since 1953. Also, couples are waiting until they are older to get married and to get remarried (National Center for Health Statistics, 1990). These statistics suggest that people are more aware of the problems of divorce, are more cautious about getting married, and are less likely to have children involved in a divorce.

Remarriage of one or more parents is a likely event for children of divorce. Of women who divorce before 30 years of age, 76 percent remarry (Glick, 1988). Even young women with three or more children have a 73-percent remarriage rate. Over half the women who divorce in their 30s and one-third of women who divorce in their 40s remarry (Glick, 1988). Given the large number of children affected by these changes, this book addresses problems and suggested interventions related to divorce, single parenting, and remarriage.

Evaluation and intervention for children and families affected by separation and divorce require a full understanding of what one might expect of children at different ages. It is appropriate to ask the following questions: Is this behavior pattern typical of children of this age, or of older children, or younger children? To what degree might this child's problems be due to father custody or joint custody? Are explosions on the part of the child on Friday and Sunday evidence of harmful visitation?

Although the research literature and clinical experience can be useful in answering these types of questions, this literature has several problems.

1. Many studies reported are case histories. Case histories can be useful in communicating individual reactions to divorce and particular intervention strategies. An understanding of particular children can inform one's

1

understanding' of the research literature, and I have used many illustrative examples in this text. In the absence of research, the case history is the only source of information available.

The case history is also a rich source of information that can be used to generate hypotheses for research. The research literature contains numerous examples of proposals from case histories that have been confirmed in the research literature. The role of family conflict on child adjustment is one example.

Case histories do have some problems, however. The absence of quantified data makes it impossible to determine whether the reader would come to the same conclusions as the author. One has no choice but to accept the author's conclusions, perhaps with a grain of salt. It is also impossible to compare one study with another. One cannot reconcile apparent contradictions between studies without information about the measures and bases for conclusions.

2. Most of the studies do not have control groups. Although comparisons within groups of children of divorce can provide useful information, statements about the effects of divorce on children are difficult to evaluate without a control group of children from intact families. For example, if a preschool age child responds to the divorce of his or her parents with anger, regressive behavior, tantrums, and whining, is that behavior significantly different from what would be expected of a child of that age from an intact family? If teenagers turn to peer groups for support after parental divorce, is that peer group orientation greater than would be expected of teens from intact families? Without control groups, such questions cannot be answered.

Even when there are control groups, potential confounding variables, such as income level, must be controlled, either statistically or by matching. Because true experimental control cannot be accomplished in divorce research (researchers cannot randomly assign half of the couples in a group to get a divorce), all designs are essentially correlational. With correlational designs, it is always possible that cause and effect are reversed or the relationship is interactional. For example, when it is reported in the literature that children whose fathers visit infrequently are also less well adjusted, it is tempting to conclude that infrequent visitation caused the children's maladjustment. It is just as likely, however, that visitation with a maladjusted child is less rewarding and that the maladjustment "caused" the less frequent visitation.

Mental health professionals should be cautious about assuming that all causes flow from the parent to the child. Troublesome behavior on the part of the child often leads the parent to respond in less warm, supportive ways.

3. Much of the research—including many of the studies cited in this book—is based on very small sample sizes. Bias in the sample may be a

greater likelihood with these small groups. How were the participants recruited? What was the parents' motivation for permitting their children to be in the study?

4. Even when sample size is adequate, biases in socioeconomic status, cultural bias in different areas of the country, initiator status for the divorce, and motive for participation may play a role in the data. Although data provided by parents and teachers are useful, each source of data may have its own source of bias. Even observation may either miss important but low frequency behavior or cause changes in the behavior.

THE IMPORTANCE OF TERMINOLOGY

Terminology is important in this text because words both reflect subtle attitudes and shape interventions. For example, this text avoids the term "broken home." Not only does such a term imply damage or inadequacy, but it interferes with strategies designed to build an alternative structure of the family that can be healthy for all members.

There is ample evidence that children in our culture flourish best in a home with two parents who love each other and their children. The assumption, however, that the absence of that structure for children dooms them to maladjustment is simply not supported by the evidence. The developmental tasks are different when divorce occurs than for an intact family. The term "intact family" is unfortunate in that, by implication, it suggests the term "broken" for divorced families. "Nuclear family" is another term for a family in which both biological parents of the children are living together; however, the term is less common. Thus, intact family is used in this book despite its unfortunate implications.

Remarriage also presents problems of terminology. Satir (1972) used the term "blended" families to reflect the coming together of two prior families. The literature also refers to "reconstituted" families. Although technically correct, this label has the unfortunate connotation of less-than-fresh orange juice. In this text, the term "remarried" families is used.

THEORETICAL ORIENTATION OF THE BOOK

Understanding the recommendations for interventions discussed in this book does not require elaborate theoretical study; the area is simply not well developed. Two theoretical bases are helpful, however:

1. The object relations theory of ego analytic thinking. From this theory comes the description of separation and individuation of the child from the parents and the developmental stages of working on that process. The bonding between child and each parent and the effect of

the premature breaking of that bond present difficult developmental tasks to the child.

2. Jean Piaget's cognitive theory. Piaget provided a structure for understanding the child's conceptualization of the world, including object permanence, cause and effect, egocentrism, time perspective, and empathy.

Each of these theories is reviewed briefly in this section. It is assumed that most readers have at least a passing acquaintance with these theories.

Development According to Object Relations Theory

When considering the impact of divorce on child development, the nature of separation from one or both parents raises questions about the nature of the bond and the child's ability to separate from one or both parents and establish the individuation process. Mahler, Pine, and Bergman (1975) suggested the following phases in development in that process, reviewed here as related to the present topic of parent divorce:

1. *The normal autistic phase.* The newborn infant is in a sleeplike state. The child is relatively unresponsive to external stimuli. Separation from primary caregivers during this phase is likely to have an impact only if the child's biological needs are disrupted. The emotional stability of caregivers following the separation and divorce may be of importance in terms of how the child progresses through the next stages.

2. *The beginning symbiotic phase.* During the second month, the infant begins to become aware that there is a "need-satisfying object" in the world. The infant acts as if the mother (typically) and child were an omnipotent system. The child begins to "split" the world into bad and good experiences. This process is the precursor to the problem of developing rigid good and bad perceptions of people at a later time. Trauma in the caretaker at this time or separation from a need-satisfying object could result in pathological splitting.

3. *The normal symbiotic phase.* In the third month, the child develops a bond with the caretaker (usually the mother), but a sense of self is still not clearly developed. If the child is experienced with joy and warmth, the child will develop pleasure in interacting with the world. If the parent is stressed and chronically anxious as a function of marital discord and separation, the symbiotic nature of the child at this stage may cause the child to experience a lack of joy and chronic tension.

a. Development of body image. According to Mahler et al. (1975), at 4 to 5 months, the child begins differentiation and the self is seen as separate from the primary caregiver. The social smile is an indication of both the separation process and the bond with that caregiver. The child may develop transitional objects, which are generally soft and smooth (e.g., a blanket), that serve to satisfy the child's need to be in contact with the mother when she is not present. By six months, the child is playing with the mother and the environment and learning to recognize objects.

Transitional objects can be used with older infants and toddlers to bridge separations from significant caregivers. Parents should be encouraged to permit the use of such objects, particularly after separation from both parents due to marital separation and the necessity for the mother's employment.

b. The early practicing period. From seven to ten months, the child is able to move away from the parent. The child is able to practice independence only in close proximity to the primary caregiver. The caregiver becomes a stable "home base" for the child. Physical contact with the caregiver results in "emotional refueling" which enables the child to develop independence from the caregiver. Because the parent often feels ambivalence about this moving away, a parent who is suffering from the loss of a marital partner may have more difficulty allowing the physical and psychological separation of the infant.

c. Rapprochement. By the middle of the second year, the child both moves away from the parent and wishes to be reunited. The child becomes afraid that separation will result in loss of love. If the parent is not psychologically available during this phase, the child's fear may seem to be realized. Availability of the primary parent during this period will result in clear reality testing, optimal cognitive functioning, and effective coping by the beginning of the third year. From this theoretical point of view, it is clear how important the primary caretaker is to the child's development and how overinvolvement or underinvolvement would inhibit optimal separation and individuation. According to Mahler et al. (1975), severe separation anxiety in the third year (a common developmental phase beginning at about nine months) may be a sign that object constancy (the concept that a person or thing continues to exist when absent) is not developing appropriately. The lack of a secure base in the parent–child relationship may increase the likelihood of such a problem.

d. Consolidation of individuality. At age three, the child develops a sense of lifelong individuality and object constancy. The child can cope with separation for fairly long periods (hours, not days) even though tense. The child is able to merge good and bad images of the parent into a single, integrated perception. This phase includes the development of the skills of verbalization, fantasy, and reality testing.

Numerous authors have pointed out that development through childhood continues to raise issues relating to separation and individuation. In Western culture, the onset of school requires a separation from parents and the ability to maintain a sense of self as separate from the parent for large parts of the day. If the parents do not provide a solid, stable base from which to make that separation, the child may have more difficulty with it. The onset of adolescence is another stage in which the child must begin again to separate and individuate. Only if the base of love and affection is secure can separation, rapprochement, and increasingly more mature individuation occur. Marital discord at this phase may result in a child who spends more time at home and is less able to separate from parents.

Development According to Piaget's Cognitive Theory

Because Piaget's theory does not focus on individual differences, its applications to stressful life events such as marital discord, separation, and divorce are more inferential than are those of object relations theory. Ault (1977) provided an excellent, readable summary of Piaget's basic theory. The four phases of development from Piaget's view, again related to the concerns of this book, are as follows:

1. *The sensorimotor period.* The child learns to use the sensorimotor apparatus, to integrate information from different sensory systems, and to develop simple mental representations of external objects. Beginning with simple reflexes, the child learns to experience the external world, to recognize its characteristics, and to manipulate it. By 18 months, the child is able to search for hidden objects. By 24 months, the child is able to think about a task prior to acting. Object permanence, as in object relations theory, is a major task of this age, although the theory focuses on inanimate objects rather than the emotional bond with the parents.

Frequent contact with both parents is particularly important from seven months of age on so that, during separation, the child can maintain an image of each parent as continuing to exist. Pictures, tapes, phone calls, and frequent visitation can facilitate object permanence.

2. *The preoperational period.* Around two years of age, the child begins symbolic functioning. According to Ault (1977), symbols are demonstrated from behaviors such as the search for hidden objects, delayed imitation, symbolic play, and language. Such symbolic ability can help the child cope with the stress of parental separation and exposure to new situations such as a new home and school. The child develops concepts of classes, ordinal position, and conservation (the concept that the number of objects is not changed by their position). Because symbolic functioning is limited and the child is unable to mentally manipulate several symbols simultaneously, the child's ability to understand the meaning of the divorce is limited. Parents can both underestimate and overestimate the child's ability to use information at this age. A child will make errors of causation ("Daddy left because I was bad") or have difficulty remembering what a long-absent parent looks like. The child may have difficulty understanding that parent–parent

relations belong to a different category of relationships than parent–child relations. A child may think, "If Mommy is mad at Daddy and can divorce him, will she divorce me if she is mad at me?"

3. *Concrete operations.* At 6 or 7 years of age, some very important cognitive changes occur that permit the child to handle a parental separation with greater ease. The child can now solve a variety of tasks through mental operations. The child can mentally check out hypotheses about cause and effect and is less likely to feel the cause of divorce. The child can understand the difficulty in the parental relationship. Time perspective becomes infinite, and the child can understand that divorce is forever. The child can do simple problem solving mentally, permitting more effective coping.

4. *Formal operational thinking.* During the final stage in Piaget's theory, formal operations, the child can perform true logic and abstract thinking, including imaginary proposals. Typically beginning around the onset of adolescence, the child becomes able to hypothesize about parental relationships and mentally try out various ideas to see if they work. As further discussed in Chapter 2, the ability to empathize is limited at first. Later in adolescence, however, the child is able to develop an understanding of why parents might behave the way they do. This abstract thinking ability can give the adolescent important coping skills in dealing with parental divorce.

THIS BOOK'S ORIENTATION FOR CLINICAL INTERVENTION

This book's basic themes, both in understanding the effects of divorce and in developing interventions, relate to the following questions:

1. Given an understanding of the age, gender, socioeconomic status, temperament, parenting history, family conflict, and other potentially relevant variables, what would one expect this child's understanding of the world to be?
2. What *is* the nature of the child's understanding of the world?
3. In what ways is that understanding distorted because of the child's developmental needs or cognitive limitations?
4. How is the child's coping maladaptive, given the developmental tasks with which the child must cope?
5. What kind of experiences can be given to the child to correct misunderstanding about the nature of the world and provide the child with alternative modes of coping?

The development of these conceptualizations is based on psychological theory, research literature, and clinical experience.

CHAPTER 2

Child Development and the Response of Children to Separation and Divorce

An understanding of child development is essential in organizing the responses of children to the separation and divorce of their parents. This chapter summarizes research and clinical literature concerning normative reactions of children to parental divorce. Those reactions can be understood in the context of attachment and object relations and the cognitive ability of the child to make sense of the world.

Psychologically, the divorce of parents is not a discrete event. Researchers in the past have tended to describe children's reactions to divorce as if the children's life pathways prior to the parental separation were identical to those of children from happy, intact families. Divorce occurs in a context that is usually characterized by chronic parental conflict, preoccupied parents who may be less sensitive to their child's needs, a reduced standard of living postseparation, and chronic stress for the child and parents. Given the great variations in how families cope with divorce, it is remarkable that there are any normative reactions. The discussion that follows, however, indicates that there are predictable pathways of children's behavior in these situations, based on gender and stage of development.

Children are almost always distressed at the separation of parents. Indeed, even when parents have been in chronic conflict, children express a preference for the intact family. Children often are unable to see the advantages of divorce until several years later. Fantasies of reconciliation are very common and may interfere with the child's ability to cope with the stress of the divorce.

The tendency to have fantasies of reconciliation declines with age. Based on a study of children aged 6 to 17, Kurdek and Berg (1987) reported that the number of hope-of-reunification beliefs is negatively related to the age of the child ($r = -.48$), so that as children grow older, they are more able to give up the belief that their parents will reconcile.

The parental divorce is earthshaking for the child. Young children typically have operated on the assumption that they could depend on the predictable availability of both parents. When that assumption proves incorrect, a child may question many other assumptions about the world; for example, whether he or she can count on the availability of *any* parent. Such concerns lead to insecure or avoidant attachment, interference with healthy object relations, and reorganization of cognitive understandings. The egocentrism of young children may lead them to conclude that a parent's absence is due to their own unlovability. Thus, abandonment by a noncustodial parent is a particularly devastating experience. With the death of a parent, the child can mourn the loss without loss of self-esteem. With abandonment, the child is constantly faced with the possibility of unlovability. It takes a mature child (for that matter, a mature adult) to adopt the perspective that the parent has a limited ability to love, rather than that the child is unlovable. The child also wonders, "If Mom has quit loving Dad, can she quit loving me?" This question leads some children to attempt to behave especially well in order to preserve their relations with their parents. Because a young child is unlikely to maintain such control for long periods of time, however, the child may begin to experience anxiety attacks or anger in anticipation of rejection. Some children become so panic-stricken by the imagined rejection by a parent that they misbehave outrageously to get the rejection over with.

Extreme behaviors, excessive misbehavior, or unusually cooperative behavior after marital separation may mask fear of abandonment.

In working with children of divorce, it is helpful to keep in mind the interpretations that children are likely to generate at different ages to make sense of the separation and divorce.

Kurdek and Berg (1987) studied common beliefs about parental divorce. Up to 25 percent of the children in their sample felt that they were not understood by friends, that their parents might want to live without them, that they might be abandoned, that their misbehavior causes their parents to fight, and that their behavior can make their parents angry with each other. These beliefs undoubtedly affect the children's adjustment to divorce.

There is a tendency to assume that the separation from the noncustodial parent is responsible for the negative effects of divorce on child development. Although that separation can be quite stressful for the child, and both children and parents focus on the separation as a major loss, professionals working with children of divorce must remember that divorce typically occurs in the context of a chronically unhappy marriage. It may be that chronic conflict, rather than the divorce per se, leads to the adjustment problems.

In our culture, children seem to flourish best in families in which both parents love each other and the children. Children do not inevitably become maladjusted if those conditions are not met, but the developmental tasks are more difficult. Chronic stress within the home also presents the child with tasks that might interfere with the ability to cope with day-to-day stress.

Nye (1957) compared the adjustment of children from divorced and from unhappy intact homes and found that unhappy intact homes presented greater difficulties for normal adjustment than divorced homes. Raschke and Raschke (1979), in evaluating 289 children from the third, sixth, and eighth grades, reported that children from intact families with high levels of conflict showed significantly lower self-concept than children from families with low levels of conflict. They found no significant difference in self-concept among children from intact, single-parent, and remarried families. Peterson and Zill (1986) noted that, for children in intact families, the level of parental conflict was strongly related to the level of depression and withdrawal in the child.

Keeping the marriage together for the sake of the children when there is chronic conflict in the family is probably ill-advised.

Mental health professionals have been giving the above advice for years; it is satisfying to know that there is research substantiating this view.

THE EFFECT OF DIVORCE ON ADULTS

Clinicians must remember that parents also are under significant stress prior to the divorce and during the adjustment period immediately after the separation. Thus, parents may have limited ability to be helpful to their children during this time.

Bloom, Asher, and White (1978) summarized a large number of studies that document the overwhelming negative effects of divorce on adults:

- The suicide rate for divorced men is three times higher than for married men.
- The risk of death by homicide is far higher for divorced people than for other groups.
- Car accidents average three times higher for the divorced than for the married. These rates double between six months prior to and six months after the divorce.
- The widowed and divorced have higher age-adjusted death rates for all causes of death combined than married people of equivalent age, sex, and race. Particularly, death by tuberculosis, cirrhosis of the liver, malignant neoplasm of the respiratory system, diabetes mellitus, and arteriosclerotic heart disease are higher for some divorced groups.

Why do men have more trouble than women with separation and divorce? There is no clear research evidence on this issue, but a variety of explanations have been offered. Women are more likely to experience stress prior to the separation (Caldwell, Bloom, and Hodges, 1984). Men are usually in more stress after the separation (Hodges and Bloom, 1984). Women are more likely to retain custody of the children and the residence of marriage, to talk to others to obtain relief from stress, and to have a highly developed social support system. Social support has been demonstrated to serve as a mediator in reducing the stress of divorce (Caldwell and Bloom, 1982). Thus, women typically experience less loss and possess better coping skills for dealing with the stress of divorce. Finally, because women are twice as likely to instigate the separation, they generally have higher self-esteem.

Women are more likely than men to be distressed about marital conflict prior to the separation. Men have much more difficulty recovering from the divorce than do women.

Having children increases the stress of marriage and lowers marital satisfaction. Having children also increases the anger and conflict after the divorce (Bloom, Hodges, and Caldwell, 1983). Parents are required to continue contact with each other for the sake of the children and are likely to resent the ex-spouse's contact with the children.

Fear and anger on the part of parents are natural responses to divorce, and dealing with those feelings must be a part of the clinician's strategy for intervention.

It should be noted that crises counseling and education are effective in reducing the stress of couples who are separating (Bloom & Hodges, 1988; Bloom, Hodges, Kern & McFaddin, 1985; Hodges & Bloom, 1986).

In addition to having emotional reactions to the divorce, the child often experiences a more chaotic home life after the divorce, further contributing to adjustment problems. Hetherington, Cox, and Cox (1979) noted in their study of preschool children that family life after the divorce was extremely disorganized for at least a year: meals were served at irregular times, the parent and children were less likely to eat together, bedtimes were erratic, young children were read to less than were children from intact families, and children were more likely to be late to school. Noncustodial fathers were less likely to eat at home, had more trouble sleeping, and had difficulty with shopping, cooking, laundry, and cleaning.

Thus the mental health professional should not overestimate the loss that is due solely to the separation and divorce. Chronic conflict prior to the divorce, parents who either did not love each other or had substantial ambivalence about each other, continued conflict after the separation, and parents under significant stress and less available to the children for emotional support may all play a role in making separation and divorce a stressful life event for the children.

CHILD DEVELOPMENT AND THE REACTION TO DIVORCE

It is important to evaluate the age-related reactions to divorce in order to anticipate the typical needs of children at different ages. Such anticipation can provide guidelines for prevention and for assessment of reactions that require more intrusive intervention because of their abnormality. The following sections review the research and clinical evidence for the effects of separation and divorce for up to two years. Chapter 3 discusses the limited number of studies on longer term effects and the role of the context in which divorce occurs.

Birth to Two Years of Age

There has been almost no research on the effect of divorce on infants. The primary problem associated with doing research on the immediate impact of divorce on infants has to do with the long delay from separation to divorce. Even though many states have relatively short waiting periods, couples often take much longer to resolve the divorce process. For example, in Boulder, Colorado, couples have a 90-day waiting period between filing for and obtaining a nonadversarial divorce. Couples, however, take an average of 13 months from separation to divorce (Bloom, Hodges, Caldwell, Systra, and Cedrone, 1977). Most studies of the effect of divorce on children do not identify potential participants in the study until the filing for the divorce, which may be a long time after the separation. Infants may move to toddlerhood during this period. More studies of families at the point of separation are needed.

Mothers are likely to obtain custody of infants. Given that they are likely to be in better psychological condition and have been more involved in infant care than fathers, such custody arrangements make sense in the average home. The average quality of the fathering of infants in the United States has been quite limited. Twenty years ago, it was estimated that fathers were spending less than a minute a day with infants under three months of age (Rebelsky and Hanks, 1971) and up to an hour a day across infancy (Pedersen and Robson, 1969). Although there may be some reason to believe that fathers now are playing a more nurturing role with infants, the amount of bonding between fathers and infants is likely to be quite limited, particularly in sex-role stereotyped homes.

How upset the custodial mother is about the separation and divorce may be far more important in determining the effect of the separation on the infant. Mothers who are tremendously upset will upset the infant. In addition, the routine and the mother's responsiveness to the infant may be extremely disrupted.

Parents with infants should take particular care to maintain routines and to reduce the exposure of the infants to emotional upset on the part of the parents.

Often, parents have difficulty obtaining quality day care for infants. A previously unemployed mother will almost always have to seek employment, because poverty (or at least a reduced standard of living) is an almost inevitable consequence of divorce. Inexpensive child care is difficult to find. A parent may repeatedly lose one sitter and seek another.

Mussen, Conger, and Kagan (1979) reviewed the literature on the influence of good child care outside the home on infant development. They concluded that children raised in a consistent, nurturant environment with another adult will develop attachments to that adult and will not have delayed development. Such children attach to both the mother and the day caregiver and show stranger anxiety and separation anxiety at the usual times. At 20 months, these children prefer the mother to the caregiver when bored, tired, or anxious. Mussen et al. (1979) recommended that in order for a day care center to be adequate for infants, there must be one caretaker for no more than three to four infants or five or six toddlers. In addition, the day care setting needs to expose the children to a variety of stimulation and an opportunity to develop new skills. They have found that children under such conditions develop as they would have had they remained at home.

Infants can handle day care quite well, provided that caregivers are warm and affectionate and provide a stimulating environment. Parents should try to maintain the same caregivers and avoid day care services with high staff turnover.

Herzog (1980) reviewed the treatment of twelve boys between the ages of 18 and 28 months whose presenting complaints were a syndrome resembling night terrors. In every case, the parents had been divorced or separated within the previous four months and the mother had custody. Herzog had been consulted within three weeks of the onset of the symptoms in each case. A characteristic pattern included falling asleep with some degree of difficulty, and waking early in the night, terrified, disoriented, and calling for help. Often, the child would cry for his father. In eight of the twelve cases, there had been a change in sleeping arrangements. In four of these eight cases, the son and mother were sharing the same bed; in the other four, the son and mother were sharing the same bedroom. Each child perceived that the father's return would stop the night terrors. Herzog interpreted the problem from the point of view of castration anxiety, narcissistic injury, fear associated with aggression mobilized by the loss of the father, and "father hunger."

In boys aged 18 to 28 months, night terrors after divorce may reflect anxiety about father loss. Reassurance, increased father contact, and removal of the boy from the mother's bedroom may facilitate reduction in the terrors.

A research study on separation in infancy and later personality development was done by Kalter and Rembar (1981). These authors looked at the marital status of families of children in an outpatient psychiatric service across a wide age range in relation to the diagnosis of the children. Such retrospective studies present problems of interpretation in that conclusions are limited to children who ultimately develop psychiatric problems and receive treatment. The results suggest, however, that particular types of problems are created by earlier divorce. Separation of parents during infancy, compared with separation of parents when children were older, was related to the child's having problems with parents that did not involve aggression when the child was in latency (6 to 12 years of age). In addition, adolescent boys whose parents separated during the boys' infancy were less likely to have problems with peers around aggressive issues.

Two to Three Years of Age

Psychoanalytic theory proposed that this period is a particularly sensitive time for divorce. Gardner (1976) stated that the younger the child, the more adverse the impact of divorce. Longfellow (1979), in her excellent review of the literature, concluded that preschool children (including the 2- to 3-year-olds) may have particular difficulty handling parental divorce. Toomin (1974) argued that the loss of the father at the 18- to 36-month period had critical implications for the separation–individuation process. Children at this age who are dealing with how safe it is to separate from a parent may find the partial or complete disappearance of a parent a frightening experience. Only when the child has a safe, trustworthy base can separation and exploration occur. When that base is threatened, either by the separation from the noncustodial parent or by chronic emotional upset of the custodial parent, the child's ability to explore and separate may be severely hampered.

Two- to three-year-olds were evaluated as part of a study of children from 2 to 18 done by Wallerstein and Kelly (1975). They studied 131 children from Marin County, California, during their parents' divorces. The children were referred by a variety of professionals in the community for help with normal reactions to divorce. In this study, children were followed for 10 years, providing a rich data base. Unfortunately, there was no comparison group of children from the same community from intact families.

The authors reported that children aged 2 to 3 showed regression, irritability, aggression, and tantrum behavior. Regression included loss of toilet training, separation anxiety, masturbation, and the use of transitional objects (i.e., the use of blankets or dolls as reassuring objects). Because these behaviors are fairly common during the "terrible twos," it is not surprising that children under stress would demonstrate similar coping behaviors. Although these data are based on a limited number of children of this age (only nine), the uniformity of reactions to the separation is impressive. Wallerstein and Kelly noted that the most severe reactions occurred when children were not given an explanation of the disappearance of the absent parent. By one year later, for all but three of the children, the major problems with aggression, fearfulness, and possessive behavior had disappeared.

Consistent with Wallerstein and Kelly's data, Neugebauer (1988/1989) noted that the majority of parents in a sample of parents with children 2 to 11 years old at the time of separation neither warned the child of the impending separation nor gave a reason for the divorce.

Parents underestimate the ability of 2- to 3-year-olds to understand and utilize information about what is going on around them. Parents should be counseled to tell children about what happened to the absent parent and why.

Three to Five Years of Age

Children aged 3 to 5 have a limited cognitive ability to make sense of the loss of one parent. As previously noted, the loss of a parent through separation and divorce can lead the egocentrically oriented child of this age to assume that it is his or her unlovability that led to the separation. It is not surprising that children of this age have difficulty understanding and appropriately coping with separation and divorce.

According to psychoanalytic theory, the major developmental process at this age that is at risk for disruption is the oedipal phase of development, in which children are developing stronger identification with the same-sex parent, developing sex-role identification and greater moral understanding and identifying with parental values. Consistent with that theoretical position, Biller (1981) noted that learning stereotypic sex roles is more critical before than after six years of age. Boys with father loss prior to age six have more trouble obtaining a masculine identity than boys with father loss after age six. Some writers have noted the likelihood of powerful guilt feelings if separation and divorce occurred during this period (Rohrlich, Ranier, Berg-Cross, and Berg-Cross, 1977; Toomin, 1974). The effect of separation and divorce on sex-role identification is discussed in detail in Chapter 8.

One common problem is the tendency of parents to use children of this age to help the parents handle their own pain. Children often move into the parental bed after the separation. Seldom does the parent who is practicing this behavior report it to the mental health professional; it is usually the other parent who raises concerns. The mental health professional should routinely ask where the 3- to 6-year-old child sleeps.

This is not to say that having a 4-year-old son move into the mother's bed after a separation results in the child's winning the oedipal conflict and being forever fixated at the phallic stage of development. Although there is a risk of sexualizing the relationship between the child and parent at an age when the child does have increased interest in the sexuality of the parent, perhaps the greater risk is the increased dependency that is supported by such behavior. Children who move into the parental bed are much more likely to continue substantial levels of immature dependency on the parent. Parents will go to extraordinary lengths to try to convince the mental health professional that changing where the child sleeps is not possible: "He is too upset to sleep alone," or "She crawls into my bed in the middle of the night and I wake up in the morning with her there." I suggest putting a lock on the bedroom door and encouraging the child to knock. If parents are frightened that they will not hear a child cry out with a nightmare (common at this age range), I suggest an intercom.

A child of either sex who is sleeping with a parent of either sex needs to be moved out of the parental bed. When the child is significantly upset and tries to move into the parental bed, the parent should provide reassurance and return the child to his or her own bed, stay with the child, and encourage sleep by sitting with the child until sleep comes, perhaps calming the child with a back rub. Then the parent should return to the parental bed.

Several research studies have looked at the reaction of 3- to 5-year-olds to the divorce of their parents. Wallerstein and Kelly (1974b; 1975) reported that regression was no longer a common response as in 2- to 3-year-olds. Perceptual motor skills had been sufficiently overlearned so that stress did not result in loss of skills. Aggressive behavior, irritability, and whiny and tearful behavior were common. Fantasy developed as a coping skill. Of the eleven children in this group, seven were evaluated as worse one year later. For most of the children who were worse, the regression was in the areas of lowered self-esteem, greater inhibition, sadness, and neediness. Although the sample was limited, the data do raise the question of whether the 3- to 5-year-olds are more vulnerable to the effects of separation and divorce than younger children.

One problem with limited samples is that chance distribution of certain types of children can influence the interpretation of data. In this case, all but one of the seven children who were worse a year later had fathers with serious problems and fairly harsh, disciplinary child-rearing strategies prior to the separation. It is difficult to know whether it was the harsh treatment before the separation, the loss of structure caused by the separation, the loss of a now more giving father after the separation, or the effect of separation on children of this age that accounted for the poor adjustment reaction of children of this age.

Hetherington et al. (1979) elaborated on a variety of issues of the reaction of preschool age children to separation and divorce. They compared 24 boys and 24 girls from divorced homes with a matched set of 24 boys and 24 girls from intact homes. The children from homes of divorce were matched by selecting children from intact homes who were similar with regard to parental age, parental education, and length of marriage, as well as child sex, age, and birth order. The authors found that preschool age children, with an average age at divorce of 3.79 years, developed more negative behavior than children in intact families. Boys had statistically significantly more trouble handling the divorce than did girls. Whereas girls were returning to the level of adjustment of girls from intact families by one year after the separation and problems had disappeared by two years, boys were still having significant problems at two years, although the level of problems was declining.

For women who were married to upper-class men, the drop in income was profound, moving them—and the children for whom they had custody—to lower-middle-class status. Poverty was seen as delaying restabilization.

One major contribution of the work of Hetherington et al. (1979) is the careful analysis of parent–child interactions. Coercive interactions were common between mother and child. Boys were particularly difficult for mothers to handle. Preschool boys would ignore an instruction from the mother, but obey the same instruction from the father. Because preschool boys in this culture are intensely preoccupied with sex-role identification, it is likely that the reluctance of boys to obey mothers is related to sex-role identification. Mothers who had custody of only boys had particular difficulties and, two years after the divorce, had low self-esteem as a parent. The boys tended to be out of control.

Wallerstein and Kelly (1975) noted that feelings of responsibility can occur for children this age, but Hetherington et al. (1979) indicated that such feelings are rare for children of this age. My own clinical experience has suggested that feelings of responsibility are relatively uncommon. There are two major reasons why a child of this age would assume responsibility for the divorce of his or her parents: First, children of this age are relatively egocentric and tend to see most things as revolving around them. It is easy for a child to turn a fight over financial matters into "You should not have bought me that jacket." And second, an assumption of responsibility may be an attempt to gain control over the situation. If the child had done something that caused the divorce, then the child could undo the divorce by reversing the behavior. Thus, some children become unusually good after the divorce in an attempt to reverse the "cause" of the noncustodial parent's leaving home.

Regardless of whether a child is being egocentric or is trying to assume control over the divorce, the child will be better off if the parents insist that the child did not cause the divorce and does not have the power to reverse the process.

In Kalter and Rembar's (1981) study, in which they looked at the diagnoses of outpatient psychiatric clinic children as a function of sex and age at the time of parental separation and divorce, they found that if parental separation occurred from 3 to 5.5 years of age, boys later had more school-related problems and less anxiety and depression than boys experiencing parental divorce at other ages. Adolescent boys who had experienced parental separation at preschool age showed less aggression toward parents and siblings than boys who experienced parental separation later. Girls who experienced parental separation during this preschool time did not have differential diagnoses during latency, were more aggressive toward parents and peers during adolescence, and had greater academic problems than did girls whose parents separated at other times. Why anxiety and depression are lower for boys if divorce occurred at this age is unknown. An expectation, at least from psychoanalytic theory, would be for greater anxiety, rather than less. For aggression, the results are easier to explain. Because boys became less aggressive and girls became more aggressive, the results suggest that later sex-role stereotypic behaviors are reduced by father loss through divorce at this age.

Relatively few studies have looked at cognitive and social functioning for preschool age children. These variables are much more commonly investigated for school age levels. Guidubaldi and Perry (1984) evaluated intellectual, academic, social, and adaptive behavior for 115 kindergarten children in a suburban school district. Single-parent status due to divorce and socioeconomic status were investigated to see which variable was more important in predicting behavior. There were 26 children from single-parent homes (23 percent of the sample).

Socioeconomic variables predicted school-entry competencies. High socioeconomic levels were associated with high intellectual levels, academic performance, and personal–social development. Single-parent status was, however, the most consistent predictor variable. It predicted academic, visual-motor, and social development. Correlations ranged from .19 to .42. Single-parent status was a stronger predictor than socioeconomic status on seven of the twelve nonintellectual criteria. Single-parent status did not predict the intellectual measures. When multiple correlations were performed, single-parent status did add predictive variation over that provided by socioeconomic status on six of the seven academic variables, suggesting that single-parent status does make a difference in academics. There were sixteen other predictors, and seldom did they add any additional predictive value. Guidubaldi and Perry (1984) concluded that the negative effect of divorce on child development was not mediated entirely by economics.

Adams (1984), summarizing seven major studies supported by the National Institute of Mental Health, noted that children who were under six when their parents divorced were three times more likely than older children to need psychological help. Such research findings raise the question about which children are at risk for maladjustment and which are likely to cope well with the stress. These questions were asked in one of our early studies (Hodges, Wechsler, and Ballantine, 1979). The participants were 52 preschool children: 26 from intact families who had never experienced the separation of their parents and 26 who were presently living in mother-custody homes. The mean age was 4.3 years. The children were enrolled in five different preschools in Boulder, Colorado. This population was predominantly white and middle class. Data included direct observation of the children in the preschool, a behavior checklist filled out by the custodial mother, and a behavior checklist filled out by the child's preschool teacher.

The first hypothesis to be tested was that children from divorced homes would manifest greater problems than children of intact homes, particularly aggression, withdrawal, dependency, and other signs of immaturity. Surprisingly, however, few statistically significant differences were obtained. The findings were obtained despite the fact that both parents and teachers reported the belief that divorce had a profound impact on child behavior.

When the data for children in the divorce group were analyzed, those children who were more likely to have problems were identified. The younger the parents and the lower the father's income, the greater the teacher-rated general maladjustment of the child. The greater the number of moves, the greater the amount of aggression in the child [$r(24) = .65$, $p < .01$]. In a multiple regression analysis, it was clear that younger parents, lower income, and number of moves were all the same variable, because young parents have not yet settled into a career and tend to move frequently. More on the role of economics and other stressors is presented in Chapter 3.

Preschool age children of younger parents with fewer resources, such as lower income and less geographic stability, are likely to have more difficulty with parental separation and divorce.

The reason that this research did not show a greater level of problems in preschool children of divorce than in children from intact families may be because of sample bias. It is impossible to determine what biases led parents of either type of family to decide to participate in the study.

The failure to find differences between the children of divorce and of intact families may be due to a series of factors:

MINIMAL EFFECTS.   It is possible that, for this population, divorce did not have a measurable effect on child behavior. There is evidence to suggest that children are not always adversely affected by the divorce of their parents.

ATTRIBUTION OF CAUSATION.   Why would parents and teachers assume that divorce leads to behavior problems in preschool age children when for Boulder, Colorado, there is no evidence to support that view? When a child from a divorced home has emotional or behavioral problems, the general assumption is that the problems were caused by the divorce. Statements such as "that child is aggressive, because he comes from an intact family" are unlikely to be made, even though they may be truer than assumptions that behavior problems in a child from a divorced family were caused by the divorce.

ATTRIBUTION OF DAMAGE.   Because of the assumption that divorce will inevitably damage the child, parents and teachers can be overly concerned about the child's welfare. Children who receive messages that they are to be pitied for their plight may develop long-term problems, but get only short-term support.

THE SOCIAL ENVIRONMENT.   In Boulder, Colorado, the divorce rate is 60 percent, substantially higher than the national average. Thus, divorce is a common event and children report that many of their classmates have experienced the divorce of their parents. One reason why children of divorce in Hodges et al.'s (1979) study were not seen as having greater problems may have to do with the common experience of divorce in that community. Divorce, while still likely to be a serious loss for children, may not be seen as depriving or unusual in a community where divorce is common. One bit of supporting evidence for this interpretation is the findings of a follow-up study (Hodges, Buchsbaum, and Tierney, 1983) using the same measures, but in Denver, Colorado, 30 miles away and with a significantly lower divorce rate. In that study, the more typical findings of greater aggression, dependency, poorer on-task behavior in preschool, poorer general adjustment in preschool, and more acting-out aggression toward the parents at home were obtained. Boys of divorce were less happy, more destractible in preschool, and less well adjusted at home than were girls of divorce.

In summary, for most studies and in most communities, separation and divorce tend to predict greater problems in preschool children of divorce, particularly in boys. The egocentrism of children of this age may lead them to assume the divorce is their fault. Economic problems in the family particularly put families of divorce at risk for children with adjustment problems.

Five to Six Years of Age

Wallerstein and Kelly (1975) found that the fourteen children aged 5 to 6 in their study also showed aggression and anxiety, restlessness, whininess, moodiness, irritability, separation problems, and tantrums. These children were old enough to understand some of the changes due to the separation. Some children did not seem to be adversely affected by divorce events. The most vulnerable group of five were diagnosed as developing childhood depressions with unhappiness, anxiety, denial, feelings of rejection, sleep disturbances, phobias, compulsive eating, aggression, and dependency.

Seven to Eight Years of Age

A major shift in cognitive ability occurs around age 7 or 8. Children move from a preoperational logic in which cause and effect are difficult to understand to concrete operations in which a greater understanding of the nature of the world is obtained. One particularly important shift is the development of an infinite sense of time. The ability to think about the future develops slowly during the preschool time, from an understanding of the near future and past to an awareness of days, weeks, and months ahead. By the age of seven, the child can understand the concept of "forever." Indeed, this understanding is why death phobia is so common at this age. In terms of the implications for divorce, the child is now able to understand that the parents intend to remain divorced forever. In terms of visitation, the child is able to tolerate long visitations and understand intuitively the return to the custodial parent. From a theoretical point of view, the greater ability to handle the information about divorce should result in reduced long-term negative consequences.

From a theoretical point of view, divorce that occurs during a child's latency period should have less impact on development than one that occurs during the child's preschool or adolescent periods. The possibility of delayed oedipal resolution due to prior marital conflict is a predictable outcome. Academic achievement may be affected (this age is the beginning of Erikson's (1963) age of acquiring a sense of industry), and the development of appropriate peer relations may be harmed. The importance of the developmental tasks of this age, the consolidation of previous stages, and the learning of peer relations and a less self-centered orientation to life suggest that the latency stage is not irrelevant to development, and several theorists have emphasized the importance of stability in the lives of children (Erikson, 1963; Sarnoff, 1976).

One advantage to the child of this age is the presence of school. Peers are more likely to be available as social support (and distractors), and the child comes in contact with a variety of adults who are not in turmoil because of the separation and divorce. In addition, the child has the opportunity to meet other children who are coping with the same stressors of marital disruption. For the younger elementary age child, however, the limits in the ability to understand the feelings of other children make it difficult to take advantage of the experience of other children. By the age of 10 or 11, children have a better developed sense of empathy, but it is reserved for people who are better known. As discussed in Chapter 10, training children in self-awareness and empathy for other children can be particularly helpful at this age.

Wallerstein and Kelly (1976a), in evaluating twenty-six children in their sample in this age group, reported that sadness, grief, depression, and fear of the future were common. In children of this age, depression resembles the sadness and grief of the adult. In younger children, symptoms of depression are withdrawal and shutdown. Deprivation feelings and intense feelings of loss in relationship to the noncustodial father were common, particularly for the younger boys (as would be predicted from psychoanalytic theory). Boys, more than girls, expressed anger at the mother for either causing the divorce or requiring the father to leave. One-quarter of the children felt pressure from an angry mother to reject the father. In school, more than half of the children had behavior changes sufficient to be reported to the interviewer by the teacher. Few children reported fantasies of having caused the separation. At the one-year follow-up, these children looked less disturbed than the younger children. Of the twenty-six children in this sample, 23 percent were worse one year later, but 50 percent had improved or continued previous progress. The intense pain had been replaced by sad resignation. A third of the boys continued to wish for reconciliation. Anger in the child was particularly likely where the parents continued to battle.

One major behavior that is common at this age is an active wish for reconciliation. Wallerstein and Kelly (1976a) reported that almost all of the children entertained such wishes. Indeed it is a rare child who does not wish for reconciliation. Such wishes would seem to be true even for children exposed to constant fighting between parents. Only older and more introspective children were likely to state, some time after the separation and divorce, that the parents were happier apart and that a reconciliation would not work.

Children should be encouraged not to provide information back and forth between households. They also should be encouraged to negotiate directly with each parent concerning rules in that household.

Forgatch, Patterson, and Skinner (1988) developed path models for understanding the effect of divorce for sixty-four mothers and their sons from 6 to 8 years of age. They investigated the precursors of maternal stress and the relationship of stress to inept discipline, leading ultimately to predictions of antisocial behavior in the child. In their model, recent hassles, negative life events, financial problems, and family health problems—common stressors in families of divorce—were all related to maternal stress. The pathway from maternal stress to inept discipline and directly to the child's antisocial behavior, as well as the pathway from inept discipline to antisocial behavior, were statistically significant.

Felner, Stolberg, and Cowen (1975) evaluated the school maladjustment problems of children from 5 to 10 years of age who had significant early school adjustment problems. Children were matched on sex, grade, city versus country residence, socioeconomic level, repeat in grade, and prior intervention. Of the 800 children in the first study, 108 had experienced parental separation or divorce and 32 had experienced parental death. Compared with children from intact families, the children who had experienced the separation and divorce of parents were more restless, obstinate, impulsive, and disruptive in class. Children who had lost a parent by death were more unhappy or depressed and moody. An additional analysis of 950 children in a new sample showed that children with parental histories of separation and divorce were significantly more maladjusted than the controls and showed heightened levels of acting out and aggression. Children who had experienced the death of parents also had significantly higher total maladjustment scores and ranked higher on scales of shyness, timidity, and withdrawal.

Professionals who liken the mourning by the young child for the divorce of parents to the mourning for the death of a parent may make incorrect comparisons. The two types of situations produce significantly different reactions in children. Divorce leads to increased aggression and disruptive behavior, and the death of a parent is associated with depression.

Nine to Twelve Years of Age

Following divorce, children 9 to 12 years of age assume more responsibility for handling the household. Parents in intact families in the United States culture underestimate children's ability to assume responsibility for household chores. Single parents need their children to help clean the house and take care of their own rooms. Sometimes major responsibilities concerning the babysitting of younger siblings occur because of the difficulty in affording day care.

Another major cognitive shift is occurring in children aged 9 to 12. While children as young as 1 ½ are capable of empathy, the ability to understand the perspective of parents does not begin until the child enters the concrete operational stage of elementary school. In this stage, the child improves substantially in the ability to see the world from someone else's point of view. This empathy is still quite limited to those people whom the child knows quite well. The average elementary-age child will participate in vicious teasing, yet children of this age can be enormously caring and concerned about the pain that their parents are going through in handling the divorce. This concern leads to *parentification of the child*, a major problem of 9- to 12-year-olds in which parent and child reverse roles. The parent who is lonely and demoralized by the divorce finds a sympathetic ear in the child. The parent begins to use the child to unload the pain of the working day and the loneliness of the evenings. One parentified child experiencing significant depression came home from school daily, cleaned the house, cooked dinner, and then listened to the mother complain about all the things that went wrong at work that day.

Brown and Samis (1986/1987) made a useful distinction between a *parental* child, who fulfills some parent functions with younger siblings, and the *parentified* child, who is expected to take care of the needs of the parent. Although the parental child may learn useful skills, the parentified child is usually overburdened and anxious.

Parents should be encouraged to use someone other than a child for the unburdening of their problems concerning the difficulties of the day or the loneliness of the nights. While children of divorce may be given more responsibility to help the family cope with the amount of work, parents should take care to avoid burdening the child with psychological needs or chores to the point of eliminating play.

Children with these burdens do not become identified as problems. They are super-responsible children. If they do come in contact with a mental health professional, it is usually because they have either developed a psychosomatic illness or depression. They are pseudo-mature rather than truly grown up. Because the maturity is not developing in a normal fashion, it is not truly balanced. The major problem from the point of view of mental health is that these people grow up into very responsible, joyless adults.

One mother described her 11-year-old daughter as extremely helpful around the house. In the course of therapy, the mother revealed that she routinely shared her adult problems with her child. The mother was urged to find friends to take that role. In an effort to encourage the daughter to be silly and spontaneous, the mother suggested a slumber party. (There is little sillier than 11-year-old girls at a slumber party, unless it is 11-year-old boys.) When the slumber party started, the daughter indicated that she had cleaned the house, and warned the guests to take care of the house. The mother told the daughter that the mother would watch after the house. The daughter started to relax, and giggles soon were coming up from the basement where the slumber party was held.

Wallerstein and Blakeslee (1989) felt that these situations are inappropriately labeled parentification, because these are not true role reversals. They preferred the term *overburdened*. Although I appreciate their argument, "overburdened" does not adequately reflect the degree to which the child is expected to take care of the psychological needs of the parent and the inappropriately heavy load of chores and responsibilities.

In a sample of 56 children from highly conflicted, divorcing families, Johnston, Gonzalez, and Campbell (1987) found that role reversal predicted poorer child adjustment. Role reversal was defined as the child taking care of a parent, soothing an angry or depressed parent, and protecting a parent from stress. Children who took care of the father had more behavior problems, depression, and withdrawal than children who did not take care of the father. If the child took care of the mother, the child had *less* withdrawn, uncommunicative behavior than did the child who did not take care of the mother.

Parentification with the divorced father seems to be related to maladjustment in the child. Parentification with the mother may lead to the pseudo-mature behavior of a super-responsible child.

Wallerstein and Blakeslee (1989) reported about parents who asked their children to decide about the parents' choices of sexual partners or potential job changes. The findings indicated that such burdens increase the likelihood of depression in the child.

London (1989) in a retrospective study on parentification as it related to present intimacy, found that college students from divorced families reported significantly more parentification in childhood than students who grew up in intact homes. Boys tended to be more parentified than girls. Mothers and fathers were equally likely to encourage the role reversal with the child. There was a small $[r(161) = -.27, p < .001]$ negative relationship between parentification and income, with lower-income families having more parentification. When family income was statistically controlled, students with high parentification in childhood were significantly more likely to report dissatisfaction with present sexual and recreational intimacy.

Divorce of parents also predicted such dissatisfaction, independent of parentification levels. Absolute levels of intimacy, however, were not related to either parentification or parental marital status.

Parentification in childhood is related to dissatisfaction with sexual and recreational intimacy in college students.

Wallerstein and Kelly (1976b) reported that the thirty-one 9- and 10-year-olds in their sample responded to the divorces of their parents with poise and courage. They characterized the children as showing soberness, clarity, and empathy for the parent. The single feeling that stood out as differentiating these children from younger children was the conscious, intense anger. About half of the children were angry at their mothers and about half at their fathers. A large number were angry at both parents. The anger was often directed at the parent who was seen (often accurately) as initiating the divorce. Fear of abandonment was common in about one-fourth of the children. Shame was a common response to the news of the separation. Wallerstein and Kelly's sample showed a shaken sense of identify, as well as loneliness and loyalty conflicts. Some children reported somatic symptoms, such as headaches and stomachaches. One-half of the children of this sample declined in school performance (see the later section on the effect of divorce on school performance in Chapter 3).

About half (14 of the 31) had fallen into depressive behavior patterns and 7 others were openly distressed. About one-fourth of the children (8 of 31) developed fierce loyalty conflicts, aligning themselves with one parent against the other. At the five-year follow-up, this loyalty conflict had disappeared.

Wallerstein and Kelly reported that one year later, the children's understanding was greater. The responses to the separation were much less intense. About half of the children (15 of the 29 available for follow-up) were doing well, although not without some bitterness about the divorce. Of the total group, 10 maintained a strong level of anger at the noncustodial parent, and about one-fourth were more distressed than at the initial interview.

Krantz, Clark, Pruyn, and Usher (1985) evaluated the cognitive appraisals of twenty-six boys and twenty-six girls of divorce, children who ranged from 8.5 to 12 years old. These children were an average of 2.5 years postseparation. The measures included a semiprojective measure of perceptions about divorce that asked the child to respond to possible thoughts a child of divorce might have in thirteen problematic situations that were described. A measure of the child's ability to generate alternative solutions to three divorce-related problems was also obtained. Reports about the child were also obtained from parents and teachers.

Boys who generated more coping alternatives had fewer behavior problems at home or school. The more adaptive the boys' evaluation of the divorce, the better their postdivorce adjustment at home. Adaptive beliefs included a positive or mixed evaluation of the divorce, optimism about the future, or acceptance of the divorce. No relationship was found between adaptive evaluations and adjustment at school. Girls in general had high levels of coping and adjustment.

Late latency boys, who can be helped to accept the divorce, to be more optimistic about the future, and to increase alternative problem strategies, are likely to show improvement in adjustment.

Kinard and Reinherz (1984) compared the behavior of 74 children in mother-custody homes with that of 320 children in intact homes. These children, about nine years old at the time of this study, were part of a cohort of children studied since kindergarten. Children who had experienced the divorce of parents had poorer parent-rated levels of attention span and withdrawal and higher teacher-rated levels of dependency and hostility. Self-concept was not related to parents' marital status. Children who had recently experienced disruption of the family had the lowest levels of teacher-rated productivity. This finding disappeared when the child's gender and the mother's education were statistically controlled.

In another study of adjustment of 9- to 12-year-olds, Wyman, Cowen, Hightower, and Pedro-Carroll (1985) compared 98 children of divorce with 170 demographically similar children from intact families on perceived competence, trait anxiety, and social support. The child of divorce had higher anxiety, lower perceived cognitive competence, and fewer social supports. For both groups, greater social supports correlated with a more positive self-view and lower anxiety.

Copeland (1985) studied 6- to 12-year-old children of divorce and their mothers. Mothers who described themselves as angry and hostile more often described their sons than their daughters as having behavior problems. Boys rated as having more behavior problems more often reported themselves as confused about the separation and as feeling guilt than did boys with fewer behavior problems. Mothers who described themselves as angry, hostile, confused, bewildered, tense, and anxious more often described their daughters as having behavior problems.

In this type of study, it is impossible to determine cause and effect or to determine the degree to which response biases may have accounted for the relationship between self-description and child description. Mothers who described themselves in a negative way, for example, may have been more negative in how they would describe anyone, including their own children.

In a study of fifty-one boys from 9 to 12 years of age, 1 to 3.25 years postseparation, Greene and Leslie (1988/1989) found that a mother's attitude toward the father had an effect on how supportive and coercive her son perceives her to be. A son's perception of the mother as being coercive was also related to his level of aggression. Maternal support of the boy did not predict the son's aggression.

Boys during late latency are likely to be more aggressive if the mother is negative in her attitude toward the father and if the mother is coercive with her son.

Stolberg and Bush (1985) analyzed eighty-two mother–child families of divorce with children from 7 to 13 years old. Families were 9 to 33 months postseparation. In a path analysis of postdivorce child adjustment, three paths were most useful.

One pathway suggested that mothers with more children described better postdivorce child adjustment. Well-adjusted mothers had better parenting techniques. Better parenting techniques predicted better social skills, prosocial activities, and less internalized pathology in the child.

Promoting improved postseparation parenting techniques is likely to improve postdivorce adjustment (particularly internalized pathology) in the child.

In the second pathway, younger children had more life changes, which were related to greater externalized psychopathology and fewer prosocial skills. These results were consistent with those of Hodges, Tierney, and Buchsbaum (1984) for preschool children and Hodges, London, and Colwell (1990) for 4th to 6th graders.

Reducing life changes for the child, particularly the younger child, is likely to reduce externalized pathology (such as aggression).

The third pathway is the effect of overt marital hostility, which predicted both externalized and internalized pathology and fewer social skills in the children. The role of parental conflict is discussed more extensively in Chapter 3.

Reducing conflict between parents may reduce psychopathology in the child and increase social skills.

Adolescence

With the onset of adolescence, another cognitive change occurs. The child moves from Piaget's concrete operational period to formal operational logic. This move means that the child gives up the relatively concrete approach to solving problems and attempts to obtain solutions on a more abstract level. It is important to understand that the child must give up concrete operational thinking before becoming effective at the formal operational level. In addition to this major cognitive change, the child has several tasks of adolescence involving proving that he or she is an individual and not a clone of the parents. These characteristics of adolescence have several implications for understanding the adolescent's response to separation and divorce:

1. *Egocentrism is high.* Egocentrism leads the adolescent to assume that everyone is just as preoccupied with his or her experience as he or she is. Adolescents tend to see everything as revolving around their experience and cannot easily see the world from someone else's point of view.

2. *Empathy goes down.* The child can no longer use the concrete operational empathy of understanding the parent, but the ability to appreciate the parents' points of view has not yet developed at a more abstract level. This lack of understanding (and sympathy) on the part of the early adolescent is hard for most parents to accept. Certainly parents undergoing separation and divorce do not find the support that the later elementary age child was giving. Not until the child is 15 or 16 years of age has the formal operational logic developed to such a point that the child is likely to start appreciating the parental point of view.

3. *Separation–individuation again becomes an issue.* The egocentrism and empathy reduction of early adolescence typical in the United States culture is functional for the task of separation from parents. Parents are typically ambivalent about allowing their children to grow up. If early adolescents were in touch with that ambivalence, combined with their own ambivalence about the same issue, separation would become significantly more difficult to accomplish. Thus, it is important for the adolescent to be oblivious to the parents' pain. When the pain is about separation from a marital partner, the adolescent is presented with an even more complex problem.

Wallerstein and Kelly (1974) reported on 21 teenagers who had experienced recent separation and divorce. They reported that all the adolescents tried to withdraw from the family to protect themselves from the pain. The withdrawal manifested itself in increased social activities or prolonged periods of staying away from home. It is difficult to evaluate the implications of this withdrawal without a control group from the same community since increased time away from home is a common characteristic of adolescence.

When the adolescent reaction to marital separation of parents is withdrawal, it is particularly difficult for the clinician to differentiate that behavior from typical adolescent independence. The clinician should take particular care in evaluating whether adolescent depression is in need of intervention.

Allison and Furstenberg (1989) analyzed data for 1,377 children from the National Survey of Children. Divorce had long-lasting effects in problem behavior, psychological distress, and academic performance. Sons of divorced parents always did less well on behavioral measures, and daughters of divorced parents did less well on measures of dissatisfaction and psychological distress. Girls tended to have larger effects than did boys. There was a clear tendency for the strongest effects to be in the youngest age group (age 12) and the weakest in the oldest age group (age 16).

4. *The adolescent makes judgments on an absolute basis.*   Ambivalence is handled by splitting. The adolescent judges a person as either all good or all bed. Thus, loyalty conflicts are likely to increase as the adolescent makes judgments about who was right and who was wrong. The ability to see both parents as having admirable qualities and sharing responsibilities has not yet developed. Wallerstein and Kelly (1974) referred to the "precipitous deidealization" of the parent (what an eloquent phrase!) as a response to the divorce. The child moves from seeing the parent as near perfect with few flaws to seeing the parent as seriously flawed and unworthy of respect. The overvalued parent is now the target of rage and underevaluation.

Parents and therapists should encourage the child to experience ambivalence and to see people as complex beings who are not all good or all bad. This balance will improve the child's ability to solve the complex relationships of adolescence.

It is difficult to predict which parent will be picked as the enemy. Some adolescents will pick the parent who leaves, but others will blame the remaining parent for not being lovable or supportive enough. Wallerstein and Kelly (1974a) reported that by one year postseparation, virtually all of their adolescent sample had been able to separate themselves from the loyalty conflicts. My clinical experience indicates that severe loyalty conflicts may continue well beyond the first year, particularly when the custodial parent continues to be deeply hurt and bitter and there is limited contact with the noncustodial parent.

McLoughlin and Whitfield (1984), in an Australian sample of teenagers of divorce, also reported continued anger toward the noncustodial father, particularly for girls when the father was involved in adultery. Because adolescents have difficulty with their own sexuality, often they will make extreme judgments of the parent who had an affair.

5. *Adolescents have difficulty with their own sexuality and the sexuality of parents.*   Wallerstein and Kelly (1974) noted that parental dating forces teenagers to be confronted with their parents' sexuality, particularly when fathers date someone not far from the children's age.

Because teenagers have difficulty with parents' sexuality, parents should minimize the teenager's exposure to that sexuality, particularly during the first year of adjustment to the divorce.

Sorosky (1977) noted that the father's leaving home can be viewed as a sexual rejection by an adolescent daughter. The teenage boy who is made the "man of the house" may have difficulty dealing with the closeness of the relationship with his mother.

This anxiety about the parents' sexuality is increased when parents enter into pseudo-adolescent behavior. Many parents who divorce when their children are teenagers have not dated since they themselves were late teenagers and may revert to those behaviors. Adolescents may find themselves apparently competing with their parents. Parents who have not dated for such a long time often were reared in sexually less permissive times and experience some guilt over their own sexual behavior. Some mothers can resent a daughter's attractiveness and youth and respond with excessive controls, inviting defiant acting out (Sorosky, 1977). Conversely, guilt can be translated into excessive permissiveness for the teenager. One parent, when confronted with "You're sleeping with your boyfriend. Why can't I?" gave her 15-year-old daughter explicit permission to have sex with boys.

In addition, the teenager is faced with information about the parents' sex lives that would never have been apparent without the divorce. As Sorosky (1977) pointed out, the parents are no longer safe sex objects. The father who is dating a much younger woman (a not unusual pattern) may find a pseudo-peer relationship with his teenage daughter or son, and thus lose healthy generational boundaries.

It is important that parents of adolescents not handle their own guilt by becoming excessively permissive toward their children. Adolescents need to be told that adults and teenagers have different rules and that a variety of behaviors acceptable for adults are not acceptable for teens.

6. *Self-esteem goes down.* The early adolescent's self-esteem is particularly vulnerable. Self-esteem in children tends to rise until age 12 and then drops until 18 years of age (Simmons, Rosenberg, and Rosenberg, 1973). When teenagers describe themselves, they are more negative than they were when younger. Feelings about how acceptable the self is is a major issue. Since the child identifies with both parents, continuing parental conflict, including character assassinations, is likely to substantially reduce self-esteem.

Self-perceived social and cognitive competence among adolescents from divorced homes was found to be lower than among adolescents from intact homes (Long, Forehand, Fauber, and Brody, 1987). When divorced parents of adolescents had high conflict, the family was also characterized by high parent–adolescent conflict and poorer school performance (Forehand, Brody, Long, Slotkin, & Fauber, 1986). Also, adolescent males were found to be more reactive than adolescent females to parental conflict, as based on self-report, mother's report, and teacher's report.

As for all other ages, whatever the therapist can do to encourage parents to decrease fighting or to decrease the exposure of the child to that fighting, the better off the child is likely to be.

Another response to divorce during adolescence noted by Wallerstein and Kelly (1974a) and other clinicians is delayed entry or accelerated entry into psychological adolescence. Those children with delayed entry may refuse to engage in the separation from parents, remaining excessively dependent. Wallerstein and Kelly (1974) reported a case of heightened parentification in which a young teenage boy took control of his mother, checking her social activities, monitoring her telephone calls, and requesting the check at restaurants. Such teenagers do not develop the peer relations that are helpful to them in the individuation process.

Accelerated entry into adolescence tends to manifest itself in early introduction into adult pleasures (i.e., sex, drugs, and alcohol). Parents undergoing separation are often so preoccupied with their own pain that they do not provide adequate supervision. For example, one 13-year-old boy came home drunk at 4 A.M., and his mother only expressed surprise that he arrived home so late. As mentioned earlier, other parents permit excessive freedom because they feel sorry for the pain that the adolescent experienced as a function of the divorce. Many teenagers who act out sexually and by using drugs may simply be wishing for external controls to be placed on them.

In terms of normal development, research findings indicated that teenagers develop the most mature levels of autonomy with a democratic level of control (Conger and Petersen, 1984). A democratic level of control is one in which there are clear guidelines for behavior, but the teenager participates in the development of the rules and of consequences for breaking them. Complete freedom and high levels of authoritarianism develop teenagers who are excessively dependent or excessively rebellious (Mussen et al., 1979).

One major concern among adolescents is the possibility for success of their own future marriage. Children who are experiencing their parents' divorce during adolescence are all seeing a marriage of some duration break up, which creates an uncertainty that marriages can last.

Adolescents can be reassured that for their own future, they are not doomed to repeat the mistakes of their parents. They can learn from their parents' mistakes.

College Students

Little research has been done on the late adolescent's or college age child's reaction to divorce of parents. In a small sample of thirty-nine college students from 18 to 23 years of age, Cooney, Smyer, Hagestad, and Klock (1986) looked at reactions to parents' divorces that occurred within the last three years. The parents had been married an average of 20.1 years prior to divorce. Sixty-two percent of the college women reported emotional problems in response to the divorce, whereas 42 percent of the men reported difficulty. Only 14 percent had sought counseling during the period of greatest upset. Holidays created problems for 85 percent of the group. The students were angrier at their fathers and more worried about their mothers. The father–daughter relationship seemed particularly vulnerable in terms of subsequent problems. Thus, even at college age, children experience considerable distress over the separation and divorce of parents.

Comparison Studies over Childhood

As part of our separation and divorce program, Bernard Bloom and I (Hodges and Bloom, 1984) evaluated the parental report of the behavior of 107 children from 1 to 18 years of age who were an average of 1.8 months after separation when the parents joined the study. People participating in the study were solicited by a deliberately ambiguous offer to participate in the University of Colorado Separation and Divorce Project. People who participated had reactions to the separation that ranged from significant distress to no distress. The parents provided descriptions of the children at entry into the study, at 12 months later, and at 18 months later (20 months postseparation).

Consistent with the studies previously discussed, younger children were reported as exhibiting more acting out than older children. Older children were seen as more depressed. Boys were described as having more problems than girls on all measures at the initial interview and on all measures except depression at 6 and 18 months.

Our study had extensive questions and long-term follow-up, but was obviously flawed by the nonrandom nature of the participants, all of whom were volunteers. Whether a person chose to answer the advertisements for the project was out of our control.

Levin (1988/1989) used the nationally representative Health Examination Survey for Children to evaluate the reaction of children to divorce. The children were 6 to 11 in the first cycle and 12 to 17 in the second cycle. Data were collected in several cycles from 1963 to 1970 and involved interviews, paper-and-pencil tests, and physical examinations. The disadvantage of these data is that they were collected in the 1960s, when divorce was less common than it is more recently. The two major advantages are the extensive, careful data collection and the representative sample of around 7,000 children.

Marital status of parents did not have an important impact on physical or health outcomes (usually 1 to 2 percent of the variance). Cognitive and intellectual functioning were affected to a greater degree, but still at a very low level (up to 2.58 percent of the variance). The effect of divorce was indirect so that when other variables affected by divorce were controlled, the level of prediction was usually minimal.

On the positive side (although still at low levels of prediction), compared with children in intact families, children living with a divorced mother had

fewer academic problems, performed better on intelligence and achievement tests, and were monitored more closely by their parent(s). However,
academic scores in general were lower for children of divorce than for children of intact families. These children of divorce also had more nighttime
problems. Boys in divorced families had better oral hygiene, were slimmer,
and had better overall health than boys in intact homes. Girls in divorced
homes had poorer oral hygiene, somewhat greater ear and hearing problems,
and poorer overall health than girls from intact families. It is a rare finding
that girls are having more difficulty than boys.

A Prospective Study of Reactions to Divorce

As previously noted, a chronic problem in interpreting research on the effect
of divorce is the fact that children are almost always first evaluated after
the parents' separation. The question can always be raised as to whether a
child's problems are due to the divorce per se or to growing up in an unhappy
home. In a very important study, Block, Block, and Gjerde (1986) evaluated
children from intact families at 3, 4, and 7 years of age. Some of these children
subsequently experienced the divorce of parents. These data made it possible
to evaluate the behavior of children of divorce several years prior to the divorce (which happened up to 11 years later). Compared with boys whose
parents remained married, boys whose parents subsequently divorced were
described as having undercontrol of impulses, higher levels of aggression, and
excessive energy *prior to the divorce*. Girls whose parents subsequently divorced were described at age three in positive terms: competent, planful, and
resistant to being victimized. At age four, these girls were described in similar, but less complimentary ways, as unyielding, not being eager to please, and
not getting along with others. They were less responsive to reason, less sex-
role stereotyped, and less calm. By age seven, these girls continued to be
evaluated in a mixed manner. They were seen as not getting along as well with
others, as being open to guilt, and as having high standards for the self and
high intellectual capacity.

   These findings suggest that the family environment prior to divorce
may play a role in affecting children of divorce. The authors suggested that
chronic marital conflict (see the discussion in Chapter 3 on this topic) and
inaccessible, upset parents may account for these predivorce behaviors of
the children. Because the behaviors occurred while families were still intact,
gender differences could not be due to mother-custody arrangements.

Studies in Which Age Was Not Taken into Account

McDermott (1970) reviewed the intake records of 1,487 children to age 14
who were evaluated at the University of Michigan's Children's Psychiatric
Hospital from 1961 to 1964. Of these children, 116 were from families
of divorce and 1,349 were from intact families. McDermott found that

duration of presenting problems was shorter for children of divorce than for children of intact families. Most had had the problem for 1 to 2 years and were 6 to 12 years of age. Home and school maladjustment were given as diagnoses more often for children of divorce than for children of intact families. Children of divorce were also characterized as running away from home more often and as having very poor home and school behavior. He classified 34.3 percent of the divorce group as depressed, but did not give a comparable statistic for children from intact families. He noted that one common problem in divorced families was the conspiracy of the mother and child to recreate the absent father by having the child identify with the father's traits.

In contrast, Morrison (1974) looked at 127 children who had already been diagnosed as having psychiatric problems and found few differences between children of divorce and children from intact families. Children of divorce were twice as likely to have problems with enuresis after age 5, as were children from intact families, but no other differences were found, including no differences in level of depression. Also, in contrast to McDermott's (1970) data, children of divorce had a longer duration of presenting problems.

Brady, Bray, and Zeeb (1986) conducted a large-scale study of the relationship of parental marital status for 703 children (from 2 to 17 years of age) referred to a nonprofit mental health clinic in Houston, Texas. Although studies using clinical populations can indicate how marital status of parents is related to the type or number of problems, they cannot indicate whether problems occur, because only problem children are evaluated. Brady et al. concluded that problematic children from separated, divorced, and remarried families and problematic children from intact families differed in type and degree of problems. These problems included less maturity, more sleep disturbances, more tension, and more hyperactive behavior for children from nonintact families than for children from intact families. Children from separated families had the most severe problems, consistent with the findings of Hodges and Bloom (1984). There were no statistically significant differences, however, between children of separation and children of divorce. Children from remarried families had more conduct problems, hyperactivity, and sibling problems than children of divorce.

Effect of Child Gender on Response to Parental Divorce

Many of the studies summarized above indicate that boys have more problems in response to the divorce of parents than do girls. Zaslow (1988, 1989), however, who extensively reviewed the research literature on this issue, raised serious questions about concluding that boys have greater problems than girls in response to divorce. A third of these studies did not indicate that boys are particularly at risk. When sample type, outcome variables, age of child, and source of data were taken into account, Zaslow found that boys from unremarried, mother-custody homes had more short- and long-term problems than girls in the same setting. Girls had more problems post-divorce if they lived with a stepfather or in father custody (see also Chapters 5 and 9). Research findings indicated that girls of divorce had more problems with heterosexual relationships during and after adolescence. Studies with children aged 13 and older generally do not show gender differences in response to divorce.

Studies Indicating No Lasting Effect of Divorce on Child Development

The prior discussion of my research (Hodges et al., 1979) suggested that children in some communities may not be adversely affected by divorce. Other studies have indicated that divorce did not result in measurable maladjustment. There is a moderately large literature that has deemphasized the effects of divorce on children.

Santrock (1975), using careful controls, reported the effect of early divorce on fifth- and sixth-grade boys and found few differences in moral development. Burchinal (1964) tested 1,566 seventh and eleventh graders in Cedar Rapids, Iowa, and found few significant differences as a function of the marital status in the home. Reinhard (1977) reported little effect of divorce during adolescence. Landis (1960) reported that college students who had experienced the divorce of their parents from ages 5 to 8 were less upset than peers who had experienced the divorce of their parents at a later age. Pitts, Meyer, Brooks, and Winokur (1965) found no relationship between divorce in childhood and any diagnostic category as compared to a control group. Gregory (1966) reported no effect of childhood divorce on 1,056 adult psychiatric patients with a control group matched for age and sex. Adult neurotics were significantly less likely to have lost a parent before age 5.

Warren, Ilgen, Van Bourgondien, Konanc, Grew, and Amara (1986) found only minimal differences between 112 children 7 to 12 years of age who were at least a year postseparation and a normal reference group. The children of divorce were not different from the norms on anxiety, defensiveness, self-esteem, parental report of behavior problems, school functioning, and family functioning. Only parent-reported home behavior exceeded test norms.

In a study of thirty-eight 3- to 6-year-olds whose parents had divorced and forty-two age-matched children from intact families, Jacobs, Guidubaldi, and Nastasi (1986) found no significant difference in social functioning for the two groups. Children of divorce were higher in verbal memory and numerical memory than children from intact homes. For the children of divorce, family support predicted total social functioning and physical well-being.

Johnson and Hutchinson (1988/1989), in an evaluation of 199 children from grades 7 to 12, found no statistical differences in overall self-concept as a function of marital status of parents. Only 3 of the 48 self-describing adjectives differed for children of divorce and intact families.

SUMMARY

There is evidence of broad effects of marital separation and divorce on child development. Young children are likely to demonstrate aggression and other acting-out behavior. Teenagers may show more withdrawal and depression. Children of divorce demonstrate a wide variety of strengths as a function of divorce. If the child is able to cope adequately with the stress of marital disruption and separation, the child may learn to be independent and more mature. In Chapter 3, the research on long-term effects of divorce and the role of other stressors are reviewed.

Developmental Course after Divorce: The Role of Context

As the child's ability to process information matures, the child begins to understand parental separation and divorce from a different perspective. Even if no new environmental stressors occur, it is reasonable to expect children's reactions to the separation to change as the children process the meaning of what is happening and cope with the stress. However, postseparation life is not typically smooth, and separation and divorce predict the occurrence of other stressful events.

Separation and divorce are often correlated with parental conflict and reduced financial resources. Parent–child relationships and parent style are influenced by divorce. Stress on both parent and child affects adaptive responses to divorce. Kalter (1987), after reviewing research literature and clinical experience, suggested that the developmental tasks of (1) handling anger and aggression, (2) separation-individuation, and (3) gender identity all may be affected by divorce. If one parent has custody and the other is peripheral or if there is sustained conflict between parents, vulnerabilities may develop in the child.

LONG-TERM ADJUSTMENT TO DIVORCE

Given the large number of variables that could affect children over time, it is surprising that children exhibit commonalities in their adjustment to separation and divorce from 6 months to 10 years later. Clearly, there are some common experiences of children that increase the likelihood of certain adjustment styles.

Six Months to 2 Years Postseparation or Divorce

According to Wallerstein and Kelly (1975), approximately two-thirds of children 2½ to 3¼ years old showed substantial improvement 1 year after parental separation. (It should be noted, however, that the sample size was nine.) These children continued to exhibit a readiness to accept and reach out to strangers and a desire to sit in a stranger's lap and hold hands.

For the 11 preschool children, aged 3 3/4 to 4 3/4 years, 7 were worse off a year later, suggesting that this age is particularly vulnerable to long-term effects of parental separation. The difficulties a year later were in the direction of increased inhibition and constriction, lowered self-esteem, sadness, and neediness. These children exhibited a need for physical contact, individual attention, and approval. Wallerstein and Kelly agreed with McDermott (1968) that the children were unable to handle their anxiety and depression through play and that their play was characterized by seriousness, sadness, and a sense of helplessness.

For early latency age children, Kelly and Wallerstein (1976) reported on the course of adjustment for 26 children who were 7 and 8 years of age. By a year later, the pain experienced initially had largely disappeared and was replaced by sad resignation. They reported that by a year later, 50% had improved in adjustment, 15% had consolidated the difficulties initially seen, and 23% were worse in adjustment.

For later latency children (31 children aged 9 and 10), Wallerstein and Kelly (1976b) reported that about 21% were still adversely affected a year later. Wallerstein and Kelly (1974) reported that of the 21 teenagers studied, most were proceeding toward stage-appropriate tasks within a year following parental separation. Those teenagers who experienced entry into adolescence with a history of long-standing difficulties had more trouble. The precise percentage of adolescents doing well a year later was not reported.

In a National Association of School Psychologists study, Guidubaldi and Perry (1985) found that, 2 years after evaluation in a previous study children of divorce continued to appear more poorly adjusted than children from intact families, based on 9 of 30 mental health measures. Boys from divorced homes continued to score higher in maladaptive behaviors. Although this study was not based on a known period following parental separation, it does give some information of changes over time in children of elementary school age.

Hodges and Bloom (1984) evaluated parental reports of 107 children from 1 to 18 years of age over a period of 20 months beginning an average of 2 months postseparation. The study found that the Disruptive Behavior Scale was higher for younger children than older children at the 6- and 18-month interviews. Depression increased with age at both the initial and 6-month interviews. Boys were having more difficulties on all four scales (Depression, Disruptive, Agitation, and Total score) at the initial interview, and on all scales except Depression at 6 and 18 months.

The child's age also made a difference in the reaction over time. Rated maladjustment increased as a function of time (over the 18-month follow-up) for children below 8 years of age. For children older than 8 years of age, although mean scores continued to increase over time, the increases were not statistically significant. These findings are similar to Wallerstein and Kelly's (1976a) results.

Professionals who suggest to divorcing parents that children's reactions to divorce will disappear in a few months are doing the clients a disservice. Particularly for preschool and early school age children, there is reason to believe that a significant number will be seen as worse off for the next 1 to 2 years. For older children, the adjustment level may not deteriorate, but improvement may not occur.

One important finding in Hodges and Bloom's (1984) study was that parents who were separated or remarried at the 18-month follow-up described their children as worse off than did parents who were divorced but not remarried. These findings for separated parents are consistent with the view that when parents are separated, but not divorced, it may be a particularly vulnerable time for children (Kalter, 1977).

Parents who remain separated without either reconciling or divorcing may be creating additional stress for the child. The mental health professional may help the child's adjustment by encouraging parents to decide what they want to do with the relationship.

Hetherington, Cox, and Cox (1979) reported on a 2-year follow-up of preschool age children of divorce and a matched group of children from intact families. They noted that by a year postdivorce, the girls had returned to a level of adjustment similar to the girls from intact families. In contrast, by 2 years postdivorce, boys were only approaching the level of adjustment of boys from intact families. By 2 years, one-fourth of the fathers and one-half of the mothers said that the relationships with their children were better than ever. Parents, however, were having difficulties with affection with their children, were inconsistent in discipline, and had poor control over their children. Positive behaviors were rarely rewarded. The divorced mothers were giving children twice as many commands as mothers from intact families, whereas the fathers were more indulging of the children.

Four to 6 Years Postseparation

Kurdek, Blisk, and Siesky (1981) evaluated the reactions to divorce of 58 white, middle class, 8- to 17-year-old children, whose parents had been separated for 4 years. They then evaluated the adjustment levels 2 years later, at approximately 6 years postseparation and divorce. By 4 years postdivorce, the children did not seem to be experiencing severe problems in regards to the divorce; however, the children's reactions toward the divorce were still primarily negative.

By 6 years postdivorce, children were not generally experiencing severe problems with regard to the parents' divorce. Children were now less likely to blame themselves for the divorce and did not think their parents would reconcile. The well-adjusted child was older, had parents who were not recently divorced, and had an internal locus of control and a high level of interpersonal reasoning. As found for the 4-year data, these children were better adjusted if they experienced infrequent visitation from the noncustodial parent. Because other data indicate that frequent visitation is best for the child, it is difficult to interpret the relationship with infrequent visitation. Kurdek et al. (1981) interpreted that finding to indicate that diminished contact might reduce hopes of reconciliation and increase awareness of parental incompatibility. Another possibility is the reduced level of conflict that occurs with rare contacts.

Wallerstein and Kelly (1980c) provided information about children's adjustment levels in their 5-year follow-up. Some of their statistics are quite sobering. Five years later, 40% of children had poor relationships with their fathers and 25% had poor relationships with their mothers. There was no longer any age effect of divorce. Children doing well came from families with low parental conflict, good quality of parenting, *regular* visitation (in contrast to the findings of Kurdek et al., 1981), absence of feelings of rejection by the noncustodial parent, personality strengths, a supportive network, and the absence of anger and depression. Wallerstein and Kelly reported that it was not possible to predict postdivorce functioning based on knowledge of predivorce functioning. In their sample, 37% were characterized as moderately to severely depressed. The authors reported that best adjustment for girls 5 to 12 years of age occurred when there was low conflict at home, the mother was not lonely, and the girls had good peer relationships. Younger girls were vulnerable to psychologically disturbed mothers. Older adolescent boys and girls were affected by the psychological intactness of the father. One of the more distressing statistics provided by Wallerstein and Kelly is that 80% of the children had not been provided with adequate explanations or assurance of their continued care.

Regardless of the age of the child (except for infants), parents should be encouraged to provide their child with some explanation of the divorce, as well as information about what is going to happen in terms of living space, when visitation is going to occur, how holidays are going to be arranged, and what the future will be like. In addition, parents having the resources for interpersonal skills should be urged to encourage their children to talk about the divorce and to ask questions.

In a longitudinal study over 5 years, Rickel and Langner (1985) examined an ethnically mixed New York City sample of 1,034 families for the effects of marital disruption as reported by the mother. From 25 to 50% of the subsamples had experienced marital disruption. Time since marital separation was not reported. At the time of the original assessment, children from fatherless homes, as compared with children from intact homes, were characterized as having greater levels of underdemanding (significant for Hispanics), delinquency, total impairment, and total symptoms. On nine scales, children living with a surrogate father (a boyfriend or stepfather) experienced more pathology than children in divorced or intact families. Five years later, the negative effect of a surrogate father had largely disappeared, as had the effect of father absence. At the 5-year evaluation, father absence led to more reports of delinquency than in father-surrogate families, which in turn led to more reports of delinquency than in intact families. Rickel and Langner suggested that although the presence of a surrogate father might be initially disruptive, the effect seems to diminish over time (but not disappear altogether).

Six Years Postseparation

In a 6-year follow-up of preschool children, Hetherington, Cox, and Cox (1985) found that 9- to 11-year old girls with nonremarried mothers were very similar in adjustment to matched girls in intact homes. For boys 6 years later, family members, schools, and the boys themselves reported more externalizing behavior. Family members also reported the boys as depressed and withdrawn, behaviors not reported by the boys or the schools.

Ten Years Postseparation

In a 5-year follow-up of 1,197 children (328 who had experienced the divorce of parents since the last interview) participating in the National Survey of Children, Allison and Furstenberg (1989) analyzed all children of divorce in the sample. Children who were 10 years postseparation were doing less well than those who were 5 years postdivorce. This finding may be due to an age effect, because children who were 10 years postseparation also were younger at the time of the separation. Based on these findings, it appears that 10 years after divorce, the negative effects of divorce are most apparent for children who were very young (2 to 7 years old) at the time of marital separation.

In a 10-year follow-up of the Wallerstein and Kelly (1980c) study (discussed in some detail in the previous chapter), Wallerstein and Blakeslee (1989) reported on the interviews of 116 of the original 131 children. The children were 11 to 29 years old at follow-up. Many of the children or young adults continued to think of themselves as coming from a divorced family. About one-half of the mothers and one-third of the fathers were still intensely angry 10 years later.

Boys in the 6- to 8-year-old range at the time of the divorce were seen 10 years later as withdrawn, aggressive, or having difficulty concentrating in school. Over a third of the young men and women 19 to 29 years old at follow-up had little or no ambition. This reported high number of young adults with lack of goals, low self-esteem, sense of helplessness, and the tendency to drop out of college for unskilled jobs has frightened divorcing parents who have read Wallerstein and Blakeslee's (1989) book. It is important to note, however, the absence of a control group in the study. Many children of affluence have never learned to work toward a goal, to delay gratification, and to be patient for the benefits of hard work. Without the control group, it is unknown whether Wallerstein and Blakeslee's results are due to parental divorce, as they suggest, or to the children's having relatively affluent parents.

Wallerstein (1984) provided a 10-year follow-up report on reactions of 30 children who were between the ages of 2 ½ and 6 at the point of the original study. These 30 children, 14 boys and 16 girls, were among the 34 preschool children in the original study. Custody had been found to be quite stable over the 10 years. Of the 30 children, 90% had remained in the custody of their mothers. Over half were living in remarriage homes, the remarriage usually occurring within 3 years of the breakup. One-third lived within an hour's drive of their fathers, revealing a surprising stability in geographic mobility, a result that may have occurred as a function of the counseling program. Of the remaining, many fathers had moved some distance, with half of the total sample of fathers living in other states.

Most of the children claimed no memories of the predivorce family. Very few remembered their emotional reactions to the divorce. No child remembered being frightened, even though this feeling was the most common reported response at the time. These children who were preschool age at the time of the divorce did not carry painful memories of the divorce. This lack of memories was in sharp contrast to the reaction of older children, who reported vivid memories of the separation and their pain.

The follow-up of preschool children 10 years later indicated that these children were not preoccupied with the reasons for the divorce, and few had clear ideas of why the divorce occurred. Few children were caught up in the bitterness between the parents.

Although the children did not continue feeling the pain of the divorce experience, over half of them still talked wistfully of life in the intact family. One-quarter disapproved of divorce. About half still had reconciliation fantasies, although these fantasies were seldom seen as realistic.

Over half of the children had close, trusting, open relationships with their mothers. Many children appreciated their mothers for how hard it was to be a single parent. Almost all children were aware of economic issues. A subgroup of children were angry at the mother and felt that she was not physically or emotionally available.

In terms of relationships with the fathers, all but one child continued to value the father. This valuing was independent of how much visitation occurred. The angriest children were those who had experienced severe economic deprivation as a result of the father's failure to pay child support that he could afford.

In another report on the 10-year interviews of only the girls in the study, Wallerstein and Corbin (1989) noted that the girls doing by far the best were the youngest female adolescents, who had been toddlers and preschool age children at the time of the divorce, a report consistent with the previously published results. Wallerstein and Corbin reported that three-fourths of these young adolescent girls were doing well in school and in peer relations, and seemed emotionally well adjusted.

Ten years after divorce, children who were preschool age at the time of the divorce seem to have no memories of the predivorced family.

Children who were in early latency at the time of the divorce (Wallerstein, 1987) and who were 16 to 18 at the time of follow-up, were seen as less well adjusted than the younger children. One-half of the boys and one-quarter of the girls were judged as doing poorly. For boys, problems were relatively minor and less serious than the next older age group. For girls, however, a quarter (i.e., 4 of 20) had had abortions. Depression was high, and there had been suicide attempts. Of these 16- to 18-year-old females, one-quarter were seen as doing poorly, and the group was seen as suffering from significant unhappiness, loneliness, and a sense of neediness and deprivation.

Children who were in early middle childhood at the time of the divorce continued to have problems 10 years later.

For the girls aged 19 to 23 at the 10-year interview, outcome was very poor. Almost 60% were seen as doing poorly, and 45% had vivid memories of unhappy times around the divorce (Wallerstein & Corbin, 1989). In another report for those now 19 to 29 at the 10-year interviews (Wallerstein, Corbin, & Lewis, 1988), the young adults felt sadness, resentment, and feelings of having missed out on growing up in an intact family. Only two-thirds were going to college in a community in which 85% of teenagers go to college. Wallerstein et al. suggested that the lower than expected college attendance may be due to economics, as most of these children lost child support on their eighteenth birthday. In another report of this age group, Wallerstein (1985) reported that 68% of the 40 young adults had engaged in illegal activity during adolescence or young adulthood, often consisting of under-age alcohol consumption or recreational drug use. Of those, 12 had been in serious activities, including assault, burglary, arson, drug dealing, theft, and serious traffic violations.

Children in late middle childhood at the time of the divorce experienced problems with sadness, limited education, and illegal behavior at the 10-year follow-up.

According to Wallerstein (1985), the adolescents had reconciled themselves to the divorce. Two-thirds felt that their parents had been ill-suited for each other and that the divorce was necessary. Many had described themselves as stronger and more independent as a result of the divorce.

Many of the young women who had experienced parental divorce reported chronic anxiety about betrayal in their own relationships. Wallerstein and Blakeslee (1989) reported this anxiety as a long-term, sleeper effect, which often was not apparent in adolescence, but became quite strong in adult life. Cohabitation was common for these young women. They sought older men whom they saw as less likely to betray them. They also may have been seeking a substitute parent, yearning for someone to take care of them. This cohabitation pattern for young women of divorce has been found in numerous other studies. Of those women who had married prior to age 20 (number unspecified), all but one had subsequently divorced by the time of the 10-year follow-up. They married men that they scarcely knew, and most relationships were violent. (As is true for all the reports on this study, the numbers are not typically given and it is difficult to determine the criteria for diagnosis.)

Fine, Moreland, and Schwebel (1983) obtained data from 100 introductory psychology students who had experienced parental divorce 7 or more years previously and compared the answers to self-report questionnaire with 141 students from continuously intact families. The average time since divorce was 10 years. They found that young adults from divorced families perceived the relationship with fathers and mothers less positively than did participants from intact families. Girls from both types of families perceived their relationships with mothers more positively than did boys. By 7 years postdivorce, there was no relationship between age at time of divorce and any dependent measures.

In this study, there was no indication that the parent–child relationships were unhealthy. Indeed, participants from divorced families rated their relationships with their parents as essentially average in quality (participants from intact families rated their relationships as above average).

Factors that were seen as reducing the negative impact of divorce on the postdivorce father–child relationship were the perception of a positive predivorce family life, a higher quality predivorce father–child relationship, parents who had more frequent contact with one another (in contrast to the findings of Kurdek et al., 1981), and higher socioeconomic status. Factors that improved the relationship between the mother and children of divorce were a more positive perception of the predivorce mother–child relationship, better adjustment of the participants at the time of the divorce, and parents who maintained a higher quality relationship after the divorce.

Hetherington (1972) investigated the behavior of adolescent girls who had lost fathers at an earlier age due to death or divorce and compared them with a matched group of teenage girls from intact families. The differences between the girls were dramatically illustrated by their behavior with the interviewer, who was a young adult male. Girls who had lost their fathers by death sat as far away from the interviewer as they could get, girls from intact families sat a middle distance from the interviewer, and girls who had lost their fathers through divorce sat as close as possible to the interviewer. The interview data from the girls and mothers confirmed the different behaviors.

Girls who had lost their fathers by death dated less and seemed frightened of men. Girls who had lost their fathers by divorce dated more often and were more sexually active. It is as if the girls who had lost their fathers by divorce were using sexuality to regain a relationship with a man.

It is likely that children of both sexes need a warm, intimate relationship with adults of both sexes for self-esteem, for normal sex-role development, and normal adult sexuality. Although a friend of the family or a relative can perform that role, participants in the Big Brothers or Big Sisters programs can also facilitate that learning.

Slater, Stewart, and Linn (1983) looked at 217 adolescents, who were an average of 16.6 years old. About one-third had come from divorced homes. Boys from divorced homes had better self-concepts and better perceptions of family environment than boys from intact homes. For girls, the opposite findings were obtained. If parents were divorced, the family was seen as having more control, more conflict, and more achievement orientation than was true if the parents were not divorced. According to these findings, boys seemed to have a relatively positive view of the divorced home and girls a relatively negative view.

Adult Adjustment with Childhood Divorce

Chess, Thomas, Korn, Mittelman, and Cohen (1983) reported on data from the New York Longitudinal Study for 132 subjects from 87 middle and upper middle class families that had been followed from early childhood to 18 to 22 years of age. Of the 132 young adults, 35 had experienced permanent parental separation, most leading to divorce. Separations had occurred before 5 years of age for 10 subjects, between 9 and 13 for 10, and between 14 and 19 for 11. Consistent with the other research found in this chapter, Chess et al. found that parental conflict at age 3 correlated with young adult adaptation ($r = .28$, $p < .01$), although this study is the first that indicated that a relationship may exist over such a large number of years. Surprisingly, they found that neither separation–divorce nor parental death was related to adult adjustment. The child's gender did not affect the correlations obtained. In an additional report on the same data base, Thomas and Chess (1984) noted that difficult temperament at age 3 also predicted adult adjustment at about the same level ($r = .29$) as did parental conflict. It should be noted that the New York Longitudinal Study was based on a relatively affluent population, and higher financial resources may offset any aversive consequences of separation and divorce.

Langner (cited in Adams, 1984) tracked 75 children of divorce and 125 children of intact families for 16 years. He controlled for effects of race and social class, a relative rarity in this area of research. As young adults, the two groups were found to have the same rates of depression and marital troubles. Adults whose parents had not separated had *twice* the arrest rate of adults whose parents had divorced—certainly data at odds with the more frequent findings of increased delinquency in children experiencing parental divorce.

Findings showed that if parental divorce occurred by 16 years of age, there was a greater risk for divorce in adult life. Glenn and Shelton (1983) found that the divorce and separation rate for adult women of childhood divorce was almost two-thirds higher than for women from intact childhood homes.

Farber, Felner, and Primavera (1985) obtained a wide range of measures for 65 late adolescent college students ranging in age from 17 to 23 who had experienced parental divorce after the age of 12. Adolescents of divorce in college who lived farther from home were more anxious, depressed, and hostile than adolescents of divorce living closer to home. Women were more depressed than men. Greater anxiety was present during the study for adolescents whose parents had been separated for shorter periods of time.

Self-blame was a consistent predictor of adjustment. Adolescents who more frequently blamed and criticized themselves were also more anxious, depressed, and hostile. Those who reported higher levels of stress related to divorce and other changes in the family also were more anxious, depressed, and hostile. Farber et al. (1985) concluded that the postdivorce environment was the most consistent predictor of postdivorce adjustment for adolescents.

Booth, Brinkerhoff, and White (1984) examined the impact of childhood divorce on the courtships of 365 college students. Parental divorce was related to a slight increase in courtship activity. If there was acrimony during and after the divorce, the courtship behavior was even more frequent. If the custodial parent remained single, courtship behavior was more frequent than if the custodial parent remarried. The authors interpreted the findings as reflecting the modeling of parental behavior. The perceived quality of courtship relationships was poorer if there was postdivorce conflict and if there was a postdivorce decline in parent–child relationships than if there was no conflict and continued good relationships. Women were more likely to be cohabiting if there was postdivorce conflict or if there was a poor parent–child relationship. The age during childhood when the divorce occurred had no effect on courtship behavior.

Lopez, Campbell, and Watkins (1988) found that adjustment was not related to whether the college students were from an intact or a divorced family. Students from divorced homes, however, had greater functional, emotional, and attitudinal independence from fathers and greater attitudinal independence from mothers than did students from intact homes. Students from divorced homes had less conflict with fathers than did students from intact homes. Conflict with mothers did not differ for the two groups.

In a study of young adult college students between 18 and 23 years of age, Drill (1986) investigated depression in 104 students from divorced families and 276 from intact families in the New York area. There was no difference in level of depression for the two groups. Students from divorced families viewed their fathers less favorably than did students from intact families.

Several other studies have looked at adult dating and marriage behavior as a function of childhood divorce. Kulka and Weingarten (1979) reported that adults from childhood homes of divorce were less likely to marry than adults from other homes. In contrast, according to Hepworth, Ryder, and Dreyer (1984), parental divorce was related to accelerated courtship. The death of a parent also led to accelerated courtship, but there was a greater tendency to avoid intimacy. The number of sexual partners was fewest for people who lost a parent to death during childhood. Those experiencing childhood divorce of parents had more sexual partners than did other groups. Adults whose parents stayed together were in the middle in terms of sexual behavior. These results are similar to Hetherington's (1972) and Wallerstein and Kelly's (1980c) findings on the effects of divorce on adolescents.

Grossman, Shea, and Adams (1980) compared 33 college students from divorced families with 261 students from intact families on measures of ego identity. Most of the children of divorce had experienced divorce when they were from 3 to 7 years old. In that study, no differences in ego identity as a function of parents' marital status were obtained. In fact, male students who had experienced divorce were higher in identity scores than students from intact families. There were no differences between students whose mothers had remarried and students from intact families. The higher ego identity scores for males of divorce are difficult to interpret. Although one could argue that divorce can strengthen coping processes, males from divorced families typically are found to have more, not less, trouble. The authors noted that, at least for their measures, no evidence indicated that negative effects of divorce continue into young adulthood.

OTHER LONG-TERM PROBLEM OUTCOMES FOR CHILDREN OF DIVORCE

The literature and clinical experience reviewed in this chapter have not indicated that delinquency, serious academic problems, depression, and suicide are likely long-term outcomes, despite findings of increased aggression, drop in school performance for a year or so, and depression among children 5 years after the divorce. When one reads the research and theoretical literature on delinquency and suicide, however, there are numerous references to "broken homes" and the effect of single-parent families.

Why do the two literatures not overlap in terms of understanding the effect of separation and divorce on children? First, there is a problem of definitions of populations. Broken homes and single-parent families are not synonymous with separation and divorce. A family can be a single-parent family for a variety of reasons, including the decision not to marry, abandonment, death of a parent, or prolonged work-related separations (e.g., the military). Each of these types of single-parent households is likely to have its own set of developmental tasks to solve. Second, there is a problem of base rates. Although suicide may be a relatively rare event in terms of absolute numbers for children, it is a common cause of death for children. The frequency may be too small to show up in the small sample sizes typically used in research on divorce and children.

Delinquency and Divorce

For a long time, an assumption in the literature has been that broken homes cause delinquency, dating back to the Cambridge-Somerville study (cited in Glueck & Glueck, 1950). Because much of this research is based on single parenting rather than divorce, it is discussed in Chapter 8 on single parenting. In summary of that research, family type seems to account for a trivial amount of the variance in delinquency, whereas economics plays a major role.

In one study of the relationship between parental divorce and young adult male crime, Mednick, Reznick, Hocevar, and Baker (1987) analyzed data from the Danish Perinatal Project. This longitudinal study was based on all 423 male deliveries that took place in one hospital from September 1959 to December 1961. Because females are seldom involved in criminal behavior, they were not included in the analysis. Young adult males from divorced families were statistically significantly more likely to be arrested for criminal behavior than were those from intact families. Time of parental divorce was not related to number of arrests. When socioeconomic status and father's criminality were statistically controlled, however, the relationship between divorce and criminality disappeared. Socioeconomic status and father's criminality were predictive of young adult criminality.

School Performance

For a long time, separation and divorce have been assumed to be major causes of school academic problems in terms of poor grades, poor school attendance, greater discipline problems, and greater likelihood of dropping out. Overall, however, research on divorce and school performance has been characterized by poor design.

One extensive study of 18,000 elementary and secondary school children in 14 states was conducted by the National Association of Elementary School Principals (NAESP) and the Institute for Development of Educational Activities (Evans & Neel, 1980; NAESP, 1980). The study looked at single-parent versus two-parent families. At the primary level, 38% of the one-parent children were low achievers, compared with only 24% of the two-parent children. At the secondary level, 34% of the one-parent children were low achievers compared with 23% of the two-parent children. One-parent children were more likely than two-parent children to be late to school, to be truant, and to receive disciplinary action. At the secondary level, three times as many single-parent children were expelled as two-parent children. Single-parent children were twice as likely to drop out of school as two-parent children.

This report, which has considerable status given its prestigious sponsors, has been criticized for using only school records, for not controlling adequately for the different levels of income in different groups, and for converting small absolute numbers into percentages, giving a misleading picture of the relationships (Staff, American Personnel and Guidance Association *Guidepost,* 1980). In addition, correlation was interpreted as cause.

In a follow-up analysis of the same data, Zakariya (1982) summarized the work of Wayne A. Barton on the effect of economics (as crudely measured by participation in subsidized school lunch and Title I programs). With this crude measure of economics, one-parent children constituted 41% of the lower income group, but only 17.5% of the total sample. Family income and student gender had a greater effect on achievement rank than whether the child came from a one- or two-parent home. Barton found, however, that when economics were held constant, two-parent children still had higher achievement than one-parent children. With follow-up analyses of 241 children, he also found that one-parent children had higher rates of absenteeism, but no differences in discipline referral, or suspension than two-parent children. Thus, there is evidence that children of divorce do have more difficulties in school.

Shinn (1978) reviewed 54 studies on academic performance and single-parent families. Of these studies, 28 were judged adequate in terms of methodology. Of these 28, 16 found some detrimental effects of father absence, 9 found no effects, and 3 found mixed or positive effects. Children from single-parent families were an average of 1.6 years behind in achievement and about .9 standard deviation units lower in IQ. Shinn noted that financial hardship, high levels of anxiety, and low level of parent–child interaction were important causes of poor academic performance for children in single-parent families.

Given evidence that financial hardship, anxiety, and low levels of parent–child interaction may play causative roles in poor academic performance for children of divorce, the mental health professional should encourage child support payments, work to reduce anxiety in the child, and help the family determine how to increase the quantity and quality of parent–child interactions.

The most carefully done investigation of the effects of divorce on academic performance was by Guidubaldi, Cleminshaw, Perry, and Mcloughlin (1983). They studied 341 children from divorced families and 358 children from intact families, matched on age, sex, and school. Children were randomly selected from schools. IQ and socioeconomic variables were controlled statistically. From each school, two first graders, two third graders, and two fifth graders were selected. Extensive differences between children from divorced and intact families were obtained, always favoring the children from intact families. Children from intact families were better on 14 of the 16 classroom behavior ratings, were absent less often, had higher peer popularity rating according to parent and teacher, had higher internal locus of control, and had higher Full Scale IQs and Wide Range Achievement Test reading and spelling scores. Their grades in reading and mathematics were higher. Children from intact families were less likely to repeat a school grade. Even when socioeconomic status was removed statistically, the relationships remained.

Boys from divorced families were particularly likely to have greater behavioral, social, and academic difficulties than girls from divorced families and boys from intact families. Girls from divorced families were found to have greater difficulty in very few areas, suggesting little divorce-related maladjustment. Older children of divorce were also more likely to have difficulties than were younger children.

Children of divorce who had gained stepfathers in early childhood were not handicapped in cognitive functioning. If there was no father substitute, then there was some cognitive deficit. Statistical control of economic factors was not rigorous, because other economically related variables could have some impact (e.g., drop in income may be more important than absolute income). This study, however, does suggest that children of divorce are at risk for problems in school.

When carefully controlled studies are performed, school performance seems to be affected by parental separation and divorce. Children may need additional emotional support, psychotherapy, structure, and tutoring to avoid reduced academic performance.

Kaye (1988/1989) tracked the grades and achievement scores in English and mathematics of 234 children of divorce and 223 children of intact families for 5 years. Immediately after divorce, achievement test scores for boys and girls were negatively affected, but grades were not. By 5 years postdivorce, boys of divorce had lower grades than boys of intact families. From the same time period, marital status of parents did not adversely affect the academic performance of girls.

When time since family disruption was evaluated for fourth graders, children from recently disrupted families had more academic problems in language and total achievement than children from early disrupted families and children from intact families (Kinard & Reinherz, 1986). These results suggest that, at least for that age group, the effect may be relatively short lived.

Teacher expectation of poorer performance for children of divorce may lead to teacher ratings that evaluate these children as poorer. There is ample evidence that teacher expectation affects how much the child will learn. For example, Santrock and Tracy (1978) showed 30 teachers a videotape on the social behavior of an 8-year-old boy. Half the teachers were told that he came from a divorced home, and half were told that he came from an intact home. Teachers rated the child perceived as coming from a divorced home as less happy, as having poorer social adjustment, and as being less able to cope with stress than the child perceived as coming from an intact home.

Kellam, Ensminger, and Turner (1977) also found that teachers' ratings of children's social adaptation could be predicted from knowledge of the child's family background. Because single-parent status is highly related to lower income, knowledge of parents' marital status could lead to teacher expectation of poor school performance.

In another study of potential teacher bias, 76 Israeli teachers were asked to evaluate a fictitious fifth-grade boy who was identified to different groups as being from an intact, remarried, divorced, or intact-conflicted parent family (Guttman & Broudo, 1988/1989). Teachers predicted that the academic functioning of a child from an intact family would be higher than for a child from an intact-conflicted family. The social and emotional functioning of a child from an intact family was predicted to be better than of children from the other three groups. A child of divorce was seen as having higher social functioning than a child from an intact-conflicted family. The emotional functioning of a child of divorce or remarriage was seen as higher than a child from an intact-conflicted family. Thus, teachers are correctly becoming more aware of the difficulties of the intact, but conflicted family.

Suicide

Adam, Lohrenz, and Harper (1973) looked at the suicidal ideation of 114 college students who had used campus mental health services, 50 from intact families, 35 who had lost a parent by death, and 29 who had lost a parent by divorce. In this sample, 50% of those who had lost a parent by death and 41% of those who had lost a parent by divorce had had serious suicidal ideation, compared with 10% of the controls. Of the 12 suicidal attempts in this population, 10 were students who had lost a parent by death or divorce.

Dorpat, Jackson, and Ripley (1965) reviewed 114 consecutive committed suicides and 121 attempted suicides in King County, Washington. This early study used "broken home" as a category, but divorce was the most common cause of parent loss. Of those who completed suicide, 50% were from parent-loss homes, but 63.9% of those who attempted suicide were from parent-loss homes. For those who attempted suicide, divorce was the most common cause of parent loss. For those who completed suicide, death was the most common cause of parent loss. In the attempted suicide group, 42.7% had lost both parents, whereas 22.8% of those who completed suicides had lost both parents. The high percentage of loss of both parents makes both of these groups atypical.

Crook and Raskin (1975) matched 115 depressed inpatients with a history of attempted suicide on age and sex with 115 nonsuicidal depressed patients and 285 normal subjects. The suicidal group had a significantly higher level of parental loss due to desertion, divorce, or separation prior to age 12 (the age set by the study) than the other two groups. Parental death was not related to suicide or depression.

In summary, there is evidence that divorce in childhood may increase school problems independent of economics and may increase the likelihood of adult suicide, particularly suicide attempts, but delinquency seems to be much more influenced by economic factors than by separation and divorce. Because most of the studies on adult suicide were performed 15 to 20 years ago when divorce was less common, there should be caution in applying the data to the present.

OTHER STRESSORS IN THE LIVES OF CHILDREN OF DIVORCE

One way of understanding the long-term effects of divorce on children is to consider what is happening in their lives during that time. Predivorce marital discord and the actual separation and divorce may be stressors that most children are capable of handling. The role of additional stressors was discussed previously in the context of research on children of particular ages. This section focuses on research on economic factors; family conflict, reconciliation, and repeated separations; cumulative effects of stress; and the effects of quantity and quality of parenting.

Economics

Substantial evidence indicates that families of divorce are adversely affected economically. Flynn (1984) cited government statistics that the single-parent family is the most significant factor contributing to the nation's higher poverty level. Single-parent families are headed mostly by women (90% of custody is mother custody, at least prior to recently enacted joint custody laws), and women earn approximately 59 cents for every dollar earned by men. Flynn noted that 75% of the poor in this country are women and children. Three years after divorce, only 19% of divorced fathers continue to pay child support payments. Even if support is paid, the amount of the award generally covers less than half the actual cost of raising a child. Even when the father has custody or does pay child support, supporting two households cannot be done for the same amount as supporting only one household.

Hodges, Wechsler, and Ballantine (1979) found that low income in families of divorce predicted child maladjustment, whereas low income was not related to maladjustment for children of intact families from the same school. In a follow-up study with a new sample of preschool children, Hodges, Tierney, and Buchsbaum (1984) found that perceived inadequacy of income and low total income predicted adjustment problems, independent of parents' marital status. Rated inadequate income predicted greater withdrawal and anxiety-depression in preschool children.

The latter study also obtained an interaction between marital status of parent and economics: Rated inadequacy of income interacted with marital status to predict level of anxiety in the preschool child. For children from intact families, rated adequacy of income had no effect on levels of anxiety-depression. For children of divorced families with adequate income, the level of anxiety and depression was the same as for children of intact families. Children of divorced families with rated inadequate income had substantially higher levels of anxiety-depression than the other three groups.

Based on a review of the literature, Herzog and Sudia (1973) argued that the negative effects of father absence on child development would be eliminated if the economic deprivation of divorce were eliminated. Blechman (1982) reviewed the literature on single parenting and the risk for maladjustment for the child. This review of the literature presented a convincing argument that prior research had so many methodological flaws that it was difficult to evaluate the effect of single parenting, independent of many other correlated and potentially confounding variables. Economic factors in particular tended to be uncontrolled. The greater frequency of identified problems in families of divorce may be due to the reduced resources of these families for solving family problems in a nonlegal manner. Blechman noted that, even when matched for socioeconomic status, samples were not comparable. Matching families by income necessarily selects families from the lower end of the income range in intact families and in the upper end of the income range for families of divorce. Blanchard and Biller (1971) found only 11 income-matched children from divorced and intact families from a pool of 297 children.

Wallerstein and Corbin (1989) found that when there was a major discrepancy in income between parents (specifically when mothers were economically disadvantaged compared with fathers), girls' psychological adjustment was poorer than when such a discrepancy was not present. Such problems were present regardless of whether the discrepancy was due to economic decline for the mother or economic advance for the father.

Thus, the behavioral problems of divorce may in part be a side effect of the economic conditions of divorce. Jauch (1977) noted that the poverty in homes of divorce, rather than divorce per se, may lead to child abuse, child neglect, delinquency, and child pathology.

Given the strong evidence that a drop in income and standard of living may play a major role in adjustment problems for children of divorce, helping professionals should do everything they can to encourage child support payments and other economic supports to families of divorce.

Parental Conflict

Most clinicians and researchers agree that interparental conflict has adverse effects on child development. Jacobson (1978b) evaluated children aged 3 to

13 from 30 families and looked at the amount of hostility that occurred between the custodial mother and ex-spouse. Jacobson found that for the preschool children ($n = 21$), interparental hostility preseparation predicted higher levels of aggression, fearfulness, and inhibition in the child postseparation. Porter and O'Leary (1980) evaluated 64 children who had been referred to a child psychological unit. Overt marital hostility was correlated with many behavior problems in boys, but not in girls. They raised the possibility that parents may be more protective of girls, avoiding shouting in their presence. In addition, girls may cope better with stress than boys. For example, girls in the study came from more discordant marriages than boys, suggesting that more marital hostility did not lead to referral for girls.

Hansen (1982) looked at the effects of interparental conflict on the adjustment to divorce of 36 preschool children. Hansen found that conflict between parents as reported by the mother had an adverse effect on child adjustment. Conflict over visitation was correlated with higher levels of anxiety in the child. Hansen also found that the content of the interparental conflict predicted child adjustment problems, but perhaps the problems themselves created the child's adjustment problems, rather than the conflict over the problem. Conflict over drinking, drug abuse, and finances all predicted problems in preschool children.

Tierney (1983) evaluated conflict between parents in a sample of 67 preschool children. Total conflict between parents as reported by the mother and father was related to a higher level of rated maladjustment in the child. Specific areas of maladjustment in the child as a function of interparental conflict included school and cognitive problems, irritability, immaturity, aggression, hyperactivity, sensitivity, and inhibition.

In a national survey of 1,423 children, Zill (cited in Adams, 1984) found that children from divorced families had fewer behavioral problems than children from intact families experiencing chronic conflict. Children from 12 to 16 who lived with fighting parents were 1.5 times more likely to be antisocial, including lying and bullying, than children living with divorced parents.

Emery (1982) gave an excellent review of the relationship between interparental conflict and children of divorce. He noted that there is a relationship between discord in intact marriages and severity or frequency of behavior problems in children. However, many of these studies were methodologically flawed. Emery noted that stronger associations between marital discord and child adjustment were found in clinic samples than in nonclinic samples, probably due to a greater range in adjustment levels in the clinic samples. Emery suggested that interparental conflict was the principal explanation for an association between divorce and childhood adjustment problems. He noted that several researchers have found that children from divorced, but conflict-free, homes were less likely to have problems than were children from conflictual, nondivorced homes.

Based on their review of the literature, Long and Forehand (1987) also concluded that parental conflict may be the major factor accounting for postdivorce adjustment problems in children. Evidence indicates that even children as young as 12 months are distressed by expressions of anger between adults (Cummings, 1987; Cummings, Zahn-Waxler, & Radke-Yarrow, 1981, 1984).

Not only is *pre*divorce conflict harmful to the child, but Long, Slater, Forehand, and Fauber (1988) found some evidence (although on a small sample) that *continued* conflict postdivorce was associated with lower grades and greater anxiety and withdrawal for young adolescents than conflict that was discontinued at the time of the divorce. When the conflict escalates to violence, there is reason to believe that the child is even more at risk for problems. In a review on family violence, Emery (1989) summarized research that family violence has pervasive effects on child development.

Johnston, Campbell, and Mayes (1985) looked at age-specific distress of 44 children aged 6 to 12 who were involved in parental postseparation disputes over custody. This sample experienced a high level of conflict, with 88% of parents being physically aggressive toward one another. Behaviors included slapping, pushing, spitting, biting, throwing objects, and threatening with guns and knives. These aggressions occurred on the average of once a month. Children had witnessed more than half of the abusive incidents. All the children were acutely distressed by the fighting and very frightened of violence. Younger latency (6- to 8-year-old) children tended to be submissive, and many tried to stop the fights. About half of the older children took sides in the fighting. Many children tried to avoid the fighting by leaving, but one-fourth of the children responded with aggression. The authors estimated that 40% of the children were passive in their adaptations and 40% merged with the angry parent and were enmeshed in the dispute. The children often worked at being good, conforming, and patient.

In another report on the same data (Johnston, Gonzalez, & Campbell, 1985), child maladjustment was predicted by role reversal of the child and the father, total disagreements between parents, and complaints by parents of the child's involvement in the dispute. In a continuation of the research program, Johnston, Gonzalez, and Campbell (1987) found that for 56 children (ages 4 to 12 at entry into the study), aggression and behavior problems increased as the children became more involved in the parents' conflicts. These findings were obtained at entry into the study and 2½ years later. In addition, verbal and physical abuse between parents predicted total behavior problems, depression, withdrawal, somatic complaints, and aggression 2 years later. Girls seemed to be more affected by parental conflict by being depressed and withdrawn. Older children were more aggressive and had more somatic complaints than younger children. At entry into the study, the sample had high levels of verbal abuse between parents (more than once a week) and physical abuse (once a month). By 2 years later, verbal abuse was once a month and physical abuse was almost nonexistent.

In another report on the same project, Johnston, Kline, and Tschann (1989) investigated 100 children from high-conflict families. Contact with the non-primary residential parent averaged 12.11 days per month for joint custody, compared with 4.05 days for sole custody. Once again, conflict interacted with access so that for these high-conflict families, children were more clinically disturbed if they had more frequent access.

In a study of 7- to 9-year-olds, 2 to 3 years postseparation, Camara and Resnick (1988) found that if divorced parents cooperated with one another (even if angry), the child had less aggression. Fathers who used verbal attacks to solve conflicts (regardless of the parents' marital status) had children who were less prosocial, had lower self-esteem, and had more behavior problems. Mothers' use of verbal attacks to resolve conflict had fewer effects on the children's aggressive behaviors. Children of such mothers, however, exhibited more parallel play (where children play side by side, but do not interact) than other children.

Wallerstein and Corbin (1989) noted that 10 years postdivorce, girls whose parents harshly judged one another were doing poorly. These parents expressed disappointment in the other parent's parenting and continued to blame the other parent for the divorce. All but one of the girls whose parents blamed each other were doing poorly (number unspecified). Girls whose parents accepted shared blame for the divorce were doing well 10 years later.

Walsh and Stolberg (1988/1989) found that greater parental hostility tended to be related to poorer parenting skills. Furthermore, even 5 years postseparation, high parental conflict was related to high levels of children's aggression. Children who witnessed parental hostility were angrier.

Tschann, Johnston, Kline, and Wallerstein (1989) developed a path model for predicting emotional adjustment based on 178 oldest children of divorce. Parent conflict again emerged as an important predictor. Its effects on children's adjustment were indirect by adversely affecting the quality of the postseparation mother–child relationship. Marital conflict predicted less warm mother–child relationships, which in turn predicted poorer emotional adjustment in children. Children who were better adjusted were female, had better infant temperament, visited the noncustodial parent more, and had better postseparation relationships with both parents.

I have treated aggressive boys from conflict-filled families by working on the conflict rather than the child's anger. It is a major accomplishment to successfully teach couple communication to parents who had been unable to talk to one another without exploding in anger. Facilitating parental communication and reducing conflict can eliminate adjustment problems in children, even without the children's being seen in therapy.

A significant percentage (but less than half) of parents in intense conflict can be convinced to reduce that conflict when it is demonstrated to them how it is hurting the children. Couple counseling can be effective in reducing interparental hostility and facilitate more adjusted behavior patterns in the children.

It is often useful during couple counseling to bring stepparents or cohabiting mates into such counseling for three reasons: (1) these individuals often play a significant parenting role and need to be included in plans for the child, (2) the presence of the significant other can help a parent who is keeping the relationship alive through conflict to accept the divorce, and (3) the two parents can be reassured that the new partners are not going to replace them in the parenting role.

Particularly important in working with aggressive children with high levels of interparental conflict is to encourage the parents to get together on discipline and to use a nonphysical form of punishment. Even simple agreements on how much television watching is acceptable, what bedtime is to be, or how many afternoon snacks are permissible are likely to be viewed by the child as evidence of cooperation, and aggression levels are likely to decrease.

Wallerstein and Blakeslee (1989) indicated a 25% incidence of family violence prior to separation and over 50% during the acute stage of the separation process. Half of the children who had observed marital violence became involved in abusive relationships in late adolescence and early adulthood. About 75% of the young adult women were victims of violence, and all the young adult men were perpetrators. Wallerstein and Blakeslee, as well as many other mental health professionals, believed that children who witness family violence are at risk for psychological problems.

It should be noted that most of the above studies have not controlled for parent–child conflict. It is likely that a parent who is aggressive toward the other parent is also aggressive toward the child. It would be difficult to determine which aggression is more negative for child development.

Jouriles, Barling, and O'Leary (1987) studied the relationship of parent conflict to parent–child aggression in 45 children from violent families. They found a strong relationship between the two $[r(43) = .56, p < .001]$. Also, high levels of parent–child aggression were related to conduct problems, attention problems, anxiety-withdrawal, and "motor excess." As is traditionally found, boys were externalizers and girls were internalizers.

Indeed, Lahey et al. (1988) argued that boys' conduct disorders may be due to having a parent with an antisocial personality disorder. In their study of 28 clinic-referred boys with conduct disorders and 34 clinic-referred boys with other diagnoses, they found that, once the factor of an antisocial parent was removed statistically, divorce had no relationship to personality disorders in the boys.

Child-Instigated Parental Conflict

Children will deliberately instigate interactions between parents to facilitate a reconciliation. Children wishing reconciliation become most anxious when parents do not interact. Even hostile interactions are less anxiety provoking than silence. One child asked his mother, a client of mine, "Is it OK to call my dad's new girlfriend 'Mother,' too?" The mother, who had not talked to her ex-spouse in 6 months, was on the phone in seconds, complaining to him that he was trying to eliminate her role as mother. I asked the mother what her son would expect her to feel in response to his question. She felt that he probably knew that she would not like his question. I suggested that he asked her the question to get her to do exactly what she did, that is, to call her ex-spouse. Indeed, it was likely that he was anxious about his father's new relationship and wanted to get his parents talking again. This case history is an excellent example of the importance of encouraging parents to keep the children out of the middle even when children place themselves there. The mother's response should have been that what the son called the woman at his father's house was between his father and himself, but that she never wanted to hear the other woman described as "Mom."

Mental health professionals should watch out for child-instigated conflicts between parents. The child may need active encouragement to stay out of parent fights. The child may also need strongly supported information that reconciliation is not going to occur (if, indeed, this information is correct), in order to discourage the child's efforts to force contact. Parents can reduce such efforts by interpreting the behavior to the child and refusing to be baited by the child's provocative behavior (easier suggested than acted on).

Reconciliation Followed by Divorce

The role of reconciliation has not been discussed frequently in the research or clinical literature. Clinicians have too frequently overlooked the impact of parents' reconciling, assuming perhaps that because children typically want reconciliation, it is not a stressor. One three-year-old child, for example, reacted relatively well to the parents' separation, but went to pieces after reconciliation. She cried frequently, showed extreme reactions to parental discord, and shadowed her parents everywhere. She now knew what she would feel if they separated again! Jacobson (1978b) found that if the divorce was characterized by previous parental separations, the child had significantly more withdrawal and less mature behavior. This research also showed that repeated separations are very hard on children. In our own research with preschool children (Hodges et al., 1984), we found that the total number of separations prior to divorce correlated .43 with ratings of dependency in the preschool child.

Repeated separations and reconciliations are very hard on children. Clinicians should encourage parents to stay in one state of habitation for a period of time and decide what they want to do. Because trial separations do not often end in reconciliation (Bloom et al., 1977), parents who are truly ambivalent about divorce should consider staying together until deciding. If the conflict is so severe that chronic tension or danger of violence is present, separation or divorce may be healthier for the children.

Kitson and Langlie (1984) found that the families of 152 reconciled couples were in high stress. Reconciled couples had higher rates of subjective distress, psychophysiological complaints, and physician visits than did the married and never separated, and the divorced. Even 5 ½ years after the reconciliation, these rates remained high. These families had a surprisingly high rate of violence, with 80 percent reporting one or more forms of domestic violence during the marriage.

Clinicians should be particularly sensitive to the high levels of stress and potential for violence in married families that have had repeated separations and reconciliations.

Abandonment

As previously mentioned, abandonment is a particularly difficult stress for children of separation and divorce. Although mother abandonment may be on the increase, father abandonment is far more likely. Abandonment would seem to be more likely when there is minimal bonding between the abandoning parent and the children. The level of bonding between traditional fathers and infants in the United States tends to be poor. Even with children of elementary school age, fathers spend only about 20 minutes per week in quality time. As the feminist movement and greater androgyny in men increase shared child care (as reflected in increases in father custody and joint custody), the rate of father abandonment should decrease. Fathers traditionally have had instrumental roles in discipline and wage earning, and only recently have showed interest in birthing, early child care, and bonding (Teyber and Hoffman, 1987).

Lack of bonding is only one reason for abandonment. Some parents find the sense of loss and pain so overwhelming that they avoid the children to reduce the sense of loss. Although these parents are intensely bonded to their children, they are unable to tolerate the sense of loss that is generated with every separation. The bonding may be combined with dependency that intensifies the sense of loss or may be due to an inability or unwillingness to complete the mourning of the lost relationship.

One father asked whether it was in the children's best interest for him to withdraw from parenting. The mother had remarried and the children liked the new stepfather. The mother would have preferred for the biological father to disappear from the scene so that she could re-form a nuclear family (a common fantasy, but not possible, as discussed in Chapter 9). The father loved the children, but was willing to give up his needs to be with them if the contact with him was not in their best interests. The clinician should always be careful with requests such as this one, because the father may be signaling that he is engaged in harmful behavior with the children and wants to withdraw to reduce his guilt and protect the children. In this case, there was no evidence of such a dynamic and the father seemed to be genuinely attached to the children. I suggested to him that his children can accept love from more than one family. Their identity would always be connected in some way to their identification with him. Abandonment by him would be harmful to their self-esteem. He was very relieved at this advice.

Children are better off getting some of their needs met than none of their needs met, even if the partial satisfaction of needs leads them to wish for more. Abandonment should be strongly discouraged unless severe pathology exists and psychological and physical protection of the children is not possible.

Teyber and Hoffman (1987) also proposed that the continued conflict between parents is a cause of father abandonment. The mother may lead the children to align with her against the father. The father feels powerless in this battle and gives up continued contact. Some parents find the rage at the other parent so noxious that avoidance of the whole family seems to be the only solution. Custodial parents have been effective in blocking (passively or actively) access to the children whom noncustodial parents have given up.

Mental health professionals are seldom contacted by abandoning parents for help with reestablishing contact with the children. When abandonment is discovered in the context of therapy for other reasons, the professional might explore whether abandonment occurred because of prior scripts of abandonment, lack of bonding, excessive dependency needs, depression at the loss and incomplete mourning, or anger at the custodial parent. While it is likely to be helpful to the child to encourage reengagement, the clinician also must evaluate the probable impact on the parent.

Estimates of abandonment rates range from 9 percent (Wallerstein and Kelly, 1980c) to 24 percent (Tierney, 1983), 29 percent (Fulton, 1979), and almost 50 percent (Furstenberg, 1988; Furstenberg and Nord, 1985).

As previously discussed, children commonly experience abandonment as personal rejection, regardless of the actual motivation by the abandoning parent. In addition to feeling this sense of rejection, children with abandoning parents dream of someday reobtaining these parents' love. Tessman (1978) described the "searching behavior" of some abandoned children, who look in the faces of strangers in shopping centers, searching for the abandoning parent. These children often experienced early abandonment and do not know what the absent parent looks like, but they assume that instant recognition will be possible. One 10-year-old child in therapy rode all over town on his bicycle on the day his stepfather was to adopt him in the hopes that he would see his father. He had not had contact with his father since he was two years old. No one knew of his father's location or had had contact with him since the divorce.

Another problem of abandonment is the possibility that the child will develop rescue fantasies to avoid the sense of rejection. For example, a child might think, "My father would be here if he could. Circumstances prevent him from seeing me. If he were here, he would not make me go to bed at 10," or, ". . . he would let me go to the rock concert." The custodial parent often resents the child's idealization of the abandoning parent and feels unappreciated. Attempts by the custodial parent to tear down this fantasy will be met with great resistance, since the child will be vulnerable to depression if he or she accepts the abandonment.

Rosenthal (1979) presented several case histories of children dealing with the sudden disappearance of a parent because of marital discord. Children showed sadness, longing for the absent parent, anger, and fear of loss of the other parent. The clinicians found that the relationship with the remaining parent was more important than the feelings about the absent parent in predicting adjustment in the child. According to Teyber and Hoffman (1987), when the father abandons, the child experiences loss of self-esteem, low initiative, depression, poor school performance, and poor peer relations.

The child who is abandoned by the noncustodial parent needs particular help in dealing with the blow to self-esteem. The child needs to be encouraged to interpret the abandonment as a problem of the noncustodial parent rather than a result of the child's unlovability. The child must also be encouraged to give up fantasies of rescue by the abandoning parent by learning to accept the implied rejection.

The Effect of Cumulative Stress on Preschool Children of Divorce

Because previous research indicated that not all preschool age children are at risk for maladjustment as the result of the separation and divorce of parents, and that economics and parental conflict affect adjustment to divorce, we decided to research what additional factors might predict which children were likely to have problems. Geographic mobility, low income, and young parents were known to be likely variables that predicted risk (Hodges et al., 1979). Age of mother, however, did not hold up as a predictor in later research. Those findings led us to look at two related variables: stress in the preschool child's and parents' life, and quality and quantity of parenting. There are two likely pathways in which the effect of cumulative stress may affect the child: (1) the child is directly affected by the stress on the family, and/or (2) the parents are so stressed that they are less available to the child for emotional and physical support.

In a separate study, Hodges et al. (1984) looked at 44 boys and 46 girls, 30 from divorced families and 60 from intact families, in terms of the amount of stress on the child and custodial parent. The two types of families did not differ in child's age, parents' ages, parents' education, or fathers' income. Total Parent Life Events was related to Total Child Life Events [$r(88) = .58$, $p < .001$], indicating a high degree of overlap, which is not surprising given that the events were occurring in the same family. First, the ability of demographic indices of stress (geographic mobility, income, adequacy of income, and age of mother) to predict adjustment was investigated. Coming from a divorced home predicted greater distractibility and more acting out. Although parents' marital status did not predict other problems, there were other findings in which the demographic indices predicted problems, independent of the parents' marital status. A greater number of moves predicted higher levels of aggression. Inadequate income predicted poor ability to stay on task, anxiety-depression, and total teacher-rated maladjustment. Lower income was related to the child's being seen as more fearful and depressed. Older mothers (compared with younger mothers in the previous study) had children with higher levels of poor task persistence and anxiety-depression.

It should be noted that although inadequate income and geographic mobility predicted maladjustment independent of marital status, families of divorce are more likely to have these stressors. In the Hodges et al. (1984) study, families of divorce moved more often, had higher rated inadequacy of income, and had lower income than did intact families.

Mental health professionals should be cautious about assuming that separation or divorce alone predicts maladjustment in preschool age children. Other stressors, particularly economic ones, may interact with divorce to predict problems. Separation and divorce lead to stressors (e.g., lower income, geographic relocation) that can cause problems independent of the stress of the separation.

Hodges et al. (1984) also examined whether the child's or the parents' stressful life events were a more potent predictor of maladjustment problems in the child. In every case, parent life events predicted adjustment better than did child life events. High level of parental stress, independent of marital status, predicted dependency, poor ability to stay on tasks, and distractibility in the child. These findings suggest that parental stress may indeed have more effect on the child than does direct stress. For children in late elementary school, both child and parent oriented stress predicted child problems (Hodges, et al., 1990).

In an extensive review of the life events and divorce literature, Sandler, Wolchik, and Braver (1988) noted consistent findings that the amount of negative life changes in the family is related to symptomatology in children of divorce. In fact, Stolberg, Camplair, Currier, and Wells (1987) concluded that life change events are the single best predictor of postdivorce adjustment in children. They noted that frequent life change events, marital hostility, and parental maladjustment all predicted children's postdivorce maladjustment.

Clinicians should be aware that parental stress is more important than child stress in predicting adjustment in the child.

Indeed, Felner, Terre, and Rowlison (1988) argued that divorce itself has no adaptive impact on children. From their perspective, predivorce parental discord, the nature and quality of parent–child relationships, hassles, life event changes, and disrupted family organization may all play more important roles in how children function.

Quantity and Quality of Parenting and Adjustment in Children of Divorce

Another major factor that might affect child adjustment is the quality of parenting. The single parent's parenting style, not balanced with a partner's perspective (see Chapter 8), may have a greater impact on the child than parenting that is balanced between two parents. The single parent under stress may also change his or her approach to the child.

Part of the negative effect of parental conflict on children may result from the affected ability of the parent to be responsive to the child's needs. For example, Tschann et al. (1989), using a path model, found that parental conflict indirectly affected a child's emotional adjustment by adversely affecting the quality of the postseparation mother–child relationship. A poor postseparation father–child relationship also predicted more behavior problems. As always, however, the direction of cause and effect is open to question in correlational studies.

The effects of economics also appear to be related to the quality of parenting. In evaluating distress in 77 custodial mothers, Braver, Gonzalez, Wolchik, and Sandler (1989) found that the mothers had experienced an average of a 30% drop in standard of living postdivorce. Drop in income and negative economic events (e.g., inability to pay bills) accounted for 21% of the variance in adjustment in the mother. If the mother was maladjusted, the quality of parenting was likely to be poorer.

In a national sample of 1,400 children, Peterson and Zill (1986) found that children who had positive relationships with both parents were less likely to have problems. Compared with children from intact families, however, children from divorced families were less likely to have good relationships with both parents. Approximately half of the children from intact families and one-quarter to one-third of the children from divorced families had good relationships with both parents. For boys, poor relationships with both parents predicted many problems. A good relationship with only the father was related to high levels of impulsive/hyperactive behaviors. Girls also benefited from having good relationships with both parents. If the girl had a good relationship with only the father, antisocial and impulsive/hyperactive problems were worse.

In a study of adjustment of children $4\frac{1}{2}$ to 7 years of age at 1 and $2\frac{1}{2}$ years postdivorce, MacKinnon, Brody, and Stoneman (1986) evaluated the families of single working mothers, married working mothers, and married nonworking mothers. They found that preschool children, especially boys in divorced mother households, received less stimulation than children in intact homes. Boys from mother-headed single-parent homes had fewer toys, games, and reading materials. Perhaps the energy required to control these boys led to less support for stimulating activities. Rosenthal, Leigh, and Elardo (1985/1986) found, however, when items with a built-in bias were eliminated from an observation scale, there were no differences in the observed environments of preschool children in one or two parent households.

Mothers' use of moderate control, rather than lax or firm control, and limited use of support systems predicted girls' social competence in divorced families (Heath & Lynch, 1988). Use of firm control and warmth, high education of the mother, and absence of guilt or critical statements by the mother were related to social competence in boys 8 to 11 years of age.

In the carefully done National Association of School Psychologists study (previously discussed), 46 elementary school age children of divorce were followed up 2 years after the initial evaluation (Guidubaldi, Cleminshaw, Perry, Nastasi, & Lightel, 1986). For boys, an authoritarian ("Do what I say because I say it") parenting style predicted poor adjustment on 22 parent- and teacher-rated measures at entry and 2 years later. Girls were less adversely affected by authoritarian parenting; they generally had higher social overinvolvement and better peer relations. Over the 2-year period, an authoritative parenting style (a blend of structure, warmth, and responsiveness to the child) seemed to be related to poorer adjustment in boys and better academic and social relations in girls. Permissive parenting led to more adjustment problems in boys, but in girls was related to better academic performance and better behavior toward the parents.

An authoritarian parenting style is particularly maladaptive for boys of divorce. Both authoritative and permissive parenting styles seem helpful to girls. It is not clear what parenting style (if any) is related to improved behavior in boys.

In a study of the quantity and quality of parenting, Hodges, Buchsbaum, and Tierney (1983) asked mothers to report on how often they gave $\frac{1}{2}$ hour of direct, undivided attention to the child. By this very narrow definition of contact, quantity of contact with parents was unrelated to adjustment in children of divorce, whereas numerous relationships were found for children from intact families. There was no difference in time spent with children by mothers of divorce and mothers of intact families.

As for the relationship between the quality of parent–child interaction and marital status, Hodges et al. (1983) reported that mothers in divorced homes described themselves at the same level of warmth and strictness as mothers in intact families. There were almost no differences in the use of different kinds of discipline (spanking; yelling; withdrawing privileges; affection for good behavior; use of guilt or love withdrawal; and rewards of food, money, or special prizes). Parental warmth and permissiveness were correlated with a variety of child adjustment measures in both types of families. For both divorced and intact families, mothers' descriptions of themselves as less warm were related to descriptions of the child as having problems in misbehavior, distractibility, and general maladjustment at home. For both types of families, children with less strict home lives were seen as less anxious or fearful at home. Parental satisfaction with the relationships with the child and enjoyment of time with the child were related to a variety of adjustment measures. One should be cautious about assuming cause and effect, however; because it is easier to enjoy a well-adjusted child, the relationship is probably interactive.

In sharp contrast are the findings of Webster-Stratton (1989), who looked at the reports of mothers and fathers in a parenting clinic for conduct disordered children. Perhaps the differences in the findings are due to the fact that the children in Webster-Stratton's study had already been identified as having problems. In Webster-Stratton's study, the children were only slightly older than the children in Hodges et al.'s study. The single mothers in Webster-Stratton's study reported themselves as significantly more stressed than either maritally supported or maritally distressed mothers. Observational data indicated that single mothers were more critical, asked more questions, and gave more commands than mothers in intact families. The children in single-parent homes exhibited more deviant and noncompliant behaviors than children in the intact family groups.

SUMMARY

The results of these studies indicate that the context in which divorce occurs determines whether separation and divorce adversely affect child development. Reconciliation, followed by divorce, creates further problems of stress on the child. Abandonment by the noncustodial parent after the divorce may place the child particularly at risk. For preschool children, cumulative stress on the divorced parent was a better predictor of child adjustment than was stress on the child. Higher quality of parenting was related to good child adjustment regardless of type of family marital status (a relationship likely to be interactional). Economic factors such as low income, inadequate income, and sharp drop in income; continued family conflict; and quality of parenting are all factors that affect that context.

CHAPTER 4

To Mediate or Not to Mediate?

Mediation in divorce refers to the use of a third party for parents to negotiate from positions of equal power the decisions of custody, parent access, property, and other assets. Only about 10% of divorces are contested in court. In the past, the others were usually settled in an adversarial relationship between two lawyers; however, that adversarial process is expensive and tends to increase conflict and the sense of unfairness. As noted in Chapters 2 and 3, if the parents continue to be furious at one another, the children suffer. More recently, mediation has been advocated as a technique to reduce conflict and costs and to encourage a win–win feeling after the divorce.

The adversarial system in divorce developed out of a history of requiring that the court find one person at fault for the divorce by "sinning" against the other. When no-fault divorce came into common use, the practices of finding one spouse at fault and of one spouse's "winning" over the other continued. Lawyers were enjoined to represent the interests of the client, not the family. Some lawyers believe that if they do not get everything they can for their client, they are performing malpractice. Therefore, any strategy that increases the likelihood that a judge will give more resources or property or grant custody of the children to one parent is fair game, even if such a move is not in the children's best interest or if the conflict permanently affects the parents' relationship. Girdner (1985b) noted that the conflict and ill-will associated with divorce is blamed on lawyers by some and dysfunctional parents by others.

Irving (1980) described North America as the most litigious area in the world. He noted that Japan, with a population about half that of the United States, has only about 3% of the number of lawyers that are in the United States. Restoring harmony rather than winning disputes characterizes the Japanese court orientation.

Mediation may be particularly needed in North American culture, because the culture has developed a style of handling disputes that may be harmful to the divorcing family.

In this chapter, the basic principles of mediation as outlined in the literature are presented, along with a discussion of what little research there is on the effectiveness of mediation. I also mention some of the concerns about mediation.

THE HISTORY OF MEDIATION IN WESTERN CULTURE

There are two major historical roots to mediation in Western culture, both perhaps related. The first is religious in origin. The Beth Din, the Jewish religious court, has a history of thousands of years and has had a major orientation toward conciliation between adversaries (Irving, 1980). As Irving noted, the Beth Din led to the Jewish Conciliation Board, founded in 1920. The purpose of the arbitration courts is to provide an impartial, third party that can help mediate disagreements without using the civil courts. D. G. Brown (1982), in an extensive review of mediation history and principles, noted that early Quakers in the United States practiced mediation and arbitration to handle disputes. The Quaker arbitration and mediation sometimes involved marital disruption. Also, Chinese immigrants formed the Chinese Benevolent Association to provide mediation (Folberg & Milne, 1988). The second major historical root is negotiations between management and labor. Techniques from both roots influenced mediation in divorce.

The earliest conciliation service in North America was the Los Angeles County Conciliation Court, which was started in 1939 (Irving, 1980). The purpose of this court was to preserve and promote family life, to reconcile families, and to provide amicable resolution to family controversy. Professional counselors began in California in 1954. For the next 20 years, approximately 1,000 families a year were reconciled, although 25% separated again within a year. In 1981, California, maintaining its lead in innovations in the area of divorce and child welfare, passed a law that required mediation to occur prior to the court hearing in every contested custody case.

The first formal private divorce and family mediation center, the national Family Mediation Association, was established in 1974 by Coogler, an attorney and family counselor. The Academy of Family Mediators is another national organization, founded as the result of differences with Coogler's organization (D. G. Brown, 1982). The Society of Professionals in Dispute Resolution, a national organization of people concerned with mediation, has a broader basis of membership with interest in helping conflicts in a wide variety of settings.

BASIC ASSUMPTIONS UNDERLYING MEDIATION

Mediation provides a setting in which the couple can feel that the divorce does not require a win–lose battle, that each person can have needs met and recognize the needs of the other person, and that the children's welfare takes precedence over hurt, anger, and need for retaliation. Girdner (1985a) noted that mediation is based on the assumption that the two parents have relatively equal power. If the parents do not have equal power, the mediator's role is to empower each participant to roughly an equal level so that relatively fair mediation can occur. Girdner noted that concern about women being less powerful in such circumstances has led some feminists' groups to lobby against institutionalized mediation.

In cases in which passivity, dependence, acquiescence, or guilt leads one person in a mediation to give up power (and perhaps to have consistently given up power throughout the marriage), the mediator has to be particularly careful to empower that person to assume an equal footing in the resolution.

Any arrangement that victimizes a member of the family should be unacceptable to the mediator. Thus, the mediator can refuse to accept agreements to which the parties previously agreed (D. G. Brown, 1982). Brown cited an unpublished paper by Lohman, who described a criterion of fairness in which the bargain would be acceptable to the extent that each party would accept the reverse situation.

Girdner (1985a) suggested that the mediator set an example by avoiding talking about custody. Girdner suggested focusing instead on how the two families plan to parent two separate households.

Ricci (1985) discussed the distinction between entitlement and empowerment. Entitlement refers to the belief in a natural or legal claim to something either by law or according to custom. Empowerment is the ability to exercise those claims. According to Ricci, the mediator must use power-balancing interventions to strengthen the weaker positions and to counteract dominant positions. Thus, the mediator should identify each person's entitlements, help both negotiate for their own best interests, objectively describe the pattern of interaction, and identify where and when to intervene.

Ricci described two potentially self-defeating patterns that women use in dealing with mediation. First, a woman may legitimize entitlements due to her role as a peacemaker who is self-sacrificing and yielding to her husband's demands in order to have a harmonious relationship. Second, the woman who feels betrayed and thus feels entitled may demand rights that are more appropriate to the old "fault" divorce.

Ricci (1985) felt that it was useful to begin mediation by asking both parties to identify their greatest fears around mediation and to build assurance to reduce those fears and rebuild trust. For example, the mother may express concerns about working toward financial independence, and the father may agree to underwrite the majority of the cost for the planning toward that independence. These traded assurances help reduce fears of manipulation and power plays.

Coogler's Structured Mediation

Coogler (1978) outlined four major areas of settlement in his structured mediation program: (1) division of marital property, (2) spousal maintenance, (3) child support, and (4) custodial arrangements. The nonprofit organization that he founded, the Family Mediation Association, has a clear set of rules, subject to revision as research provides additional information about the best way to proceed.

Coogler's book provided a set of very useful appendices, including two orientation booklets that explain to clients what mediation is and how the legal system works. The book lists 45 rules on how the mediation is to proceed, including arbitration if the mediation is not successful. Coogler also provided a guide in his book for negotiating and drafting marital settlement agreements, and examples of forms used by the Family Mediation Association. Distinctive features of Coogler's approach include the use of an advisory attorney and of an initial temporary agreement (Grebe, 1988).

According to Coogler's approach, an impasse in mediation occurs if the mediator declares one, if either party declares one and the mediator agrees, or if 10 hours of mediation has occurred and either party declares an impasse. Clearly, the pressure is to have both parties stay with mediation for at least 10 hours to try to obtain a settlement. Grebe (1988) noted that Coogler's approach was toward restructuring the family, not dissolving it.

Coogler outlined several stages in the five-session, 10-hour mediation process:

1. *Orientation.* At this stage, the mediator provides information to the clients. Each party receives an identical package of material, including orientation information; the rules; forms for personal data, financial data, monthly expenses, emergencies, future goals, seasonal expenses, and debts; an analysis of expenditure; a predivorce or postdivorce mediation–arbitration agreement; a temporary custody and maintenance agreement; and a release for audio-taping for research.

2. *First hour of the first 2-hour session.* After putting each spouse at ease and explaining the general procedure, the mediator asks the parties to reach agreement on procedure. The mediator looks for opportunities to reinforce even this level of agreement. The parties then work on developing an agenda, including temporary support and custody arrangements, identification and division of marital property, spousal maintenance, child support, and child custody and visitation arrangements.

3. *Second hour of the first 2-hour session.* If there is no controversy over custody, visitation is discussed during the second hour. Also, the marital property is discussed. The basic assumption on division of marital property is a 50-50 division; however, parties may discuss why it might be fair to make a different division. If the anticipated budgets for two households exceed

the family income, the family must find additional sources of income or reduce the budget. Coogler, Weber, and McKenry (1979) noted that the amount
of child support necessary should be determined prior to the question of
custody so that money is not used as manipulation in the mediation. The
focus is on each individual's responsibility, not on how one spouse can solve
the other's problem.

4. *Hours 3 through 6.* The focus during this time is on division of marital
property, support, and custody arrangements. If couples cannot complete
these issues within the first 4 hours, the mediator must consider whether it is
useful to continue or whether to declare an impasse. This decision is crucial
by the end of 6 hours. Most couples decide to extend the time by adding 4 or
more hours.

5. *Hour 7.* If agreement has occurred by the end of 6 hours, the couple
meets with an advisory attorney for the next hour.

6. *Hour 8.* The advisory attorney brings the final settlement agreement
to this session. Usually only minor changes are required at this stage.

7. *Hours 9 and 10.* When custody is in dispute and all other issues are
resolved, the issues of custody and visitation are reserved for the ninth hour.
Visitation is decided before custody. An agreement is made prior to this
meeting as to whether the children will participate in this discussion and why.
If they attend, children need to be told at the meeting explicitly *by each parent*
that they have permission to express whatever they wish in this meeting.

*When children participate in mediation sessions, the ground rules and rea-
sons for the meeting need to be explained in age-appropriate language. Children need explicit, verbal permission from each parent to say what they wish.
The mediator should verify with the children that this communication was
accomplished.*

Coogler (1978) provided theoretical discussion of how mediation works.
He felt that achieving resolution of conflict requires that (1) the physical
well-being of each party be maintained, (2) feelings of self-worth of each
party be maintained, (3) each party respect or tolerate the opposite party as a
person (not requiring approval of that person's morals or values), (4) all relevant facts and options be considered and used in reaching a resolution, (5) the
consequences of all available options be considered before resolution, and
(6) the resolution be chosen by both parties, even though other choices were
available.

*Demands for meeting individual needs and for winning should be deempha-
sized in mediation, and cooperation must be supported.*

If the couple seeks mediation early after the separation, escalation may not
yet have occurred and cooperation is relatively easy to establish. If mediation

is delayed until the battle has already begun, developing the proper atmosphere supportive to mediation is considerably more difficult.

Once the decision to divorce has been made, couples should be encouraged to begin mediation early in the separation process to avoid escalation. If the decision to divorce has not been made, couple therapy could be used to aid in making the decision.

Irving's Mediation Procedure

Irving (1980) proposed that the goals of mediation are to help the family come to an amicable settlement, to protect the children's interests as primary, and to help parents and children understand that divorced couples remain mothers and fathers. Irving recommended that even when the couple has already resolved the issues about the children, it would be useful to have the couple mediate to ensure that the welfare of the children is protected.

Irving proposed that prior to mediation, an agreement must be made to exclude the mediation process from the adversarial process. The agreement must exempt all meetings, information, and offers that occur in mediation from subsequent court proceedings. A precondition of mediation is that the mediator cannot be called to testify or produce documents in the courtroom. This agreement makes it possible for the parents to consider alternatives without worrying that such considerations would be used against them later. Irving recommended that the mediator meet privately with the lawyers, accountants, or any other relevant people to clarify the rules and maximize the fact-finding phase of the mediation.

Prior written agreements that exclude mediation proceedings from any subsequent litigation are highly recommended to avoid legal manipulations or prevent paranoia from rendering mediation ineffective. Clear written communication about guidelines and rules provided to the clients and their lawyers can protect the clients' rights and the mediator's well-being.

Because mediation has communication as its base, support for improving communication between family members lies at the core. The mediator monitors the communication patterns and clarifies for the family how to correct faulty communication. As in family therapy (mediation is *not* therapy), the mediator encourages family members to communicate directly with each other.

To encourage communication between family members, the mediator should ask each family member to express concerns, questions, and answers directly to the other family member involved. By avoiding the role of translator, the mediator gives training in direct communication.

The mediator may provide information, alternative choices, and advantages and disadvantages of particular options, but tries to maintain neutrality and not side with any family member. The decisions are made by the family members, not the mediator.

Irving (1980) divided the mediation process into three phases:

1. *The initial phase: exploration.* In this phase, each family member is asked to tell his or her story. The mediator empathizes with each in order to communicate acceptance, understanding, and support. The focus is to determine where each person stands and what each person wants to accomplish. In addition, the mediator wants to understand each person's feelings, self-perceptions, and unique problems. This phase may be held between individual family members and the mediator. In this phase, the mediator provides emotional support and helps identify the problems.

2. *Second phase: problem solving.* In this phase, joint interviews with the couple or entire family are held. Each person is asked to explain his or her goals and wants. The mediator reviews what each person has said and how that person is understood by the other family members. When an impasse occurs, the mediator reframes the conflict by broadening the perspective and offering alternatives. The mediator's goal in this phase is to obtain sufficient factual information to find a solution, develop and identify alternatives, and evaluate the probable outcomes of each alternative.

3. *Final phase: resolution.* The final phase is highly structured. The purpose of this phase is to detail what each party will do in the general form of a contract. If anyone violates the agreement, there is immediate feedback. Irving recommended crisis intervention or individual therapy (outside mediation) if one or more family members have such high levels of resentment as to prevent proper separation. The mediator's goal in this phase is to help the couple select one of the alternative solutions to each problem, develop an agreement as to the steps to implement that alternative, and formulate a way of following up on the success of the agreement.

Irving also recommended setting firm minimum limits for mediation and a maximum number of sessions (generally two). When the maximum number of sessions has not resulted in agreement, there are three options: (1) adversary through the courts, (2) binding arbitration, and (3) advisory arbitration. Following advisory arbitration, the arbitrator's report is available to the court if one or more parents do not accept the advice. No information is confidential, and the participants must understand the change in the rules. Irving saw arbitration as less desirable than mediation because it removed the responsibility for arriving at a decision from the parents. To preserve the confidentiality for mediation, Irving recommended that if mediation was not successful and the conflict moved to arbitration, the arbitrator should be someone new.

Haynes's Divorce Mediation

Haynes (1981) came to divorce mediation from a background in labor mediation. As part of the decision as to whether mediation should occur, Haynes noted that it is important to determine whether the couple has sufficiently developed their thinking about divorce. If either party still desires reconciliation, mediation is likely to be ineffective. The mediator may want to refer that party to a psychotherapist to resolve the conflict over whether to divorce.

Mediation begins with a separate meeting with each party to discuss division of resources. Each person is asked to develop a list of family expenses for the past year and to estimate a budget for the new life. After the economics have been agreed upon, the mediator defines property items that have emotional value to either or both of the parties. Once the economic resources and wants in terms of items are defined, the mediator identifies areas of common agreement. The symbolic issues are then identified. Using labor statistics, the mediator helps both parties understand the likelihood of a drop in the standard of living in an effort to reduce postdivorce resentment over the financial consequences. The mediator strikes trades for items of emotional value. The process is designed to help each party respect the other, perceive the process as fair, and keep his or her own dignity.

Haynes used Federico's (1979) divorce adjustment process model to determine at which stage of divorce the couple is operating. Federico's stages, as described by Haynes, were:

1. *Deliberation.* The possibility of divorce has been raised by one or both of the parties. The initiating party may try one of two strategies to make the decision the fault of the other spouse:

a. *Provocation.* The initiator tries to force the other spouse to make the decision. Sometimes an affair that is "accidentally" discovered can have this purpose.

b. *Sabotage.* The initiator provokes the other spouse until the latter retaliates in anger. The angry response is used by the initiator to justify leaving. A therapist, not the mediator, needs to identify and work with these strategies.

2. *Litigation.* Once the lawyer is contacted, the couple may try to work out the relationship.

3. *Transition.* The period of transition follows the physical separation. This period is characterized by irrational behavior that can be upsetting, overwhelming, and panic producing. If the couple is in this stage, the therapist or mediator will have to repeat ideas several times.

4. *Redirection.* This period occurs when the couple as individuals are able to make independent decisions. This period involves learning mastery over skills formerly performed by the spouse, giving up fantasies about sex

with the other partner, feeling financially secure, giving up bitterness and anger, and looking toward new relationships.

Although the therapist may have specific roles for each stage, the mediator has a limited set of goals that are not therapy oriented. In the first three stages of divorce development, the mediator's goal is to problem solve. In the fourth stage, empowerment and skill development are the primary goals.

In discussing custody mediation, Haynes suggested refocusing the mediation from custody (which he defined as residential or physical custody) to maintaining a coparenting orientation. Joint physical custody apparently was a rare outcome for Haynes, but is likely to be more common now.

For custody mediation, the parents are asked to complete three tasks: (1) list why the children should live with them, (2) list the accommodations that they are willing to make to facilitate the other parent's access to the children, and (3) list the accommodations that the other party would have to make to gain custody. These lists may provide an idea of which parent really wants custody and which might be using custody requests as a bargaining tool. Although I feel that this technique can be highly useful as part of the custody mediation process, my experience indicates that a significant number of parents both genuinely want custody and feel deep attachment to the children.

The ultimate goal of mediation is to provide each child with direct and open lines of communication with each parent. Haynes worked toward helping the parents get out of the role of mediating between the children and the other parent and encouraging each parent to contact the children and discuss issues directly. The techniques of encouraging such communication were clearly derived from family therapy. When the issues are between the parents, rather than between parent and child, the children also need to be kept out of the middle.

Haynes described some very useful process variables in mediation:

1. *Referral.* The source of referral can be used diagnostically to predict the stage of the divorce adjustment process of one or both parties. Referral by a source other than a therapist or another mediator is likely to be a good predictor that the couple is ready for mediation.
2. *Blockages.* Resistance to the fee or to the process may indicate that one or both persons are not ready for mediation. If the couple needs a therapist rather than a mediator, it is important to either change to that role or refer the couple elsewhere.
3. *Power.* The basic assumption of mediation is to equalize power. Haynes saw power as developing through control of income, rejection of the other partner, and resistance of a settlement.

As have others who have developed models of mediation, Haynes outlined steps for the sessions:

1. *The first session.* Establishing the mediator's credibility, explaining the process, clarifying the expectations, and developing empathy are goals of the first session. A data base for mediation is acquired. The first session typically lasts 1 hour, and subsequent sessions are likely to last 1 ½ hours. The appendix to Haynes's book provides sample handouts explaining the process and a sample budget form. Haynes also provided useful questions and helpful wording for collecting the basic data.

2. *The second session.* This session involves review of the budget. Unequal power distribution is a focus.

3. *Individual interviews.* In individual interviews, each party fills out an individual interview form, designed to review perceptions of the marital disruption and the strengths of each party. As part of this process, the mediator legitimizes feelings, sets goals, and develops a family data profile about basic living arrangements, initiation of the divorce and feelings about it, strengths of each party, resources, feelings, power, self-esteem, and goals shared and not shared.

4. *Negotiating sessions.* Based on work by Morley and Stephenson (1977), Haynes defined four major components of negotiation. First, there must be some joint decision making. Second, each party has mixed motives, with a wish to reach agreement and an investment in the original emotional relationship. Third, each party has a different order of priorities for the same set of items. Finally, the process requires talking prior to acting.

The mediator begins these sessions by indicating the areas of agreement or near agreement. This process sets the tone for the negotiation. Then the mediator slowly works through the items of minor disagreement, alternating items that require minor accommodations from each spouse. This process develops a spirit of give and take. Trading becomes a common strategy. Haynes provided a relatively extensive set of case studies that are helpful in demonstrating his principles and providing specific techniques.

All major forms of mediation include power equalization, emotional support for reaching preliminary agreements, and trades on minor and major issues.

Musetto's Family Therapy Mediation

Musetto (1980) described an intervention into custody and visitation disputes that he developed over 10 years that used family therapy strategies for helping the families. When he began to help with custody and visitation problems, he observed that the problems were similar to the marital and family problems that he saw in practice. His approach, although referred to as family therapy in his book, is essentially family mediation. All family members are seen together to help them assume responsibility to solve the problem in a constructive way. Family accountability is the theme of the therapy.

Although this approach is nonjudgmental in that rulings are not made about who is right or wrong, issues are raised where the therapist feels that responsibilities are being failed. Family members are reminded that they have responsibilities toward each other, including the children's responsibilities to the parents. Three or four sessions are usually required to reach a compromise. After explaining the purpose of the meetings, the therapist provides one major ground rule: Everyone is to be heard without interruption. The family background and history of each spouse are taken. A marital history is taken, with a focus on what factors prevent resolution of the conflict.

It is recommended that family history be obtained to determine the family system issues that interfere with resolution of the conflict.

The clinician's role is to create an environment of communication and cooperation. The clinician supports both parents by indicating that a custody struggle is an expression of concern for the children. The clinician supports positive connotations of each member's behavior. Paradoxical prescriptions in which the person is encouraged to increase the defenses or resist change are used to reduce resistance to change (see Chapter 13 on family therapy).

The therapy focuses on helping the parents see how the problem is affecting the children. Parents may be asked to meet alone and work out a compromise. Further compromise is reached by using common grounds of agreement, for example, that children should have contact with both parents.

Unlike other custody mediation techniques, if the parents cannot obtain agreement, the therapist then makes a recommendation to the court. The mixing of these roles is seen by others who write about mediation to have the potential problems of increasing anger in the sessions and using the therapist for the adversarial battle.

Group Mediation

One of the more unusual innovations in the area of mediation is the group-based mediation model developed by Campbell and Johnston (1986/1987). The described impasse is seen as developing at individual, interactional, and external social levels. Using an impasse model, they developed a group model of intervention, which they applied to 80 divorcing families characterized as enmeshed, litigious, angry, and ambivalent, and as having moderate to severe pathology or stress.

Prenegotiation Counseling Phase

For the first four sessions, the parents were separated and joined each of two concurrent groups, and the children met with peers. Significant others, including kin, were invited where appropriate. The children's group focused on providing information, identifying feelings, learning coping strategies, and discovering how to stay out of parents' fights. The goals of the first four sessions were as follows:

1. *Session one.* The purpose of this session was to raise parents' awareness of their children's needs. The session began with a 15-minute lecture on child development and divorce. Parents were asked to carefully observe their children and to more carefully support the children's needs for both parents, as well as for stability, continuity, coherence, parental cooperation, and parental responsibility.

2. *Session two.* The focus at this session was on increasing awareness of the impasse or need not to settle. A 15-minute lecture on impasse was given, including discussion of common impasses occurring for that group.

3. *Session three.* The goal of this session was to increase parents' sensitivity to the effects of the parental conflict and to help the child out of the conflict.

4. *Session four.* At this session, to help parents resolve the impasse, the leaders labeled the problem and helped the parents put the problem aside. For parents still entrenched, the focus was on the reality of the situation and the costs and benefits of alternatives.

Negotiation or Conflict Resolution Phase

The two parent groups were combined for three 3-hour sessions, as follows:

1. *Initial transition to negotiation stage.* The first joint session tended to be tense because the two spouses were meeting together for the first time. Some regression of conflict usually occurred. The group was presented with a working agenda to produce a coparenting agreement.

2. *Actual negotiation stage.* In one or two sessions, each family's situation was dealt with one at a time, beginning with couples able to do some sharing and cooperating. These couples provided models for the group. Techniques from the literature on conflict resolution were frequently used.

3. *Implementation phase.* One or two additional couple mediation sessions were held, if needed.

In a study of the effectiveness of group versus couple mediation, Campbell and Johnston (1986/1987) found that the group took 40% fewer staff hours and about half the time for mediation. Both interventions had 80 to 85% success rates at reaching agreements, but group families were more likely to resolve future disagreements on their own (65% vs. 87% for couple mediation), suggesting that couple mediation had less generalization to new problems.

A Social Learning Theory Approach to Mediation

Stuart and Jacobson (1986/1987) described a social learning theory approach that has a different set of concepts to describe the process. Not surprisingly, the goals and specific strategies overlap with the models previously described. Using systems theory, social exchange theory, and cognitive behavior theory, they developed some basic and useful strategies.

Some of the goals common to most mediation theories include:

1. Gain divorcing partners' acceptance of the process.
2. Adopt a conciliatory set.
3. Facilitate communication.
4. Direct attention to present-oriented resolutions.
5. Find creative ways to resolve differences.
6. Help the couple to feel relatively satisfied with the agreement (a two-winner model).

The following techniques are used in Stuart and Jacobson's approach:

1. Decentered understanding is used to facilitate each partner's view of the other partner's perspective.
2. The partners communicate through the mediator until partner communication can occur at an effective level.
3. The "divided brownie" technique is used, in which one partner divides the property, and the other chooses.
4. Because people tend to devalue what they have won in mediation, the mediators must work to help the couple value the outcome and remind them of the costs of litigation and the inevitable sense of loss in any divorce.

Mediators can facilitate continued compliance with mediated agreements by taking into account the tendency of the parties to question the mediated agreement. It is natural that each party would be more aware of his or her own loss than that of the other party. Parents need to be reminded how much they and the children have gained by avoiding the court proceedings.

A Psychodynamic-Based Perspective of Mediation

Wallerstein (1986/1987) noted that in the mediation process, the children's needs are often ignored, parents often cannot separate their own needs and wishes from those of the children, and some parents may wish themselves rid of the children and at the same time develop psychological dependence on the children. From Wallerstein's perspective, the mediation process works because it discourages ego regression in the parents, protects parents both from the fear of their own anger and from the anger of the other parent, and provides a safety zone for negotiation. Wallerstein classified adversarial parents into three categories: people in search for benign authority, people who are fighting for the child, and people who remain enmeshed.

MEDIATOR BEHAVIORS

Vanderkool and Pearson (1983) analyzed the behaviors of two-person mediator teams of mental health professionals and lawyers in the Denver Custody Mediation Project. The mediators had been trained in workshops led by Kessler, Milne, and Coogler, with written materials by Black, Joffee, and Haynes. Analysis was from 35 taped mediations and 22 written summaries for 15 mediators. The following is a summary of the patterns of mediation found:

1. *Orientation.* All mediators worked on creating an atmosphere to support mediation and to build trust. Two styles were used, an informal egalitarian one and a more formal, task-oriented one. Empathy for each party was emphasized.

2. *Defining issues.* Five issues were typically addressed: custody, visitation, division of property, child support, and spousal maintenance. Issues were defined and clarified. Some structure was useful, but nonstructured approaches tended to interfere with mediation. Children, grandparents, and new spouses were often included. Children were typically interviewed separately and information shared with the parents. All signs of generosity and agreement were reinforced. Small issues were addressed first to set the stage for bigger ones.

3. *Resolving divorce issues.* Emotions had to be ventilated and controlled. Interrupting, ascribing motives, and denigrating were forbidden. Reframing behaviors in more sympathetic terms was helpful in reducing rage, and provided new ways of looking at the other spouse's motives, for example, by moving from "custody" to a "time sharing" perspective. Brainstorming generated alternative solutions. If a solution was obtained that did not satisfy both parties, compromises were negotiated.

Vanderkool and Pearson found that the mediators who were most effective in reaching a joint agreement in mediation were those who were highly directive, active, and in control of the sessions.

Whether Children Should Be Included in the Mediation

Drapkin and Bienenfeld (1985) proposed that it generally is useful to include the children in the mediation process. Children may be relieved to have a third party trying to consider their feelings. By including the children, the mediator maintains the focus on parenting. This approach is particularly important when the parents are engaged in a bitter battle and claim that the children are doing fine.

In a survey of 124 California public mediators, Paquin (1988) found that 52% of mediators believed that preschool children should have input into the mediation process and 92% felt that school age children should have some input. In practice, however, only 15% of the preschoolers and 29% of the adolescents were requested to give input. Preschool children were most often seen with parents, whereas school age children were seen without parents. Mediators were divided on whether to ask children where they would like to live, and about half never asked. (See Chapter 6 on custody evaluations for further discussion on this issue.)

Drapkin and Bienenfeld (1985) felt that including the children is inappropriate in two situations. First, the child need not be seen if both parents see the children's needs in the same way and have similar plans for how to meet the children's needs (rare in court-ordered mediation). Second, children under 3 years of age should not be seen.

For children seen separately from the parents, a type of play therapy may be the most supportive environment. Drapkin and Bienenfeld recommended against asking questions of the child, and instead developing a supportive environment in which the child can be self-expressive. Children should be carefully informed about why they are seeing the mediator. Young children should be allowed to explore in an informal setting with play materials. The authors felt that children 6 to 10 do better if given a chance to be physically active while talking. Paper and colored pens are recommended, as well as child-sized table and chairs. Other play therapy techniques include using small, bendable dolls to set up the child's family structure and ask questions about the family; asking the child to make three wishes (useful for children 3 to 5); and creating imaginative stories. The limits of confidentiality should be carefully explained, particularly limits about child abuse.

In individual contact with children, the mediator should be very careful to explain that what is being said is not confidential, particularly if someone is being hurt.

Children between the ages of 10 and 18 are interviewed more directly. The mediator should ask specific permission to share concerns that the child has with the parents. If the child fears punishment or anger, the mediator should share with the parents general impressions and observations, but not verbatim remarks.

Other Process Recommendations

D. G. Brown (1982) suggested that initial sessions be oriented toward impartiality, trust, and confidence. A triangle of chairs is recommended to facilitate communication.

Ricci (1985) felt that it was useful to begin mediation by asking the couple to identify their greatest fears around mediation and to build assurance to reduce those fears and to rebuild mutual trust. For example, the mother may express a need to work toward financial independence, and the father may agree to underwrite the majority of the cost for the planning toward that independence. These traded assurances help reduce fears of manipulation and power plays.

Erickson and Erickson (1988) also noted the need for bargaining from interests (what parties need) rather than position (what parties want). They suggested focusing on the greatest fear of each partner during the first session to reduce resistance. Their descriptions of the procedural strategies focused on full disclosure, use of "I" statements, and positive language. The mediator must first define issues, narrow them, control the discussion, define interests and needs, and bargain with fairness, empowerment, and dignity.

Emery and Wyer (1987) noted that standards of practice for mediation are just emerging. Confidentiality may or may not be protected by law. The courts may be able to order testimony from a mediator. The use of independent legal review and whether mediation should be mandatory are other professional issues to be resolved.

RESEARCH ON THE EFFECTIVENESS OF MEDIATION

As noted by Johnston, Campbell, and Tall (1985), there has been no research on which subpopulations mediation might help most. The few outcome studies have made claims of success from 48 to 80%. D. G. Brown (1982) quoted unpublished studies that reported reduced costs of 75% and decreased relitigation by one-third using mediation instead of adversarial approaches.

In a study of 12 cases of mediation (Kressel, Butler-DeFreitas, Forlenza, & Wilcox, 1989) with high levels of parental conflict and pathology, 9 cases were satisfactorily resolved. Kressel et al. identified an "interpersonally dysfunctional" parent in 8 of the cases (usually the father). The dysfunction was characterized by a narcissistic preoccupation with one's own needs, disparaging and dismissive attitudes toward the other parent, encouraging the child to be disrespectful to the other parent, destructive behavior during mediation, and an inability to acknowledge any responsibility for the problem. Although the interpretation of results are severely limited by the small sample size and subjective interpretations, the findings are sufficiently interesting and reasonable to warrant follow-up research.

Bahr (1981) evaluated the economic efficiency of mediation from published and unpublished documents concerning the programs of four geographic areas. In evaluating the cost to taxpayers, he found that courts with a mediation service cost about 10% less than a court without mediation service in Los Angeles, 50% less in Australia, 50% less than a custody evaluation in Minnesota, and about 10% less in Toronto. Bahr estimated that $9.6 million in court costs and $88.6 million dollars in legal fees would be saved yearly in the United States if court mediations were available everywhere.

Mediation was also a factor in compliance with court orders. In Minnesota, 26% of people using traditional child custody determination returned to court within 2 years, whereas only 10% of people using mediation did so. As Bahr noted, these results were confounded by the lack of random assignment to conditions. More difficult cases may not have been referred for mediation. In Wisconsin, 34.3% of families returned to court following traditional custody determination, and 10.5% following mediation. In Connecticut, no data were available on the adversarial group, but more than two-thirds of families using mediation said the agreement had been maintained.

Irving, Bohm, MacDonald, and Benjamin (1979) attempted to look at postdivorce adjustment. This study involved random assignment to either mediation or custody evaluation. At a 6-week follow-up (which is far too brief a time for thorough evaluation) of 228 clients, three times as many mediation clients as adversarial clients reported that things had gotten "much better" (25% vs. 9%).

Mediation is likely to lead to higher satisfaction rates, lower relitigation rates, and significant financial savings to the parents. When mediation is unsuccessful, however, the total cost is likely to be higher.

Koopman, Hunt, and Stafford (1984) compared a structured mediation sample (using Coogler's, 1978, model) of 31 agreements, and a nonmediated sample of 31 agreements from the same jurisdiction. Both samples were compared with published data on 162 lawyer-initiated, adversarial cases in Connecticut. They did not report any statistical analyses, but descriptive statistics were useful in discerning the consequences of the different approaches. An additional problem was that the data for the first two groups were collected in the central east coast region so that geographic locale was also not controlled.

In this study, higher levels of joint legal custody resulted for the mediation sample (88%) than for the adversarial (0%) and Connecticut samples (4%). Maternal physical custody was most common for the latter two groups. Mediation also produced high levels of detailed visitation agreements (96%), compared with the adversarial and Connecticut groups (38 and 8%, respectively).

Koopman et al. (1984) suggested that mediation provides for the "best interests of the family" in that it is likely to reduce relitigation around child-related issues, finances, education, residential location, and medical and life insurance security. In addition, they noted that 100% of the mediation agreements acknowledged that development means change and that all agreements provided arrangements for mediation for future changes.

In the initial analysis of the 61 couples who completed mediation in the Denver Custody Mediation Project, Pearson (1981) found that 51 went beyond one session. Of those, 30 came to a final agreement. The mean number of sessions was 4.2, requiring 5.6 hours. Of those couples who agreed, 75% (70% in the final evaluation) chose joint custody, typically with primary physical custody with one parent and generous visitation with the other. Of those who did not agree, 21% accepted joint custody. In a randomly assigned control group, only 14% chose joint custody, and only 8% of those who rejected the offer for mediation chose joint custody.

Pearson and Thoennes (1982) found some evidence of reduced cost to parents for mediation, although not always, with about $200 saved. The state saved from $5,610 to $27,510 per 100 cases mediated. Time was saved only if mediation was successful. Personal satisfaction with the mediation was high, with two-thirds of the couples highly satisfied. Even with unsuccessful mediation, 81% of couples said they would recommend mediation to others.

In a longitudinal analysis of the Denver Custody Mediation Project (Pearson & Thoennes, 1984a), participants were interviewed (1) as soon as they were identified as being in a custody dispute and accepted mediation, (2) 3 months following final orders, and (3) 6 months after the second interview. The short-term effects for couples involved in mediation, compared with couples involved in the adversarial process, included higher user satisfaction, better reported relationships between former spouses, and more satisfaction and higher compliance with orders. More visitation, more joint custody arrangements, and more generous visitation terms were reported for the successful mediation group. The long-term (9 months postdecree) effects for participants in this group, compared with those in the adversarial group and unsuccessful mediation group, were that they felt more optimistic about solving future problems with the ex-spouse without going to court, felt more satisfied with the decree, reported fewer serious problems, and reported more compliance with the terms of the order. They also reported more enjoyment of joint custody and more visitation.

Compared with the adversarial approach, successful mediation seems to result in some financial advantage, significant improvement in problem solving, a better relationship with the former spouse, more compliance with court orders, and greater support for long-term visitation frequency.

Pearson and Thoennes (1985, 1988) extended their Denver project data base to include 300 individuals who were interviewed 5 years postmediation (originally in 1978 or 1979), 100 individuals who had contested the divorce through the courts in 1981, 100 noncontested divorce cases from 1981, and a sample of individuals who had contested divorces in 1978. Of those in mediation, only 13% filed for modifications in court, whereas 35% of those in adversarial divorces filed for modifications (Pearson & Thoennes, 1988).

Surprisingly, for the 1978 sample with the couples 5 years postmediation, noncustodial parents reported higher visitation frequency if the divorce was processed through the courts in an adversarial manner (80%

regular visitation) than through mediation (60% regular visitation) (Pearson & Thoennes, 1985). When the data were reported by custodial parents, 60% of the adversarial group reported regular visitation and only 46% of the successful mediation group reported regular visitation.

For the 1981 sample, 30% of the mediation group, 30% of the adversarial group, and half of the noncontesting group reported that visitation rarely or never took place. When noncustodial parents were reporting, none of the successful mediation group reported infrequent visitation, whereas about 30% of the nonagreement mediation group and 30% of the adversarial group reported infrequent visitation. Thus, whether successful mediation improved postdivorce visitation frequency depended on to whom you were speaking.

For the prospective study population, initially the noncontesting group reported about half as many visitation problems as the contesting groups (45 to 50% of the cases had three or more problems). By the final interview, 9 months later, all groups reported three or more problems in about 30 to 40% of the cases, except for the noncontesting group, which was at about 25%.

Child support for the 1981 sample was becoming irregular by 1 year postdivorce, regardless of the group to which the individual belonged. Nonpayment of support was a problem for both successful and unsuccessful mediation groups and for both contesting and noncontesting groups. The increase in problems over time was greatest for the adversarial group.

Parental descriptions of the children's behavior on a behavior checklist did not differ as a function of contested or mediated group status. Pearson and Thoennes (1988) concluded that there has yet to be demonstrated a measurable benefit to the children of divorce whose parents went through mediation rather than adversarial procedures.

There is as yet no demonstrable benefit to children of parents using mediation instead of adversarial procedures. Parents, however, are less angry, tend to save time and money, and are less likely to return to court.

Kelly, Gigy, and Hausman (1988) reported on 106 couples who went through mediation and 225 adults (including 47 couples) who went through a two-attorney, adversarial process. The two groups did not differ in level of anger prior to the process, but the mediation group was more likely to have children (83% vs. 54%). Those who completed mediation, compared with those who quit, were more willing to mediate, were more involved in mediation, were less angry, and had higher self-esteem. No demographic variables and none of the 21 first-session variables predicted successful mediation.

At the completion of mediation or 6 months after entry into the study (for the adversarial sample), self-report indicated that mediation had not reduced anger for the men, but women in both groups were less angry. Mediation had increased cooperation between spouses, although women in mediation had become less positive about the divorce.

In another report on data from the same project, Kelly (1989) reported that mediation helped women feel that they were more able to stand up for themselves, whereas men in mediation were less likely than men or women in the adversarial groups to feel that way. Of those in mediation, 76% of the women and 62% of the men felt that the mediation helped them to be more reasonable. The mediation groups, compared with the adversarial groups, were more satisfied with the property settlement, saw the settlement as fairer, and felt that the custody and visitation agreements were better for the family. A significant percentage of women (38%) felt that child support was inadequate regardless of group.

Emery and colleagues (Emery, 1988; Emery & Jackson, 1989; Emery & Wyer, 1987a, 1987b) developed an experimental evaluation comparing 40 couples randomly assigned to mediation or litigation. Mediation resulted in a 67% reduction in cases going to court hearings in Virginia and a 75% reduction in Los Angeles County. Emery (1988) noted that in Los Angeles, where there is mandatory mediation if there are custody or access disputes, 55% of the couples settled without court intervention. Fathers in mediation were much more satisfied with mediation than fathers in litigation. Mothers in litigation tended to be quite happy with the results, so mothers in mediation could not have been more satisfied. Mothers in the two groups, however, were more similar than fathers, and mothers in litigation were more satisfied with the outcomes than mothers in mediation. In contrast to Kelly's (1988) results, mothers in litigation felt that they had won more than did mothers in mediation. Indeed, mothers in court tended to obtain sole custody more often than mothers in mediation. Emery and Wyer (1987b) suggested that if fathers have more to gain with joint custody in mediation, advocates of mediation need to be advocates on financial issues of concern to women.

In litigation, if one parent felt he or she had won, the other felt a loss ($r = -.47$). In mediation, if one parent felt he or she had won, so did the other ($r = +.33$), suggesting that a win–win philosophy is possible in mediation.

From the perspective of how much is lost or won, the outcome in mediation may be less advantageous to mothers than in litigation. Mediation, however, is more likely to foster a win–win orientation. If both parents feel that they win, the whole family benefits and does not leave one parent resentful of the loss.

Stull and Kaplan (1987) compared mediated and adversarial divorces from a sample of 58 parents with two children. None of the parents had been previously married. They volunteered for the study after being contacted from court records (some had been in a court-based mediation) and a private mediation service (62% had had some mediation). Descriptions of the pre-divorce relationships between spouses did not differ. After the divorce, parents who had mediation talked to the younger of the two children more than did parents in nonmediated divorce. There were no differences in parent–child relationships for the older children. The older child of the mediation group (as compared to the older child in the nonmediated group) was seen as more involved in school, less likely to use drugs, and less likely to break the law (without police involvement). The younger child of mediation was doing better in school, but was less affectionate with the responding parent than was the younger child with nonmediation parents. The volunteer nature of respondents always makes selective participation in a study a potential confound in the reports.

IMPASSES IN MEDIATION

Moore (1988), in one of the best, relatively brief summaries of the mediation process, described useful techniques for handling impasses in mediation. He noted five major areas that influence impasse:

1. *Relationship factors.* Emotions, misrepresentations, stereotypes, and repetitive negative behaviors can interfere with the ability to mediate.
2. *Data problems.* In determining answers to certain questions (e.g., What are child development needs? How much money is needed for additional education?), Moore suggested the use of a "data mediator," an independent third party who can respond with expert information in a particular area.
3. *Competing or incompatible interests.* As others have noted, it is important to move away from a positional statement ("I want to win") to an interest-based bargaining ("I want time with the children").
4. *Structure of the relationship.* This area deals with exploitation, isolation, intrusion, and marginalization of a person in the relationship.
5. *Diverse values.* Focus on behaviors rather than values. Change the focus to an interest conflict. Search for a superordinate goal (What is best for the children?). Use cognitive dissonance to loosen rigid positions.

It is useful to use a third party to provide information on children's developmental needs or finances. In this way the mediator can avoid the appearance of taking sides with one parent.

Johnston, Campbell, and Tall (1985) reported on factors that led to a mediation impasse. They found that the greater the number of levels or components of an impasse, the more complex and entrenched the divorcing family was. They listed the following factors:

1. *Unholy alliances and coalitions.* Divorcing partners allied with mutual friends, extended kin relationships, and families of origin. Displaced conflict

occurred with a divorced spouse experiencing a failed remarriage or cohabitation relationship. Coalitions also were formed with helping professionals who, after hearing only one side of the story, encouraged an uncompromising aggressive position. The adversarial stance of the legal system through tactics of the attorney also fueled the fight. Even when the attorney made charges out of context and in the most unfavorable light possible, spouses saw the strategy as coming from the other spouse, not the attorney.

When externally fueled disputes were identified, the authors recommended encouraging the divorcing parties to divest themselves of the individuals encouraging the battle. If it is not possible to get the divorcing parties to recognize the interference and disengage themselves, the mediators should ask permission to work directly with the external agents, seeking to work with those most open to change.

2. *Character pathology.* A large majority of disputing parties who reached impasses had indicators of character pathology. These patterns did not always fit the traditional diagnostic categories. In a significant number of cases, the disturbed behavior occurred only in the area of the divorce relationship. In other areas, these people seemed to be well adjusted. Such encapsulated areas of pathology may well have played a significant role in the divorce itself. Several subtypes were identified:

a. *Legacy of a destructive marital relationship.* From a family system perspective, the "mutual crazy making" of some families leads them to habitually provoke, attack, and regress around the weakest areas of psychological functioning. Johnston et al. advised unhooking the spouses from each other, both to avoid the traps and to take responsibility for not attacking the other's defenses.

b. *Traumatic or ambivalent separations.* There are two types of traumatic or ambivalent separations. In one type, the ex-spouses have negative and polarized views of each other with no grounding in current reality. They are so anxious about the crazy or dangerous behavior of the other that they act out their fears and fight to protect the children from imaginary dangers. Traumatic separation involving sudden abandonment, discovering secret plotting, secret affairs, and explosive incidents of violence are examples of traumatic separation that tend to increase distorted views of the other spouse. Under such circumstances, the spouses have avoided each other and an opportunity to disconfirm the distorted view could not occur. With traumatic separations, the therapist should try to help the spouse search for reasonable explanations for the suddenness of the separation. The therapist should work to provide a safe arena for the exchange of factual information and improved communication.

The other type involves one spouse's maintaining an idealized image of the other and engaging in a constant search for reconciliation.

The authors saw both types as separation engendered. These couples sometimes go through periodic separations and reconciliations in which they get closer to intimacy and then experience explosive anger. Deep erotic attraction is combined with hostility and dependency. For many, the marriage partner was their first love. The ambivalence is sometimes related to complementary and opposite personality styles, which leads to attraction as well as problems.

For the spouse with idealized images, Johnston et al. recommended confronting the spouse with the dichotomy between the idealized view and wish and the reality. Separation is encouraged by drawing clear boundaries and business-like roles.

3. *Intrapsychic elements.* Certain intrapsychic conflicts, such as feelings of rejection, loss, humiliation, helplessness, anger, and loneliness, are generated by the separation and loss.

a. For many, the battle is a defense against narcissistic injury. Wanting custody is a way of addressing the narcissistic injury and labeling the other spouse as inadequate.

b. For others, the conflicts are a defense against experiencing a sense of loss.

c. For some, the arguments are expressions of a need to ward off a sense of helplessness.

d. For still others, the arguments are a defense against guilt.

Musetto (1980) described a series of underlying motives that can keep the dispute from being resolved. He recommended asking whether any factors, such as drug abuse, alcoholism, sexual or physical abuse, psychosis, or previous neglect of the children, might prevent a parent from being granted custody. As other mental health professionals have suggested, he did not consider psychopathology in the parent a sufficient criterion, in of itself, to rule out custody.

Girdner (1985a) indicated that mediation may not be appropriate for enmeshed or autistic couples. The stage of divorce can influence whether the couple is ready for mediation. When mediation might be an injustice to one or more parties, Girdner suggested referral to a therapist prior to mediation.

Pearson and Thoenness (1984b) noted four conditions under which mediation seemed contraindicated: (1) allegations of child abuse or neglect, (2) multiple social agency or psychiatric service contacts, (3) severe postdivorce conflict with frequent court appearances, and (4) serious psychiatric problems or erratic, violent, or severely antisocial behavior.

Johnston, Campbell, and Tall (1985) identified several personality characteristics that led to chronic battles: the borderline disordered parent, who had a characterological need to fight; the obsessional parent, who enmeshed the ex-spouse and others in minute details; and the paranoid, psychotic parent, who had projections and symbiotic ties with the children. They indicated, however, that these problems made up a remarkably small percentage of families who had reached impasse.

OPPOSITION TO MEDIATION

D. G. Brown (1982) noted that not everyone is uniformly enthusiastic about mediation. Although some have claimed that the adversarial method is quicker and cheaper, no data have been provided to support these claims. Several people have noted concerns about the ethics of lawyers "representing" both parties in a dispute resolution, a practice that violates the lawyers' code of ethics. Others have claimed that mediators may be practicing law without license.

Other expressed concerns are that mediators may be too ready to accept agreements rather than fairness and that power equalization may not occur. Girdner (1985a) cited cross-cultural research that indicated that unequals reach settlements that reflect the inequality.

Another problem with mediation is that when it fails, the expense of the divorce increases. If the divorce fails in mediation and goes to mandatory arbitration, the new arbitrator must be paid, and if the process goes to court, the cost of mediation is added to the cost of an adversarial divorce. In the absence of generally recognized standards of practice, these issues are yet to be resolved. D. G. Brown (1982) extensively reviewed these issues.

SUMMARY

The available evidence suggests that mediation is far superior to court-resolved battles, for the well-being of both the parents and the children. Relitigation, postdivorce conflict, and costs are likely to be lower. Mediation seems to be less effective when coalitions of family and friends are formed, when there is severe psychopathology in one or both of the parents, and when couples are enmeshed or autistic.

Effective divorce mediation is conceptually difficult and, although it uses some of the same theoretical skills as psychotherapy, the interventions are very different. Because skill and knowledge are required, formal training and supervised experience are recommended.

CHAPTER 5

Custody Evaluations: Types of Custody, Parents, and Problems

No study has been done of the validity of procedures for determining child custody. To do such a study well would be extremely difficult. A researcher would have to do the typical assessments and then randomly assign children to different custody arrangements. It would then be possible to determine whether any assessment tools predicted adjustment in the child as a function of the custodial arrangement. Obviously, however, such a study will never be performed. Enough is known about parent–child bonding, parenting styles, consistency in environments, and general child development to demonstrate that such a study would be enormously damaging to the welfare of many children.

Such a difficulty does not mean that child custody evaluations are invalid. Research is steadily increasing an understanding of variables that affect children in different custody arrangements and in different parent access patterns. There is a substantial literature on the importance of parent–child bonding, affection, and discipline. Some arrangements, such as joint custody, gained popularity prior to an adequate research base. More recent research has provided information about the conditions under which joint custody would be appropriate. Research on determining the validity of allegations of sexual abuse during custody disputes also has had a major impact on the court's ability to make decisions in custody decisions. Other important research has been done on the adequacy of parenting by lesbian mothers. In contrast, however, the research on gay fathers is still quite meager. After a review of the historical context of present-day custody decisions, research on various custodial arrangements is reviewed.

HISTORY OF CHILD CUSTODY

Reppucci (1984) wrote that the first concern for the welfare of the child in divorce proceedings in the United States occurred in 1881. According to Foster and Freed (1978), who reviewed the historical antecedents of custody, the first concern for the welfare of the child in custody was in England in

1817, when the poet Percy Bysshe Shelley lost custody because he was an atheist and accused of immoral conduct. Prior to 1920, however, children were considered property of the father and were typically given to the father if a divorce occurred. In the United States, the father's right to custody was never absolute (Foster & Freed, 1978). Generally, it was assumed that the father was best for the child because of his ability to provide protection and nurturance as well as maintenance and education (Weiss, 1979). Several changes during the late 1800s and early 1900s led to modifications in that attitude. With the movement from an agrarian society to an industrial society, the labor force led fathers to become primary wage earners in factories, while women became primary child care providers in the home (Clingempeel & Reppucci, 1982).

During the early 1900s, Freud's theory of child development was becoming popular. People were becoming increasingly aware that early childhood was strongly influenced by the emotional bond between the mother and the child. In addition, in the later part of the nineteenth century, there was an increasing attitude that the family protected the child from an impersonal world. Mother love became an important aspect of child development (Weiss, 1979). In England, the Guardianship of Infants Act of 1925 gave equal rights for custody to both parents (Ricks, 1984). At the same time in the United States, Judge Cardozo wrote a child custody opinion based on "the best interests of the child." This criterion for child custody rapidly became accepted throughout the United States. Today, most states use this criterion for child custody.

It should be noted, however, that the best interest of the child is seldom used as the sole criterion for deciding custody. For example, Derdeyn (1975) noted that the interests and needs of the biological parents are given greater weight than those of the child. Surprisingly, Felner, Terre, Goldfarb, et al. (1985) found that in an unnamed northeastern state, only 15% of lawyers and only half of the judges included best interests of the child as one of the five most critical factors in deciding custody.

The best interest doctrine that currently prevails gives the judge or referee a great deal of discretionary power. Deciding which parent is in the best interests of the child can lead judges to use criteria that include "fault." The advent of the "no-fault" divorce (1970 in California) was enormously helpful in reducing the amount of anger and pain associated with being able to obtain a divorce. The Uniform Custody Code adopted by many states declared that conduct of a parent that did not directly influence the child should not be considered as part of the custody evaluation. As noted by Weiss (1979), however, judges may be influenced by evidence of immorality (which may reflect that a parent is sexually active outside of marriage). In addition, some judges are reluctant to award custody to a parent who had an affair that was the precipitating event that led to the divorce. Such an award can have the appearance of rewarding "immoral" behavior.

TERMINOLOGY

It is not possible in two chapters (Chapters 5 and 6) to describe all the problems and suggested solutions that could be helpful in making custody decisions. Indeed, entire books have been written on making custody evaluations (Group for the Advancement of Psychiatry, 1981; Parry, Broder, Schmitt, Saunders, & Hood, 1986; Skafte, 1985). The purpose of these two chapters is to help mental health professionals understand the issues involved in custody evaluations that will affect children and some of the consequences of those decisions. Prior to reviewing the custody evaluation process and the research on the effects of various custody decisions, some definitions of terms are useful.

Sole Custody

In sole custody, historically the most common form of custody, the legal responsibility for the child is given entirely to one parent. Usually, residential custody is included in the custody arrangement. Prior to the development of joint custody arrangements, mothers obtained custody in about 90% of the cases, fathers in about 7.5% of the cases, and others (usually other family members) in about 2.5% of the cases. Frequency of custody nationwide since the advent of joint custody arrangements has not been published.

Joint Custody

Joint custody is a confusing term because the lay public confuses legal responsibility issues with physical location of the child. In many jurisdictions, joint custody technically refers to legal responsibility, not physical location. It is possible for parents to have joint responsibility for the rearing of the children, even though the children have primary residence with one parent.

A couple once came to me for consultation. The wife said that the husband wanted joint custody and she wanted sole custody. She noted that she would have preferred him to be more traditional in terms of expecting less involvement with the children. When I inquired what each spouse meant by joint custody, she said "joint time" and he said "joint legal responsibility." At that point, he commented that he was glad to let the children live most of the time with her. She said that she was glad to have him share legal responsibility. It was the shortest successful consultation I have ever done.

Split Custody

In split custody, one or more children go with one parent and the rest go with the other parent. Most mental health professionals recommend against split custody on the grounds that such an arrangement could compound the sense of loss for the children. Chasin and Grunebaum (1981) recommended split custody, however, if the children are chronically destructive to one another.

Split custody should be considered if the interactions between siblings are destructive. If split custody does occur, it may be important to arrange visitation in such a way as to provide an opportunity for the children to interact. One problem of split custody is the possibility that the children will feel rejected in not being chosen to go with a particular parent and feel jealousy about the chosen child. If split custody is being considered, the needs of the children must be paramount to the parents' needs. Under most conditions, it is most appropriate to keep the children together.

Guardian *Ad Litem*

A guardian *ad litem* is an attorney appointed by the court or jointly agreed on by the two parents to serve as representative for the children's interest in the divorce proceedings. Although such representation can be very helpful to the children, lawyers often do not like the role. The client is not an adult. Payment can be difficult. Many lawyers are not trained in what issues affect the best interests of a young child. Parents can be upset by the role because it increases the cost of litigation and can add another layer of complexity to the case.

Theoretically, the guardian *ad litem* role can provide increased legal protection for the rights of the child. In practice, there has been little use of the role in court. Pearson, Munson, and Thoennes (1983) reviewed 100 contested child custody cases in Denver, Colorado, for the years 1972 to 1976 and 60 cases in 1966, which was prior to the passage of the Uniform Marriage and Divorce Act (1970). Of the 146 cases reviewed, only 7 cases involved the appointment of a guardian *ad litem,* all after the passage of the Uniform Act. These 7 cases made up only 4.8% of the total sample, and 4 were made by the same judge. Their data indicated that the guardian *ad litem* role was used in particularly difficult cases since in 5 of the 7 cases, a third-party custody award was made. The judges apparently used the lawyer in that role more as a fact finder than an advocate.

When guardian *ad litem* lawyers were appointed, they played different roles, including no role at all. Pearson et al. (1983) found that the guardians were inactive in 3 of the 7 cases. For the other lawyers, the roles were quite diverse, from a "psychologist's mouthpiece," to fact finder, to advocate. A guardian *ad litem* may be particularly useful when neither parent is psychologically healthy and abuse or neglect are real possibilities.

The Tender Years Doctrine

The tender years doctrine refers to the assumption that the young child's best interests are served by being with the mother. In the United States, concern that very young children were best served by being with the mother dates back to 1830 (Foster & Freed, 1978), but did not become common until the 1920s. The age considered "tender" has been variously interpreted by different courts. Some courts have set the range at birth to 6 years, others to 9 years, and still others to 12. Weiss (1979) noted that the upper age to which the tender years doctrine was applied seemed to increase over time.

If the presumptive criterion is placement with the mother, the father must prove the mother unfit, rather than simply that he is a better parent. Several states repealed the tender years doctrine during the 1960s and 1970s. The change in attitude concerning the tender years doctrine occurred for three reasons: (1) the doctrine was clearly discriminatory against fathers, (2) there was a growing recognition that fathers could make very adequate parents even for very young children, and (3) the position that young children were better off when there was a parent at home caring for them was weakened when it was recognized that the majority of custodial mothers became employed (Weiss, 1979).

There is no evidence that gender of parent defines quality of parenting for a child of any age.

Interestingly, after the tender years doctrine was declared unconstitutional in Alabama, there were no subsequent increases in father custody awards or in custody requests from fathers (Santilli & Roberts, in press).

The Reversion Doctrine

The reversion doctrine has been used to support a biological parent's rights over that of a guardian (Goldzband, 1982). Thus, if a stepparent adopts a child as part of a remarriage and the custodial biological parent dies, the courts are likely to award child custody to the noncustodial biological parent. It is clear that this doctrine may come in direct conflict with the "best interests of the child." Indeed, some courts have given the child to the adoptive parent, so the reversion doctrine does not always hold up. Some jurisdictions specifically prohibit a reversion policy. Hoorwitz (1982) noted that biological parental rights do not tend to prevail in custody decisions in which there was a surrender of the child, abandonment, persistent neglect, or unfitness.

PROBLEMS IN ACCEPTING CUSTODY ASSESSMENTS

Beware the False Custody Battle

Not every request for custody evaluation is made in good faith. Lawyers sometimes complain that a client has not provided them with all the information that they need to provide an adequate case. Lawyers, like everyone else, hate to lose. They can get very angry at a parent who fails to mention physical abuse or major battles that have been observed by others. The client's failure to mention these problems may be an indication that the parent was only going through the motions of a custody battle and did not want to win. As painful and as expensive as these battles can be, why should a parent develop a false custody battle?

1. The custody battle is a continuation of the anger that the parents have felt toward one another. ("Why should I let you win anything?") One referee told me of an agonizing case in which there was much bitterness between the parents. The parents were apparently equally competent to be parents (at whatever level that was), and it was not at all clear which should get custody. The referee painfully decided that the mother should receive custody. The mother promptly turned the custody over to the father, indicating that she had never really wanted custody, but wanted to prove to the father that she could win over him.

2. A parent may be afraid that the children would interpret a willingness to let the other parent have custody as an indication that the children are unloved or are willingly abandoned. ("I fought for you, but the judge wouldn't let me have you.") This communication allows the noncustodial parent to reassure the children that he or she was not abandoning them.

3. Sometimes custody battles are used as bargaining tools in the divorce. ("I will drop my request for custody if you will be willing to accept lower child support payments.") Fearful that they might not win, parents have accepted such blackmail to avoid the possibility of losing the children.

4. The parent has unresolved feelings from childhood. ("I don't want to do to them what was done to me.") These custody battles are often attempts to avoid imposing on the children an unresolved anger or hurt from childhood.

Mental health professionals should recognize that requests for custody can be very complex. Although such requests can come out of a genuine feeling of affection and belief of superior parenting, they also can originate from anger, fear, and manipulation. Careful evaluation of explicit and implicit reasons as to why each parent wants custody is needed.

Inappropriate Custody Wishes, but True Custody Battles

There are various inappropriate justifications for custody battles in which a parent truly wants custody, but does not have any particular bonding to children or any sense of what is better for their welfare.

1. *Control.* A parent may request custody as a continuation of a control battle in the marriage. This reason is similar to the first reason given

for false custody battles, but here the parent will want custody and will keep it.

2. *Revenge.* A parent may want custody to hurt the other parent.

3. *Parentification of the child.* Musetto (1980) noted that when a parent has become dependent on the child, a custody request may be a wish to continue that dependency relationship. Loss of the child may evoke memories on the part of the parent of his or her own earlier deprivation, exploitation, or neglect.

Parents preoccupied with control or revenge or who are dependent on the child will often make desperate and dramatic attempts at custody.

PROFESSIONAL JUDGMENT VERSUS BIAS

One reason custody evaluation is so difficult to do well is that all professionals carry unexamined assumptions about mother–child relationships and father–child relationships that are a function of the professional's own childhood. In a study in which a large number of lawyers, psychiatrists, psychologists, and social workers (half male and half female) were asked how they make custody decisions, Woody (1977) found that expert witnesses make judgments that may be unrelated to the merits of the case. Older professionals tend to show more preference to the mother and are more likely to be influenced by a traditional morality. Never-married professionals give greater weight to emotional ties and less support to the mother. Women psychiatrists and psychologists are more likely than women social workers and lawyers to favor the mother over the father for custody.

Girdner (1985a) suggested that preconceptions by the court and mental health professionals concerning "appropriate" behavior for men and women present problems for both sexes. Women have fought against sexual discrimination in the workplace and other public areas, and men are starting to fight in the private domain of family life. Fathers' rights groups have claimed that the 90% mother custody rates and the tender years doctrine have unfairly discriminated against father custody. Polikoff (1982) argued that the reverse is true: Fathers usually do not want custody, but when they do want it, they have substantial chances of winning. Such statistics, however, ignore fathers who do not try for custody because they believe they cannot win.

Polikoff cited studies that found that from 45 to 63% of fathers who requested custody obtained it. Polikoff noted that courts have supported father custody because (1) the father is financially better off than the mother; (2) mothers, not fathers, are criticized for being employed; and (3) remarriage of the father, not the mother, is seen as providing a supportive stepparent. She cited specific court cases to support her point of view.

Mental health professionals have a great deal of difficulty being objective when they use different criteria for assessing normality in men and women.

Girdner (1985a) performed an ethnographic analysis of 18 months of court behavior in child custody decisions. Fathers had to justify lower levels of past involvement with the children. The father had to show that the mother did not perform the role of mother adequately or that he had excelled beyond that normally required of a father. If the father deviated too much in the direction of parenting, the role violation might work against him in the custody process. When a father takes over household tasks, the tasks are seen as unnatural and done for instrumental reasons rather than as acts of love (which is motherly). For mothers, the problem was that role expectations were quite high so that it was not difficult to find occasions where the mother deviated from them. One bias that Girdner noted was that sex acts by a mother were seen as "self-gratifying animal acts," whereas the father's sexual behavior may be overlooked. The mother's attorney attempted to show that the mother was an excellent mother, and the father's attorney tried to show the mother had fallen below standards. Girdner (1985b) noted that parents will use neighbors to testify to trivial facts ("He was able to cook a pot roast" or "She let the child out without a coat on a chilly day") to push for fitness of each parent.

In a study of 60 mothers challenged for custody, Chesler (1986) made similar arguments that when fathers fight for custody, they often win without regard to fairness. Mothers have lost custody for having nontraditional religious orientations or political opinions and have been blamed if the husbands were guilty of child abuse, incest, or spousal abuse. Only 13% of fathers who won custody had done housework or primary child care in the marriage. Chesler also noted, as have others, that any imperfection in the mother was a sign that she is unfit, but that parenting in the father was often ignored. Chesler found that 59% of fathers who won custody had abused their wives, and 36% had kidnapped their children. She found that two-thirds of the fathers said that they sued for custody for some economic reason, one-third for control issues, and almost one-third for anger at the wife for pre- or postseparation sexual behavior.

The mental health professional needs to be particularly sensitive to attitudes about sex roles and psychological health. It is useful to ask the question as to whether a particular evaluation would change if the behavior were by the opposite gender parent.

Hare-Mustin (1976) felt that mental health professionals may place more emphasis on exhaustively evaluating the degree to which the mother meets traditional sex-role stereotypes than on evaluating the father. If the mother fails to meet these characteristics, the mental health professional may recommend that the child go to the father. Hare-Mustin criticized mental health professionals for bias in what constitutes parental capacity, given that there is almost no research on what parental capacity is.

THE EFFECTIVENESS OF CUSTODY DECISIONS

Remarkably little research has been done on the effectiveness of custody decisions. Although mental health professionals advise the court about attachment bonds, parenting skills, mental and physical health, stability, and continuity of care, no research indicates whether such predictions are correct in terms of subsequent parent–child relationships. In the next sections, the literature on father custody, joint custody, split custody, and grandparent custody is reviewed. Because mother custody has been the norm, there is no section on it. The research tends to compare other custody arrangements with mother custody. Certainly, mothers who do not have custody often feel stigmatized and under stress (Fischer, 1983; Fischer & Cardea, 1981; Rosenblum, 1986). As the norm changes to alternative arrangements, perhaps the mother who chooses to relinquish custody or is court ordered to do so will feel less inadequate.

Father Custody

Characteristics of Fathers Who Obtain Custody

Because the nurturant role has traditionally been assigned to mothers, fathers who sought custody in the past were suspect. With a move toward androgynous parenting, fathers are increasingly interested in having custody of their children even in the absence of evidence that the mother is a poor parent.

Fathers and mothers do have different patterns of parenting (Lewis, Feiring, & Weinraub, 1981). As a group, fathers in intact families spend much less time in one-to-one interactions with the children. They are more concerned than are mothers with sex-role development. They spend less time with caregiving activities, but more time in play. In observational studies, however, there have been few differences observed between the behaviors of mothers and fathers. Lewis et al. concluded that fathers appear to be as sensitive and as concerned with child rearing as are mothers.

Lamb (1981), in naturalistic home observations, found that infants aged 7, 8, 12, and 13 months showed no preference for mother or father in terms of attachment, but preferred either parent to an unfamiliar visitor. By 2 years of age, boys showed preference to fathers but girls still showed no preference.

In a study of the characteristics of fathers who obtained custody and fathers who did not seek custody, Gersick (1979) compared 20 custodial fathers and 20 noncustodial fathers in terms of demographic variables, families of origin, participation in child rearing, sex-role orientation, and characteristics of the divorce. Men with custody were more likely to be closer to their own mothers than their fathers and more likely to be later born children with both brothers and sisters. The relationship to the father was respectful, but relatively unemotional. Perhaps stereotyped sex-role training was reduced, leading the father to be more androgynous in orientation. The family of origin was seen as competent, the father was a provider and protector, and the mother was able to give great warmth and intimacy. Most of the custodial fathers wanted more closeness to their fathers as children and may have given greater importance to the father–child bond because of that lack.

Based on interviews with a small sample of custodial fathers, B. Johnson (1985) noted that these fathers were strongly influenced by their relationships with their own fathers. Fathers who engaged with the children with the greatest zeal and enthusiasm were those who felt the most ignored by their fathers during their own childhoods. Those fathers with comfortable relationships with their own fathers tended to model the warm, tender relationships with their own children. Fathers who felt victimized by their own fathers' violence tended to have a more friendship-oriented, but less intense, relationship with their children.

In Gersick's (1979) study, men who felt that they were wronged, betrayed, or victimized were more likely than others to seek custody. Involvement of the ex-wife in a relationship with another man was common for fathers with custody and rare for noncustodial fathers. In 18 of the 20 cases in which the father obtained custody, it was with the pretrial consent of the mother.

A father who seeks and obtains custody is likely to have had more androgynous training from the family of origin. He also is more likely to be angry and resentful of the ex-spouse. He may have had inadequate fathering. Seeking custody, regardless of which parent seeks it, can be an expression of affection and bonding, compensation for an inadequate childhood, or an expression of rage and revenge.

Turner (1984) evaluated 26 divorced fathers who had won a contested divorce and found that they fell into two categories: (1) 9 fathers who had been actively involved with their children throughout the marriage and wanted to continue that relationship, and (2) 17 fathers who had not been actively involved in parenting prior to divorce and who waited until 2 years after the divorce to seek custody. Interestingly, the second group accounted for almost two-thirds of the sample. The small sample size limits generalizability, however.

Fathers who sought custody at the time of divorce were characterized as having had a close father–child relationship during the marriage; as being pleased with the pregnancy; as being involved in birthing, infant care, and at least half of child care activities during marriage; and as wanting a close relationship with the child. Fathers who sought custody some time later did not have these characteristics and wanted custody because of anger at the ex-wife, because of restrictions or denial of visitation, or because they felt that the ex-wife was a poor parent (e.g., due to alleged alcoholism, neglect, or abusive behavior). Fathers who sought custody immediately also were more positive about the beginning of the marriage, felt that the separation and divorce were a tremendous loss, wanted reconciliation, and had a more friendly relationship with the mother postdivorce than did fathers who sought custody later.

Risman (1986) found that fathers who obtained custody tended to feel adequate as homemakers and were comfortable with their roles as single parents. Fathers with custody would seem to fare better than fathers without custody. Custodial fathers have been demonstrated to be less depressed and anxious and have fewer adjustment problems than noncustodial fathers (Stewart, Schwebel, & Fine, 1986). Such custodial fathers are as well adjusted as fathers in intact homes.

G. L. Greif (1987) gathered follow-up data over a 3-year period for fathers who had custody. Of those who continued to participate in the study, 28 remained custodial single fathers and 22 had remarried. Almost 7 years after getting custody, the single father was not satisfied with his social life or with being single. Loneliness was a continuing problem. Of the original 61 fathers with custody, only 5 had relinquished custody, indicating that father custody has a relatively high stability.

The Effectiveness of Father-Custody Arrangements

A major study of different custody arrangements was accomplished by Luepnitz (1982). The study's focus was on comparing 16 families with mother custody, 16 with father custody, and 18 with joint custody. These families had a total of 91 children, and were about 3.5 years from the final separation. Children were evaluated for self-concept, and the family was evaluated for home atmosphere, parent adjustment, and family functioning. Luepnitz found no advantage to mother-custody homes. The emotional climate of father-custody homes was just as positive as that of homes headed by a mother. Parents were able to develop cross-gender skills. Mothers became more involved in work, money management, and care maintenance. Fathers became less involved with work, spent more time with children, and learned to cook, sew, and do laundry.

The most extensive research on father custody has been done by Santrock and Warshak (1979; Warshak & Santrock, 1983a, 1983b). They studied 64 white, middle class families with children from 6 to 11 years of age, half boys and half girls. One-third came from father-custody homes, one-third from mother-custody homes, and the remainder from intact homes (the 1979 report was based on a slightly different number of children). In spite of the relatively small number of children in each category, this study is extremely important because it is one of the few systematic, carefully measured studies comparing type of custody. Children were an average of 8.3 years old and about 3 years postseparation. Recognizing that previous articles on father custody were based on case histories and parent report and seldom on direct measurement of the children, the authors developed a multimethod evaluation approach that included observation of a structured parent–child interaction, a parent interview, and a child interview.

The parent–child interviews indicated a clear relationship between type of custody and child adjustment. Children living with the same-sexed parent were better adjusted than children living with the opposite-sexed parent. Boys in father-custody homes were less demanding than were girls in father-custody homes and were more mature, sociable, and independent. Girls in mother-custody homes were better adjusted than boys in mother-custody homes. Boys in father-custody homes performed more competently socially than did boys in intact homes, and girls in father-custody homes did less well than girls in intact homes. Children from mother-custody homes showed little difference from children in intact homes.

When the interviewer ratings were examined, similar results were obtained. Children in same-sex parent custody arrangements were rated as more socially competent than children living in opposite-sex arrangements. Boys in father-custody homes were also rated as more honest, more appealing, and having higher levels of self-esteem. Girls in father-custody homes were rated as low on these dimensions.

In a study comparing 37 mother-custody and 10 father-custody families in which the child was between 7 and 10 years of age and 2 to 3 years postseparation, Camara and Resnick (1988) found that mother-custody boys and father-custody girls had the highest levels of aggression and behavior problems and the lowest levels of self-esteem. Not surprisingly, boys were more likely than girls to initiate or respond with aggression during free play. Mother-custody girls were the least likely to generate or support aggression during free play, and boys from two-parent families were the most likely to do so.

In general, fathers seem to do better with boys than with girls and mothers seem to do better with girls than with boys. Specific individuals may not follow this pattern. The magnitude of differences in terms of benefits of same-sex parent custody was not sufficiently strong to lead to the conclusion that it should be used as a guide to custody arrangements. Fathers and mothers may be differentially beneficial to each gender child as a function of the child's age. An interaction that has not yet been tested in research is child's age by child's gender by parent's gender.

In the Santrock and Warshak (1979; Warshak & Santrock, 1983a, 1983b) studies, fathers with custody were much more likely to have children in contact with the noncustodial mother than custodial mothers were to have children in contact with the noncustodial father. The children in contact with other caregivers were rated as warmer, more sociable, and more conforming than children with less contact with other adults. The authors interpreted these results to mean that these children obtained higher quality care from the other adults and had custodial parents with less depleted resources.

It is interesting to note that parenting style was important in the child's personality development, regardless of the type of custody. An authoritative parenting style, which involves parental warmth, clear rules, and extensive verbal interaction, was related to higher levels of social competence in the child than was a laissez faire or authoritarian parent style. Authoritative parenting style also resulted in lower levels of anger and demanding behavior (Santrock & Warshak, 1979). The parenting styles of high levels of permissiveness (laissez faire) and high levels of power-oriented strictness (authoritarian) interacted with type of custody. Authoritarian child rearing by mothers did not seem to affect a child's social competence, but mothers using laissez faire styles had children with little warmth, high anger, high demanding behavior, and little conformity. A laissez faire style by fathers had no apparent effect on social behavior compared with other styles, but fathers with authoritarian parenting had children who were higher on anger and lower on independence compared with children raised by other parenting styles.

Regardless of which parent obtains custody, an authoritative parenting style with warmth, clear rules, and open verbal interchange best serves the child. Custodial mothers with laissez faire parenting style and custodial fathers with authoritarian parenting style are particularly likely to put the child at risk for less mature social behavior. Consultation with parents is recommended under such circumstances.

The old folklore that the mother is always better for the child is clearly disproved by Warshak and Santrock (1983b), who also noted that such data cannot be used to support reversal of previous custody arrangements. In addition, they noted that these results were obtained only 3 years after the separation and that little is known about long-term effects of different custody arrangements.

Warshak (1987) reported that single fathers felt overburdened by the workload (which tends to be true of single mothers as well). Families that agreed on father custody tended to be less conflictual. If the mother had relinquished custody without the father's request, the father was more angry and anxious and the postdivorce conflict was higher. Warshak noted that two areas in which custodial fathers often need therapeutic help are in accepting the custodial arrangement and improving parenting skills. Fathers often need help in fostering a postdivorce coparenting arrangement. Warshak also emphasized the importance of supporting and facilitating the mother–child relationship.

Father-custody families are likely to need specific help. A father may have more difficulty than a mother in accepting the custodial arrangement, particularly if given no choice. He is also likely to need consultation around parenting skills. Both the custodial father and noncustodial mother need help in supporting the mother–child relationship, just as a father might need help in a mother-custody arrangement.

Comparing 62 children who were from 6 to 16 years old, half mother custody and half father custody, Schnayer and Orr (1988/1989) found no differences on children's self-perceptions or their behavior as rated by the parents. Economic level was a predictor of behavior problems, with lower income related to more problems, a finding often noted in Chapter 3.

Mothers Who Relinquish Custody

Rosenblum (1986) interviewed 20 noncustodial mothers who voluntarily relinquished custody. A subset of these mothers chose to leave to accommodate the husband's wishes or needs. They felt that they were leaving the husband rather than the children. These mothers maintained frequent contact with the children after the divorce. Another subset relinquished the mother's role, felt failures as mothers, or enjoyed the parenting role less than the father. Rosenblum noted that mothers tended to be stigmatized regardless of the reason for leaving.

Split Custody

G. L. Greif (1990) reported on the only study of split custody found in the literature. Only 4% of divorce decrees in Baltimore in 1987 were split custody. In two national samples of 1,136 custodial fathers and 517 mothers without custody of at least one child (a Parents Without Partners sample), Greif evaluated the causes of split custody. Split custody usually evolved over time and was not in the original decree. Fathers had custody of some of the children if the children were making the choice, if the mother could not handle the child, or if a male role model was seen as needed. Split custody developed from sole custody if (1) one parent remarried and there was stepparent–child or parent–child conflict, (2) the child wanted a two-parent family, (3) there was a parent–child clash (with remarriage), or (4) the child moved to a new developmental stage in which a change for only that child was seen as appropriate.

At present, no studies have evaluated children's adjustment in split custody arrangement or the effect of separation of siblings.

Joint Custody

History of Coparenting and Joint Custody

The concept of joint custody was recognized as early as 1905 (Black & Cantor, 1989). Not until the latter part of the 1970s, however, was joint custody offered as the solution to the problem that each parent might be equally deserving of custody. If both parents are relatively equal in terms of parenting quality and if continued contact with both parents is helpful for psychological development, splitting responsibility (and often time) between the parents may be a good solution. Even though the model of joint legal custody was to promote equal time, there usually is a primary residential parent in joint custody cases. Wolchik, Braver, and Sandler (1985) reported a primary residential parent in three-fourths of joint custody cases in Arizona. Recent evaluations in California suggest the same pattern, with the mother primary in 75% of cases, the father primary in 10%, and joint time in only 15%.

Galper (1978) developed the term "coparenting" to refer to the equal involvement of both parents in the caring for the child. Coparenting requires mutual respect and some harmony between parents. It is an agreement that both parents are intimately involved in rearing the children. One parent does not have the right to move to another city and automatically take the children along. If such a change were to occur, it would be a mutually agreed upon decision.

Ahrons (1979) identified three patterns of joint legal custody families, which she referred to as "binuclear families":

1. Parents who are good friends. These parents choose to live in the same neighborhood so that the children can attend the same school and maintain the same playmates. Shared time with both parents and children occurred.
2. Parents who are cordial. These parents share responsibility fairly equally, but seldom spend time together. These families rely heavily on the telephone for communication. These parents have more unresolved anger.
3. Parents who are disengaged with each other except in a formal manner. These parents tend to be bitter enemies. The nonresidential parent is the most displeased with the arrangement and has less involvement with the child.

A 1980 California law established joint custody or sole custody as the preferred legal arrangements. It was hoped that joint custody would better protect the economic well-being of children. Judges must consider joint custody if either parent requests it, even after other custody arrangements have been awarded (Clingempeel & Reppucci, 1982). Even though California law did not make joint custody presumptive, the courts acted as if it were. By the mid 1980s in Los Angeles, joint custody was being awarded about 45% of the time (C. A. Richards & Goldenberg, 1985). More recently, in light of evidence that some circumstances make joint custody ill advised, judges have been more cautious about ordering joint custody.

As Derdeyn and Scott (1984) noted, concern for the criteria that should be used to determine successful joint custody has been given less weight as the enthusiasm for joint custody has increased. Part of that enthusiasm came from the courts who were freed from the painful decision of having to decide which parent is best for the child.

Early articles on joint custody were very supportive of the concept and gave strong support (Abarbanel, 1979; Ahrons, 1979; J. B. Greif, 1979; Messinger, 1976; Ramos, 1979). In the late 1970s, some concerns were raised about when joint custody was appropriate (Abarbanel, 1979; Ramos, 1979). By the mid 1980s, several authors were showing concern (Derdeyn & Scott, 1984; Irving, Benjamin, & Trocme, 1984; Volgy & Everett, 1985).

Studies in Which Most Couples Voluntarily Chose Joint Custody

Ahrons (1979) reported data from 41 divorced parents who had court-awarded joint custody in California. The children ranged from 1 to 17 years of age, with an average of 11.7 years. These divorces involved joint legal responsibility, but not necessarily joint time. The minimum time in the secondary household ranged from a couple of hours per week to 50% of the time.

The greater the amount of conflict between the two parents, the lower the amount of nonresidential parent–child involvement ($r = .43, p < .01$). The more supportive the relationship between the two parents, the more parent–child involvement there was likely to be ($r = .53, p < .001$). The few divorced spouses who had bitter conflict had little or no postdivorce involvement with each other.

Parents who had a "best friend" relationship had continued coparenting relationships. As might be expected, anger tended to be moderate to low between these parents. These parents were strong supporters of joint custody. The coparenting relationship that characterized all but a few of the parents remained child centered.

Steinman (1981) evaluated 24 couples who voluntarily chose shared physical custody. The residential time arrangements ranged from 50-50 to 67-33. In half the homes, the children split residences every 3 to 4 days. Twenty-five percent arranged a week-to-week schedule. The others had varied arrangements, alternating every day, every 2 weeks, every 3 months, and in one case every year.

The parents in this study were described as maintaining a strong ideological commitment to joint legal custody and open access. They actively valued each other as parents. The children felt that they had two "psychological parents." They expected and received nurturing, discipline, and guidance from both parents.

Although the parents liked the arrangement, one-third of the children felt overburdened by the demands of maintaining two households. Children typically knew when household switches would occur. About 25% experienced confusion and anxiety about their schedules and switching. Of those, half were girls in the youngest group (4- and 5-year-old). Four 7- to 9-year-old boys also struggled to keep up with the schedule. One said, "The big problem with joint custody is that you have to remember where the spoons are."

Ilfeld, Ilfeld, and Alexander (1982) looked at 414 consecutive custody cases in Los Angeles court over a 2-year period. They compared the relitigation rate for joint custody (138 cases) versus sole custody (276 cases). Both sole custody and joint custody cases were based primarily (91% of sole custody and 86% of joint custody) on agreement between parents. They also examined 18 cases in which families were given joint custody without both parents' consent. Relitigation rate for the joint custody families was 16% at the end of 2 years. There were half as many relitigations involving joint custody as sole custody cases ($p < .001$). Only six (33%) of the nonagreeing joint custody cases had been involved in relitigation, which was almost the same percentage as for the sole custody sample (32%). Thus, Ilfeld et al. concluded that the data did not support the belief that both parents must have a commitment to joint custody for it to work. In contrast, Hauser (1985) evaluated the effectiveness of joint and sole custody arrangements and found a high relitigation rate.

Irving et al. (1984) presented preliminary results of a large-scale study involving questionnaire results for 201 parents (75 couples and 51 individual parents), all of whom were involved in a shared parenting arrangement. The Joint Custody Project was initiated in Toronto in 1982.

Of the sample, most had at least some university or postgraduate education. The majority had been married only once, the marriage lasting an average of 9 years or more. Typically, the parents had two children, one aged 7 to 13 and the other aged 5 to 10. Although the parents reported a high level of conflict at the time of the separation, feelings were generally more positive by the time of the study. Many former spouses continued to live within a short ride (46%) or walking distance (32%) from each other, and 75% were within five miles. Although joint legal custody with shared access may discourage geographic mobility, those who choose joint legal custody may be less distressed and feel less need to move. The decision to share parenting was almost always initially suggested by one spouse or the other (85.3%), seldom by lawyers or mediators. About 50% of the parents spend equal amounts of time with the children.

Some parents indicated that joint custody worked from the beginning, but these were a minority (36%). The ironing out process took up to a year (32%), but some parents reported fairly early success (41.8%). Most parents felt that their relationship with the former spouse was moderately friendly and either remained the same or became more positive over time. Satisfaction with coparenting was high, with 77.4% overall satisfaction and 86.2% satisfaction with the schedule. Twenty-three percent of the children were upset for a time following a shift in residence, an issue not addressed in other studies.

According to Irving et al. (1984), predictors of successful outcome for joint custody were commitment to parenting, reasonable communication skills, flexibility, the ability to circumscribe or separate marital conflict from the children, and good faith with regard to the arrangements. Poor success occurred when the cause of the divorce was a break of trust (e.g., an affair), guilt, or feelings of being coerced by the mediator.

Luepnitz (1982, 1986) compared joint custody with sole custody. This study had only 11 families with joint custody. Most joint custody children were satisfied with the amount of contact they had with each parent. These children maintained an appropriate parent–child relationship with both parents, whereas sole custody children developed an "avuncular" relationship with the noncustodial parent.

Luepnitz reported both disadvantages and advantages of joint custody. Disadvantages were that parents felt that they were tied to ex-spouses in a way that did not occur in sole custody arrangements, that they could not easily move out of town, and that the movement of children between households was a hassle. Reported advantages included the following: fewer court battles over money occurred than in sole custody families, child support payments were more likely to be paid to the single mother, both parents had a built-in break from parenting, and both parents felt that it was useful to have the perspective of two parents in disciplining and felt that they could rely on each other for child care.

Although joint custody mothers have seen their sons as having more loyalty conflicts than mothers with sole custody, children in the two types of families reported no differences in loyalty (Shiller, 1986). Shiller reported that joint custody boys did not experience more adjustment problems than boys from mother-custody homes. Boys in joint custody felt comfortable expressing negative feelings toward both parents, whereas boys in maternal custody expressed fewer negative feelings toward the mother. Boys in joint custody were not more likely than boys in sole custody to have reconciliation fantasies, as some in the literature have suggested might happen, and were less likely to yearn for the absent father.

D'Andrea (1983) compared 24 fathers in joint custody with 22 noncustodial fathers with visitation. Fathers with joint legal custody spent much more substantial time with their children. Joint custody, compared with noncustodial sole custody, was related to statistically significantly higher paternal involvement in terms of self-perceived knowledge of and influence on the child.

Voluntary joint physical custody seems to increase the children's satisfaction with access to both parents and maintain both parents in parental roles.

In a study of 121 families over a 2-year period, Nelson (1989) found that joint custody led to more parental access to the child and that more parental access was related to more communication between parents and *more conflict* between parents by 2 years after the divorce.

In a study of 133 children within 30 months of parental separation, Wolchik et al. (1985) evaluated the impact of joint legal custody for one-third of the sample. Children were an average of 11.1 years old in the joint legal custody group and 11.7 years old in the mother-custody group. In three-fourths of the joint custody group, there was a primary residential parent.

Self-esteem was significantly higher for children in joint custody than for children in maternal custody. Both boys and girls of joint custody families reported more positive experiences in the last 3 months than did children in maternal custody. Boys in joint custody reported fewer negative experiences than boys in maternal custody.

Wolchik et al. reported that symptomatology as rated by both parents and children did not vary by group or child's gender. Because the participants were from a state without presumptive joint custody, parents were self-selected into groups. Therefore, it is not possible to tell whether joint custody per se was responsible for the differences between group or whether the parents who approve of joint custody are different on other dimensions (e.g., they fight less).

Wallerstein and Blakeslee (1989) indicated that joint physical custody was particularly well suited for elementary age children. Fathers in joint custody were less likely to abandon at 2 years postdivorce. There were no clear benefits of joint over sole custody in terms of the child's adjustment.

Benjamin and Irving (1990) evaluated 201 Toronto parents involved in shared parenting and found a variety of correlations of satisfactory arrangements. Parents who were satisfied with shared parenting were less bitter and more positive about the preseparation relationship with their former spouse and saw marital conflict as only mild or moderate. Parents dissatisfied with shared parenting tended to see the preseparation conflict as extreme. Satisfied parents were more open to shared parenting from the start, whereas dissatisfied parents felt coerced, enticed with a less expensive divorce, encouraged toward a reconciliation, or guilty over the divorce.

In all these studies, the question of cause and effect cannot be assessed. Perhaps joint custody produces better adjustment. Alternatively, those parents who wish to have joint custody may have better child-rearing skills and greater parental involvement, which in turn predict better child adjustment. Another possibility is that when children are better adjusted, parents may be less likely to consider the other parent a "bad" parent, and be more willing to consider joint custody.

Thus, data indicate that if the parents are willing to try joint custody, the child seems to benefit. Some parents seem reluctant to try joint custody, but do attempt it for the benefit of the child, and often are able to work out the arrangement.

Unfortunately, the limited research on joint physical custody has not permitted judgments of the most appropriate residential time arrangements according to child's age. It is unknown whether a particular pattern facilitates or interferes with good adjustment. Other mediating factors, such as parental conflict and the child's age, gender, cognitive abilities, and temperament, have not been evaluated.

Studies Indicating Problems with Joint Custody

Steinman, Zemmelman, and Knoblauch (1985) were among the first to document problems in joint custody. In their study of 48 joint custody families followed for 3 years, 22 were referred by the courts for disputes and one or both parents were opposed to joint custody. Three groups were identified:

1. *Successful* (27% at 1 year). These parents were satisfied.
2. *Stressed* (42% at 1 year). These parents were stressed and frustrated by the joint custody, but felt it was good for the children.
3. *Failed* (31% at 1 year). These parents were extremely distressed and chronically dissatisfied.

Litigation in the divorcing process was uncommon in the successful group (15%), common in the stressed group (65%), and very high in the failed group (86.6%).

When they evaluated personality characteristics of parents in each group, Steinman et al. found that parents in the successful group responded to the divorce with mild depression and guilt. Anger was low and hostility toward the spouse was generally suppressed. In the stressed group, severe and long-standing emotional problems were common. Both the stressed and failed groups had higher incidences of alcohol problems (about 65%) than the success group (23%). Most importantly, the failed group was characterized by unmitigated anger, but no guilt, sadness, or positive attachment to the other parent. These parents blamed the other parent for their problems and any problems the child was having. Because these parents had low self-worth, the trauma of rejection from the other partner was experienced as an intolerable assault. It should be noted that physical abuse was common in the failed group (45%) and stressed group (50%), and lower but still distressingly common in the successful group (23%).

According to Wallerstein and Blakeslee (1989) in their 10-year follow-up of Wallerstein and Kelly's (1980c) sample, all the children in joint physical custody had trouble changing residences. Indeed, high numbers of transitions made adjustment more difficult rather than less. Some children needed several hours to calm down. Children had particular trouble adjusting to two different schedules.

Parents sharing child custody should choose a common bedtime for both households, and develop common rules for snacks, television watching, and chores. Similar patterns are likely to reduce stress for the child.

McKinnon and Wallerstein (1986) found that preschool children did not benefit from joint custody, but there was no clear evidence of greater harm. Children 1 to 3 years of age who did poorly with joint custody had parents in chronic conflict. Children from 3 to 5 seemed to have more problems with joint custody than the younger children, and 10 of the 16 children in this category were doing poorly.

In a study of 7- to 9-year-olds 2 to 3 years postseparation, Camara and Resnick (1988) found that if divorced parents cooperated with one another (even if angry), there was less aggression in the child. Fathers who used verbal attacks to solve conflicts (in either divorced or intact families) had children who were less prosocial, with lower self-esteem, and more behavior problems. Use of such verbal attacks by mothers had fewer effects on children's aggressive behaviors. Children of such mothers exhibited more parallel play (where children play side by side but do not interact) than other children.

Researchers at the Center for the Family in Transition (Johnston, Kline, & Tschann, 1989; Kline, Tschann, Johnston, & Wallerstein, 1989) obtained longitudinal data on 100 children of divorce in very high-conflict families. These families had been referred to counseling services after failing to obtain agreement through mediation or lawyer negotiation. They evaluated the adjustment of the oldest child from 1 to 12 years of age in an ethnically diverse population. There was more frequent contact with the nonprimary residential parent in joint physical custody (12.11 days) than in sole custody (4.05 days). Two years after entry into the study, 98% of these families had joint legal custody. Of the 100, 35 children were in joint physical custody, 53 in maternal physical custody, and 12 in paternal physical custody. Adjustment of the child was not related to type of physical custody.

There is no evidence that any type of custody arrangement is better for children of high-conflict families.

In these high-conflict families, the more frequent the access, the more maladjustment in the child, including total behavior problems, depression, withdrawal, and somatic complaints. Girls' emotional and behavioral adjustments were more seriously harmed by frequent access than were boys'. Another important predictor of adjustment problems was the degree to which the child was caught up or used in the parents' conflict. Difficult temperament as a baby also predicted behavior problems.

Frequent access for high-conflict families does not seem in the child's best interest. The mental health professional should encourage the parents to keep the child out of the conflict. Girls and children with difficult infant temperament are particularly at risk.

At times, a court may find that the parent who is the "better" parent is also the one who is increasing the conflict. The court is reluctant to allow a parent to blackmail by increasing the conflict, but must decide based on what is best for the child, not necessarily what is "fair." High-conflict families, at the time of the divorce, have a high rate of violence. There is now evidence that spousal abuse has much the same psychological effect on children as does child abuse.

Age of the Child and Joint Physical Custody

Few studies have reported the pattern of parent access and age of the child. Stahl (1986) noted that parents felt that there were occasional problems for the child of moving between homes, but most parents were satisfied. In this group of nonrandom joint custody families, the families with very young children tended to have rigid schedules. These schedules were "somewhat complex" and designed to satisfy the needs of the parents rather than the child, but also took into account assumptions about the needs of the young child. For teens, schedules were dissolved and the teens decided on the time to move back and forth. Because the level of satisfaction is quite high for this select sample, compared with samples from other studies, it is difficult to interpret the results.

The case histories described by Atwell, Moore, Nielsen, and Levite (1984) indicated that there were problems with joint custody mainly for the younger children. For example, an alternating 3-month block created problems for a 2-year-old, a split week pattern was related to provocative and oppositional behavior for a 2 1/2 year old, anxiety for a 5-year-old, and dependency in a 2 1/2 year old (who did not have obvious psychopathology).

C. A. Richards and Goldenberg (1986) looked at fathers having joint physical custody of young children (under 6 years of age). Even though the sample was quite small ($n = 10$), the study is of particular interest because few studies have looked at such young children in joint custody. The fathers were spending an average of 24 hours of waking time a week with the children, considerably more than the average of 14 hours a week estimated for fathers in intact families. Fathers were quite positive about the experience. They often felt anger toward the mothers due to work overload and often felt that the mothers were not doing their share of the child care responsibilities. Many of the fathers felt that the impetus for the divorce had come from the mothers' wishes to leave the marriage and child-rearing responsibilities. Most fathers were bitter due to that perception and were not prepared for the difficulties of caring for very young children. At least in this small sample of fathers, the picture of a manipulative father with little interest in the children did not hold.

McKinnon and Wallerstein (1988) were particularly concerned about the needs of very young children. Such children may experience fears of abandonment in response to relatively brief and long separations. Wallerstein and Blakeslee (1989) felt that joint physical custody was particularly stressful for 4- to 5-year-olds, even more so than for 3- to 4-year-olds in their sample. A number of courts have ruled that joint physical custody is inappropriate for children of tender years or of parents who are overtly hostile. The exception was with parents having close geographic proximity and similarity (Clingempeel, Shuwall, & Heiss, 1988).

Irving et al. (1984) noted that joint physical custody is inappropriate for very young children or for children with emotional problems who experience the frequent changes as confusing and anxiety provoking. There is no discussion as to what is the lowest appropriate age for joint physical custody and how frequently changes can occur. I know of no references that suggest that joint physical custody is appropriate for preschool children.

Clearly some children, particularly younger ones, have difficulty with joint physical custody.

The recommendations concerning visitation patterns given in Chapter 7 are appropriate for consideration for joint custody. As Clingempeel and Reppucci (1982) noted, evidence of multiple attachments and the lack of evidence for harm to social–emotional development from day care raise questions about what coparenting arrangements would be appropriate for young children. Rarely do parents request joint physical custody for infants. When they do, the mental health professional needs to be prepared to decide the best pattern of residential changes for a young infant. As discussed in some detail in Chapter 7 concerning the length and frequency of visitation in young children, there is some reason to believe that infants can easily tolerate frequent contact with two parents if each parent has daily or almost daily contact with the child. Under such conditions, the child will bond to both parents.

No one has looked at the effect of daily changes in where the child sleeps, but intuitively it would seem that frequent changes would be unnecessarily confusing to the child. Clingempeel and Reppucci (1982) noted that children under 3 might require the greater stability of single-parent residential custody. They also noted, however, that continued relationship with both parents is highly useful to these children.

It is not known whether repeated separations due to alternating residential care would lead to adjustment problems in very young children. Fay (1985) is one of the few people to provide specific recommendations for parent access patterns for joint custody of infants. He recommended two patterns, depending on whether the mother is breast feeding the child. His recommendation for starting overnight visits anywhere from 3 to 6 months and beginning 50-50 time division at 1 year seem to be unusually open. The recommendations in Chapter 7 are much more cautious regarding overnight visits and the timing of 50-50 custody.

Thus, although there are theoretical positions on the effect of alternating residences, only some case histories and almost no empirical data are available to guide clinicians. If both parents are having almost daily contact with the child and the child has a relatively easy temperament, the child can probably handle physical joint custody, provided that the child sleeps in only one house. If daily contact is not likely (and few divorced parents are on such good terms as to permit such frequent contact), joint physical custody may be a goal to achieve as the child becomes older.

Joint physical custody is probably inappropriate for infants and toddlers, although the question has not been researched. For 3- to 5-year-old children, joint physical custody should be considered only if both parents have frequent, almost daily contact with the children. If such frequent contact is not feasible, it may be more appropriate to have physical custody initially with one parent with frequent visitation for the other (see Chapter 7). Under such conditions, parents can slowly increase the amount of time that the child spends with the less frequently seen parent until equal time with each parent has been developed (by age 6 or 7).

Basically, there are no guidelines about what pattern of change is best for joint physical custody. Part of the decision about the best pattern may depend on the ease with which the child has access to the other parent and to friends. For school age children, changes of less than 1 week would seem to be very confusing.

Clingempeel and Reppucci (1982) reported on a joint residential arrangement in which a child changed residences *and schools* every 2 weeks. Supposedly, the child adjusted well to this situation, but given the incredible complexity of that life, it is reasonable to propose that the child adjusted well in spite of, rather than because of, that residential arrangement. The courts are charged to devise plans that are in the best interests of the child, not plans that can simply be tolerated. The failure to see symptoms in the child does not prove that no harm is occurring or will not become apparent sometime in the future. The fact that a child can survive such a program does not mean that optimal adjustment will occur.

Joint Custody and Parental Relocation

Sometimes problems arise when one parent remarries and job opportunities develop in another geographic area for that parent or the parent's new spouse. To handle the parents' wishes to have shared residential time, suits for sole custody (or primary geographic custody) occur. The judge then has to decide what is best for the child or rule that the parent who is changing the agreement is at risk for losing custody. Even long-distance families can consult over important decisions that affect the children's lives; however, joint physical custody does not work well over long distances. For young children, the long separations can interfere with attachment. For older children, alternating school years (a common arrangement) interferes with peer relations. Often, the parent who gets the child for the first year or two then claims that the child should remain at that home to have continuity of activities, schools, and peers.

Recommendations for Successful Joint Custody

Irving et al. (1984) noted that good predictors of outcome success include commitment to parenting, good communication skills, flexibility, the ability to circumscribe marital conflict from the children, and good faith in following the arrangements. In a study of lawyers and judges from a northeastern state, Felner, Terre, Farber, Primavera, and Bishop (1985) mentioned the following as standards for joint custody: a good relationship between parents with cooperating positive communication, shared goals, and a low level of conflict.

Indices of successful joint custody (i.e., parental self-report of satisfaction) noted in Coller's (1988) review of the literature included:

1. A firm belief that the other parent is competent
2. A firm belief that the other parent is important to the child
3. Geographic proximity
4. Relatively high compliance of child support awards
5. Relatively low levels of relitigation (although there is some debate on this issue)
6. Increase in contact by the parent with less access (clearly a problem in high-conflict families)
7. Low parental burnout from full-time parenting
8. Children who in general prefer joint custody (although perhaps not in high-conflict families).

Coller also recommended six reasons to avoid joint custody:

1. Inability for a parent to care for the child, whether mental, emotional, or physical
2. Significant substance abuse
3. Expressed desire of a parent not to participate in joint custody
4. Great geographical distance in the case of very small children when frequent changes of residence are unmanageable
5. Intractable overt hostility over time between spouses despite mediation.

Irving et al. (1984) mentioned several contraindications for shared physical custody:

1. Very young children
2. Children with emotional problems for whom the arrangement is confusing and anxiety provoking
3. Parents who use their children as a weapon or whose anger toward their former spouses persists
4. Court-ordered joint custody, which is often less satisfactory.

When remarriage occurs without a long-distance move, J. B. Greif and Simring (1982) felt that joint physical custody works better than sole custody. Feelings of loss are reduced. Joint physical custody gives the remarried couple significant time together without parenting and reduces "instant" parenting needs.

Conclusions

Emerging research evidence indicates that joint custody and especially joint time are contraindicated in families with severe conflict. Another concern that has been increasingly expressed is that joint custody creates financial problems for the mother. Many states vary child support payment based on the amount of time the child spends with each parent. With equal time, mothers often obtain no financial aid (C. A. Richards & Goldenberg, 1985), but the cost of a home with space for children is constant whether the child stays 90% or 50% of the time. Seldom are mothers with lower initial income adequately compensated for the true "fair share" of raising children. In situations in which the parents enter the agreement voluntarily and are willing to make the time and energy to support the other parent, joint custody seems to be helpful to the child.

The Association of Family Conciliation Courts has compiled a useful handbook that includes some of the previously mentioned references in addition to others (Folberg, 1985; Milne, 1979). Articles on the psychological impact of joint custody, case law, a sample joint custody agreement, and an annotated bibliography are included.

Grandparent Custody

Wilks and Melville (1990) noted that in 75 custody cases reviewed by the Family Court Clinic in Toronto, 11% had grandparents as applicants for custody. In 67% of those cases, the grandparents had been involved in child rearing, and in 74%, the child had lived for some period of time in the grandparents' home (22% of the time without the parent). Typically, these grandparents were found to be neither in conflict with their own child nor overinvolved with the grandchild.

Kennedy and Keeney (1988) noted that in the United States in 1981, 3.7% of children under 18 who were unmarried or noninstitutionalized were living with someone other than their own parents. Based on the 1970 census, about 40% of these children were living with a grandparent. The authors formed a support group of 24 grandparents (out of 54 who were invited) who were rearing a grandchild without the child's parent present. Several grandparents had had the child from birth, but had no legal award of custody. Another group had temporary care of the child, and it was understood that the parent maintained custody and would become a full-time parent again. Those who chose to participate in the groups were far more likely to have uncertain custody status. Nonattenders (who seemed less concerned about their role) were far more likely to have legal custody. Attenders tended to have temporary custody, informal custody, or no custody. This uncertainty was reflected in greater anxiety on the grandparents' part and greater conflict with the child's biological parent. Of the attenders, it was likely that the parent who left the child with the grandparent was an only or youngest child, and that the parent had a hostile, dependent relationship with the grandparent.

At present, no research has been done on how well children reared by grandparents fare or whether the reasons for grandparent custody play a role in predicting a child's welfare.

ETHNICITY AND CUSTODY EVALUATIONS

Although mental health professionals have suspected that ethnicity makes a difference in divorce and custody issues, they have not had the research to support these suspicions and have not had the training in understanding ethnic differences. Professionals have based their studies on experience or intuitive knowledge or used the same criteria across cultural groups. Thus, evaluators have tended to use classical criteria for Hispanic and black families, although there is reason to believe that custody recommendations should be culture bound. Certainly, attachment between parent and child differs in various cultures. As a start, an entire issue of the *Journal of Divorce* (Everett, 1987) was devoted to minority and ethnic issues in divorce. There were three articles on black families, two on Hispanic, and one on Catholic Italian women. As an example of information from those studies, Fine and Schwebel (1987) argued that data on children's and adults' reactions to divorce and single parenthood may not generalize to blacks and that blacks, as a group, may cope more successfully than whites. It should be noted that none of these groups is homogeneous in that different subcultures exist within each. What is desperately needed is research on different Asian groups.

HOMOSEXUAL PARENT AND CUSTODY OR ACCESS

Prior to recent changes by the American Psychiatric Association on whether homosexuality is a criterion for maladjustment, homosexuality was grounds for denying custody. Indeed, in many court jurisdictions, it continues to be a decisive factor. Judges have been concerned about the stigma for the child, the possibility of peer ridicule, the possibility that the child might grow up to be homosexual, and the likelihood that the child might have inappropriate sex-role behavior (Harris, 1977; Hitchens, 1979/1980). Hitchens noted that a high number of custody battles involving a homosexual parent are between a lesbian mother and another relative, often the child's grandparent. Ironically, such battles are often with the parents of the lesbian mother, who have already demonstrated that a child of their upbringing can end up homosexual.

Kirkpatrick, Smith, and Roy (1981) did a careful study of 20 boys and 20 girls, half living in homes with lesbian mothers and half with heterosexual mothers. They used an extensive mother interview and tested the children. The testers were blind as to the type of family to which the child belonged. The maternal interests of the two types of mothers were the same. Lesbian mothers were more interested in breast feeding than heterosexual mothers. The marriages had been the same length for the two types of families. The lesbian mothers did not cite sexual dissatisfaction as the reason for the divorce (as might be expected), but indicated that the absence of psychological intimacy was the basis. Heterosexual mothers listed drug use, alcohol, other women, psychotic behavior, and physical abuse as reasons for divorce. Visitation patterns were the same for the two families, and there were no differences in gender development in the two groups of families. The lesbian mothers were more concerned about providing adult male figures for their children than were the heterosexual mothers. In addition, Kirkpatrick et al. found that children of lesbian mothers were as well adjusted as children of heterosexual mothers. Waters and Dimock (1983) likewise noted that there is no evidence that homosexual parents have any particular deficit in parenting ability.

In a review of four studies, Nungesser (1980) found that the majority of lesbian mothers were committed to nonsexist child rearing and that 80% of the children of lesbian mothers had male role models. Golombos, Spencer, and Rutter (1983) evaluated 27 lesbian single mothers and 27 heterosexual single mothers, with a total of 75 children from 5 to 17 years of age. They interviewed the mothers and the children. There were no differences between the two groups in gender identity, sex-role behaviors, or sexual orientation (for those children who were old enough to evaluate sexual orientation).

R. Green (1982) also compared 58 children of 50 lesbian mothers with 43 same-age children raised by 34 divorced heterosexual mothers. He obtained no significant differences for femininity, masculinity, sexual identity, ratings of peer group popularity, and gender of peer group. Hoeffer (1981) studied 20 lesbian and 20 heterosexual single mothers and their only or oldest child, age 6 to 9. She found few differences on measures of sex-role behavior. The mothers had little impact on boys' behaviors because the mothers were infrequently involved in encouraging particular play. Boys were just as sex typed regardless of type of family and were more sex typed than the girls.

In a fascinating discussion of family dynamics involving a lesbian mother, her lover, and the children, Hall (1978) reported behaviors of the lover that are remarkably similar to dynamics of remarried families as discussed in Chapter 9. The new partner either felt pressure to be a "supermom" (like many stepmothers) or to set limits on misbehavior (like many stepfathers). Children often felt threatened by loss of attention from the biological parent, just as in heterosexual remarried families.

Knight (1983) noted that the evidence was strong that economic deprivation was far more powerful as a predictor of the quality of child rearing than was having a lesbian mother. Lewin (1981) and Lyons (1983) felt that the primary source of difference between lesbian mothers and heterosexual mothers was the fear of loss of custody, and some mothers reduced property settlements in exchange for not having the homosexual orientation brought up in court.

Few studies have looked at the adequacy of parenting by homosexual fathers. B. Miller (1979) interviewed 40 gay fathers and 14 of their children. The sample was a snowball volunteer sample ("can you give me the name of a friend in the same situation"), so sample bias is a problem. No participants reported molesting their sons, and none was aware of any molestation from gay friends. Although Miller felt that adult heterosexual males were a greater sexual risk to children than adult homosexual males, supporting data are limited.

Of the sample's 27 daughters and 21 sons old enough to evaluate sexual orientation, only 3 daughters and 1 son were self-reported to be homosexual, figures similar to or lower than the number that would be predicted from heterosexual families. In this study, harassment of the children for having a gay father was not a problem. Daughters were more accepting than sons, and sons were more accepting than their mothers.

Clinical experience has suggested that gay fathers can be just as caring and concerned for the child's welfare as lesbian mothers. Higher levels of homophobia for males may lead to fewer cases of custodial homosexual fathers than custodial heterosexual fathers, but I have seen no data on the frequency of custodial homosexual fathers or mothers.

It should be remembered that there is no evidence that homosexuality is passed from one generation to the next (an issue that is important only if the task is to reassure the court that homosexuality is an unlikely outcome). Harris (1977) noted that sexual orientation identity takes place some time between infancy and middle childhood and is not passed from parent to child. One could argue that nothing is wrong with a parent deciding to rear a child with a homosexual orientation, but the courts and many mental health professionals (who are willing to accept the adult decision to be homosexual, but not the imposition of that decision on a child) are likely to disagree.

In any family, it is important to evaluate that a child is not being exposed to sexually explicit material or to adults' sexual behavior. Questioning may need to be more explicit in an evaluation with a homosexual parent, because norms concerning parenting behavior are less well defined and the "coming out" behavior (and concomitant increase in self-esteem) may conflict with "hiding" something about the homosexuality from the children.

SEX ABUSE ALLEGATIONS IN CUSTODY EVALUATIONS

It is generally believed that children rarely make false allegations of sexual abuse. Because child abuse is recognized as extraordinarily harmful to children during childhood and subsequent adulthood, allegations of child sexual abuse during a custody evaluation tends to bring the evaluation to a halt, and the accused is denied access. An emerging literature, however, suggests that such allegations made during or immediately after separation and divorce are not always true. An important issue is how to handle an allegation of sexual abuse in the middle of a custody or access battle, when the allegation was not made before and there is no real corroborating evidence.

The Association of Family and Conciliation Courts' Research Unit (1988) conducted a study to try to evaluate the frequency of such allegations and the degree to which such allegations could be substantiated. The association evaluated cases of alleged sexual abuse in 12 jurisdictions over a 6-month period. Over 9,000 cases involving custody or visitation disputes were seen. Of these, 169, or 1.5%, had allegations of sexual abuse of one or more of the children. Of those cases, abuse probably did occur in approximately 50%. In 27% of the cases in which abuse was judged not to have occurred, the false reports were judged deliberate. In the other cases, actual circumstances were not clear or the report was judged to be sincere but incorrect.

Even though it is more likely that sexual abuse allegations are false when made during a custody or access conflict than when made in other situations, there is reason to believe that a significant number of such allegations will be substantiated. Lawyers, the court, and mental health professionals must proceed with caution.

Gardner (1989) argued that the recent increase in information about sexuality through the media and sex education in the schools means that children across a wide age range have explicit information about sex. The fact that a child is aware of sexual behaviors can no longer be used as a criterion for whether abuse has occurred. For example, inappropriate exposure to sexually explicit materials can lead to a child's sexualized behaviors. Also, in several cases, a child has shown highly sexualized behavior because of association with an abused child, who was acting out the abuse in peer play.

True Allegations

Mian, Wehrspann, Kaljner-Diamond, LeBaron, and Winder (1986) evaluated 125 children under 6 years of age who had been sexually abused. Typically, the children younger than 6 were sexually abused by a family member, whereas almost three-fourths of the children over 6 were abused by someone outside the family. Physical symptoms indicating that young children had been sexually abused included vaginal discharge, bleeding, sexually transmitted diseases, bruises in the genital area, and abdominal pain. Psychological symptoms included nightmares, disruptive behavior, clinginess, and fearfulness. Only 18% showed specific sexual behavior, including sexual play, masturbation, seductive behavior, and inappropriate knowledge. Wehrspann et al. found intrafamilial abuse much more common in divorced families.

Morris (1989) argued that mental health professionals may be too quick to dismiss true allegations when made in the context of a divorce. She noted that there are several reasons why abuse may begin at that time. The marriage may have helped to contain the sexual impulse on the part of one parent. The emotional upset of the divorce may lead a potentially abusing parent to the child for emotional support. This latter problem may be exacerbated by the child's movement into the parental bed, a common behavior after a divorce, particularly for 4- to 7-year-olds. Finally, the anger that the perpetrator may feel toward the ex-spouse may be expressed in sexual abuse toward the child. Morris argued that the impulsiveness, anger, rigidity, and lack of empathy that are common in sexual abusers may also increase the risk of divorce itself. Faller (1991) made similar arguments as to increased risk for abuse after separation. Of her 136 cases of allegations of abuse during divorce, 52 fit this situation.

MacFarlane (1988) also noted reasons why true allegations may arise for the first time during the divorce proceeding. Incestuous fathers may resort to such inappropriate behaviors under stress, and divorce may be such a stressor. The child may be afraid of the abusing parent, and the separation may give sufficient protection for the child to risk revealing the abuse. Also, the child may be terrified of visiting the abuser alone and reveal the abuse to avoid such a visit. Faller (1991) noted that in her clinical experience, about half of mothers who discover that their husbands have sexually abused the children will divorce them.

False Allegations

MacFarlane (1988) noted that the allegations that arise during divorce proceedings often involve a very young child, age 2 to 4, who is unable to provide a clear explanation of what, if anything, happened. She believed it rare for the parent to deliberately falsify an allegation, but fearful parents might misinterpret a child's statements of behavior. She also noted that increased attention and nurturance given to a child who has made statements that sound like abuse can reinforce the child's verbal report. MacFarlane, like others, noted that "coached" descriptions devoid of any elaboration and use of adult terminology were indicative of false allegations. When repeated many times, the statements can sound like they were memorized. The evaluator's problem is to determine the quality of the original statement.

A. H. Green (1986) felt that allegations of incest and sexual abuse have increased in custody disputes. He felt that false disclosures are relatively rare, but that they do occur under the following conditions:

1. The child is "brainwashed" by an angry mother. The accusation often has a core of reality.
2. The child is influenced by a delusional mother. These mothers often have made accusations before concerning sexual misconduct. They also constantly interrogate their children about the alleged events leading to a "folie à deux."
3. The child's allegations are based on fantasy.
4. The child deliberately accuses the father of incest for revenge or retaliation.

Green noted that false disclosures present a different diagnostic picture than true disclosures. False cases are characterized by easy disclosure, absence of negative affect, use of adult sexual terminology, the child's check-ing with the accusing parent when telling the story, the child's willingly confronting the accused in the accusing parent's presence, the child's being comfortable when alone with the accused, the accusing parent's being para-noid or hysterical, and the child's having no symptoms of sex abuse.

Green's (1986) proposal was strongly criticized by Corwin et al. (1987), who felt Green's approach was based too much on opinion and too little on data. In rebuttal to Green, they argued:

1. Only difficult, ambiguous cases are referred to specialists, creating false impressions of base rates.
2. Green presented one case history as an example of a false accusation, that subsequent evidence proved was a true accusation.
3. Abused children use denial and dissociation that may lead them to appear unafraid of the perpetrator.
4. Children as young as 3 can accurately report experiences.
5. Sometimes accurate reports are given easily unlike Green's proposal.
6. Checking with the mother is a common behavior of young children in an ambiguous situation and is not indicative of brainwashing.
7. Adult terminology for genitalia is used by some families as a matter of course.
8. Being comfortable with the accused is an unreliable indicator of false allegations.
9. Green depends on a set of symptoms, but 1 out of 5 sexually abused children show no symptoms.

Thus, they argue that Green's criteria are not consistent with research findings and may mislead someone into thinking that a true allegation is false. The complexity of proper diagnosis raises serious questions about the utility of case history approaches to differentiate false from true allegations.

Bresee, Stearns, Bess, and Packer (1986) felt that mothers who had influ-enced a child to make a false report were relatively easy to identify. The mothers were unable to give much information. They were reluctant to have the child interviewed alone and were unwilling to consider the possibility that there was an interpretation of the facts other than molestation. These mothers were eager for the child to testify, unlike mothers with genuine complaints (who worried about the effect testifying would have on the child). The retri-bution was so important that these mothers pressed for an investigation de-spite the effect on the child. These mothers also shopped around for a professional who would support them.

Blush and Ross (1987) gave a case history of a 7-year-old girl who had reported that her father had sexually abused her sister. Without any addi-tional evidence, the report led to severing the parental rights of the father. Later, the girl told a similar story of herself being sexually abused on the school bus. An investigation ultimately revealed that the girl made up such stories to retaliate against those at whom she was angry. Blush and Ross labeled the phenomenon as the SAID syndrome, which stands for Sexual Allegation in Divorce.

Gardner (1989) noted that he required a court order to agree to do an assessment and to have access to all parties in an alleged abuse case. He recommended that, in the assessment, the examiner should learn the family's words for body parts. Open-ended questions are extremely important in the examination. According to Gardner, children invent answers to specific questions.

Morris (1989) noted that children who had not been abused respond to sexually anatomically correct dolls in a different way than do abused children. When left alone and observed unobtrusively, young children who had not been abused show curiosity about the doll, poke fingers in the orifices, and quickly become bored and look for something else to do. Abused children respond with aggression, repeat contact with the doll's genitals, and repetitively perform acts with the dolls. Gardner (1987, 1989) expressed doubts about the use of anatomically correct dolls in assessment. He felt that the uniqueness of the dolls draws attention to the genitalia and may mislead the evaluator.

Gardner (1987) developed an extensive Sex Abuse Legitimacy Scale, based on an extensive set of criteria for evaluating the veracity of sex abuse allegations. There are 50 items given three different weights based on Gardner's clinical experience as to how differentiating they are. He used 10% or less of the maximum score to indicate fabrication and 50% or more to indicate a true allegation. The typical abused child:

1. Was hesitant to divulge
2. Was fearful of retaliation by the accused
3. Felt guilt over consequences to accused
4. Felt guilt over participation
5. Gave specific details of the abuse
6. Gave a credible description
7. Told a consistent story
8. Showed frequent episodes of sexual excitement
9. Considered his or her genitalia damaged
10. Exhibited sensitized play
11. Described threats or bribes
12. Had no Parental Alienation Syndrome (a label Gardner coined)
13. Told story of abuse at time other than during a custody battle.

Gardner also described 13 more child characteristics he felt were less central but important, and several characteristics of the accused mother and the accused father.

While Gardner gives an elaborate pseudo-scientific scoring procedure, he provides no justification for specific items, for scoring rules or validation of the scale. Gardner's scale would seem to be an elaborate case history approach.

Blush and Ross (1987) also provided guidelines for typical characteristics of the complaining parent (mother or father) and for the alleged perpetrator (male or female). The characteristics, less systematically scored than Gardner's (1987) criteria, are summarized below.

Personality characteristics common to complaining mothers include:

1. The mother presents herself as fearful and a victim of manipulation, coercion, and abuse.
2. The mother presents herself as a "justified vindicator" with a wish for prosecution before proof has been demonstrated.
3. The mother may be psychotic (although this is rare).

Common personality characteristics of the complaining father (much rarer) include:

1. He is intellectually rigid, with a need to be correct at all times.
2. He has been constantly critical.
3. He usually makes allegations against the mother's boyfriend and sees the mother as a passive supporter of the situation.

Common personality characteristics of complaining children include:

1. They have a limited verbal ability to talk about feelings.
2. They are too immature to comprehend the politics of divorce.
3. They give responses that appear to be rehearsed.
4. They quote the same phrase as the complaining parent.
5. They use age-inappropriate language with no awareness of the meaning of what they are saying.
6. They will talk about the alleged incidents without prompting questions.
7. They are inconsistent in their telling of the incidents.
8. They lack the appearance of being traumatized.

Common personality traits of the alleged male perpetrator include:

1. He is an inadequate personality and passive-dependent.
2. He seems socially naive.
3. He assumed a "caretaker" role with the mother during courtship.
4. He earns love by yielding to the demands of the spouse.

Neither the Blush and Ross criteria nor the Gardner criteria have been subjected to systematic research, however. Although suggestive from a clinical point of view, the accuracy of the predictions awaits confirmation in research.

Perhaps the most developed strategy for assessing the veracity of sex abuse allegations has been criteria-based content analysis of the child's statement of abuse. Raskin and Esplin (in press) noted that truthful stories tend to have a series of elements that differ from those of stories that are made up. Their approach is based on the work of Undeutsch, who in the 1950s developed a technique he called "statement reality analysis." The child's story must be obtained with as little intrusion of the interviewer as possible, and structured questions are asked only after an open-ended interview.

Based on the European literature on statement analysis, Steller and Koehnken (1989) developed 19 specific content criteria divided into five categories: general characteristics, specific contents, peculiarities of content, motivation-related contents, and offense-specific elements. In a study cited by Raskin and Esplin (in press), after analyzing the stories of 40 sex abuse allegations of children from 3 to 15 years old, they divided cases into 20 cases with strong indications of actual sex abuse (confessions and/or physical evidence) and 20 cases in which the allegations were of doubtful veracity (all denied by perpetrator, subsequent recantation by child, no corroborating evidence, or polygraph examinations). When the criteria-based content analysis for veracity was applied, the distributions for the two groups were nonoverlapping, giving strong support for this technique.

There are no proven, highly reliable ways to evaluate whether sexual abuse has occurred. Gardner's (1987) scale has yet to be validated in research. The criteria-based content analysis approach may be the most promising approach to analyzing the truth of the child's story. Although it is frightening to miss a sex abuse case, it violates a basic tenet of the justice system to accept such allegations without evidence and may do a grave injustice to an innocent parent. Allegations, whether substantiated or not, do indicate a family in trouble and in need of professional intervention.

SUMMARY

Custody evaluations require specification of the criteria for custody and awareness of child development. It is important to monitor potential biases in the assessor. Proper custody evaluation requires an understanding of the effects of mother custody, father custody, and joint custody on child development. Joint custody has been surprisingly effective, even when there is a significant level of parental conflict. At severe levels, however, joint custody seems to be contraindicated. Allegations of sexual abuse in the midst of a custody evaluation raise complicated questions. Although some may have validity, others may be generated at the instigation of an anxious or psychopathological parent.

CHAPTER 6

Strategies for Custody Evaluations

Given the complexity of family relationships, the problem of predicting future stability given the upset over divorce, and the problem of changing developmental needs over time, the task of determining the best interests of children of divorce is indeed difficult. The evaluator has the additional burden of trying to predict future parenting based on present parental personality and behavior (Beaber, 1982). As Beaber noted, accurate data are difficult to acquire due to the intense motivations of the parties involved.

General issues involving joint custody, mother versus father custody, split custody, homosexual parents, and allegations of sex abuse were discussed in detail in Chapter 5. In this chapter, specific strategies for gathering information and descriptions of recommendations and actual practices by professionals are described.

PRECUSTODY EVALUATION NEGOTIATIONS

Mental health professionals should avoid representing one party against the other party in a custody battle, unless serious harm might befall the child by failing to do so. Mental health professionals may box themselves into difficult situations by representing one side. Just as the court has decided that the best interests of the child must be served, the mental health professional's first responsibility is the welfare of the children. When the mental health professional represents one parent, the other parent will see the professional as an adversary and will resist the process. Therefore, to best evaluate which parent is more appropriate or whether joint custody is reasonable, the mental health professional needs to be in equal relationships with both parents (Chasin & Grunebaum, 1981). It is also extremely important that the evaluator avoid assessing only one or some of the parties in question (Weithorn & Grisso, 1987). Although joint representation is ideal, sometimes circumstances prohibit equal access. Under such conditions, the assessor should not make any evaluative statements or opinions about any party not directly assessed (Weithorn & Grisso, 1987). Despite the usefulness of an impartial position, evaluators play this role in only half the cases, according to a national survey of 82 experienced child custody evaluators (Keilin & Bloom, 1986).

The mental health professional should make every effort to be in a neutral position for custody assessment with equal access and equal relationships with both parents. Representing one parent against the other in a child custody dispute is likely to lead to inappropriate assessment and recommendations. The mental health professional should represent the best interests of the child, not of either parent, regardless of who is paying for the service. Thus, it is useful to require that the evaluation reports be sent to both lawyers and to the court. The evaluator should also avoid situations in which only one or some of the parties are evaluated.

If the evaluation is being done at the joint request of two lawyers, the mental health professional should obtain an agreement in writing prior to the evaluation that the report will be submitted to both lawyers and the court. Without such a stipulation, the evaluator should obtain a court order signed by the judge. If the court orders the evaluation, such an agreement is not necessary.

At the beginning of negotiations and prior to contact with the parents, it is useful to establish a working relationship with the attorneys involved (Goldzband, 1982). Although a team approach may be somewhat more expensive, it may correct for biases held by a single evaluator (see Chapter 5). A team approach, however, was endorsed by only half of the experienced custody evaluators in Keilin and Bloom's (1986) survey.

The mental health professional should not allow a lawyer to read a report and decide at that point whether the report would be useful in court. If the assumption is that the report is focused on the child's best interests, legal strategy should not be the basis for deciding whether the report is used by the court. If the assessment is being done in response to a court order, the court should stipulate that the report must be sent to both sides.

Each parent should have a written explanation of the evaluation process, the limits of confidentiality (there are none), the procedure for billing, and a list of who will receive the results. Chasin and Grunebaum (1981) provided a copy of such a basic contract. Prior to starting the evaluation, this explanation should be distributed and, for safe measure, a signed agreement indicating understanding of these rules should be obtained.

Suarez, Weston, and Hartstein (1978) and Skafte (1985) suggested that a stipulation of the ground rules be signed in court. The ground rules should indicate that evaluation can include the parents, the children, and any other person deemed necessary by the evaluator (e.g., grandparents, new spouses, living partners, housekeepers, child care workers, teachers). Suarez et al. suggested that the stipulation also require that the parents provide any pertinent records or files, including previous psychiatric evaluations, medical files, and school records. The request should also include police records, medication, and statements as to whether anyone has received psychotherapy. The content of psychotherapy should be protected from evaluation (see the discussion as to why later in this chapter).

The stipulation should include information about fees and who pays them. Fees for expert testimony may be additional to fees for evaluation. Suarez et al. (1978) also indicated that the evaluator should have at least a week's notice prior to a court appearance. Some states require that the report be available a minimum number of days prior to court. Skafte (1985) noted that without the court order, the mental health professional can be vulnerable to lawsuit if either parent claims at a later time that the evaluation was not done with his or her permission.

I recommend that payment be done in advance, as does Goldzband (1982). It is extremely important, however, that concern over payment not be an issue for the mental health professional in deciding which parent is best suited for custody. Concern over payment or anger at nonpayment can affect the decision making process, even for the mental health professional who conscientiously avoids being influenced by that problem. In addition, one parent is likely to be dissatisfied with the report. It is very difficult to get an angry parent to pay for services.

Mental health professionals should collect the anticipated fees in an escrow account prior to beginning the evaluation. They should not complete the report if additional fees have not been paid.

AVOIDANCE OF DUAL-ROLE RELATIONSHIPS

A mental health professional who interacts with any party in a business, professional, or personal relationship and then is involved in a custody evaluation with that person is involved in a dual-role relationship, which is unethical (Weithorn, 1987). It is very important that psychological assessors be aware of the unique characteristics of performing custody evaluations. As Weithorn noted, complaints against psychologists involved in custody evaluations represent a major source of the caseload of the American Psychological Association's Ethics Committee.

MODELS OF CUSTODY EVALUATIONS

The following would seem to be a desirable model for custody evaluation:

1. Have several interviews with each parent alone. Parents need to be reminded that nothing in the interview is confidential. If a parent asks whether he or she can say something off the record, the answer should be "no." The mental health professional should never get in the position of promising something that cannot be kept secret. Skafte (1985) indicated that there are advantages to seeing the parents together for the first interview, even though the level of tension in the interview tends to be high.

2. Hold several interviews with each child alone. Gardner (1976) recommended observing young children, seeing preschool age children two or three times, and seeing older children three or more times. Children also need to be informed that the information obtained is not confidential. The evaluator should try to protect the children in terms of the relationship with each parent whenever possible.

3. Interview each parent and the children together.

4. Interview teachers, babysitters, and other significant people in the children's lives. If grandparents play a significant role, they should be interviewed. If one or both parents are in a new relationship to which the children will be exposed, that person should be seen. Chasin and Grunebaum (1981) also recommended seeking out conversation with significant others, including grandparents, housekeepers, friends, teachers, physicians, neighbors, and psychotherapists.

5. Schedule a home visit. This visit allows determination of the safety of the home setting and provides additional information about the sensitivity of the parents to the children's needs. Beaber (1982) also recommended observations of parenting *in vivo*.

6. Invite the parents to submit other information. Chasin and Grunebaum (1981) tell parents that not only will the evaluation team speak with them, but that the team will read any material that the parent might want to submit and talk with anyone whom the parents feel has information that would help the court make a custody decision.

Barnard and Jenson (1984) recommended a joint session with the parents, separate sessions with each parent, sessions with all children, separate sessions with each child, and sessions of the mother and children and of the father and children. They added two interesting sessions: mother and extended network and father and extended network.

In a home with two children, the above model could take 20 to 40 or so staff hours, not including team meetings to pull together the information and write the report. In a more complex or difficult evaluation (e.g., where there are serious accusations that must be investigated in some depth or where more children are involved), the staff time may be considerably longer. In addition, the custody team can expect to be required to testify in court, permitting cross-examination of the report and its implications.

Private custody evaluation can cost from $1,000 to $5,000 for a simple evaluation and much more for complex battles. This cost puts private custody evaluations out of reach of most families, who may already be paying substantial legal fees for a contested divorce. Given that their income is already being stretched by now serving two households, it is understandable that 90% of divorces have uncontested court battles.

The British Columbia Service Delivery Standards

In a rare move in the area of child custody assessment, the British Columbia Corrections Branch (Robinson, 1985) developed a set of standards for custody and access assessment in 1985. These standards defined mediation, conciliation, and custody assessment procedures. The law provides a family court counselor to perform the assessment, but private evaluations are permitted.

The best interest of the child is the primary consideration for custody determination. The British Columbia law specifically excludes from consideration behavior of a parent that does not affect the child.

All parties in the assessment are notified that nothing is confidential and that they have the right to withhold information. This limit to disclosure protects people from self-incrimination. Other people contacted as part of the investigation, however, do not have that right to confidentiality.

In the first interview, the family court counselor tries to meet with both parents, preferably in one of their homes. The counselor asks for the names of other people who can provide information. If the parents live in the same area as the counselor, the counselor observes the child in the presence of both parents, jointly or separately. The observation should be done in the environment in which the child might be placed, if possible. This requirement applies regardless of the child's age.

The child's views are obtained in a manner appropriate to the child's age. The child is not asked to make a choice. It is recognized in the standards that such a choice might be damaging to the child. The child is simply given an opportunity to express feelings.

The report, which must be prepared by one person, is provided to every party at least 5 days before the hearing. The counselor informs the parties that they have the right to ask any questions to clarify the contents of the report prior to the hearing, but dispute of the content must occur in court. The report should identify sources of information, provided that such sources do not damage constructive or essential relationships.

Developing assessment standards is a very exciting innovation for a jurisdiction. Although the evaluator has wide discretion about how to collect information, some information is required for all evaluations. Such a data base provides a common set of criteria for all assessments and an opportunity to research the effectiveness of the process.

Additional Evaluation Procedures

Some teams use additional evaluation procedures, based in part on the professional roles of the team members. Dr. Lanning Schiller (personal communication, 1985) has found it expedient to obtain most factual information through a long written questionnaire rather than an interview. The interview is reserved for more probing questions.

Psychological testing is most commonly done as part of the evaluation of children and parents. Bonding with each parent can be evaluated using projective techniques. Thematic Apperception Test evaluations can be helpful. For example, when a child sees all adult women as angry and controlling, the examiner can combine that information with other obtained information to describe the child's parent perception. Use of the Minnesota Multiphasic Personality Inventory (MMPI) can catch some false negatives that were not apparent in interviews, and projective testing can be helpful in detecting borderline pathology in a person who seems quite healthy on interview.

No custody evaluation should be based solely on test results. The implications of test materials are given meaning only in the context of other information.

Although both lawyers have the right to see the test materials, the psychologist should not explain the process by which recommendations arise from the test materials. Learning to interpret test materials takes years. In spite of knowing that interpretation is not a simple process, some psychologists feel compelled to answer questions that cannot be answered. If the well-meaning psychologist tries to draw an inference from a single piece of information, he or she is setting up himself or herself for a cruel and effective cross-examination that can discredit the testimony. Because idiosyncratic experiences may lead to particular perceptions (although why the child chose to remember that particular perception is another matter), it is always possible that one perception has limited meaning. Because it is the *pattern* of perceptions on projectives that permit valid inferences about the child's functioning, the psychologist should refuse to answer questions concerning the interpretation of individual responses.

Weithorn and Grisso (1987) warned against the use of psychological assessment procedures that have not been validated for divorce situations. Indeed, some people have argued that psychological tests have little if any utility in custody evaluations. The MMPI, for example, was validated on clinical samples. In the custody evaluation situation, people have a vested interest in looking good and are often quite anxious. Under such circumstances, people may distort some answers.

Evaluators should be warned against the use of psychological assessment procedures that may not be valid for use in divorce evaluations. In particular, "homemade," unvalidated assessment procedures may create ethical problems and invalid data.

Family Interview

Relatively few evaluators start with family interviews. Musetto (1980), however, recommended beginning an evaluation by seeing the parents and children together unless the level of anxiety is too strong. The advantage of a joint meeting is to emphasize the fact that custody and visitation evaluation is a family problem and the family needs to be responsible for solving it. The interviewer talks to the family about the joint responsibility for the problem, rather than focusing the blame on one particular person. Musetto felt that "psychological" parents should be willing to acknowledge their own contribution to the family problem.

Musetto discussed a systems analysis of families. Following Bowen (1976), he noted that families tend to form triangles. To maintain a relationship, parents may divert attention to children or to issues. Because the family is a system, the whole family contributes to maintain the status quo. When there is a problem between two family members, the question must be raised as to the role of other family members in maintaining that problem. Family interviews give the evaluator an opportunity to understand those dynamics and to help the family accept responsibility for the problem and the solution.

Bentovim and Gilmour (1981) used a family therapy model of assessment and intervention. They proposed a model in which a *focal hypothesis* was generated to understand family functioning (i.e., a primary theme to explain how the family operates). The *surface action* described ways in which the family normally nurtured and socialized with each other. If the surface action is pathological, it may reflect a rigid repetitious behavior that overrides individual needs. Professionals can become enmeshed in such systems. Consistent with Bowen's (1976) orientation, *depth structure,* or more enduring family scripts from historical child rearing, is analyzed in terms of family system issues from the family of origin or family of procreation.

Bentovim and Gilmour proposed seeing together all significant family members and professionals and seeing them in various combinations. Interactional tasks between parents and children were used to avoid parental attempts at convincing the evaluators of a point of view. With infants, the task may involve caretaking. With toddlers, play, setting limits, separations, or reunions might be used. With older children, the parents were asked to talk about the divorce situation and to ask for wishes and opinions from the children. Genograms, that is, diagrams of family history, were used to collect information, and life books for the children were used to describe complicated life situations.

Parent Interview

A variety of criteria are useful in evaluating parenting. Gardner (1976) suggested starting the parent interview by giving the parent the opportunity to tell the interviewer anything on his or her mind. The Group for the Advancement of Psychiatry (GAP) (1981) suggested the following criteria for evaluating parents: basic mental health status, personality functioning, past personal history with particular reference to their own childhoods, degree of flexibility in accepting feedback to their parenting responsibilities, probable method of restoring missing mate (cooperative or noncooperative), and ability to form treatment alliance where their children are concerned. Parents should be questioned about suicide and homicide attempts, as well as their own childhoods, especially concerning divorce and how it was handled, abuse, alcohol, drugs, discipline, and affection. Evaluation of parental scripts may provide information on areas to explore about present parenting.

Other useful questions include:

1. Why do you want custody of the children? (This question is an obvious one, but it may produce some surprising answers. Common answers include the affectionate bonds with the children and a wish to protect the children from the inadequate parenting of the other parent.)

2. Every family has different ways of expressing their love for each other. Some touch a lot. Some say that they love each other. Others just know it. How do you express affection for the children? How do they express affection for you? (This is essentially the same question that I recommend asking the children.) What do you see as true for the children's other parent in terms of affection?

3. How do you provide for discipline for the children? What do you think about spanking, yelling, taking away privileges, grounding? How often do these punishments occur? For what behaviors? What do you see as true for the children's other parent in terms of discipline?

4. Do you consider yourself to have deficiencies with regard to handling the children (Gardner, 1976)?

5. What is the child's history? Was the pregnancy wanted? Was birth control being used? How was the pregnancy? What was the labor and delivery like? Before the birth, did you have any preference for the child's sex? How did you feel about the baby? How was the infancy? Did the mother breast or bottle feed? Why? What was the child's temperament (biological rhythms, eating regularity, eating ease, sleep patterns, attachment)? What is the history of childhood diseases? Childhood accidents? When were the milestones for sitting up, walking, talking, and toilet training? (These answers are notoriously inaccurate.)

6. What complaints does your spouse make about the way you handle the children (Gardner, 1976)?

7. What activities do you enjoy with the children? What activities bore you or irritate you?

8. What do you hope for the children in terms of your dreams for them? (This is an adaptation of one of Gardner's questions.)

9. What do you see as the needs of children in general at this age? (Ask this question regarding the age of each child.) How do you think things are going to change in terms of the children's needs?

The following questions were suggested by Chasin and Grunebaum (1981):

1. What is the ideal custody arrangement for your family? Why?
2. How would it affect you if the other parent got custody?
3. Joint custody involves equally shared decision making and may or may not involve equally shared child care. What would be its benefits and drawbacks for your family?
4. What aspect of your ideal arrangement would you be willing to negotiate?
5. Describe each child's daily routine, friends, teachers, likes, dislikes, interests, fears, skills, and problems. For each problem, describe the remedy you feel would be most effective.
6. What are your strongest assets as a parent? What are your weaknesses?
7. What are the strengths and weaknesses of the other parent?

   I particularly like one of Skafte's (1985) questions: "If you had custody of the children, how often would you like them to see the other parent?" It is important to assess the understanding that each parent has concerning the children's needs to have contact with both parents. Indeed, California law requires that some preference be given to the parent who is most willing to support access to the other parent.

Skafte (1985) proposed that the parents be interviewed in a joint session. She felt that information obtained by such an interview outweighed the tension produced. Joint assessment might provide useful information on the likelihood that joint legal custody would work. She suggested beginning the interview with questions concerning the history of the relationship, the effect of having children, parenting, child care responsibilities, changes in relationships with the children, the decision to separate, changes in the children's lives after separation, desire for custody, and plans for the children. She also suggested asking each parent to assume that he or she had custody and to describe the allowed access to the other parent.

Skafte then provided an additional set of questions for interviewing each parent separately. These questions focused on the parent's own childhood, young adulthood, marriage, separation, feelings about the children, feelings about custody and how the parent expects to handle it, expected allegations from the other parent, and thoughts about visitation.

D'Andrea (1983) used a measure of "fathering," developed from J. B. Greif (1979) and Roman (1977, cited in Abarbanel, 1979), that could be used for evaluation of parents of either gender. Each parent is asked who has been responsible for:

1. Routine daily care and safety of the child
2. Intellectual development

3. Physical development
4. Teaching the child how to behave
5. Recreational activities
6. Emotional development
7. Religious development
8. Moral development
9. Giving the child a sense of being a part of the family
10. Financial decision making affecting the child.

A measure of perceived knowledge of the child was obtained by the number of "I don't know" responses to the questionnaire.

Beaber (1982) listed 10 criteria for parental competence and 8 more subtle criteria if the parents are roughly equal on the first 10. Examples of the 10 primary criteria include the ability to abide by court orders; to properly feed, clothe, and shelter the child; and to provide some minimal amount of love and caring. Examples of the more subtle criteria include the ability to model, reinforce, and encourage positive character traits; to provide a stimulating home environment; to play and teach the joy of play; and to provide for cultural, sports, and intellectual resources outside the home.

Child Interview

The GAP (1981) report proposed the following areas to be included in the child evaluation: basic mental health status, previous developmental course, coping with grief and the desire to restore the missing parent, attachment to parents, phase of development, degrees and severity of psychological impairment and treatment if any, and ability to use substitute objects as resources in lieu of missing parent.

Lewis (1974) raised some difficult questions concerning information given to the primary school age child concerning the purpose of the interview and testing: If it is clear to the child that confidentiality is not present, will the data be limited because of the child's defensiveness? Will the child feel betrayed when learning of the information given the court? Should the child be encouraged to open up old wounds, when a therapeutic relationship does not exist and follow-up is not going to be possible?

Even though the child may be more defensive or try to distort information to fit wishes, providing a child with the information concerning the purpose of the interviews and with the limits of confidentiality is likely to produce less harm to the child later than concealing such information. The mental health professional has an obligation to protect the best interests of the child not only in terms of the custody decision, but also in the custody evaluation process. The evaluator should discourage the child from opening up unresolved areas to a greater degree than can be handled easily and should request more time with the child if inadvertent stress occurs as a function of the process.

Chasin and Grunebaum (1981) proposed that the evaluator should tell the parents exactly what the parents should say to the child about the interview. They suggested that the parents say something like, "You are going to see someone who will help us decide the best way for us to take care of you after the divorce. He won't hurt you or give you tests. (This latter comment should be changed if tests are to be administered.) He wants to play with you. He wants to understand you." They then suggested telling the parent that the first question to the child would be, "What did your parent tell you about your visit to me?" If the child does not or cannot answer, the assessor should provide some structure and then proceed.

In meeting with the child alone, the type and wording of the questions must be altered to take into account the vocabulary and developmental needs of the child. Gardner (1976) provided a list of useful questions that might be asked of the child. Some of the questions are indirect; others directly ask the child to describe feelings about the family. Examples are:

- A child is ashamed to tell his father about something. What is it?
- Act out what you would do if you found that you had magic powers.
- Tell about a time when your feelings were hurt.
- If you had three wishes, what would they be? (This is a standard child interview question.)
- Tell something about your father that gets you angry.
- What are the worst things a child can say to his or her mother?

Remember that attachments and conflict change over time and the overall pattern is more important than single responses.

Skafte (1985) proposed merely observing children under 3. For children from 3 to 5, she suggested play evaluation:

1. Mommy's house, Daddy's house. This play uses stuffed animals, dolls, puppets, or small figures that have parents in two locations. Such play develops a fantasy to tap relationships with each parent. Skafte gave several examples of questions that would be helpful in developing the fantasy.
2. Calling Mom, Calling Dad. The evaluator develops a fantasy of a telephone conversation with each parent. The child is then encouraged to play the role of the parent while the evaluator plays the child.
3. If you could change yourself into an animal, what animal would you be, and why? This game is a standard projective device for young children. It is also helpful to get the child to imagine each member of the family as an animal and report which animal and why.
4. If you could have three wishes, what would they be?
5. Island Game. Skafte recommended developing the fantasy in some detail. The child is on an island and has everything he or she needs. The

child is lonely because no one else lives there. A magic fairy gives the child the chance to have someone with him or her. Who would the child choose? Then have the child add another person on the island. (Skafte recommended drawing the island and people to increase involvement.) The child is then given the chance to have anyone on the island. Skafte ended the fantasy by having everyone go back to the land where they lived and live happily ever after. (I like Skafte's variation of this common assessment technique. The child's order of preference is assessed, but the child is not left with a fantasy of isolation from either parent.)

For 5- to 8-year-olds, Skafte included:

1. Make three wishes.
2. Tell in whom you can confide. In this game, the child is given a moral dilemma and asked how to solve the problem and to whom the child would go for help to solve the problem.
3. Name the best and worst features of living with each parent.
4. Draw your family.
5. Complete the sentences.

For children 10 years of age and older, Skafte proposed:

1. Draw your family.
2. Complete the sentences.
3. Name the worst and best things about being with each parent.

If the child is over 8, I find it useful to ask the same questions of the child that I ask of each parent, rephrasing the questions to make them appropriate. T. W. Miller and Veltkamp (1986) added family doll play and imaginative stories as part of their recommended assessment. Building on Despert's fables to assess potential stressful life experiences for children, they derived 11 fables to assess the child's feelings and fears: Anger, Worry, Incest, Discipline, Spaceship, Drug/Alcohol, Abandonment/Left Alone, Fear, Dream, Separation/Divorce, and Parental Violence. Preliminary use suggested that the content of the stories was extremely useful for identifying themes in the child.

Weithorn and Grisso (1987) noted that of the several assessment procedures that might be considered for custody evaluations, the Children's Reports of Parental Behavior (Schaefer, 1965) seem to be a useful tool with acceptable psychometric properties.

Should the Child Be Asked with Whom He or She Wants to Live?

The GAP (1981) report indicated that although a child's opinion about custody has relevance, it should be considered as only one part of the evaluation and should not determine custody. As many as 20 states have statutes that require taking into account the child's preference if the child is over 10 years old (Reppucci, 1984). Older children are more likely to be asked for their preference (Felner, Terre, Goldfarb, et al., 1985), but judges and lawyers reported difficulty in knowing how to weigh the child's preference. Some states require that older children's preference be honored unless there is strong reason not to do so (Weiss, 1979, p. 331). This requirement is most unfortunate, given the evidence that children may be placed under significant stress by that evaluation. Franklin and Hibbs (1980) noted that depression may result as a reaction to expressing a preference for one parent. The child could feel even more divided in terms of loyalties due to expressing a preference.

Mental health professionals should not ask children with whom they want to live and should advise the court to avoid asking children the same question. If the judge or referee insists that such a question will be asked, request that it be given in chambers without the parents present. There are a variety of ways to assess how the child feels without a direct question. If the child feels compelled to indicate a preference without being asked, the opportunity to talk should be given. The interpretation of the meaning of that communication should be based on the context.

It is advisable to avoid asking the children which parent they want for a variety of cogent reasons. Children will answer this question for many wrong reasons. First, regardless of the logic of the answer, the choice places the child in the position of accepting one parent and rejecting the other. Even if the parents can accept that choice (and many parents are hurt and angry at the choice), the child is at risk for carrying guilt for that rejection.

Second, some children will make a request based on their view of the best deal they can make for the quality of life: Which parent has the latest bedtime? Which parent does not censor television watching? Which parent is most permissive or seldom punishes? Although this strategy is reasonable from the child's point of view, it may not be in the child's best interests.

Third, some children try to decide which parent most needs them (particularly the children aged 10 to 12). One girl told me that she was choosing her mother because her mother was emotionally upset and would have trouble getting along without the daughter. The girl was closer to her father, but saw her father as stronger and able to survive without her help. The girl was petrified that the choice would invite rejection from the father, but felt it was the only decision she could make. In this case, it would be far better for the court to decide that the child's best interests were not to take care of the mother. Children will often not tell the judge why a particular choice was made, because they recognize that the truth would undermine their strategy. In addition, the child may have little insight as to why a particular choice seems correct.

Fourth, the child may feel compelled to punish the parent whom he or she sees as responsible for the divorce (Weiss, 1979). Out of anger (and limited cognitive ability to understand empathetically why a parent might decide that a relationship is harmful), the child may reject a parent who may be of more benefit to that child's long-term development.

Chasin and Grunebaum (1981) reported a case in which the child felt so much guilt at testifying against one parent, that the child was never able to reestablish the relationship. They also noted that another problem with asking for children's participation in the decision is that indelicate or dishonest handling of the child by any of the professionals involved may lead the child to distrust the legal and therapeutic process.

Clearly, some parents coach the children as to what to say to the judge when this question is asked (Reppucci, 1984). It is difficult, if not impossible, for the court to ensure that such pressure does not occur.

Finally, there is an ebb and flow of attachments that children have with parents. Sometimes they are more attached to one parent and other times more to the other parent. It is unfortunate that a relatively irreversible decision is made, based on the timing of that varying attachment.

Mental health professionals may recommend that custody be given to one parent, not because the child needs the particular parent at the moment, but because the next developmental stage would make one parent better. No child has that perspective.

If the mental health professional does not ask the child for parental preference, what choices are there? The nature of each parent–child bond can be evaluated without actually asking the child for a preference. The following questions can be useful in determining that preference:

1. When you have a problem, to whom do you go?
2. When you are sick, whom do you ask for help?
3. When you wake up in the middle of the night with a nightmare, whom do you ask for help? Why?
4. Which parent do you play games with? Which games?
5. Do you have any hobbies? Does either parent help you?
6. How is anger expressed in the house?
7. How are you punished? Who does the punishing? How do you feel about it? What are you punished for?
8. If you are happy (had fun at school, got a good grade), which parent would you tell?
9. What do you imagine it would be like if you spent weekdays with mother and weekends with father (Chasin & Grunebaum, 1981)?
10. In which home would you like to spend school nights and why? In which home would you like to spend weekends and why?

Data from Pearson, Munson, and Thoennes (1983) on how often children are interviewed by judges or by investigation teams indicated that such interviews are surprisingly rare. In Denver, Colorado, judges were reluctant to interview children of any age. (It would not be surprising, however, to find regional differences on this issue.) In their data of 100 cases from 1972 to 1976, the judge interviewed the child in only 8 cases. Judges found it difficult to talk to young children. One judge indicated that younger children only cried that they wanted both parents. The mean age of the few children who were interviewed was 11.1 years. In no case was a child interviewed by a judge prior to setting temporary custody orders, an important issue because temporary orders often become permanent.

Parent–Child Interview

Although there are no guidelines about what questions might be asked during the joint parent–child interview, the important issue is the evaluation of how the parent and child interact. When asked to think about a question, does the parent listen to the child's opinion? Does the child listen to the parent's opinion? Does either interrupt the other? How does the parent handle inappropriate behavior on the part of the child? Misbehavior on the child's part during the interview puts the parent at considerable stress, since the parent knows that an evaluation is occurring. Some parents let the child have more freedom than they would in private on the incorrect assumption that mental health professionals value permissiveness. If the parent puts no limits on the child, the professional should request that limits be set, and see how well the parent can accomplish that goal. Remember that boys aged 4 to 6 do not tend to obey mothers.

Another important dimension to evaluate in the parent–child interview is nonverbal behavior. Where does each sit? Does the child cling to the parent or show indifference? Is there evidence of bonding? Does the parent show a wish to protect the relationship between the child and the other parent? Suarez et al. (1978) encouraged the use of a one-way window whenever possible and to observe the parent and child during unstructured play activity as well as the more structured story telling activities of the Thematic Apperception Test or Children's Apperception Test. Chasin and Grunebaum (1981) observed parent–child interactions around a structured task. A parent might be asked to guide a 3-year-old child in building a structure of blocks or making a puppet play. For older children, the task might be to jointly plan a vacation.

The GAP (1981) report suggested the following dimensions of evaluations for parent–child interactions: What is the spontaneous response of the child to the parent? Is the parent viewed as an asset—and if not, why not? How in tune with the child is the parent? Is the parent "listening" or "telling"? How psychologically nurturing is the parent?

The evaluator must keep careful notes about all interactions, observations, and testing information, and never depend on memory on the assumption that an interaction can be recalled later. Usually, particularly for more complex and angry cases, there is significant delay before a case reaches court. The evaluator may have to wait months and perhaps even years before testifying.

A Measure of Parent–Child Behavior

McDermott, Tseng, Char, and Fukunaga (1978) developed the Parent–Child Interaction Test to measure parent–child behavior. Each parent was asked to work together with his or her children to tell stories about a modified set of the Children's Apperception Test cards and to build together a wooden block tower. Each parent–child interaction was videotaped. McDermott et al. evaluated the child's behavior on degree of comfort, initiative, spontaneity, fantasy expression, range of feelings, and separation behavior. The parent was evaluated on attachment, empathy with and sensitivity to the child's own level, monitoring the child's needs, discipline, guidance, consistency, patience, intellectual stimulation, emotional expression, spontaneity, physical closeness, encouragement, and acceptance.

Although no data were presented to indicate whether such a systematic approach improved the quality of custody decisions, McDermott et al. felt that the test was of significant help. A 2-year follow-up of child adjustment was of limited usefulness, however, because the data were used originally to make the decisions of custody. Thus, it was impossible to determine whether use of the test would have improved the decision making process. Although the authors indicated that the test provided dramatic information about the effects of particular custody arrangements, they did not present the means of the scales or the analyses, so it is impossible to determine whether everyone would come to the same conclusion. They indicated that their data supported terminating visitation rights in cases in which the custodial parent strongly opposes visitation or strongly dislikes the former spouse and pressures the children to have similar attitudes. Again, there are no data on the adjustment of children when such visitation is eliminated. McDermott et al. also noted that for two cases, strong religious orientation masked an inability to tolerate spontaneity and autonomous thinking.

In the aforementioned national survey of 82 child custody evaluators (Keilin & Bloom, 1986), all evaluators interviewed the mother, the father, and each child. Psychological testing occurred in three-fourths of the cases, and parent–child interactions were observed in two-thirds. Home and school visits were endorsed as practices by only 30% of the evaluators.

Criteria for Custody

Chasin and Grunebaum (1981) recommended using the following criteria for determining custody. They recommended favoring the parent who:

1. Is most likely to foster visitation and who shows the most objective and respectful attitude toward the other parent. Again, it should be noted

that the laws in some states give greater weight to the parent who is more willing to support visitation with the other parent.

2. Will maintain the greater continuity of child contact with relatives, friends, neighborhood, schools, and so forth.
3. Has the best child-rearing skill.
4. Shows the greater humanity, consistency, and flexibility in handling the child.
5. Is the one to whom the child is most deeply attached.

Woody (1977), in his study of custody determinations of mental health professionals, found that the following criteria were used:

1. Love and affect between each parent and the child
2. Other emotional ties
3. The length of time in an emotionally or psychologically stable environment and the importance of continuity for the child
4. Mental health of each parent.

If there is a conflict in the above values, so that a decision cannot be made from those principles, mental health professionals also give greater weight to the parent who:

1. Will provide geographic stability
2. Has a good health history
3. Has traditional morality.

The GAP (1981) report proposed five major principles of custody determination:

1. Custody decisions should be a part of the process of the developmental change in a family.
2. Family ties and family continuity have an importance that transcends divorce.
3. The history of mental illness in a parent does not in itself preclude effective parenting.
4. Prevailing values regarding family styles do not necessarily correlate with parenting capabilities.
5. A child's opinion in custody disputes has relevance, but it is only one part of the evaluations and should not alone determine custody.

Dr. Lanning Schiller (personal communication, 1985), also recommended considering the capacity of each parent to facilitate child growth, awareness of child development, avoidance on the part of the parent of role reversal, identification with the child, and satisfying the parent's own needs from the child.

Felner, Terre, Farber, Primavera, and Bishop (1985) found that 74 attorneys and 43 judges from a northeastern state gave greatest value for custody to (1) emotional stability and ability to care for the child and (2) time availability of each parent, stability of living arrangements, child care arrangements, and financial resources. One-half felt that the child's wishes were important and one-third felt that the child's gender and emotional maturity were important.

Musetto (1980) proposed that custody be awarded to the psychological parent (a term used by J. Goldstein, Freud, & Solnit, 1973). He defined the psychological parent as one who acknowledges his or her own contribution to the family problems, allows the children to express genuine feelings, accepts the responsibility for being a parent and expects some fair consideration from the children for the efforts, and neither infantilizes nor parentifies children. Psychological parents provide support, stimulation, guidance, and limits. They care for the child's physical needs. They help the child control instinctual urges, support moral development, and provide empathy. They are good models for identification. The psychological parent supports the loyalty of children with both parents and encourages positive contact with both parents. Psychological parents support their children's relationships with grandparents and extended family on both sides. Psychological parents do not want custody to force reconciliation, secure financial aid, or replace a lost child.

In their survey of 82 experienced child custody evaluators, Keilin and Bloom (1986) found the following factors to be given greatest weight for sole custody: expressed wishes of the older child, a parent's attempts to alienate the child from the other parent, the quality of emotional bonding of the child with each parent, the psychological stability of each parent, and the parenting skills of each parent.

In a study of reasons why judges pick a particular parent for primary residential custody, Sorensen and Goldman (1989) found great variability of responses. Seven factors accounted for most of the variance. Social deviance, the child's wishes, the psychological assessment, and quality time were rated as moderately important and of increasing weight, whereas family unity (including access to relatives and keeping siblings together) was seen as much more important. Less important were parental supports and tradition factors.

When parents were asked what should be the criteria for custody (Lowery, 1985), three factors emerged:

1. Concern for selecting a parent who was both in a position for and would give a high priority to child rearing
2. Concern for maintaining the child's social network, including relatives and the noncustodial parent

3. Concern for conventional cultural values, such as a good education and religious and moral training.

Making an "Impossible" Custody Decision

If the above recommendations were all that were involved, many mental health professionals would be willing to participate in custody evaluations. Often, however, the trade-off is in terms of values. One parent is loving, but chaotic. The other parent is more distant, but stable. Which value is more important, affection or stability? Generally, the negative impact of the less desirable characteristics has to be weighed in the trade-off with the more desirable.

An additional problem that complicates custody evaluation is the problem raised when one parent is better at providing for needs at one developmental stage, but the next stage is probably more easily handled by the other parent. One advantage of joint residential custody is that the child can get a different set of needs met from each parent. If the home environment of the parent who is not appropriate for that age child is severely detrimental, the child may not be able to wait until residential custody switches to get those needs met.

It is not unusual for a mental health professional to conclude that the problem is not which parent is in the best interests of the child, but which parent provides the least harm. Additional protections, if needed, should be included in the recommendations.

Fine (1980) recommended several criteria for determining the least detrimental alternative:

1. The custodial parent should enjoy a nurturing and psychologically appropriate relationship with the child.
2. The custodial parent should have the capacity to be a nurturing and mature parent.
3. The custodial home should be able to provide for the needs of the child: food, shelter, education, medical care, and special needs.
4. Siblings should not be separated in the custody disposition. (See the discussion on this issue in Chapter 5.)

THE CUSTODY EVALUATION REPORT

The custody evaluation report should be written by the custody evaluator and provided to lawyers on both sides and to the court. The report should begin with the question being asked by the court, which is usually, "What custody decision is in the child's best interest?" Next, a summary of the data used to reach a recommendation should be listed. The total amount of contact with each person involved and the types of interviews, tests, and other spoken and written data should be listed (Lewis, 1974). Following that information, the basis for the conclusion should be given. The report should not include comments that require professional training for a reader to understand. If possible, the report should give positive support to both parents in terms of each one's strengths. The report should not be biased to support the conclusion. It should simply contain the facts, the opinions formed from those facts, and the conclusions.

Awad (1978) noted that it is useful to give each party's version of the history of the marriage, separation, and the pros and cons of the current arrangements. As in court testimony, jargon should be avoided. Awad also recommended that for situations in which there is no clear-cut recommendation, it is useful to report the situation as precisely as possible and to list the advantages and disadvantages of each alternative.

Skafte (1985) gave an excellent example of report writing, including common mistakes that therapists-turned-custody-evaluators are likely to make. She particularly stressed keeping the report as short as possible (i.e., 7 to 10 single spaced, typed pages) by eliminating irrelevant details.

Feedback to the Contesting Parents

Some evaluators prefer to have joint meetings with the parents to provide feedback on the report. Others prefer to meet separately with each parent and that parent's lawyer to provide information concerning the findings and to explore each parent's feelings about the report. Careful feedback can increase acceptance of the report by both parents. Suarez et al. (1978) recommended that the initial stipulation indicate that the feedback should be given to the two lawyers (without parents present). They suggested that the feedback session be used to explore with the lawyers constructive alternatives and the role that the lawyers might play in facilitating those alternatives. The purpose of the meeting is also to find alternatives to litigation. While the meeting with lawyers provides information about how the evaluation was done, findings of the evaluation, and recommendations, Suarez et al. indicated that the evaluators must be firm in discouraging claims and counterclaims that reinstate a courtroom battle.

Evaluation of Custody Reports

Clawar (1984) proposed criteria for evaluating the respectability of a custody report. Those criteria, which serve as useful reminders to custody evaluators to take care in evaluation and writing, include:

1. A full history. Have appropriate data been collected?
2. Credentials of the author of the report or expert testifying on the report. Have experts limited their testimony to their area of expertise?

3. The ability to duplicate or replicate the findings. Are procedures and findings sufficiently detailed to permit replication of the process?

4. The amount of time involved in evaluation.

5. One fact a case does not make. Does the report focus on patterns or themes?

6. Consulting or supportive opinions. Was collaboration used?

7. Relevancy of material. Were tests used appropriately for the questions asked? How recent is the material on which opinions were based?

8. Source of referral. Was the report potentially biased based on the source of contact for hiring the professional?

9. Clarity of report. How clear is the report?

10. Language usage. Is it neutral or adversarial? Are the technical terms vague?

11. Reporting office behavior and testing versus behavioral observation outside the office. What is the context in which observations were made, and can the conclusions be generalized to other contexts?

12. Self-critical. Does the report indicate its own limitations?

13. Conclusions. Were the conclusions based on the material used for the evaluation?

TESTIMONY IN COURT

Testimony in court depends on the presentation by lawyers and the testimony by witnesses, which might include the parents, the child, neighbors, and mental health professionals. Expert witnesses are those who are recognized by the court as having special training and experience that enable them to draw conclusions from findings of fact and hypothetical situations. Lay witnesses, which include parents, children, relatives, neighbors, teachers, and friends, are supposed to restrict their testimony to things that they have observed and may not comment on or draw conclusions about what they have not observed.

One problem with expert testimony in the area of mental health is that there is folk wisdom in the culture about what is best for children. Judges often have strong opinions about how children should be raised. A judge would not presume to contradict a medical pathologist concerning evidence and opinion as to the cause of death, but may feel quite comfortable telling mental health professionals that their opinions about children are wrong.

Should a Psychotherapist Testify?

Mental health professionals who have had a therapeutic relationship with a client who is involved in a custody dispute should have second thoughts about how useful that testimony would be to the court. Girdner (1979) noted that judges and lawyers have difficulty with the testimony of expert witnesses who are therapists for a variety of reasons:

1. Judges and lawyers see therapists as too influenced by verbal behavior, which the legal professionals consider not very reliable. Legally trained people feel that mental health professionals draw opinions that seem to be based on hearsay evidence.
2. The client's feelings, emotional needs, and perceptions are not directly observable and are considered irrelevant.
3. There is a major value difference between judges and mental health professionals. Mental health professionals work hard at avoiding value judgments about behavior. Judges may then conclude that therapists have no values at all.

Awad (1978) strongly recommended that therapists refrain from giving any report to the evaluation team if this action would interfere with the therapeutic relationship. A clinician seeing a client, *particularly a parent,* should not volunteer an opinion on the custody of a child. The therapist knows little about the capacities of the other parent or the attachment and choice of the child.

Therapists should be reluctant to participate in a custody evaluation by providing expert testimony on behalf of their client. First, the therapist has not had equal access to both parents. The view of the other parent is based entirely on hearsay evidence that would be vulnerable to aggressive cross-examination. Second, the therapist is not in a position of making a judgment of the relative merits of the two parents. Finally, the therapist is an advocate of the client, but expert testimony should be given in the position of being an advocate of the child.

When the child is the client, the therapist should be cautious about extrapolating from therapy information to assumptions about the adequacy of parenting. The therapist may see the parents through the child's eyes, and that perception can be distorted through needs and developmental stage.

If asked to participate, the therapist should decline, informing the client and/or the lawyer why the information would not hold up in court and why such information might be harmful to the client. Clients may not anticipate the questions that a therapist may be asked, and the answers may be painful or embarrassing. In addition, if the testimony does not result in help to the client, the therapy can be seriously damaged. Even therapy terminated prior to the trial may be damaged or "undone" by court testimony.

It is not unusual for the client to want to use the therapist in court when the client feels that he or she has the therapist's support. Perhaps the therapist said, "If indeed your husband is doing that behavior with the children, it could be substantially harmful to the children." The client may focus on the single statement, without considering other testimony that might come out in court. Confidentiality usually cannot be partially released.

Therapists also should avoid giving referrals to other mental health professionals for custody evaluation. The outcome of that evaluation could contaminate the therapy. The same is true for providing referrals for lawyers.

Testifying under Protest

Mental health professionals as a group hate to testify in court. They tend not to understand the rules for evidence. They dislike the strategy of a hostile attorney trying to discredit their credentials. Such attacks can tap vulnerabilities that most of us have concerning our competence. A therapist who has had any association with a case can be subpoenaed to testify. Some mental health professionals become involved because a parent requested consultation concerning a separation or divorce, liked (or misconstrued) those comments made by the professional, and then informed the lawyer.

Therapists, particularly child therapists, often do not want to get involved in the custody battle. Because confidentiality is controlled by the parents and not the child, the therapist may be in a painful position if either parent decides that the therapist's testimony could be useful. The therapist can request the judge to keep the child's welfare protected by avoiding testimony from the therapy. If that request is denied, the therapist can request that such evidence be given in chambers so that the parents would not be informed about the child's concerns.

Courtroom Dynamics

Because most mental health professionals do not know the rules of courtroom performance, it may be useful to review them. In her analysis of court behavior, Girdner (1986) noted that the discourse of a custody hearing is structured by legal categories that were derived from procedural and substantive law. Such rules cover who can be spoken to, by whom, when, and how. The rules also structure what can and cannot be said. These requirements for lawyers lead them to manipulate the rules of evidence to present evidence to support their case, to discredit the evidence of the other side, and to prevent the other attorney from doing the same.

Professional Witness Behavior

As a professional witness, a mental health professional should adhere to the following guidelines:

1. *Dress professionally.* Judges are offended by dress that does not reflect proper respect for the court. Credibility can be lost if dress is too casual.

2. *Be prepared to present your name, address, and professional qualifications.* Expect to have those qualifications challenged if the opposing lawyer expects your testimony to be unsympathetic to his or her point of view. Do not be defensive about those qualifications. It is up to the judge to decide if your experience qualifies you as an expert witness. You do not gain anything but credibility problems by questioning the right of a lawyer to examine your training or experience.

3. *Be polite.* Address the judge as "your honor." Speak slowly and clearly, particularly if there is a court recorder. Avoid jargon. Assume that the court will know words in general use, but not technical words. It is better to avoid technical words rather than constantly explain their meaning.

4. *Do not use diagnoses* (Gardner, 1976). It is not the therapist's role to provide a diagnosis, so avoid diagnostic terms altogether. Avoid arguments over the meaning of technical terms. A lawyer is likely to pull out a dictionary and read the definition.

5. *Do not joke or wisecrack* (Gardner, 1976). Although you may want to communicate that you are not intimidated and are relaxed on the stand, joking may communicate that you are not taking your role seriously.

6. *Use direct quotes whenever possible.* Do not quote one parent about the other (Gardner, 1976). You can refer to allegations, but be very careful to call them allegations. If you make the mistake of accepting as fact something told to you by one parent, you can lose credibility. It is acceptable to say the following: "I was given the following information from Mrs. X. I do not have direct knowledge of the veracity of this information. I can state, however, that if such behavior occurred, it would have the following effect on children." It is also acceptable to present such testimony in the form of hypothetical situations, if requested to do so by one of the lawyers. If a hypothetical situation presented by a lawyer differs in important ways from the case at hand, indicate that your answer is limited to those conditions and that other conditions would potentially lead to different conclusions.

7. *Do not state cause and effect in absolutes.* Given the nature of prediction in mental health, it is seldom the case that A always causes B. It is acceptable to talk of high-risk behaviors or evidence that such behavior has already adversely affected the child. Be ready to admit that you are not certain as to outcomes.

8. *Take notes and refer to them.* It is useful to refer to notes to provide the exact time and length of contacts for the evaluation. *Never* take to court any notes that you would feel uncomfortable having the entire court review. Either lawyer can ask to see your notes and can read them in court. You may be required to bring all notes and all files you have on a case. *Never* keep notes that would be embarrassing to have read in court.

9. *Know what to expect from questioning.* The lawyer who expects you to be sympathetic will tend to ask open-ended questions that allow you to

develop detailed answers. The lawyer who sees you as antagonistic will ask questions to be answered "yes" or "no." Do not be upset if you are not allowed to develop an answer. Do not hesitate to refuse to answer a question if it cannot be answered simply.

10. *If you are not given an opportunity to say something that you think is important for the judge to make a decision, do not try to squeeze into your testimony.* Rules of evidence will generate an objection and you may be prohibited from speaking. Tell the judge at the end of your testimony that you have testimony that you have not had an opportunity to provide that you think may be of use to the court in arriving at its decision. In most family relations courts, you will be permitted to give your testimony.

11. *Do not bias your report.* Give a full report of the findings of fact, including information both favorable and nonfavorable to your conclusion. Admit freely valid points that are at odds with your point of view.

12. *Do not be apologetic about your fee.* You will be asked what you charge. You are charging for your time, not your support.

13. *If you are treated rudely by a lawyer, respond with marked courtesy.* When vigorously attacked on the stand (not really as common as people imagine from television watching), I have found it useful to deliberately slow down and relax and answer the question.

14. *Watch out for distortions of previous testimony.* If you are incorrectly quoted, point out the error.

15. *Be prepared to lose.* While your investment in the child may lead you to be indignant if the court chooses to ignore your recommendations, be glad it is not your decision. On one occasion, I had my advice followed, only to learn later that the parent I recommended was an abusing parent. I am glad to give the court my opinion based on the information that I have, but I do not want the responsibility of making the final choice. Always recognize that your information may be limited and your ability to predict the future may be flawed.

AVOIDING RELITIGATION

Any move that mental health professionals can make to reduce anger and the likelihood of relitigation is likely to benefit the child. In preparing the evaluation, the mental health professional can do the following to reduce relitigation:

1. Carefully interpret the recommendation that supports the integrity and self-esteem of each parent.
2. Avoid "loaded" evaluations that agree with the description of one of the complaining parents. If the report seems to agree with the

complaints of one parent, using a vocabulary that differs from that used by the accusing parent is more likely to avoid feeding the conflict between parents.

3. Spell out possible solutions to as many anticipated problems as possible. For example, avoid the phrase "liberal visitation." Permit change in the agreement, if it is with the mutual consent of both parties. Consider how to establish visitation schedules as a function of the child's developmental stage (see Chapter 7) and how out-of-state moves should be handled. Consider mediation or arbitration as required alternatives to relitigation.

4. Consider supporting joint custody. Ilfeld, Ilfeld, and Alexander (1982) found that the relitigation rate in joint custody arrangements was one-half that in sole custody arrangements.

SUMMARY

Careful evaluation, balanced and fair approaches to both parents, extended interpretation, and professional presentations of information are all necessary in performing an effective evaluation. Although these procedures do not ensure that the best interests of the child are served, failure to provide such standards does ensure that the child's interests are not served.

CHAPTER 7

Visitation/Parent Access: Patterns and Problems

A father insists that his 10-year-old daughter visit him every other weekend regardless of birthday parties, play groups, or other invitations. He is convinced that his ex-spouse instigates all such requests. The daughter is becoming chronically angry at her father for his position.

A 9-year-old boy waits at the window wondering if his father will pick him up. The mother is fuming at the delay in her weekend plans and is distressed at her son's pain. When he asks, "Why is Dad so late?" she would like to say, "Your father is chronically irresponsible and has never shown much love for you." Because she is afraid to alienate her son from what little affection he gets from his dad, she simply says, "I don't know."

The Uniform Marriage and Divorce Act (Foster, 1973) provided the following visitation provisions:

1. A parent not granted custody of the child is entitled to reasonable visitation rights unless the court finds, after a hearing, that visitation would endanger the child's physical health or significantly impair his emotional development.
2. The court may modify an order granting or denying visitation rights whenever modification would serve the best interests of the child; but the court shall not restrict a parent's visitation rights unless it finds that the visitation would endanger the child's physical health or significantly impair his emotional development.

Such a straightforward description of parent access seems quite reasonable, yet parent access is one of the most troubling parts of the divorce process and often a cause of relitigation. Limited information is available to guide lawyers and mental health professionals concerning the most appropriate arrangements for children of different ages. For example, relatively little research has been done on how visitation affects child adjustment. No one really knows whether the best interests of the child are served by visitation patterns that include alternate weekends, alternate holidays, and 6 weeks in the summer. Although theory offers an answer, theory is rarely supported by empirical research. Thus, caution is necessary in proposing a particular visitation schedule.

Parent access may perpetuate interparental conflict by requiring parents who were unable to maintain a marriage to negotiate times, places, and activities. As mentioned in Chapter 3, chronic conflict increases the likelihood of poor adjustment in the children. R. S. Benedek and Benedek (1977) noted some areas of conflict between parents related to visitation:

- Dealing with each other in visitation provides a constant reminder of the marriage and its failure.
- Visitation may serve as a source of spying on the other family.
- The child may experience conflicts of loyalties.
- There is a lack of flexibility, which prevents normal childhood activities.

Courts have little patience with parents who continually litigate as a way of solving chronic disagreements. The courts have difficulty in establishing an objective view in determining which story to believe and have limited resources for dealing with a chronically irresponsible parent. Although a parent who does not follow court orders is in contempt of court, most judges are reluctant to use it against parents. Also, although it might be possible to limit the contact between an irresponsible parent and the child, most judges consider visitation to be the child's right as well as the parent's. Punishing the child for the parent's irresponsibility seems inappropriate. In addition, there is general agreement that visitation with the noncustodial parent is good for the child (with the possible exception of an abusing or severely psychopathological parent). Therefore, limiting visitation to punish the irresponsible parent may damage the child.

Clearly, the most desirable visitation pattern is likely to change as the child gets older, yet visitation agreements that are jointly obtained or court ordered rarely suggest change as a function of the child's age. Even the child's wish to visit is likely to decrease and increase as a function of developmental stage or the changes in attachment that normally occur for children. Intact families tend to tolerate the ebb and flow of attachment that children show toward parents. For example, a child might prefer to walk with the mother at the beginning of a year, prefer walking with the father later that year, and prefer the mother again a few months later. If the parents are comfortable with their relationships with the child and each other and do not compete for affection, these changes cause little or no parental anxiety. Parents from divorced families, however, often do not tolerate this cycle of affectional ties. A child's preference for one parent produces competition, often marked by a parent's beliefs that the other parent intentionally caused the child's "alienation."

Divorced parents have difficulty tolerating the ebb and flow of children's attachment. A mental health professional should help them understand that it is normal for children to have more intense or less intense affectional ties over time.

Visitation limits the authority of the custodial parent (Weiss, 1979). While the custodial parent is given the power to make the crucial decisions that affect the child's life, the noncustodial parent receives some control over the child during visitation. J. Goldstein, Freud, and Solnit (1973) proposed an extremely controversial policy giving the custodial parent absolute control over visitation. They suggested that the noncustodial parent should see the child at the discretion of the custodial parent and have no legal rights to visitation beyond the wishes of the custodial parent. This recommendation has generally been disregarded by the courts and mental health professionals. Weiss (1979) felt that such a policy would reduce the beneficial contact between the child and the noncustodial parent. Furthermore, limiting visitation might occur as retaliation against the noncustodial parent rather than because of potential harm to the child. Thus, in most cases, the child would be victimized by a policy that gives too much control to the custodial parent.

Some custodial parents may not want the sole responsibility of deciding visitation. Hoorwitz (1983) felt that giving too much power to one parent increases the need for competition and revenge for the parent out of power. He also noted that although eliminating visitation might temporarily reduce conflict, the child needs to learn that conflict is inevitable in life.

THE FUNCTIONS OF VISITATION

Visitation serves a variety of important psychological functions. It is important to keep these functions in mind when evaluating particular visitation patterns or determining whether an ongoing visitation pattern has been successful.

1. *Visitation agreements protect the child's rights for access to the noncustodial parent.* Courts have typically determined that frequent visitation is generally in the best interests of the child. Except in cases with child abuse or severe psychopathology, courts are reluctant to block visitation entirely.

The custodial parent is often hurt by and angry at the noncustodial parent. The child's wish to please the custodial parent may place the child in a very rough position. The wish to see the noncustodial parent may invite upset and rejection. Clear visitation rules free the child from some of the psychological pressures of pleasing each parent.

Although visitation agreements that permit liberal and frequent visitation may seem helpful to the child, failure to designate some pattern of visitation may place the child in the position of having to request visitation. Such requests may jeopardize the child's relationship with the custodial parent.

2. *Visitation agreements protect the rights of the noncustodial parent.* Less discussion has focused on the degree to which the custodial parent controls the access of the noncustodial parent to the children. Indignation over imagined or real harm to the children, and anger over the increased financial issues, jealousy, and competition between parents may lead the custodial parent to deny visitation to the noncustodial parent.

Even if parents are cordial at the time of divorce, the potential remains for later disputes. Control of visitation becomes an issue for these parents when one separated parent enters into a romantic relationship with someone else. Failure to pay child support also can lead to battles over visitation.

Even when the separating parents are cordial at the time of separation, the mental health professional should recommend to the parents that they consult a lawyer (better yet, two lawyers) and work out a written agreement for visitation that would assume that they are no longer cordial. To avoid relitigation, the stipulated agreement should include procedures for conflict resolution when parents cannot agree. Mediation and arbitration are examples of such procedures.

3. *Visitation agreements protect the emotional bond between the child and both parents.* Substantial research indicates that children need contact with adults of both sexes for balanced development (see Chapter 8 on single parenting). Assuming that neither parent is grossly pathological, it is important to maintain the child's affectional bond with both parents. Basic trust and self-esteem are maintained in the child by having predictable parents who care. The child's primary means of understanding what it is like to be an adult of a particular sex is established by having continued affectionate contact with the parent of that sex. Although children can resolve these issues with one understanding parent and without any contact with the other parent, the task is certainly easier with continued affectionate contact with both parents when possible. In addition, the child's understanding of self is based partly on his or her understanding of who the parents are. The child needs to integrate this understanding into the self-concept.

4. *Visitation provides alternative role models for the child.* One disadvantage of single parenting is that the number of ways to solve problems is limited by that parent's repertoire. With visitation contact, children can learn to use the problem solving skills of both parents. In addition, role limitations of each parent restrict the child's ability to solve problems of living, such as how to cook, sew, fix cars, or repair household articles.

5. *Visitation provides the custodial parent with relief from the parenting role.* Although the courts are unlikely to use this criterion for deciding visitation, custodial parents have often felt the need for some relief from the parenting role. Single parenting is an unrelenting, demanding job. Work, meals, house cleaning, and parenting all give little time for oneself and no

time to be sick or to have a sick child. Visitation provides some relief from responsibility, and many custodial parents look forward to the weekends with no children.

VISITATION FREQUENCY

Visitation Frequency and Age of the Child

This section summarizes the literature on how often visitation occurs a function of the child's age and the time since divorce. Although no studies have been reported on visitation patterns with infants, several studies have described visitation patterns for children of preschool age through adolescence.

Maccoby, Depner, and Mnookin (1988) provided normative data on overnight visits for very young children according to age and family size. For children under 2 years of age, 42.5% of only children and 39% of children with one or two siblings visited overnight. For 2- to 4-year-olds, 62.5% of only children and 55% of children with one or two siblings stayed overnight during visitation. Overnights peaked for 5- to 7-year-olds, with about two-thirds staying overnight (less for children in three-child families). Although spending more than 3 nights during a 2-week period was relatively rare for children of all ages (10 to 15%), children 2 to 4 years of age were most likely to spend 3 or more nights during a 2-week period (20%).

Tierney (1983) collected the first systematic data on preschool children. She evaluated 32 boys and 35 girls of divorce. Of the 67 children, 64 were in mother-custody homes. The decision for the visitation pattern was made jointly by the parents; in only eight cases was the visitation pattern determined by the courts. In 52% of the cases, only "reasonable and liberal" visitation was indicated.

For the preschool children in Tierney's study, the range of visitation ranged from no contact to daily contact. The typical frequency of visitations was bimodal, with 24% having no contact with fathers and 24% having contact every 2 weeks. Duration of visitation ranged from an hour or less to 2 to 5 months. Most typical was several days (40%). There was no relationship between the child's age and visitation frequency or consistency. The child's gender was unrelated to frequency, duration, or consistency of visitation as reported by the mother or the father.

In their study of children from 2 to 18 years of age, Kelly and Wallerstein (1977b) and Kelly (1981) reported that at the time of the divorce, about two-thirds of the children were visited about twice a month. Visitation frequency was as high as one to three times a week for about half the children, but only about one-fourth had overnight visits, usually the 6- to 12-year-olds. One-fourth of the children had almost no contact with the noncustodial parent, and 5% had no contact. Only 20% of the children were satisfied with the amount of visitation. Boys aged 11 to 18 were most often satisfied with visitation. Those with the greatest satisfaction, however, were 7-to 8-year-olds with visitation two to three times a week, within biking distance of each parent, and with free access to each parent. Children liked brief contacts only if they were frequent and combined with overnight visits. Resistance to visitation occurred in 11% of the sample, usually in children over 9 years of age, but even these children continued to visit.

By 18 months postdivorce, 60% of the children were seeing the noncustodial parent at least twice a month. The number of overnight and weekend visits had doubled during that time. Although duration of visits had increased, frequency had decreased. At 18 months, 29% continued to visit once a week, compared with 42% at 6 months. Younger children had more frequent visitation, peaking at 7 to 8 years of age (averaging about once per week). These children were reported as longing for more visits. Adolescents visited more often than 9- to 12-year-olds, a finding that is at odds with the view of adolescents as more withdrawn from parents. Age differences in visitation depended somewhat on the child's gender, with boys aged 2 to 8 and girls aged 9 to 18 visiting most often with their fathers.

Adolescents demonstrated a sharp drop in visitation frequency between the 6-month and 18-month interviews. Adolescents seemed content with an occasional visit lasting several hours. Weekend and overnight visits were rare. Girls visited fathers much more frequently than did boys, often once or twice a week. Infrequent and no visitation was occurring for 25% of the children; this pattern was most typical for the 9- to 18-year-old group. By 18 months, the amount of abandonment (i.e., no visitation at all) was 8%, a small amount compared with Tierney's (1983) 24%.

At the 5-year follow-up (Kelly, 1981), visitation frequency had remained at a fairly high level for a substantial number of the children, suggesting that the decrease in visitation leveled off after 18 months. Kelly noted that mothers who were committed to supporting the father–child relationship played a major role in facilitating the high rate of visitation. One-third of the children had not changed in their visitation pattern since the 18-month interview, and 20% had increased the frequency of visitation. Weekly visits were common for 25% of the sample. About 20% of the children visited two or three times a month, usually alternating weekends. Another 20% visited monthly. Vacation and holiday visits had increased due to the greater number of children who lived geographically distant from the noncustodial parent. Erratic, infrequent visitation was occurring for about 17% of the children, the same number as at 18 months. The statistics for children with no contact were also the same as at 18 months.

One-fifth of the children did not like visitation at the 5-year follow-up. The child often felt hurt if the father was self-absorbed or intensely involved with other activities or people. Infrequent visitation routinely caused hurt. Younger children interpreted infrequent contact as evidence of their unlovability.

In Wallerstein and Blakeslee's (1989) 10-year follow-up, most of the children experienced visitation on a regular basis. One-third were seeing their fathers at least once a month even 10 years later. Only 10% saw their fathers less than once a year. Late adolescent girls were more erratic in their contact (Wallerstein & Corbin, 1989). These high rates of contact may be influenced, however, by the facts that the Marin County study was designed to keep fathers involved and that the area is relatively affluent. Particularly interesting data about visitation from Wallerstein and Blakeslee's study was the discrepancy between the perceptions of the noncustodial fathers and those of the children. Most fathers felt that they had done reasonably well with their postdivorce parenting, but three-fourths of the children felt rejected. The amount of visitation was unrelated to the degree of felt rejection.

Warshak and Santrock (1983b) examined the child's feelings about visitation. More than two-thirds of the children felt that the frequency of visitation was inadequate to meet their needs. Only 3 of the 64 children aged 6 to 11 years wanted less visitation; 62% wanted more visitation. These children expressed a great deal of satisfaction with the visits. Half of the children rated the noncustodial parent as nicer to be with since the divorce. No children in the study reported not enjoying the most recent visit, and 87% said they enjoyed it a lot.

Hirst and Smiley (1984) reported the access pattern for 147 (out of 200 invited) families in the Brisbane, Australia, area. The families were selected from court records from January to September 1977. Mothers had custody in 88% of the families. On the average, there were two children per family, ranging in age from 1 to 17 and averaging 9.8. The modal time since separation was 3 to 4 years.

The study reviewed the frequency of five visitation patterns occurring at the time of the interview: free access (9%), flexible regular access (13%), rigid regular access (13%), irregular access (33%), and no access (32%). Only 17% of the cases had fortnightly arrangements, a finding particularly significant in that every other weekend was a common guideline in that jurisdiction.

As others have found, visitation generally decreased over time, with 50% decreasing during the first year following separation and only 9% increasing. Where free access was occurring, the families tended to be pleased with the arrangement. Surprisingly, where visitation had ceased, 83% of the custodial parents were also happy with that arrangement. Most parents viewed regular but rigid visitation negatively, a finding that is important for considering how specific court-ordered visitation should be. Hirst and Smiley (1984) felt that lack of flexibility and cooperation between parents may limit future visitation.

According to Warren et al. (1986), children aged 10 to 12 with 11 or more problems were more likely than children with fewer problems to have less visitation with the noncustodial parent, to have parents who disagree more on parenting, and to have a custodial parent who is less satisfied with the coparenting agreement.

Neugebauer (1988/1988) interviewed 40 children of divorce from 7 to 18 years of age. The parental separation had occurred at least 4 years previously.

Children reported a very strong preference for flexible, unrestricted access. Younger children wanted more time, and older children wanted more flexibility. If the child was emotionally close to the noncustodial parent, the wish was for more access. Children expressed dismay over the lack of individual time alone (i.e., without siblings) with the noncustodial parent.

Isaacs and Leon (1987) compared 70 white and 26 black divorced families and found that noncustodial black fathers visited far less often than white fathers. Sixty percent of black fathers visited their children no more than once a month, compared with 26% of white fathers. In addition, 23% of black fathers and only 8% of white fathers never visited. Isaacs and Leon also explored whether there might be racial differences in the mother's self-reliance. Indeed, when mother's self-reliance, mother's extended family, and father's residential proximity were taken into account in a multiple regression analysis, race no longer predicted visitation frequency.

Furstenberg and Nord (1985) analyzed the National Survey of Children data (see also Furstenberg, 1988; Furstenberg, Peterson, Nord, & Zill, 1983). This study is particularly important because the data are based on 423 divorced families who were from a nationally representative sample of households containing children aged 12 to 16 years (7 to 11 years in the original 1976 interviews). They found a sharp reduction of noncustodial parent contact over time (particularly in low-income families) and a high percentage of adolescents (60%) who had not seen their noncustodial fathers in the last month. Ten years postseparation, 49% of the children had not seen their noncustodial parent in 5 years, and only 28% had seen the parent in the previous month. Even if the visit occurred the prior week, only 10% of those parents had given help in homework and only 20% had worked with the children on a project (Furstenberg & Nord, 1985).

Furstenberg and Nord felt that such figures suggested a very limited child-rearing role for noncustodial parents. More than half of the children complained that outside fathers were not giving the affection that the children felt they needed, and almost as many said that the fathers did not make consistent, clear rules and were not firm enough. However, a majority said that they seldom argued with their nonresidential parent, and that they felt loved, appreciated, and trusted.

In summary, visitation frequency declines over time. Younger children are less likely to stay overnight, but most report wanting more contact than they typically get. Visitation frequency peaks for 7- to 8-year-olds and is less for 9- to 12-year-olds. Older children want more flexibility. Adolescents visit only occasionally, the visit lasting several hours. The frequency of total noncustodial parent abandonment several years after divorce may be as high as 50%.

The Prediction of Visitation Frequency

It is important for mental health professionals to recognize which families tend toward reduced visitation contacts in the future. This section describes research on the variables that predict a child's frequent, continued contact with the noncustodial parent.

Hodges, Landis, Day, and Oderberg (in press) found that if fathers were actively involved in infant care and interacted with the infant regularly during the first year of life, visitation by those fathers was more frequent when the child was 2 to 3 years of age. Pre-separation conflict was related to irregular post separation visits.

In their follow-up study at 5 years postdivorce, Wallerstein and Kelly (1980c) provided relevant information about visitation. Fathers who were depressed after the separation often found it extremely painful to visit with the child and often avoided visitation. If the father initiated the divorce, he often felt guilt at leaving an affectionate parent–child relationship. Guilt led to either a reduction in visitation or an initial upsurge that was not maintained. Parents' intense anger also played a role in determining visitation patterns (Kelly, 1981). Bitter custodial parents often tried to severely limit visitations or to sabotage those that were legally permitted. One strategy was to entice children from wanting visitation by providing more attractive alternatives. Setting up medical appointments, parties, or lessons were other strategies used by custodial mothers to prevent the noncustodial father from having access to the children.

Hodges and Bloom (1986) found that visitation increased if the custodial parent participated in an intervention program designed for newly separated individuals, whereas the noncustodial parent's participation in the program did not affect visitation. This result suggests that the custodial parent maintains much of the control over the noncustodial parent's access to the children. Participation in the program may have increased custodial parents' awareness of the importance of maintaining contact between the children and each parent.

Wallerstein and Kelly (Kelly, 1981; Kelly & Wallerstein, 1977b; Wallerstein & Kelly, 1980a, 1980b) found a variety of factors related to an increase in the frequency of visitation. These factors included open yearning for visitation by children, especially those under 9; strong commitment by many fathers; the open support of half of the mothers for visitation; children who expressed pleasure in visitation; children who were not angry at the father for the separation; fathers who were lonely, psychologically intact, and not depressed; fathers who were economically secure and better educated (not a strong relationship); and low conflict between parents.

Tierney's (1983) study of preschool children and visitation looked at predictors of visitation, such as conflict and quality of parenting. Total amount of conflict between parents was related significantly to frequency and consistency of visitation. Greater conflict was associated with less frequent and less consistent visitation. In particular, general conflict explained 16 to 36% of the variance, whereas conflict due to visitation explained 10 to 64% of the variance in visitation. Conflict was generally not related to duration of visits.

Tierney also looked at the child's behavior during the visitation as a predictor of visitation patterns. Visitation was less frequent as children became more withdrawn or regressive. Such relationships do not imply causation, however. Surprisingly, there was no correlation between child aggression levels and visitation pattern.

Using unpublished data from a study on newly-separated adults, David Stevens, a doctoral student, examined five domains that might relate to visitation frequency: (1) demographic variables, (2) parental discord variables, (3) stress variables, (4) decision to separate variables, and (5) visitation pattern variables. The following are preliminary analyses of those data:

1. *Demography.* Noncustodial parents visited less frequently if their own parents had ever separated. Visitation was more frequent when the noncustodial parent was living with fewer adults rather than more. Visitation also decreased as the number of times the custodial parent had moved increased.

2. *Discord.* Visitation decreased as postdivorce discord increased.

3. *Stress since separation.* Stress levels were unrelated to visitation patterns.

4. *Decision to separate.* Visitation was more frequent when the noncustodial parent was more responsible for the decision to separate. In addition, the more the noncustodial parent was in favor of the decision to separate, the more frequent the visitation. Perhaps guilt or lack of anger by the noncustodial parent made visitation more frequent.

Low visitation frequency was related to high frequency of spouse's neglect of the home, predivorce physical abuse, verbal abuse, high levels of predivorce money problems, high levels of seeing the spouse's nagging as a contributing factor to the divorce, and high levels of drug and alcohol use. Higher levels of visitation were related to seeing infidelity as a contributing factor in the divorce.

5. *Visitation variables.* When the noncustodial parent saw the visitation arrangement as satisfactory to the child, visitation was more frequent. For noncustodial parents, more frequent visitation was related to taking greater levels of responsibility in parenting the child.

When all the statistically significant variables were entered into a multiple regression equation to determine how well frequency of visitation could be estimated, several variables were independent from each other in predicting frequency. For noncustodial parents, higher visitation frequency was related to fewer adults in the noncustodial household, fewer problems with friendships, and sexual problems being a major complaint prior to separation. For custodial parents, visitation frequency increased when the custodial parent cited low levels of neglect of the home, high number of money problems, sexual problems, and geographic proximity of parents as a factor contributing to the separation.

Kurdek (1986) found no relationship between child's age, child's gender, length of separation, and maternal stress. He separated the sample of 91 custodial mothers into two groups, low and high parental conflict. One child from each family was randomly selected, an advantage in design over several other studies that either used all children or preselected which child to study. In studies that use all children, the effect of one family may be counted several times in the statistics. When one child (such as the most distressed or the oldest) is selected, there is a potential bias in the data that may be difficult to generalize to other populations. There were 45 boys and 46 girls from 6 to 17 years of age, with a mean age of 10.24. The effect of age on the relationships was statistically removed. Kurdek found that frequency of visitation was positively related to regularity and length of visits *and* highly related to child support regularity ($r = .70$). Frequency was more common in families with low environmental change than in families with many geographic moves.

In a 5-year longitudinal study of children of divorce, Braver, Wolchik, Sandler, Fogas, and Zvetina (1987) followed families with at least one child under 15 who were within 9 weeks of filing for divorce. The study is commendable because of the large sample size (341 fathers and 271 mothers) and the high percentage of participating families of those eligible (60%). As others have found, the longer the time since the separation, the more infrequent the visitation. The involvement of the noncustodial parent in a new love relationship was also related to reduced visitation frequency. If the noncustodial parent (94% fathers) had a higher education, visitation was more frequent, and more frequent visitation was understandably related to greater child support payments and more enjoyment of the visits. Gender of the noncustodial parent, income and support from relatives were not related to frequency.

Problems with visitation were frequently reported by both custodial and noncustodial parents. Custodial mothers complained that the father was a bad role model, exposed the child to unacceptable language or bad influences, spoiled the child, left the child upset after visits, was not on time for transitions, drank and/or used drugs, or ignored the child. Noncustodial parents complained of the blocking of visitation by the custodial parent, child support, short notice changes, overcontrol, visitations contingent on payments other than child support, or errands and chores. They also complained of transition times.

Camplair and Stolberg (1987) found that the more time the child spent with the noncustodial parent, the fewer the life changes reported by the parent. This finding suggests either that frequent parent access provides a stabilizing influence or that fewer life changes make access easier to provide.

As might be expected, the more frequently the child talks to and sees the noncustodial parent, the better the custodial parent sees the relationship of the child and the other parent (Petronio, 1988). Petronio also reported that children visit more often with noncustodial mothers than noncustodial fathers, as reported elsewhere.

Isaacs (1988; Isaacs, Montalvo, & Abelsohn, 1986) has been following the parent access patterns and child adjustment in 103 families over a 5-year period. The 1988 report is a summary of the first- to third-year findings. Unlike many other studies that have been predominantly Anglo and middle class, this sample was varied demographically, with 77 white mothers and 26 black mothers. Education of mothers ranged from less than high school to professional training.

Children ranged in age from 2 through 17, with a median of 8. The sample size prohibited a breakdown by age groups, but it would have been helpful to have analyses that included age as a variable. One problem in interpreting the data is that the child having the most difficulty with the separation was selected from each family for analysis. Thus, the data are not representative of even the volunteer sample that was obtained. However, it might be assumed that the reactions are at least the worst found in the family (the median and mode number of children in the family was two). Isaacs found that both regularity and frequency of visitation in the first and third year were positively related. Fathers with a schedule saw their children with greater frequency than those without a schedule, again raising questions about the advisability of "liberal" visitation patterns.

Koel, Clark, Phear, and Hauser (1988) provided extensive information concerning joint and sole legal custody agreements for 700 divorces in Cambridge, Massachusetts, from 1978 to 1984. They found that in 46.8% of those cases, reasonable visitation with reasonable times and reasonable notice was the specified agreement. Thus, although regular visitation is more likely with a schedule, almost half of divorcing couples do not specify a schedule in the divorce agreement. Couples who were on friendly terms were more likely to establish a schedule. About 80% of women who had friendly relationships with the ex-spouse had children with regular visitation schedules, whereas only 37% of women who described their relationships as neutral or hostile had children with schedules.

Camara and Resnick (1988) found that the amount of interparental conflict was not significantly related to frequency of visits or of other parent–child contact. Conflict was negatively related to duration of visits for noncustodial mothers and the child ($r = -.58$, $p < .05$) and less so (nonsignificantly) for noncustodial fathers. Child gender had no effect on visitation variables. Noncustodial fathers saw their children more often than noncustodial mothers. Cooperation between parents did predict parent access. Noncustodial parents with cooperative relationships with their former spouses visited their children more frequently ($r = .47$, $p < .001$), had significantly more phone calls and correspondence ($r = .52$, $p < .001$), and had longer visits ($r = .55$, $p < .001$).

In summary, more frequent noncustodial parent access occurs if:

1. There is a regular visitation schedule.
2. Parents are cordial.
3. The custodial parent encourages visitation.

4. The noncustodial father is not depressed.
5. The father is better educated.
6. The child wishes to visit.
7. The child is not withdrawn or regressed.
8. The noncustodial parent was from an intact family.
9. The noncustodial parent lives alone.
10. The noncustodial parent seldom moves.
11. The noncustodial parent decided on the separation.
12. Child support payments are more regular.
13. It is close in time to the separation.
14. Remarriage has not occurred.

PATTERNS OF VISITATION AND CHILD DEVELOPMENT

Although personality theorists have not developed recommendations for visitation that cover the developmental span from birth to 18 years, theorists have focused on the visitation patterns of young children. Numerous theorists have recommended that the visitation pattern should take into account the child's time perspective, thus ensuring a sense of continuity of care and affection, particularly for very young children (J. Goldstein et al., 1973; Lewis, 1974; Tulloch, 1976).

From an object relations perspective, attachment and self–other awareness require stable, affectionate, responsive care. From a Piagetian point of view, object permanence, time perspective, and cause–effect thinking affect a child's understanding of visitation.

The development in time perspective has a predictable path during the preschool years. The child slowly understands that "wait a minute" and "wait an hour" have different meanings. For the young child, "tomorrow" is an undefined, infinite time away, yet the child slowly learns the meaning of the word. "The day after tomorrow" is a far more complex concept (thus making weekend visitations a potentially confusing pattern for the young child).

The concept of "tomorrow" is seldom understood by 3-year-olds, but most 4-year-olds understand it. By age 5, "the day after tomorrow" is conceptually understood, but a week may be a vaguely conceived time period. By 6 or 7 years, the child can count and can understand a week or a month. By 7 or 8 years, an infinite time sense develops so that the child understands the concept of "forever."

Because the time perspective of children is variable and changeable before the age of 7, visitation agreements for children under 7 should take into account the child's time perspective. Children can endure longer and longer visitations as they approach age 7, from hour-long visits to weekends to weeks. If the visitation pattern violates the short time perspective of the child, the child may have difficulty remembering the absent parent and will not be able to understand intuitively when he or she will return to the custodial parent. The results may be insecurity, anxiety, and difficulty in establishing a firm identification with either parent. Basing the visitation patterns strictly on chronological age could be a mistake, however, because each child has a unique age pattern for learning time concepts.

VISITATION PATTERNS AND CHILD ADJUSTMENT

Only one study has looked extensively at the variables that predict children's reactions to the visitation itself. Johnston, Campbell, and Mayes (1985) studied the distress and symptomatic behavior of 44 children aged 6 to 12. All the children were involved in severe postseparation disputes over custody and care. The children were evaluated an average of 3 years, 3 months postseparation.

Only three children were able to make the transition between parents without stress, and these children were given clear permission to be with and enjoy the other parent despite the ongoing conflict between parents. All the other children were typically symptomatic at the time of transition. Because children were making an average of two transitions a week, they were frequently stressed.

The mildest reactions reported by Johnston, Campbell, and Mayes (1985) were quieting and withdrawal at transition. Parents reported "spaced out" behavior and unresponsive reactions. More distressed reactions included high anxiety, apprehension, tension, and restlessness. If the conflict was long standing or if there had been violence, the child was quite apprehensive and vigilant. Almost three-fifths of the children resisted going on visit and returning, and two-fifths demonstrated some type of somatic symptom at the time of transition. Parents used the children's problems as proof that the visitation was harmful. These children were quite upset by a chaotic schedule. The most distressed were those whose access patterns were never made clear and whose plans kept changing. Flexibility meant more parental fighting. Children also reported being highly distressed at meeting the other parent accidentally during a nonvisitation time. They did not know how to respond.

Children whose parents are in severe conflict show a high frequency of symptomatology at times of transition. Unpredictable visitation times increase children's stress.

Studies Not Analyzed by Age Groups

In a study of children with a wide range of ages (6 to 17) but no subanalyses by age group, Kurdek (1986) found several relationships of visitation pattern and child adjustment. He analyzed data separately for low- and high-conflict families, looking at child adjustment ratings based on mother and teacher reports. For children in low-conflict families, pattern of access (frequency, regularity, and length) was related to few adjustment variables. The mothers reported only one relationship with adjustment that was statistically significant (longer visits were related to less child maladjustment). Teachers were more likely to rate lower personal and social competence in the child if the mother reported that frequency of noncustodial parent access was *less* frequent and if visits were *more* regular. For children in high-conflict families, frequency of visitation was negatively related to teachers' reports of externalizing and internalizing behavior problems. Longer visits were related to lower personal and social competence and more internalizing. Thus, the findings are mixed, with about one-fourth of the correlations indicating difficulties with more noncustodial parent involvement and three-fourths of the correlations indicating advantages to more noncustodial parent involvement. The findings also indicated that noncustodial father access is particularly helpful to a child in cases of high parental conflict; however, it may be the high degree of contact that is fueling the fires on the conflict.

In an expanded sample for a 2-year follow-up of a study previously discussed, Johnston, Gonzalez, and Campbell (1985) studied 56 children post-divorce who were aged 4 to 12. They found a dramatic decrease in verbal aggression (to once a month), although physical aggression had almost completely stopped. Verbal and physical aggression between parents at baseline did not predict child adjustment at baseline, but did predict greater levels of depression, withdrawn and uncommunicative behaviors, somatic complaints, and aggression at the 2-year follow-up. In particular, the father's involvement of the child in the dispute was predictive of later problems. In extremely high-conflict families, high frequency of visitation was related to more problems in the child. Thus, the effect of intense parental conflict may show up in the child's behavior some time after the conflict has begun to abate.

In a 5-year prospective study, Isaacs (1988) found that neither frequency nor regularity of visitation was related to child adjustment for the first year. By the third year, regularity of visitation predicted social competence. Again, cause and effect are not evaluated by this correlation: Regularity may lead to greater social competence, but social competence also may lead the noncustodial father to want to visit more regularly.

Isaacs also found an interaction of visitation and family conflict. For children without a regular visiting schedule, the more the parents had conflict over visitation, the more the child had behavior problems at the first and third years. If there was a schedule, there was no relationship between the number of parental arguments and the degree of behavior problems in the child. Isaacs felt that if there was no set schedule, the child may have been more threatened by parental arguments, fearing that the visits might stop.

"Liberal visitation" with permission of both parents is a common phrase in divorce agreements (46.8% according to Koel et al., 1988). Given Isaacs's findings that a lack of a schedule seems to protect the child from conflict and increases the frequency of visitation, however, it is reasonable that such liberal visitation agreements are misguided.

Specific schedules in divorce agreements encourage more visitation and may protect the child to some degree from parental conflict.

In an impressive causal modeling of family process after divorce, Tschann, Johnston, Kline, and Wallerstein (1989) looked at predictors of adjustment for 351 children aged 2 to 18 who were the oldest in their families. Of these children, 73% were in mother custody. Greater number of hours with the visiting parent was related at statistically significant levels to a warmer relationship with the father, less postseparation conflict, and higher levels of emotional adjustment. The magnitudes of the correlations were relatively low, however.

A few studies have differentiated the effects of noncustodial parent contact as a function of the child's age. The consistent point of view in this text is that the child's developmental stage should have profound effects on the interpretation of the divorce and future parent access on child development. The related studies are reviewed in the following sections.

Preschool Age Children

Tierney (1983) looked at the effects of frequency, duration, and consistency of visitation patterns for mother-custody families and adjustment in 67 children from 3 to 5 years of age. In addition, she looked at the child's time perspective to determine whether visitation that was consistent with that time perspective facilitated adjustment to visitation. Other variables she investigated were parenting quality and parental conflict.

Given that there was ample evidence in the literature that parental conflict was harmful to the children and that conflict and visitation might interact, Tierney looked at the effect of visitation patterns for children with parents who had low conflict levels. She found that frequency of visitation was negatively related to the father's ratings of the child's adjustment, with infrequent visitation related to high father-rated levels of maladjustment in the child [r $(23) = -.36$, $p < .05$]. Frequency was unrelated to the mother's or teacher's ratings of the child. High levels of consistency of visitation as reported by the mother and the father were related to high maladjustment scores as reported by the mother and the father on the Louisville Behavior Checklist [r $(39) = .37$, $p < .01$, for the mother; $r(25) = .37$, $p < .05$, for the father]. When the subscales of the Louisville Behavior Checklist were related to visitation consistency, inconsistent visitation was related significantly to school disturbance problems, neurotic behavior, normal irritability, fear, aggression, and inhibition. Thus, for preschool children, the findings are similar to those reported by Johnston, Campbell, and Mayes (1985).

For preschool children, consistent visitation is an important predictor of adjustment.

Tierney (1983) also looked at whether visitation patterns would predict adjustment when the mother's parenting quality was high. Under these conditions, low frequency of visitation was related to the mother's report of total behavior problems in the child [r (30) = $-.31$, $p < .05$], with low frequency related to more problems. Low frequency of visitation for this group was related to school disturbance problems, hyperactivity, and dependency.

The correlation demonstrating a relationship between low frequency of visitation and maladjustment in the child as seen by the father would tempt a conclusion that low frequency of visitation causes maladjustment. It is just as likely, however, that a father whose child is maladjusted would find those visits as less rewarding; thus, the maladjustment could cause the infrequent visitations. Probably, both are true and the relationship is interactive.

Professionals should remember that although parent behavior can cause specific adjustment levels in the child, children's adjustment problems also can lead to that behavior in the parent. Professionals should be cautious about assigning blame for particular family interaction patterns. If noxious behavior on the part of the child is the cause of the parent's behavior that causes concern, simple recommendations for change in parental behavior are likely to be ineffective. Family therapy approaches may be needed to affect the interactive process.

Hetherington, Cox, and Cox (1979) reported that, except where there was conflict and ill will between parents or severe disturbance in the father, frequency of the father's contact with the child was associated with both a more positive adjustment in the child and better functioning in the mother.

School Age Children

In a study in which most children were school age, Kelly and Wallerstein (1977b) did not report systematic analysis of the relationship between visitation frequency, duration, or consistency and adjustment. They reported few instances in which frequent visitation was harmful to the child. In those instances, severe pathology in the noncustodial parent was manifested during visitation. Examples included sexual abuse and a case of a child's being exploited as a servant during visits. Kelly and Wallerstein did not feel that pathology alone was grounds for eliminating visitation altogether.

A more extensive analysis of visitation on this project at the 5-year follow-up provided more information (Wallerstein & Kelly, 1980c). This report noted no correlation between the predivorce father–child relationships and the relationship at 18 months postseparation. About 25% of the fathers were closer to their children after the divorce than before, and 25% had markedly deteriorated in their relationships.

D. S. Jacobson (1978a) reported on visitation time and adjustment of 51 children who had experienced parental separation within 12 months of the interview. Children ranged from 3 to 17 years of age. The mean time since separation was 140 days. Time lost with each parent was determined over a 2-week period. Children had typically lost an average of 21 hours of time with the mother from before the separation, dropping to about 73 hours (a 22% decrease). Time lost with the father was about 33 hours per 2-week period, dropping to about 20 hours (a 62% decrease). Generally, the more time lost with the parent, the greater the maladjustment. Greater time lost with the father was related to more problems in the areas of aggression, inhibition, cognitive disability, and overall severity of maladjustment. Only the child's sensitivity level was significantly affected due to time lost with the mother. Jacobson then analyzed the data separately for children 3 to 6 and 7 to 13. Although time lost with the father was inversely related to adjustment for each group (i.e., the more time lost, the poorer the adjustment), the relationship was stronger for the older children.

Lowenstein and Koopman (1978) looked at the relationship of visitation pattern and adjustment in boys aged 9 to 14. In this study, 20 boys and their mothers and 20 boys and their fathers were studied. No relationship was obtained for the child's self-esteem levels and the custodial parent's gender. Also, no relationship was found for self-esteem and time in a single-parent home, or for self-esteem and quality of parental relationship. Self-esteem was related to whether the boys saw the noncustodial parent at least once a month or less than once a month (this frequency of visitation was selected for analysis and should not imply that data supported once a month as the critical cut-off point). Boys who saw the noncustodial parent more than once a month had higher self-esteem. Although the small sample size probably does not permit a breakdown by gender of custodial parent, it is unlikely that significance could have been obtained without inclusion of both groups in the results.

Regardless of the custodial parent's sex, when parental conflict is low and pathology in the noncustodial parent is low, data seem to suggest that frequent contact with the noncustodial parent is important for a child's self-esteem.

Hess and Camara (1979) evaluated 16 families of divorce and 16 intact families with children aged 9 to 11. When visitation was addressed, they found that boys saw their fathers more frequently for longer periods of time and were in touch more often between visits than were girls. For boys and girls, the quality of the relationship with the father was related positively to duration of visitation, but not frequency. Neither frequency nor duration of visitation was significantly related to adjustment. However, high quality of the father–child relationship (for both intact and divorced families combined) predicted low aggression ($r = -.41$, $p < .01$), good social relations ($r = .54$, $p - .001$), and good work effectiveness in school ($r = .40$, $p - .01$).

Kurdek and Berg (1983) evaluated the adjustment of 34 boys and 34 girls, averaging about 10 years old, in terms of the children's attitudes toward the separation, understanding of the divorce, locus of control, and interpersonal understanding. In addition, they evaluated the mother's description of the child's attitudes, emotional reactions to the divorce, and environmental change; of the mother's social support system, divorce adjustment, and current stress levels; and of the interparental conflict. Teachers also provided a description of the children's personal and social competence. Results were similar to those found by Hess and Camara (1979). Adjustment in the child was unrelated to frequency of visitation, regularity of visitation (not mentioned by Hess and Camara), or phone contact with the noncustodial parent. Children's divorce adjustment was related to a variety of variables, including time spent *alone* with the noncustodial parent. Visitation duration that is shared with the parent's date or cohabiting partner may not be as important as exclusive visitation time. Given the tendency for noncustodial parents to share visitation with live-in boyfriends or girlfriends, this information is important to share with parents.

Noncustodial parents should ensure that significant visitation time be spent with the child alone, without the inclusion of significant others.

Adolescents

Few studies have looked at visitation issues in adolescents. Adolescents frequently determine their availability to either parent. Following interviews with children 7 to 18 years old, Neugebauer (1988/1989) noted that adolescents had a strong preference for flexibility in parent access. Southworth and Schwarz (1987) interviewed 104 female college students, 52 from divorced families and 52 from intact families. Those who had experienced parental divorce were selected only if the divorce occurred when the child was 9 to 16 years of age and if the child had lived with the mother after the divorce. The amount of postdivorce contact with the noncustodial father was significantly related to the daughter's perception of current acceptance and consistency of fatherly love, with more contact after the divorce predicting greater feelings of acceptance and constant love at the time of the study. Indeed, for daughters who experienced frequent contact, the level of perceived acceptance was as high as for daughters from intact families.

Although they did not specifically study visitation and adjustment issues, Springer and Wallerstein (1983) did evaluate the adjustment of 14 adolescents from the larger Wallerstein and Kelly (1980c) study. They reported that the adolescents experienced significant internal conflict regarding visitation. Their wish to spend time with friends conflicted with concern about hurting their parents' feelings. They frequently expressed anger about parents' failure to include them in visitation planning. Teenage girls had particular problems with spending extended time with their fathers. Perceiving their fathers as adult men created anxiety in some of the adolescent girls. Fathers often shared that anxiety. If the father–daughter relationship was good the anxiety was overcome. If, however, this anxiety occurred in the context of a poor father–daughter relationship, the daughter rejected continued contact. The young adolescent boys did not generally experience as much anxiety in visiting with fathers.

Father–adolescent daughter visitations may need some professional help if either or both parties experience moderate levels of anxiety regarding the visit. For adolescents, research findings are contradictory concerning whether frequency of parent access is related to adjustment.

Abandonment

Awad and Parry (1980) noted that if a parent is alive but not available, the child will fantasize about him or her. According to them, the fantasy is a combination of the memory of the parent, the projection of the child, and the often negative projection of the custodial parent. Of necessity, the child will develop an egocentric and usually negative explanation as to why the noncustodial parent is abandoning. Loss of self-esteem is a common outcome. Awad and Parry also noted that abandonment can lead to concerns about having to depend on a single parent for survival, leading to increased anxiety. Isaacs (1988) also found that the father's disappearance or infrequent contact has negative effects on child development.

Having no contact with the noncustodial parent generally has a negative effect on the child. Cases involving abuse or parent psychopathology are likely to be exceptions to this principle.

RECOMMEND VISITATION PATTERNS BY AGE OF CHILD

Parents, lawyers, and judges all would like a formula to simplify the difficult problem of determining parent access after divorce. This section is an attempt to provide guidance. Because the research is meager, it is likely that these recommendations will undergo extensive revision over the next few years. It should be clear that the child's developmental needs are only one consideration and that no simple table of access patterns by age of child is likely to be helpful.

Certain assumptions underlie the recommendations given in this section:

1. The child has a reasonably strong affectionate bond with both parents.
2. Both parents have a basic understanding of children's needs.

3. Both parents can adjust to children's changing needs as a function of developmental changes.

4. Both parents can provide for the physical safety, nurturance needs, emotional support, and interest and ability to interact regularly with the child.

Violation of these assumptions might lead to a recommendation to increase or restrict visitation, depending on which parent has the problem.

The Context in Which Development Occurs

It is tempting to provide the developmental guidelines and then indicate contextual issues; however, it is important to understand the *contexts* in which such guidelines should be considered. The following 16 (not exhaustive) important issues need to be taken into consideration:

1. *If the child is an only child and there are no special considerations,* consider the developmental guidelines.

2. *If the parents have tried a developmentally inappropriate pattern with apparent success over some reasonable period of time,* consider that the child may be very adaptable. Evaluate whether there are symptoms of problems that are ignored by the parents, such as difficulty at transfer, unusual levels of dependency, unusual levels of detachment, or spaciness. If no symptoms are present and the pattern is not widely divergent from the guidelines, acceptance of the deviation might be appropriate.

3. *If the child shows symptoms of attachment problems,* consider evaluation by a mental health professional.

4. *If the child shows symptoms at transition from leaving one parent,* consider (a) that visitation problems may exist (e.g., psychological abuse, sexual abuse, neglect, conflict); (b) that the child may attempt to please the parent who is being left; and (c) that the child may find leaving that parent less painful if everyone is upset or angry.

5. *If the child shows symptoms at transition from leaving both parents,* consider that the child (a) has difficulty with loss; (b) is trying to please both parents; and (c) has a difficult temperament and has difficulty with any change.

6. *If an older sibling is present for parent access times, and the child is bonded with the sibling,* consider some longer duration visits.

7. *If the child is not bonded with the sibling(s),* consider the developmental guidelines.

8. *If the parents have chronic conflict,* consider (a) third-party transfer; (b) sole custody; (c) regular, predictable visits; and (d) reduced frequency of transfers.

9. *If the nonprimary parent is psychopathological,* consider reducing visitation frequency and duration. Also consider supervision or termination.

10. *If the nonprimary parent is an abuser,* consider supervision or termination of parent access.

11. *If the child has a difficult temperament,* consider longer visitation duration and fewer changes. Consider providing stability in terms of where the visitation occurs.

12. *If the child is severely alienated from the parent,* consider very brief visits (½ to 1 hour), with or without supervision.

13. *If there is great geographic distance between parents,* consider frequent visits if the child is young, provided such visits are financially feasible. Half the time, have the primary parent take the child to the nonprimary parent for visits with nightly return to the primary parent. Half the time, have the nonprimary parent travel to the city of the primary parent. Avoid long visits for very young children. For children over 7, long visits tend to be better tolerated (see later section on long-distance visitation).

14. *If there has been a long break in parent access with a wish to reinstate contact,* consider phasing in a schedule to let the child get used to the formerly absent parent and rebuild trust. If trust is absent in the child or the primary parent, consider a phase-in with supervision.

15. *If the custodial parent is socially isolated, is under stress, has few friends or relatives available to share child care, and has low income,* consider increasing visitation duration with the noncustodial parent to relieve the custodial parent from constant child care responsibilities.

16. *If the child has an easy temperament and the parents want to change the guidelines,* consider some compromises, but evaluate the effect on the child. Often, visitation schedules are related to convenience for the parents rather than the child's welfare.

Developmental Guidelines

The recommendations discussed below are based on minimizing the risk to the child. Provided that the parents are "good enough," that visits occur without stress, and that other basic needs are provided, the visitation patterns described below are designed to produce no additional stress for most children at each stage.

Infancy

BIRTH TO 6 MONTHS OF AGE.   Based on research in the 1960s and 1970s, it is clear that infants do not develop attachment bonds to only one person, but can become securely attached to several parental figures. Attachment is not related to who feeds the child and changes diapers, but rather to who provides talk, play, cuddling, and rocking. Attachment is determined by the quality of the adult–infant interaction.

According to Sroufe (1979), the primary developmental issue in the first 6 months is physiological regulation and the primary infant need is smooth routines. From 3 to 6 months, the child needs a reduction of tension, with sensitive, cooperative interaction between the infant and caregiver. Visitation should not interrupt the ability of the two families to provide these routines.

An important function of visitation during this period is to facilitate sufficient contact that the noncustodial parent will develop affectionate bonds for the child. The foundations for attachment by the child are also being set at this time. Although such bonds can develop later, it is much more difficult.

Although there is no research on noncustodial father–infant visitation (rarely is the mother noncustodian for infants), some inferences about multiple attachment and infant needs can be drawn from several studies. According to the U. S. Department of Labor, in 1979, 40% of mothers with children under the age of 3 were employed. By 1988, half of married women with infants under 1 year of age were employed (Bureau of the Census, 1989). Schachere (1990) estimated that by 1990, 60% of mothers with preschoolers were employed. Thus, a large percentage of children are separated from their mothers from a very early age, regardless of the mother's marital status.

Research on families with two wage earners demonstrated that fathers in these families are more active in child care (Pedersen, 1981). In observations of 5-month-old children from families with either one or two wage earners (Pedersen, 1981), there was no difference in the quality of either parent's caregiving behaviors. Mothers in both types of families spent more time than fathers in feeding. Mothers who worked spent more time in verbal interaction with their babies than did nonworking mothers. Fathers in families with two wage earners actually interacted less with infants than fathers in families with one wage earner, perhaps because the mothers' needs to interact with the infants after work crowded out the fathers.

Bowlby (1969) proposed that from birth to 2 months of age, the infant is at a preattachment stage, with undiscriminating social responsiveness. The infant needs social stimulation, but will respond to any adult who provides that stimulation. At the same time, the child is slowly learning to recognize parenting or caregiving figures. From 2 to 6 months of age, the child shows greater responsivity to familiar figures, and smiles more and vocalizes more to familiar adults. At 4 to 6 months of age, the infant becomes wary of unfamiliar people (Bronson, 1972). The infant frowns, breathes heavily, and perhaps cries when a stranger approaches.

From day care research, it is clear that very young infants can tolerate contact with adults other than mothers. Kagan, Kearsley, and Zelazo (1978) compared children from 3½ months to 29 months in day care versus home care. They found that for *high-quality day care,* there was no effect of day care on language, cognitive functioning, and attachment with adults or with parents. High-quality day care meant warm, consistent care in a day care center with a ratio of no greater than four infants for each adult caregiver.

In research with infants from economically disadvantaged homes (often true for mothers after divorce), of the children in day care who were under 12 months of age, 47% were anxiously attached (Vaughn, Gove & Egeland, 1990). Of the children placed in day care between 12 and 18 months, 28% were anxiously attached. Even for infants not in day care, 18% were anxiously attached. Consistent with those data, Schachere (1990), in her review of the attachment literature for working mothers, noted that if the infant is in nonmaternal care for 20 hours or more a week, the child has an increased likelihood of developing insecure attachment. Clearly, very young infants of economically deprived mothers are at risk for disruptions in attachment. If about half (but clearly not all) of young infants can handle such intensive day care without harm, obviously some infants can handle visitation without harm, *provided that the visitation is both frequent and predictable* and that day care is consistent and high quality.

Based on data on day care for working mothers, infants may be at risk for insecure attachment with the divorced primary caregiver.

Skafte (1985) noted that short, frequent visits are much better for infants than longer visits spaced far apart. Skafte recommended daily contact of a few hours as ideal; however, practical considerations may prevent such an arrangement. If both parents are employed, it would be difficult for both custodial and noncustodial parents to find enough waking hours in the day to have quality time with the child. Skafte recommended that no more than 2 days in a row go by without time with the noncustodial parent.

Dishon (1985) noted that professionals concerned with object constancy in the parent–child bonding would be concerned about separating the child from the primary parent (usually the mother) for more than brief periods, prior to 30 to 36 months of age. Bentovim and Gilmour (1981) also raised concerns about long-term reactions to separation from the primary caregiver to whom an infant is attached. They also emphasized the importance of continuity.

Thus, the recommendation for visitation for infants is the opposite of what often occurs in the thinking about frequency versus duration. Parents whose schedule or preferences lead to less frequent visitation want to compensate for that reduced frequency by increasing the duration. Although such a compensation is appropriate (and perhaps preferable) for school age children, it is not recommended for infants.

For infants from birth to 6 months, a frequent and predictable visitation pattern is recommended. The more frequently the noncustodial parent can be available, the longer the duration should be. For infants who can be visited only once or twice a week, visitation should not exceed 1 or 2 hours. Infants visited every day or every other day can develop attachments to the noncustodial parents that can maintain their security. Stability of child care location should be maintained. Subject to the needs and abilities of the custodial and noncustodial parents, such visitation could be for 1 hour or part of a day. Overnight visits are likely not to be in the child's best interests, because, infants' eating and sleeping arrangements should be as stable as possible.

SIX TO 18 MONTHS.   True attachment to parental figures begins around 6 months of age. Sroufe (1979) noted that the issue for development at this age is the establishment of an effective attachment relationship, and the caregiver's role is to provide responsive availability. Stranger anxiety often begins at 6 or 7 months and peaks at 8 to 12 months. Children will show apprehension and possibly cry when picked up by a stranger and will calm down when held by a consistent parental figure. Attachment is not limited to the mother. The child can attach as well to the father and to a child caregiver. Children with multiple caregivers will be more comfortable with strangers and will show less intense responses. Also, the stranger anxiety response will be delayed if there are multiple caregivers. The response to strangers seems to be related to the infant's ability to recognize that the situation is strange and to recognize the inability to do anything about it.

For the same reason, separation anxiety becomes more common during this time. Infants who previously showed no distress at a parent's leaving, begin to cry when parents leave the house. Separation anxiety typically develops at about 8 months of age, peaks from 1 to 1 1/2 years of age, and can remain quite strong at 2 years of age. For infants 12 to 18 months of age, if the father is present, the separation response to the mother may not occur, even in the presence of a stranger.

Given the reactions of infants 6 to 12 months of age to strangers and to separation, the frequency and duration of visitation depend in part on the prior contact of the infant with the noncustodial parent. If that parent has participated frequently in child care, the frequency and duration of visitation can be greater.

If the 6- to 12-month-old child has had little prior contact with the noncustodial parent, visitation should be initially short and frequent to provide familiarity and comfort to the infant.

In the latter part of this period, the child begins to explore and master the environment (Sroufe, 1979). The parent or caregiver must provide a secure basis for this exploration. Because the child is capable of walking and beginning speech, both the custodial and noncustodial parents must provide safe environments. Safety in the environment is a requirement at all times, but becomes a more crucial issue as soon as crawling begins.

S. Goldstein and Solnit (1984), in giving advice to noncustodial parents, noted that children under 3 quickly lose feelings of attachment to people whom they do not frequently see. For example, a young child may show stranger anxiety to a parent not seen for several days. Skafte (1985) also recommended that no more than 2 or 3 days pass without the noncustodial parent visiting the child. Skafte recommended against overnight visits at this age.

As for younger infants, short visits of 1 to 3 hours are recommended if visitation frequency is low. If contact is regular and frequent, the child can handle visitation that lasts part or most of a day. The noncustodial parent should recognize that the infant of this age needs predictability and familiarity. Visitation will work best when visitation occurs in the same location every time. Overnight visits should be considered less than desirable and used only when other considerations are more important (e.g., to support bonding between the child and noncustodial parent or to accommodate long distances). In these cases, some instability to the child may be worth the trade-off.

Frequency of visitation for the infant should vary according to the noncustodial parent's sensitivity to the infant's physiological and psychological needs. The infant needs to be fed and kept warm and comfortable. Most parents recognize the physiological needs. Some parents are less sensitive to the infant's psychological needs—to be held, talked to, stroked, and played with.

The child's temperament may also help determine frequency and duration of visits. An easy child will handle liberal visitations. A slow-to-warm-up child may need a slower transition to more frequent and longer visitations. A difficult infant may require less frequent and shorter visitation. Noncustodial parents will find a difficult infant less rewarding to have around and may request less time; however, the needs of the custodial parent for relief from a classically difficult infant can be profound.

For infants, temperaments should be taken into account in setting the visitation pattern.

Toddlers

The task of toddlers, aged 18 months to 3 years, is individuation (Sroufe, 1979), that is, becoming an individual separate from the parents. The child needs firm support both in terms of limit setting and freedom to explore. The "terrible 2s" is an important developmental stage. The child must be given permission to resist the parent on unimportant issues, but required to obey in areas of safety, self-control, and social interaction. The child who is too resistant may have too many pressures for new skills or obedience to handle. Because children's time perspective is increasing and they can remember people whom they have not seen for several days (but not weeks or months), children can tolerate longer times between visits as well as longer visits.

Skafte (1985) recommended entire days and overnights by the time the child is 3. She also felt that entire weekends are too long for such young children.

Children from 18 months to 3 years of age can handle less frequent visitations than can infants, but consistency and frequency are still important. An 18-month-old child who is visiting only on weekends can handle parts of a day. By 3 years, the child can spend an overnight without harm; however, weekend visits are still not recommended. (Several times a week rather than a long weekend are more helpful to the child.) Long visitations during summer vacations are not recommended. Although the exact length of a long visitation during the summer for this age child is not known, a child familiar with and bonded to the noncustodial parent can handle 3 to 4 days. A child who has not had frequent contact with the noncustodial parent (e.g., due to geographic distance) should not be separated from the custodial parent for more than 1 or 2 days.

Children of this age should not be required to travel to a distant geographic location for an extensive visit with the noncustodial parent. If the parent has not had regular visitation, one parent should travel to the other parent's location and the noncustodial parent can have short, regular visits for part of a day. In many cases, however, such a program is not economically feasible.

Preschool Children

Children aged 3 to 5 are learning to manage their impulses, develop sex-role identification, and develop peer relations. The parents need to provide clear roles and values and flexible self-control for the child (Sroufe, 1979). For preschool children, Awad and Parry (1980) recommended frequent, brief visits and advised against day-long or overnight visits. Other clinicians have indicated that children of these ages can tolerate day-long and overnight visits quite well. According to Tierney (1983), low-conflict and high-quality parenting may be very important. Tierney also indicated that children of this age are more affected by predictability than by frequency and duration of visits.

For preschool children, professionals should take into account that conflict between parents and high-quality parenting may be more important than pattern of visitation. Given low conflict levels and high-quality parenting by the mother, the professional should emphasize the important of consistency. Children from 3 to 5 benefit from highly predictable visits. Given low parental conflict levels, frequency is important. If quality of parenting by the mother is high, frequency of contact with the noncustodial father correlates with adjustment. Support of more frequent visitation should be the next level of priority after consistency. Because these recommendations are based on correlations, and cause and effect are not established, they should be considered tentative.

Skafte (1985) approved of long weekends, holiday time, and blocks of time for summer vacations for the 3- to 5-year-old child. She recommended that children go no longer than a week without contact with each parent.

Preschool age children can handle weekend visits during the year and week-long visits for holidays and summer vacations, if limited in frequency. It is not known what the maximum long visit can be that will still benefit the child. Visits of longer than a week may still be inappropriate without visitation with the custodial parent. If longer visitations are necessary because of distance or planning problems, the parents should be advised of methods to help these children handle such visits (see the section on long visitations for young children).

Primary School Age Children

SIX TO 10 YEARS OF AGE.   During this stage of development, the child is involved in moving from the parents as the primary sphere of influence to teachers and peers. The child learns to play cooperatively, to be industrious and creative, and to see the world from another person's perspective. The child's time perspective permits long separations from parents while maintaining affectional bonds. The research summarized in the section on visitation and adjustment suggests that most children of this age do not find every other weekend, alternate holidays, and 6 weeks in the summer a plan that provides enough contact with the noncustodial parent. Quality of bonding and "good enough" parenting are likely to be very important in determining whether children wish for more visitation. Frequent visitation and liberal opportunity to have contact with the noncustodial parent should be permitted if the level of conflict between parents is not increased severely by that contact.

During this age period, the child is usually not ready for totally nonstructured visitation. Some visitation contact should be specified and predictable to the child. Spontaneous contact can be of enormous benefit to the child who can interpret the wish by the noncustodial parent to initiate contact beyond that required as an indication of affection and enjoyment. Such spontaneous contact is beneficial to the parent and the child only if the custodial parent is not competitive or resentful of that contact. Contact by phone or letter between visits can also increase the child's sense of being loved and enjoyed.

While predictability is important during this age, the child is also increasing contact with peers and having greater opportunities for parties, overnight stays with friends, and recreational sports. The noncustodial parent who insists on visitation without regard to the 6- to 12-year-old's wishes to participate in these activities may invite resentment and rejection. Also, the custodial parent may try to use these activities to block the other parent's access to the child. Although flexibility is useful, it is generally best to "trade times" to take into account the child's wishes rather than to use such activities to reduce the frequency or duration of visitation.

For primary school age children, the visitation pattern should minimize the interference with peer relationships.

Skafte (1985) felt that the appropriate schedule for many families was every other weekend with some time after school or in the evening during the off week. Research evidence suggests, however, that many children would find such a schedule too limited.

If the two parents have a reasonably cordial relationship, visitation more frequent than every other weekend may be desirable. At 7 or 8 years of age, children who have contact with the noncustodial parent several times a week are the most content with visitation. Contact once or more during the week is helpful. Children seem to benefit from more contact with the noncustodial parent rather than less, but the time of maximum benefit is not known. Flexibility within some general scheduling of visitation is helpful. When conflict between parents is high, children benefit from a more structured, predictable pattern of visitation. Long visitations during the summer are acceptable, but some contact with the custodial parent, either through visitations or phone, is desirable.

ELEVEN TO 12 YEARS OF AGE.   Based on the research on visitation satisfaction, some reduction in visitation, particularly for boys, may be appropriate at 11 to 12 years of age. Skafte (1985) noted that peer involvement at this age may lead children to want less contact with the parents and a more flexible visitation schedule. As she noted, sometimes spontaneous activities can enrich the relationships.

At ages 10 to 11, boys in particular seem to prefer less contact, perhaps only every other week, with the noncustodial parent. If the child prefers to maintain weekly contact, this amount of contact should be permitted.

Adolescence

Divorce creates special problems for the adolescent. Just when the teenager needs to separate from the parent, the parent separates from the teenager. Emotional upset on the part of one or more parents makes it more difficult for the teenager to separate. Although visitation plans for teenagers often include plans for every other weekend, Kelly (1981) noted that teenagers usually have contacts that last only several hours. Seldom do overnight or weekend visits occur. A teenager required to stay home with a parent for a weekend is likely to see that requirement as being grounded, rather than as an opportunity to develop a relationship. Because teenagers tend to spend more waking, non-school hours with friends than with family, long weekend visitations are likely to interfere with age-appropriate developmental needs.

Visitation for adolescents should take into account that teenagers do not need contact of long duration with either parent. Weekend visitations may interfere with developmental needs to separate from both parents. Contact once or twice a week for an hour or more may be enough contact. Some contact should occur each week or every other week.

HOLIDAYS AND VACATIONS

As Skafte (1985) noted, it is important to develop family traditions and strengthen family bonds through holidays. therefore, children should have the opportunity to celebrate each holiday with each parent, by alternating specific holidays with each parent. When both parents live in the same community, it is possible to split important holidays, such as Christmas or Hanukkah, so that the child can spend part of each holiday with both parents. For example, many families successfully split Christmas by having the child spend Christmas Eve with one family and Christmas day with the other. Other families change visitation at noon on Christmas day.

Skafte also noted that family vacations can be an important time for developing relationships. She recommended, and I agree, that children under 3 should not go on extended vacations. For children from 3 to 5, several short vacations are more beneficial than one long vacation.

VISITATION PLANS THAT ACCOUNT FOR CHILDREN'S CHANGING NEEDS

The problems of setting visitation plans are the same as those involved in determining custody arrangements. Children have different needs at different times of their development. Visitation agreements seldom take into account these changes over time. Tierney (1983) noted that parents of preschool children seemed to adjust visitation to the age of the child, even when the written visitation agreement permitted longer visitations. Although the good will of parents and the awareness of the child's needs may permit individual negotiation that benefits the child, it is generally better to provide written plans that take the changing needs into account.

Because the child's ability to tolerate or benefit from specific visitation patterns is not solely dependent on age, plans for evaluation (perhaps including mediation) on a regular basis may be appropriate. For parents not good at negotiating, the child's needs will be better served by approximating the changing needs in the divorce agreement. Thus, an agreement might indicate that the visitation pattern would be at a particular frequency and duration until age 3, another pattern until age 5, a third pattern until age 9, and a final pattern at age 10. The agreement might indicate that for the teen years, the visitation pattern would be negotiated with the teenager involved, but would be at least 2 hours per week and no more than every weekend.

VISITATION PLANS WHEN CHILDREN IN THE FAMILY ARE IN DIFFERENT DEVELOPMENTAL STAGES

Families seldom split visitation based on the ages of the children. All children usually visit the noncustodial parent together. Except for infants, such visitation plans make sense for the children. When the preschool age children are bonded to one another, the presence of siblings can serve to provide the stability that frequent visitation could provide, and a child of a particular age might be able to tolerate longer visitation than might be recommended for a child of that age without siblings. Perhaps some average of the children's ages might serve as a guideline for determining the best pattern. Regardless of other children's ages, infants should still not be subject to overnight visitations. Likewise, although primary school age children might desire frequent visitations, the older brother or sister in high school might prefer shorter times. It is reasonable to have visitations of varying lengths, taking the different children's developmental needs into account.

Such a variable program must also take into account the needs of the custodial parent to be relieved of parenting responsibilities for some period of time. Single parenting is an exhausting job, and many custodial parents look forward to the visitation time as an opportunity to be alone for a while.

GRANDPARENT VISITATION

C. L. Johnson (1988) noted that in a study of 50 grandmothers who lived in the same area as a divorcing child, the grandparents played a significant role in reducing the stress of divorce for their adult child. Of the sample, 89% provided babysitting and 75% provided economic help (22% gave regular income maintenance). Thus grandparents can be a major source of support. When the parent and grandparent do not live in the same community, contact with the grandchild can be quite limited, however.

Because the grandparent–grandchild relationship can be a special one of affection, the pain of some grandparents about the loss of contact with their grandchildren after divorce can be profound. Typically, the parents of the noncustodial parent have sharply reduced contact with their grand-children (Gladstone, 1987). Particularly if the noncustodial parent is aban-doning, the custodial parent may find contact with the grandparents painful. Most states have given grandparents the right to petition for visita-tion time with the child, provided the best interests of the child are pro-tected (Derdeyn, 1985).

Gladstone (1987) collected data on 80 Toronto grandmothers whose grandchildren were affected by parental divorce. Patterns of access to the grandchild were more likely to change if the grandparents' adult child did not retain custody. Some parents and grandparents moved closer to one another for emotional support. Often, grandparents provided day care or a more spacious or appealing setting for visits than the parent's home. Decrease in visiting was associated with unresolved conflicts be-tween the grandparent and adult child or difficulties in renegotiating the relationships with the parents of the grandchild. Another difficulty can arise if remarriage occurs. Adoption by a stepparent may divest a grandparent (whose adult child is noncustodial) of visitation rights even in states in which grandparents have a right to petition for visitation (Bowser, 1982).

There are potential problems with grandparent visitations, although chil-dren clearly can benefit from healthy relationships with their grandparents. For example, if the custodial parent is employed, if the noncustodial parent has liberal visitation time, and if both sets of grandparents want time with the child, the custodial parent may have little time with the child. Grand-parent visitation laws also ignore the fact that the grandparent–parent rela-tionship might be strained and that the children can be caught in the middle in that conflict. According to Derdeyn (1985), courts have resolved requests for visitation under such strains in both directions, granting visitation in some cases and denying it in others.

In a study of 8- to 21-year-old children of divorce, only 10% liked the amount of visitation with their grandparents (Funder, 1989). Almost half wanted to see less of the maternal grandparents, and two-thirds to see less of the paternal grandparents. Monthly visits were considered too often by these children.

Provided that the grandparents can be properly supportive to the parents and the grandchildren, some grandparent visitation should be encouraged under most conditions. Given the findings of Funder (1989), the amount of visitation should be limited. S. Goldstein and Solnit (1984) did not feel that legally mandated, court-enforceable grandparent visitation rights were in the child's best interests. They felt that such an arrangement interfered with the custodial parent's ability to be in full charge. Derdeyn (1985) felt that giving grandparents such rights could exacerbate chronic conflict. Derdeyn also noted that such visitation could foster competition between grandpar-ent and parent for parenting the child and lead grandparents to try to assume a former, rewarding (and now inappropriate) role.

WORKING WITH VISITATION PROBLEMS AFTER THE DIVORCE

A variety of family dynamics may predict visitation problems. When one parent enters into a new relationship, problems often increase. When one parent dramatically changes his or her lifestyle, it is not unusual for the other parent to have serious concerns for the child's welfare. A variety of problems with visitation also are involved with parental psychopathology. Examples include a parent who involves a child in role reversal such that the parent is getting primary needs met from the child, a narcissistic parent, and a parent who demands the child's loyalty and insists on the child's rejection of the other parent (see parent alienation syndrome, discussed below).

"Proof" of Poor Visitation

The mental health professional needs to beware of accepting parental reports of the child's emotional upset immediately prior to or after visitation as proof of poor quality of visitation with the noncustodial parent. The child may be responding to the reactions of the custodial parent who gets upset around the time of visitation. When the child also gets upset, the custodial parent can feel justified in trying to block visitation. Also, separation may be more tolerable to the child when everyone is angry. The child may deliberately provoke everyone so that he or she can tolerate the pain of leaving each parent.

Upset at transition times has been demonstrated to be related to chronic conflict between parents for elementary age children (Johnston, Campbell, & Mayes, 1985). Thus, children may show high levels of both psychological and physical symptoms at the time of transition in response to the dispute between parents. R. S. Benedek and Benedek (1977) also noted that children act out around visitation and that such behavior does not necessarily indicate a bad visit.

Finally, anger can be a child's technique to keep the parents communicating with each other. Children who wish for reconciliation find noncommunicating parents an almost intolerable situation. Even battles are preferred to parents who never communicate, because parents who do not talk can never reconcile. The child may set up the parents around visitation to force communication.

Mental health professionals should be cautious in interpreting the meaning of an upset around visitation. Although the visitation may be damaging to the child, and certainly investigation of the quality of the visit is called for, a variety of other reasons may account for the child's being upset, including trying to please the custodial parent, having difficulty with separation, and forcing contact between parents.

R. S. Benedek and Benedek (1977) recommended counseling for the parents for such problems. Termination of visitation should be considered only after a thorough evaluation.

S. Goldstein and Solnit (1984) noted that a parent who argues that there is substantial evidence of harm because of the child's resistance to the visits is often received by the courts with little sympathy. Courts may order the visitation to continue on the grounds that the custodial parent influences the child's attitudes and, if the visitation is discontinued, the child will be deprived of contact with a parent to which the child is entitled. In addition, Goldstein and Solnit noted that opposition to the visitation by the custodial parent might lead to a weakening of the child's relationship with the custodial parent because it undermines trust.

Irregular or Nonexistent Visitation

The problem of a noncustodial parent's irregular or nonexistent visitation is particularly difficult. Ultimately, the courts cannot force a reluctant parent to visit. Even if the coercion was successful, the argument could be made that the parent could sabotage the visit in such a way as to prevent it from being useful to the child.

Mental health professionals should try to work with a noncustodial parent to diagnose why visitation is rare or nonexistent. The willingness of such a parent to talk may be a sign that negotiation (or therapy) could increase visitation.

The elimination of visitation often leads a child to feel low self-esteem. As discussed elsewhere, the child may consider the parent's disappearance to indicate that the child is unlovable. Unlike the death of a parent, an unexplained or unresolved disappearance prevents mourning.

Chronic Irresponsibility on the Part of the Custodial Parent

Angry parents can be expert in manipulating one another. The custodial parent may schedule special activities, such as church activities or dental work (which of course are seen by the custodial parent as essential to the proper development of the child), during the visitation time. In such cases, neither the parent nor the child is present when the noncustodial parent shows up. Alternatively, the noncustodial parent may keep the custodial parent waiting for hours before picking up or delivering the child, thus ruining the custodial parent's plans. Also, the child may be delivered hungry or tired.

Remarriage

The presence of a significant other for the noncustodial parent can create resistance to visitation from any of the parties involved. The child may resent the loss of attention from the noncustodial parent. A stepparent may have difficulties with the intrusion into the family life.

Brand, Clingempeel, and Bowen-Woodward (1988) evaluated 40 Caucasian, middle income stepfather families and 22 Caucasian, middle income stepmother families. All families had been remarried less than 3 years, and all families had a child from 9 to 12 years of age. The frequency of visits with the noncustodial parent was related to three measures of stepparent–stepchild relationships. No relationships were found for boys. For girls in stepfather families, visitation frequency with the noncustodial parent was higher if the girls had more positive behaviors directed toward them from their stepfathers. For girls in stepmother families, frequency of visits with the noncustodial mother was negatively related to the child's rating of the stepmother's love. There was no relationship found between frequency of visitation and adjustment in the child.

Much more will be discussed about the problem of the stepfamily in Chapter 9.

LONG VISITATIONS FOR YOUNG CHILDREN

Many families cannot provide for the somewhat brief, but frequent visitation that is recommended for children under 7 years of age. Long visitation for young children may increase risk because of the child's difficulty in maintaining an image and attachment for the absent parent for long periods of time. In addition, the child has difficulty perceiving the return to the custodial parent at an intuitive level. Long visitation periods thus place the child in the position of being constantly separated from a parent without an awareness of when he or she will return to that parent.

Parents can do a variety of things to aid a child in adapting to a relatively long visitation that is necessitated by vacations, great geographic distance, or the intractable nature of the separation conflict:

1. *Increase object constancy for the young child.* With long separations, the young child has increasing difficulty in maintaining an image of the absent parent. Photographs of the parent, cassette tapes of favorite bedtime stories in that parent's voice, and frequent phone calls can help bridge the memory of the absent parent for the young child. Many homes have videocassette recorders, and video cameras are relatively inexpensive to rent. Several videocassettes of the absent parent would be helpful to the young child. If the absent parent is in the same area, visitation with that parent would be desirable, even during the 6-7 week summer visitation. The custodial parent must provide some groundwork with the noncustodial parent, particularly if the noncustodial parent is involved with a significant other. The last thing a new spouse wants around the house is a picture of the ex-spouse; however, perhaps the child can be given a special place to keep

material. Phone calls also can be intrusive, but planning may reduce resentment generated by them. The stepparent may need counseling to understand the child's needs and reduce pressure on the entire family.

2. *Avoid or minimize long-distance travel for children under 3.* For children aged 3 to 5, nonstop airline flights require an escort both ways. Usually, if there is a plane change, an escort is required for children to age 8. Thus, having the parents travel rather than the child may save money and reduce stress on the child.

When a child under 3 years of age lives some distance from the noncustodial parent, that parent should try to go to the town of the custodial parent and visit the child regularly for several days. Alternately, the custodial parent could go with the child to the town of the noncustodial parent and provide similar access.

3. *Maintain stability of the environment in terms of familiar objects.* The child should be encouraged to take to the noncustodial parent's house familiar objects, toys, dolls, and transitional objects (e.g., a "Linus blanket") to help reassure the child that the environment has not changed too dramatically.

4. *Maintain familiar routines.* Parents should be encouraged to maintain comparable bedtimes, types of rewards and punishments, and even familiar food. When a child is visiting in another part of the country, even favorite particular food brands could be sent along. Careful preparation is necessary, because a stepmother may be quite insulted if a child shows up with a suitcase full of food. She may misinterpret the behavior as an indication that the mother does not believe that the child would be adequately fed at the new home! It is enormously upsetting to young children, however, to find that nothing is familiar, not even the taste of their favorite macaroni and cheese.

5. *Help the child comprehend the passing of time.* Use visual aids on calendars to increase the 4- to 6-year-old's understanding of the time for his or her return home. This technique can be helpful for young, elementary age children as well.

Newman (1981) listed numerous ideas for helping a father maintain a relationship with a distant child. The ideas are creative ways of making letters and phone calls more fun and of maintaining the relationship. Suggestions include how to stay involved with teaching the child and understanding how the child is doing at school through quizzes, stamp collecting, games, jokes, riddles, and other fun things to do over the phone.

TERMINATION OF VISITATION

Awad and Parry (1980) indicated that visitation should be completely terminated under three conditions:

1. The harm to the child outweighs the benefits. The noncustodial parent may be significantly disturbed. Awad and Parry found the most likely diagnoses of noncustodial parents who are damaging to children with *any* contact are paranoid/obsessional personality or narcissistic personality.

2. The custodial parent gets extremely upset at visitation, which places the child in a chronic stressful situation. Although Awad and Parry felt that such a problem could justify termination of visitation, I caution overuse of this criterion. California law requires that custody preference be given to the parent who would most likely protect the access to the other parent. A parent can use (consciously or unconsciously) increased upset as a form of blackmail to coerce the other parent out of the picture. Knowledge that such behavior would be weighed by mental health professionals would increase the frequency of such behaviors.

3. The choice of the child. Awad and Parry proposed that when a child refuses visitation, whether based on neurotic or realistic reasons, visitation may be denied. To the contrary, I propose that in many (but not all) cases, very brief visitations can provide the opportunity for the child to develop a relationship with the noncustodial parent, should the intensity of opposition decline. The visitation should be only as long as the child can tolerate. Even a half hour a month gives some opportunity to negotiate a relationship. Clearly, if the child increases outrageous behavior to indicate opposition, visitation may have to be terminated.

Visitation should not be terminated without a formal assessment as to why the problem exists. Individual (custodial and/or noncustodial parent) consultation, couple therapy, or noncustodial parent–child therapy should be seriously considered as interventions to avoid termination of visitation.

Supervised visitation can be helpful in obtaining a diagnostic evaluation as to why the child is adamant against visitation. (See the section later in this chapter on supervised visitation for abusing parents.) Awad and Parry recommended supervised access with the custodial parent observing so that anxieties on the part of the parent strongly opposing visitation might be reduced by having fantasies disconfirmed.

Awad and Parry (1980) cautioned the mental health professional against overuse of elimination of visitation rights. If a parent believes that the outcome of custody could block access, the battle for custody is likely to be extreme. The anticipation of access on the part of the noncustodial parent may reduce the intensity of the battle, since even the losing parent can continue to have a relationship with the child.

VISITATION TERMINATION AND PARENT ALIENATION

Gardner (1987) coined the term "parent alienation syndrome" to describe those cases in which the child is so alienated from the noncustodial parent as to refuse contact. The parent alienation syndrome is characterized by unrelenting statements of hatred for the rejected parent and that parent's relatives. Often the reasons for the hatred are trivial. The hatred is typically completely supported by the accepted parent, who usually gives the child the power to decide whether to visit and may support in a variety of ways the rejection of the other parent. In cases in which the parent is actively programming the child against the other parent, Gardner recommended that the court immediately transfer the child to the so-called hated parent and that the child have no contact with the accepted parent for a month or two. There are no data on the success of such an approach. For young children, such a drastic move could interfere with the attachment process. In cases in which the accepted parent accepts that the hatred is not in the child's best interests and is willing to work with the other parent, such an extreme solution is not necessary.

It is difficult to intervene to reinstate visitation if the child is old enough to be strongly willful on refusing to visit. Family therapy with the custodial and/or noncustodial parent and the child is recommended for many of these cases.

VISITATION AND THE SEVERELY MALADJUSTED PARENT

Visitation patterns recommended earlier in this chapter were for use when both parents are reasonably cordial and lacking of severe pathology. Visitation may have to be limited, however, when one parent has difficulty in maintaining boundaries for anger, parental role, and narcissism; is psychologically abusive; has borderline personality problems; has trouble separating the parent's perspective from the child's; uses the child as a pawn in the battle with the other parent; or pushes the child into a loyalty battle for alienation of affection from the other parent. (These criteria were suggested by Dr. Lanning Schiller, personal communication.)

When the custodial parent has such problems, the question must be raised as to whether a proper custodial decision was made by the court. Several states recommend that custody be awarded to the parent who is willing to support visitation with the other parent. Any of the above problems, if held by the custodial parent, would make such support difficult. If the noncustodial parent is even more pathological, it is clear that visitation should be limited, because the reaction of the custodial parent to the visitation produces such stress for the child as to be potentially damaging.

When the noncustodial parent has such problems, the child must be protected from the pathology by limiting the visitation to a very low level so that the custodial parent's strength can be generally available to the child. When the pathology is quite severe, visitation may have to be eliminated. However, because of identification problems for the child and the potentially damaging effects of fantasy with visitation eliminated (see the discussion in the next section), supervised visitation is probably more appropriate. (Supervised visitation is discussed in the next section.)

Visitation and the Sexually or Physically Abusing Parent

The anger that mental health professionals feel toward abusing parents leads them to want to punish the parent by restricting or eliminating visitation altogether. However, as stated before, the criterion for visitation patterns is the best interests of the child. Thus, the question becomes whether it is in the child's best interests to have continued contact with an abusive noncustodial parent. Limitations are appropriate in some instances, namely where the parent is so psychologically damaged that any contact is harmful. In general, however, the child benefits from having some contact with an abusing parent in several ways:

1. Although many abusing parents can be quite loving, they may have a problem with self-control that is harmful to the child. If the child can be protected from the impulse control problem, there can be substantial benefits from the affection.
2. Prohibiting visitation can be damaging to the child's self-esteem in a variety of ways. For example, a parent may be so damaged that he or she cannot be permitted to see the child, inviting reduction in self-esteem through identification problems. In addition, the child's fearfulness of the parent's pathology can increase through fantasy (R. S. Benedek & Benedek, 1977; Hoorwitz, 1983).
3. If the child decides that the court's decision to isolate the parent was inappropriate, the child may develop rescue fantasies. For example, a child may think, "My father would visit me and take care of me better (and not make me go to bed so early or restrict what I eat or restrict what I watch on television) if they would just let him come." Normal resentment for age-appropriate restrictions in freedoms can increase and be prolonged when such rescue fantasies are maintained.

Although the foregoing arguments encourage some form of visitation even for abusing or psychopathological parents, such visitation should occur only if there are adequate safeguards to protect the child's well-being. It would be better to have no visitation at all than to subject a child to a physically or psychologically dangerous home setting. Courts have a great deal of difficulty balancing these two values. A traumatized child may be retraumatized if required to visit a feared parent.

Armstrong (1985) documented several case histories of inadequate controls when courts appeared to give excessive weight to the value of noncustodial contact over child protection. For example, she described case histories of courts that ignored mothers' reports of child sexual abuse by fathers, choosing to believe the fathers' denials. In one case, a mother was sent to jail for refusing to send her children to visit the father who had repeatedly molested them. In another case, the father's mother was assigned supervision responsibility for the visitation of a 4-year-old daughter, but this grandmother apparently did not provide adequate controls. This supervision continued despite evidence of genital abrasions and labial burns. The same court ordered visitation even when the father was found to be sexually abusing the child, on the assumption that to terminate visitation would be harmful to the child. The court ordered treatment and supervision even when it was felt that neither would be effective. In all these examples, it is difficult to imagine that visitation value was more important than protecting the child. The child's welfare should take precedence, and visitation is less important than protection from such abuse.

False allegations of sexual abuse apparently do occur, usually around a divorce proceeding. Blush and Ross (1987) noted that such allegations can occur to block visitation. (See the discussion on sexual allegations in divorce—the SAID syndrome—in Chapter 6.)

Supervised Visitation for Abusing or Psychopathological Noncustodial Parents

The child's welfare must be protected. A parent with impulse control problems cannot be permitted to impose those problems on the child. The most obvious protection of the child is to provide supervised visitation.

Family members may be unable or unwilling to control pathological interactions. I recommend against use of people who have emotional ties with either parent or of teenage babysitters who may be unable to handle intimidation or recognize psychologically abusive behavior. Ringler-White (1982) noted that having a mental health professional available for supervision permits the court to have professional advice when the visitation pattern is too irregular to be useful to the child or the behavior during visitation cannot be controlled even under supervision.

The visitation supervision program at Children's Hospital in Denver, Colorado, was described in some detail by Ringler-White. This service provides feedback to the court on a regular basis (e.g., every 6 months) about whether the visitation supervision plan should be changed. The service has three different levels of supervision. First, the program provides a visitation exchange program. Children are dropped off and picked up under the supervision of a staff member. Parents never have to interact. This plan is helpful when parents cannot negotiate visitation plans, when one or both parents cannot follow the plans agreed on, and when the parents cannot control the anger that they feel toward one another. This plan is not used when the child's safety may be in question.

Second, monitored visits are provided. A staff member listens to the visit through microphones and observes the interaction from time to time through a one-way mirror. If necessary, the staff member can intervene directly with support, limit setting, or recommendations. This plan is used when limited supervision is sufficient to protect the child.

Third, complete supervision is possible whereby a staff member observes and listens to the entire visit through a one-way mirror and audio system. With more severe problems, the staff member may be present in the room during the visit (a requirement that may be necessary when the child is exceptionally fearful and needs the reassurance of another person in the room). If there is significant risk of physical violence or self-destructive behavior even under this amount of supervision, the supervision is terminated and the hospital will not agree to further supervision.

As can be guessed, such a program is expensive in staff time. Therefore, parents have to pay a significant amount for the service. When the choice is paying for supervision or not having any contact at all, the parents often prefer to have some contact. Abusing parents may have a significant amount of guilt about their past behavior, and continued contact can reassure themselves as well as the children that the impulse control problems do not mean the children are unloved.

Lawyers looking for visitation supervisors sometimes arrange to hire advanced graduate students in clinical psychology on an hourly basis. The graduate student is less expensive than a private practicing clinician or public service facility. Retired teachers, social workers, or other retired mental health professionals also may provide less expensive supervision. The graduate student or retiree might welcome an opportunity to earn extra money. In addition, the graduate training enables the student to provide professional-level input to the courts in determining whether supervision or visitation should be discontinued (although there are problems with such advice, as noted below).

Stott, Gaier, and Thomas (1984) described a supervision program staffed by church-affiliated volunteers and another coordinated by staff of a Salvation Army Community Center.

Armstrong (1985) noted that there is some resistance by the court to ordering supervised visitation. It is, after all, babysitting of adults. Also, it may represent prior restraint, that is, punishment for a crime that has not yet been committed (although in many cases, the abuse has occurred). The question of how long the supervision should continue is also raised.

Other problems with supervision of visitation have yet to be worked out. Because supervision is costly, it is generally not possible to have extended visitation times. More importantly, it is difficult to know when to change the visitation pattern. Because the abuse may be a low-frequency behavior, which occurs only when the parent is frustrated or alone with the child, the absence of abuse during supervised visits may not be sufficient to predict the likelihood that abuse will not occur if supervision was terminated. Simply because a parent is able to control the abuse for short visits when the parent knows someone is watching, that parent may not have such control without the supervision. Behavioral scientists are not very good at predicting low-frequency loss of control in people who have already demonstrated a tendency toward that behavior. No research has yet been done on supervision of visitation.

If no pathological behavior is present during the observation, if the parent seems to be in better self-control, and if the parent develops better understanding of the child's needs, it may be possible to make a transition toward less controlled circumstances, particularly for older children capable of reporting on the visit. Transitions might include moving from the observation room or controlled playroom to the community with supervision continuing; moving to the home of the noncustodial parent with supervision continuing; having supervision at the beginning and end of the visit, but having the middle of the visit unsupervised (permitting pre- and postvisit evaluation of the physical and psychological state of the child and parent; moving to observation only at the end of the visit; and moving to observation every other visit. If the child or either parent is substantially anxious about such transitions, I recommend continuing some structured supervision of the visitation.

The ability to predict future violent behavior is very poor. Supervisors should be very cautious in indicating that future violence or danger would not be likely. For legal protection, visitation supervisors should agree to participate only if a legal contract prevents a lawsuit in case of future damage. Such an agreement should also indemnify and hold harmless the supervisor of all costs that might occur as a function of any report or action by the supervisor. Although supervised visitation is a solution to the problem of potential harm to the child, moving toward unsupervised visitation is a much more complex problem. In some cases, supervision may have to continue indefinitely.

Hoorwitz (1983) suggested a gradual increase in visitation time and recommended the type of activities that would be preferable. For example, if a child is fearful or angry, Hoorwitz suggested that the noncustodial parent be taught to "woo" the child with cards and letters.

If a child continues to show significant anxiety or acting out with supervised visitation, it must first be determined whether the child is expressing the anxiety or anger of the custodial parent. If the custodial parent is having significant problems with the visitation, working with that parent may be helpful. If the anxiety or anger is not related to the behavior of the custodial parent, the child may be experiencing significant problems being with an abusing parent. Under these conditions, reduction in visitation time, or even elimination of visitation, may be necessary.

REINTRODUCING PARENT ACCESS AFTER A LONG SEPARATION

A request for renewed parent access after years of no contact can be a source of considerable anxiety for the custodial parent and the child. The custodial parent is likely to resent the intrusion and resist any contact at all. The custodial parent often feels that he or she has done all the work and the parent who abandoned deserves no consideration.

Typically, such a request follows the introduction of a new partner in the life of the absent parent. This partner may urge the parent to renew contact with the child. Sometimes, an absent parent may have been doing significant work on personal problems, and makes an internally motivated resolution to reestablish contact. Usually, the child will benefit from finding out who the absent parent is and reestablishing some affectionate relationship. Families should avoid, however, moving too quickly into such a new relationship as both the absent parent and child may be overwhelmed.

When there have been long periods without contact, even for older children, there should not be a sudden introduction of long visitations. Initial visitations should be relatively short, slowly increasing in duration to permit the development of a relationship without fear.

A 14-year-old girl who had not seen her father for 5 or 6 years was quite frightened of a 2-week visit with a father 1,500 miles away when contact was reestablished. The relationship would have a greater likelihood of working well if the first contact were for a long weekend or short week and anxiety were lower. Ringler-White (1982) noted that some parents meeting their child after a long separation welcome supervision. The noncustodial parent can see the mental health professional as a resource for advice on how to handle the visitation. Supervised visitation also can calm the custodial parent's and the child's fears. Having a chance to talk to a neutral party about those fears can be quite helpful.

In a study that examined requests to reinstate access after a long period of no access, Eagle and Sheaffer (1989) studied 44 families in which the noncustodial parent requested access and the custodial parent opposed. Records were obtained from the Family Court Clinic in Toronto. Last access had ranged from 1 to 7 years earlier, and 11 of the children had not seen the noncustodial parent in more than 3 years. Clinicians recommended unsupervised access in 11 cases, supervised access in 10 cases, and no access in 27 cases. A recommendation for no access became more likely with length of time since the last access. For example, for no-access recommendations, an average of 2.5 years had passed since the last access. For access recommendations, 11 months had passed since the last access.

Access was denied for various reasons: the child's wishes; a perception that the visit would have negative emotional consequences on the child; the negative perception of the custodial parent toward the noncustodial parent; the noncustodial parent's character, psychosis, or lack of interest; potential physical danger to the child; and the noncustodial parent's new relationship. For the 18 children who specifically requested no access, the clinicians granted the request for 13. Clinicians never recommended no access if the child requested access. Although the custodial parents were concerned about kidnapping in 12 cases, the clinician recommended no access in only one of those cases.

REDUCING VISITATION PROBLEMS

Several strategies can be used to reduce visitation problems.

1. *Define visitation time.* I recommend highly structured visitation agreements, specifying exact time and definition of terms. A phrase can be added permitting "liberal visitation with the mutual consent of both parties." When one parent enters into a romantic relationship, liberal visitation often becomes less liberal. Vacations and school holidays also need to be defined. When does spring vacation begin: 2:00 P.M. Friday before the vacation or 8:00 A.M. Monday when school would have been in session? Is a week-long visitation 7 or 9 days long? If phone calls are permitted, how often, when, and for how long?

Johnston, Campbell, and Mayes (1985) studied 44 children aged 6 to 12 years whose parents had high levels of parental conflict. These children wanted set, regular visits. The children were upset by chaotic schedules, particularly those that kept changing and were never made clear. Flexibility meant more fighting. Almost 60% of the children resisted changing from either parent and 40% percent had some somatic complaint at the time of transition.

With high levels of parental conflict, children benefit from highly predictable visitation. Flexibility can be built in once the stress and conflict go down.

2. *Use a third party for transfer.* Reduction in angry communication and the use of an observer reduce irresponsible behavior. See the section on visitation and the physically or sexually abusing parent.

3. *Arrange for parent counseling.* Parents must be shown how the fighting hurts the child and how the child needs positive relations with both parents to protect his or her self-esteem. Parents can be taught to reduce attacks on each other and to support each other's relationship with the child. Bentovim and Gilmour (1981) described a family therapy interactional approach to helping families deal with custody and access problems. Chapter 13 gives examples of other family therapy approaches.

4. *Reduce stress on the child by increasing the commonality of rules at each household* (e.g., bedtimes, television watching, eating of sweets). Children can learn that different households have different rules, but the more constant the environment across households, the less stress.

5. *Build in developmental needs of the child in scheduling visitation.*

6. *Build in the use of mediation as a form of dispute resolution.*

7. *Protect the child's access to both parents.* If one parent needs to move a long distance, parents should be required to mediate on a plan that will protect the access of the child to both parents, taking into account the developmental needs of the child.

8. *Arrange for child counseling.* Children can receive counseling or therapy to be taught how to protect themselves from psychological abuse. For example, it can be helpful to children to understand that some problems come from the parents and are not the children's fault.

Mental health professionals should help parents anticipate problems prior to the onset of visitation. If the guidelines are introduced prior to the development of problems, the severity of problems may be significantly reduced.

SUMMARY

Visitation should generally be encouraged and supported. Problems of visitation can often be solved by consultation with family members rather than limitation of visitation. Parent consultation, therapy, and mediation can be effective in reducing visitation problems. Access of some kind is beneficial to most children, and frequent access is important in the absence of severe pathology. Grandparent visitation can be useful to the child if such visitation does not undermine the authority and bonding of the parents with the child. In cases of abuse, supervision of visitation can protect the child from harm and reduce harmful fantasies.

CHAPTER 8

The Unique Problems of the Single Parent

Single-parent families share several characteristics that increase the likelihood of certain strengths and problems in the developmental pathways of the children. These children tend to be given more responsibility, are more autonomous, and are more likely to have housekeeping skills. Despite these advantages, there are numerous disadvantages that increase the probability of problems in these children's development. This chapter reviews the research and clinical experience and gives recommendations about how to better serve the needs of single-parent families.

Laosa (1988) noted that in 1980 the percentage of families in the United States headed by a single mother ranged from 9.5% for Asian groups to 41.8% for black groups. The average for the United States was 12.2%. In 1980, 40.4% of single-parent mothers were divorced, 27.8% separated, 8.9% widowed, and 18.3% never married. In no ethnic group did single-parent fathers with custody constitute more than 5% of all families, and the average for the United States was 2.5%. Thus, the typical single parent continues to be a mother, and the most common way in which she became a single mother is through divorce.

This chapter reviews some special problems of the single-parent household. Chapters 2 and 3 reviewed the research and clinical evidence on the effect of divorce on child development. Those chapters evaluated the effects of exposure to chronic family conflict and loss of contact with one parent. This chapter looks at one of the longer term effects of divorce, single parenting. The clinician needs to remember that the effects of divorce are complex, and various responses may be due to the stress of chronic conflict, the strain of the divorce process, the economic effects of divorce, and the effect of having only one parent.

The two most salient problems of the typical single parent are economics and energy. Most single-parent families have fewer financial resources than do intact families. In part because of problems of financial resources and in part because of the enormous time demands of parenting, most single parents are exhausted. Child rearing, done well, is extraordinarily time consuming, even for two parents. To do this task alone is a burden that is difficult to imagine if one has not been through it (I was raised in a single-parent home). The single parent cannot afford to be ill. No matter how sick the parent, the children still must be fed and cared for. When the child is ill, the single parent may have to stay home (and sometimes lose pay) or leave the child alone. Two-parent families in which both parents are employed have similar problems with child care, but they usually have greater financial resources and can share the workload.

Single-parent families may have problems for a variety of other reasons:

1. The entire culture is organized around two-parent families. School districts often do not have policies that permit mailings to two different addresses concerning school activities. The degree to which two-parent families are accepted as the norm is demonstrated by the fact that even in communities in which the majority of children are no longer living with both biological parents, the schools and child-related organizations are oriented toward two-parent families.

2. Single parenting limits the wisdom of the family (Blechman & Manning, 1976). Because no parent can have the full range of competencies that can be provided by two parents, the quality of problem solving is unlikely to be as good in single-parent families.

3. Emotional support may be more limited.

4. Sex-role development can be impaired by the absence of one parent. Although the absence of a parent can lead to more androgynous orientation, substantial evidence shows that a child's perception of the meaning of belonging to a particular biological sex (and feeling good about that belonging) is determined in part by exposure to warm close relationships with adults of *both* sexes. The issue of sex role is discussed in detail later in this chapter.

5. The child may show concern over separation and abandonment. If the divorce resulted in an abandoning parent, the child, particularly the child aged 3 to 7, may develop concerns about being left alone. This concern over abandonment may develop from fears that misbehavior or angry thoughts will lead to parental rejection. A child may think that if one parent "gets rid of" the other parent because of dissatisfaction with behavior, the same thing may happen to the child. It is difficult for a child to understand that a parent–child relationship has different dynamics than a spousal relationship.

When a child shows concern over parental death, it is sometimes helpful to emphasize how the child will be cared for if the parent is ill (this wording is particularly helpful if death has not been articulated by the child). If the noncustodial parent is involved with the child, abandonment fears due to death are less likely.

My mother informed me that when I was 6, I had intense anxiety when she was even mildly late from work. I was obsessed with the possibility that she might be killed in an automobile accident. (Death phobia, as has been mentioned, often shows up around age 7 or 8.) There was nothing she could do to reassure me that sometimes she had to work a few minutes late or traffic was heavier than usual. One day, I asked what would happen to me. She informed me that she had a will and that I would live with an aunt and uncle. Since I liked that family, my anxiety disappeared. My mother said it was like turning off a faucet. The egocentrism of the young child is focused around "What will happen to me?" It does not occur to the child to worry about what the death would mean to the parent. Only with the empathy of later elementary years does the concern about the shortened life enter into the child's distress.

Concern over abandonment may be particularly acute for children from ages 3 to 7. Magical thinking leads children of these ages to believe that angry thoughts can lead to severe retaliation. School phobias are often based on hostile, dependent relationships with a parent in which the child must protect the parent from the consequences of the angry thoughts. Children may need reassurance that parenting is forever and that they will not be abandoned by the remaining parent. Children with concerns about the death of the custodial parent may need information about what will happen to them should the death occur.

6. The parent's concern about the implications for child development of being raised in a single-parent household can itself lead to problems in child rearing. Some parents raise the standards of strictness to protect the child from the tough world "out there." Others feel the need to compensate for the trauma of single parenthood by overindulging the child. Neither parenting style is in the best interests of child development.

7. Child care may be a constant problem. Finding high-quality, inexpensive child care for young children may be impossible. For older children, the latchkey may provide protection, but no supervision. In one junior high school, one group of latchkey boys deliberately misbehaved so they would be kept after school. Such "punishment" was seen as a preferred alternative to boredom.

8. When the single parent is the mother, finances tend to be a major issue. The burden of single parenting requires more money, and yet women are less able to obtain it. On the average, single mothers earn about 46% of the amount earned by single fathers (Norton & Glick, 1986).

Weiss (1984) noted that even 5 years after separation and divorce, the income of single mothers was about one-half that of married mothers. Whereas welfare and food stamps were used by only 4% of lower income, married households, two-thirds of lower income, divorced mothers received welfare in the first year after separation and one-half received food stamps. This heavy use continued at the 5-year evaluation mark.

Child support payments represent only 11.6% of single divorced mothers' incomes. Never-married, unemployed, nonwhite, young, and low-income single mothers receive the least help from child support payments and are in the greatest need (Fletcher, 1989).

9. Single parenting may encourage inappropriate use of the child as confidant or adviser. (See the discussion on parentification dangers in Chapter 2.)

10. The single parent may be traumatized by the loss of the other parent and may never feel complete or whole (Mendes, 1979). This parent tries to act as both parents to the child and to compensate the child for the loss of the other parent. Such efforts lead to stress, fatigue, anger, guilt, and failure.

A parent who tries to fulfill all roles for the children needs help to attain a more realistic expectation about what is possible or reasonable. This parent needs help in more appropriate problem-solving techniques to solve the needs of the parent and the children.

11. The parent who feels overloaded with work may give older children too much responsibility for the care of younger siblings, producing stress for the older child. Also younger children can sometimes resent the authority of the older child, particularly when the ages are close or when the older child handles the authority in an arbitrary or hostile way (Mendes, 1979).

When an older sibling is given parental responsibility for a child, the clinician should be sure that the parent makes the lines of authority clear. In particular, rules should be clear and authority to impose sanctions should be well defined. Neither child should be subject to the tyranny of the other. In particular, the parent should be sure that the older sibling has adequate maturity to provide control and safety. Minuchin (1974) warned that such a role may be harmful to the older child's development.

THE STIGMA OF SINGLE-PARENT FAMILIES

Substantial evidence indicates that there is significant stigma to belonging to a one-parent family, even in this age of common divorce. Stigma tends to be greater for families of divorce than widowhood, where sympathy often plays a greater role (although sympathy itself can be a problem, as discussed in Chapter 2).

A single parent told me the story of her son's experience in a scout troupe. The scoutmaster indicated that the family was like the tepee, with three poles holding it up: the father pole, the mother pole, and the child. Without each member of the family, the tepee could not stand! This is a most unfortunate message to give a child from a single-parent family: "You are flawed" or "There is something unnatural about your family."

In Boulder, Colorado, another parent informed me that the family found difficulty getting sponsorship in their church because the church did not want to sponsor a single-parent group. In Boulder, 60% of marriages end in divorce.

Other evidence of stigma for single-parent families comes from research. In a study in England, Ferri (1976) asked teachers to rate parental interest in children. Teachers rated single parents, particularly divorced single mothers, as less interested in their children's performance. Single mothers who were widows were considered to be as interested as intact families. Despite these attitudes, the frequency of school visits did not differ for single mothers and two-parent families. Single custodial fathers did have a lower level of parental school contact. Fathers on their own, in this case particularly widowers, were seen as less interested in their children's progress. When social class was controlled statistically, the significant differences disappeared, suggesting that economics plays a major role in the bias against single parents.

Santrock and Tracy (1978) found that teachers saw children from divorced homes as less happy, lower in emotional adjustment, and poorer at coping with stress than children from intact homes. Similar findings were reported by Kellam, Ensminger, & Turner (1977), who found that teacher ratings of children's social adaptation could be predicted from knowledge of the family background, in this case income. Because single mothers have incomes 52% below the incomes of fathers, who are the sole support of their families, this bias could also explain why children of divorce are more often seen as more damaged or poorly adjusted.

Ratings of children from single-parent households may be biased. Children from single-parent households due to death of a parent may receive sympathy, whereas children from divorced homes may be stigmatized.

IS THE RESEARCH ON SINGLE-PARENT HOUSEHOLDS BIASED?

The above discussion on stigma and single-parent families suggests that research based on the judgments of teachers and others in the community about the adjustment level of children from single-parent families compared with those from intact families may have biased results. Research on single-parent households also may be biased for other reasons.

Interestingly, the literature on single parenting is relatively independent of the literature on divorce. This area of research is tremendously flawed. The most apparent flaw has to do with the fact that the research does not always indicate the reason why single-parent status occurred. Many studies treat single-parent status as a unitary classification, as if death, divorce, desertion, or never having been married have the same psychological effects. As a dramatic example of the differences, when a parent is lost due to death, the remaining parent is able to participate in the grieving process. In death, the absent parent is often idealized. After divorce, the remaining parent is likely to view the absent parent as an enemy. The image of the absent parent can have a profound impact on the family members. Research discussed later in this chapter demonstrates that the cause of single-parent status can make a significant difference in research findings.

Blechman (1982) convincingly argued that research on single parenting is so flawed that it is questionable what is really known about these families. Problems listed in Blechman's review include the following:

1. Studies frequently confounded income and social class. When income was statistically controlled, the relationship between family type and adjustment became trivial.
2. Studies often failed to take into account cause and length of parent absence, sex of single parent, and amount and type of contact with absent parent.
3. Studies sometimes matched the upper income group of single families with the lower income group of intact homes. In a study supporting Blechman's concern, Blanchard and Biller (1971) obtained only 4 matched sets of 11 children from a pool of 297 children.
4. Unrepresentative samples were common.
5. Other important variables were realized income, occupational prestige, availability of flexible working hours, perceived environmental control, precipitous drops in income, and drops in status.

THE SINGLE-PARENT FAMILY FROM EACH MEMBER'S POINT OF VIEW

The Child's Point of View

Blechman and Manning (1976) noted that the single-parent child has several disadvantages compared with the two-parent child. There is one less parent to help solve problems. There is no second parent to appeal unfair decisions. Less parental time and attention are available. The single parent also provides a narrower perspective and can train the child in fewer skills.

Schlesinger (1982) asked 40 children for their perceptions of the advantages and disadvantages of living in a single-parent household. These children, who averaged 14.9 years old, had lived in single-parent households for an average of 4.7 years. It is most interesting that some items they named appeared on both lists:

Advantages	Disadvantages
Closer to mother	Not closer to father
More responsibility	Smaller dwelling
Helping in household	Helping in household
Getting along with siblings	Coming home to empty house
More friends	More responsibility
Trusted more	Moving to new area
Moving to new area	Not getting along with siblings
Closer to father	Fewer friends

It is clear from the above lists that single-parent status can lead to diametrically opposed outcomes. The child may perceive that the loss of a parent can increase or decrease the number of friends and that increased responsibility is a blessing or a curse.

The Mother's Point of View

Brandwein, Brown, and Fox (1974) noted that single-parent mothers are at a disadvantage from several points of view. First, their economic power is quite limited. Economic discrimination against women has been extensively documented. Even though the majority of men do not continue support, the courts are reluctant to take legal action against nonpaying fathers. Second, single-parent mothers command less authority in society. They are taken less seriously and respected less than men. Third, single-parent mothers are less likely to obtain homemaking services.

Quinn and Allen (1989) extensively interviewed 30 single white mothers, all employed outside the home. Lack of money was the primary concern of 80% of the women. Lack of time to accomplish all the needed tasks was a serious concern for all but two. Child care was a major concern for two-thirds, and 70% worried about the children's quality of life. These women had low self-esteem and felt badly about their failure to provide an idealized two-parent family for their children.

Because mothers are more likely to obtain physical custody (even in joint legal custody arrangements), the economic and physical burden of child rearing is particularly likely to fall on mothers. Single mothers (as well as married mothers) spend 10 to 20 more hours per week in all kinds of work than nonparents (Burden, 1986). While performing well on the job, it is at the expense of physical and emotional well-being. In a study of mothers' distribution of time in single- and two-parent families in California, Sanik and Mauldin (1986) found that single mothers and married mothers provided the same amount of nonphysical care to their children.

Evidence suggests that single mothers spend the same amount of time as married mothers in communication with their children. It is a myth that children of single-mother households suffer from lack of attention.

Work overload is a particularly high risk to employed single mothers. Single mothers accomplish their work overload by spending less time on household tasks, child care, personal care, and volunteer time. Both single and married *employed* mothers spent less time in recreation than unemployed mothers (Sanik & Mauldin, 1986).

The Father's Point of View

Relatively little research has been done on the single-father family because the frequency of such families has been relatively low in the past. Schlesinger (1982) listed the problems of single-parent fathers, which included:

1. *Financial problems.* The single-parent father may not be able to get public assistance.
2. *Child care.*
3. *Social life.* It is interesting to note that although fathers identify problems maintaining a social life as a single parent, this problem was not mentioned in the studies on mothers.
4. *Homemaking.* Basic housekeeping chores (e.g., buying groceries, washing dishes and clothes, and mending clothes) can be difficult skills to learn for the first time as an adult, particularly for strongly sex-role stereotyped males.
5. *Personal problems.* Men in general seldom seek professional help or friends to deal with role strain.
6. *Community support.* Such support seems lacking for single fathers.

Smith (1976) indicated that single fathers tend to adjust well if they have had anticipatory socialization, prior experience in child rearing, education in child development, previous participation in household responsibilities, previous participation in child discipline, and experience in nurturing the children.

In discussing the problems of single parents regardless of sex, Bray and Anderson (1984) noted that role overload was a common problem. Money was a constant problem. Groceries, meals, child care, and discipline all were demanding. Such parents also felt more intensely the fear, hurt, and anger of the children, without the buffer of another parent. Similar problems were mentioned by Frey (1986).

Because there is not another parent to serve as a buffer or source of social support, single parents are more vulnerable to the hurt and anger experienced by their children. Such potential enmeshment may increase the pain of parenting and lead to inappropriate problem solving.

Keshet and Rosenthal (1978) studied 128 fathers with children under age 7. These fathers were typically noncustodial, upper middle class professionals. They remained very active and in close contact with their young children. Their initial reaction to single parenthood was the feeling of having failed their children, regardless of whether they had initiated the separation. They experienced significant fear in learning the new roles. They felt overwhelmed at the thought of assuming the parental role on their own and questioned their competence as caretakers. Frequently, the fathers did not know their children's likes or dislikes. They found planning, organizing, and anticipating the needs of the children to be difficult.

Risman (1987) compared the behavior of custodial single fathers with the behavior of single mothers, dual-paycheck married couples, and one-paycheck married couples. The study looked particularly at widowed or deserted single fathers who did not voluntarily choose that role ($n = 55$). This aspect of the design allowed assessment of the father's ability to parent even when he did not ask for that role.

Parent's gender and being a single parent (regardless of gender) were equally strong in predicting parent–child intimacy. Scoring high on a measure of femininity (regardless of gender) was the best predictor of intimacy. However, because nurturance tends to be a "feminine" trait, the ability to nurture may be one of the areas measured. Single fathers and dual-paycheck mothers had the same levels of femininity (Risman, 1987).

Risman and Park (1988) concluded from additional analyses that the custodial parent's gender was unrelated to parental attachment, household organization, and child development. Being employed and continuing to be the primary caretaker (as before the separation) were related to reports of positive child development.

THE EXPRESSION OF AFFECTION IN
SINGLE-PARENT HOUSEHOLDS

In a two-parent family, the spousal bond existed before the parent–child bond. In healthy families, this bond is stronger than the parent–child bond. When the bond between one parent and a child is stronger, the parenting role can become confused and a coalition against the other "unreasonable" parent may develop. In single-parent families, the absence of another parent tends to encourage a coalition anyway. Triads tend to prevent two-person coalitions aligned against the third (Blechman & Manning, 1976). Divorce or widowhood intensifies the parent–child bond (Blechman & Manning, 1976). The loss of a parent can reduce competition, increase interactions, and improve the affection expressed between parent and child. This bond can become so strong that the parent and child will resist any intrusion and the parent is prevented from developing a successful remarriage.

One side effect of this intensification of the affectionate relationship between the parent and child is the parentification process (discussed in Chapter 2). The child begins to care for the parent by cooking, cleaning, and providing reassurance. Young children may join the parental bed. Adolescents cannot separate from the parent, particularly if the parent is depressed. Parents begin to discuss with their children work-related problems or their romances. Blechman and Manning (1976) indicated that the intensification of the parent–child bond is more likely if the child is the same sex as the parent, particularly for females.

Single parents should be encouraged to maintain their parental roles. Parents should be encouraged to find an adult friend to share feelings about work or dating and to avoid sharing those feelings with the child. A peer relationship with a child can lead to premature adult responsibilities for the child and is sometimes quite anxiety provoking.

DISCIPLINE IN SINGLE-PARENT FAMILIES

A common problem is the single mother who is referred for clinical help because she has problems with a 13-year-old son. These situations often have similar family patterns. The family has been ineffective in terms of discipline. The child never learned self-control. He left elementary school with its relatively tolerant, warm atmosphere and entered junior high with its much higher demands for self-control. Without self-control, the son starts failing in schoolwork. The mother responds by moving to excessive strictness. For example, I have seen several mothers enforce long-term (a month or more) groundings that were ineffective. At the same time that the son developmentally needs to separate from the mother, the mother is trying to exert increased control. When this intervention is ineffective, the teenager either rebels by passively withdrawing from school and home or actively refusing to cooperate at any level. Not surprisingly, these families are difficult to treat.

In the family where the discipline has broken down and the parent no longer has control over the child, individual treatment tends to be relatively ineffective. Family-oriented therapy is more likely to return the control of discipline to the parent.

Heath and MacKinnon (1988) evaluated the social competence in 80 children from 8 to 11 years of age in single-parent families. For male children, higher levels of social competence were predicted in a multiple regression by *higher* levels of education of the mother, mother's acceptance of the child, and use of firm control and by *lower* levels of psychological control (using $p < .10$, a lax criterion). For girls, higher social competence was predicted by lower use of a support system by the mother and less use by parents of firm control ($p < .05$). Mothers used lax control more for sons than for daughters, and lax control predicted less social competence in boys. For girls, moderate control was related to social competence.

In a study that compared single-parent families with intact and remarried families, Amato (1987) found that children in single-parent families perceived themselves as having less father support, less control, and less punishment, and as having more autonomy, more household responsibility, more conflict with siblings, and less family cohesion than children from intact families. Autonomy was expressed in more lenient bedtimes, clothes buying, and going out.

Blechman and Manning (1976) felt that two-parent families have more reinforcement power than one-parent families. They argued that single-parent children are involved in more aversive control of parents. Blechman and Manning indicated that single parents have difficulty diluting the children's aversive control. If the child is successful in controlling the parent through tantrums, crying, misbehavior, or chronic illness, the parent finds parenting less rewarding and may actively resent the child. The parent begins to feel that the efforts at being good to the child result only in bad being given back. The danger of such a dynamic is that the parent becomes tempted to withdraw positive interactions. The fatigued parent can get into a coercive cycle with the child in which the parent tends to ignore positive behaviors and respond only when the child has misbehaved. Blechman and Manning felt that successful interactions in the single parent must be based on positive rewards.

Children who are ignored for positive behaviors can develop fears of nonexistence. Such children will misbehave to get a parental response, reassuring themselves of their ability to have some impact in the world. Working with such parents requires intensive support from the therapist to energize the parents to provide support to the child.

Sack, Mason, and Higgins (1985) investigated the retrospective report of 802 Oregon adults about the use of abusive punishment in their childhoods. The random sample of adults was asked about the ways in which they were punished as children, the reasons for punishment, and the age at which this punishment occurred. Punishment was coded as abusive for answers such as being hit with a fist or knocked unconscious, and as serious but less severe for answers such as severe whippings in areas other than the buttocks.

Abuse was more common in single-parent households. Either parent was equally likely to be the abuser. Well-established abuse occurred in 9% of single-parent households (regardless of cause of single status) and 5% of two-parent households, a statistically significant difference. For divorced parents, the abuse level was 14%. The data did not provide information about whether the abuse occurred before or after the separation. Participants who said that they got along with their fathers best reported no well-established abuse regardless of the reason for the family breakup or the gender of parent (although the father was judged the most compatible parent in only 19% of the cases).

The second National Family Violence Survey comprised a national probability sample of 6,002 households. In this study (Gelles, 1989), single parents were not found to use physical violence toward children more than other parents, but rates of severe and very severe violence were substantially higher in single-parent households. Single-parent custodial fathers were particularly likely to abuse. For fathers below the poverty line, single fathers were 4.2 times more likely to abuse than fathers in two-caretaker families (including married and cohabiting fathers). Their abuse rate was 406 per 1,000, an extraordinarily high rate.

Abuse is more likely from custodial fathers living below the poverty line. Abuse is also more likely in families with rapidly accumulating stress. Single parenting would seem to produce sufficient stress as to increase the likelihood of abuse. The mental health professional should help the parent to avoid physical punishment and coercive hostile interactions. Impulse control and cooling off periods may be helpful when anger is out of control. Use of nonphysical punishment, rewards for appropriate behaviors, cognitive explanations for rules, and bonding facilitation are likely to be more effective.

FATHER ABSENCE AND DEVELOPMENT IN BOYS

As previously stated, much of the research on father absence is flawed because the reason for father absence is not included as a variable. In many of the studies, it is also not possible to determine whether children have any contact with the fathers. As Biller (1981) noted, many children who visit with their fathers may have more actual contact with their fathers than children in father-present homes. Biller also noted that father-absent children may not be paternally deprived if there is an adequate father surrogate. Competent mothers also compensate for the lack of a father and may give a child a more positive view of adult men than the intact family with a weak, ineffective, withdrawn, or passive father.

Masculine Sex Role

Substantial evidence indicates that masculine sex roles are affected by father absence. Sears, Maccoby, and Levin (1957) found that father-absent boys were less aggressive and had less sex-role differentiation in doll play activity than father-present boys. Many other studies indicate that father-absent boys are seen as less aggressive, less masculine, and more dependent.

Hetherington (1966) felt that father absence before age 4 or 5 affected masculine development. She reported that 9- to 12-year-old, father-absent boys were less masculine, were more dependent on peers, and engaged in fewer physical contact games. Biller (1969) set the age of importance of father absence for sex-role development at 4 or 5. Santrock (1970) found differences in sex-role development in boys when separation occurred before and after 2 years of age. Boys who became father absent before age 2 were less trusting, were less industrious, and had more feelings of inferiority than boys who became father absent between ages 3 and 5.

Hodges, Wechsler, and Ballantine (1979) found that mother-custody, preschool age children of divorce were less sex-role stereotyped. Boys were less aggressive than the comparison group of boys from intact families. Vess, Schwebel, and Moreland (1983) found that the more postdivorce conflict, the more "feminine" children of both sexes were.

There is nothing intrinsically valuable about appropriate sex-role behavior. Indeed, it can be argued that defining appropriate behaviors by biological sex only limits behavior. The evidence is overwhelming, however, that boys with inappropriate sex-role development have lower self-esteem and are more likely to be rejected by peers. Therefore, anything that the mental health professional can do to foster positive images of being male in boys is likely to benefit them. In addition, it would be valuable to provide a warm, caring, positive adult male role model for boys without fathers to increase the chances of boys having high self-esteem for being male. Reinforcing assertive behavior can be of value to both boys and girls. Eliminating effeminate mannerisms in boys without fathers is helpful and does not indicate that important feminine sex-role stereotyped behavior (e.g., interpersonal sensitivity) is undesirable.

One of the strange manifestations of behavior in boys that I have not seen discussed in the literature is the development of stereotypic mannerisms that clearly communicate an effeminate identification. These mannerisms are strange because they are exaggerations of feminine behavior that rarely appear in girls. I have observed father-absent boys exhibit grossly exaggerated hip swings while walking that simply did not appear in girls. Other boys develop the "limp wrist" that is the stereotype of male femininity, but relatively rare in girls. These behaviors can be discouraged and more masculine behaviors supported without necessarily encouraging a "macho" orientation toward the world.

Several studies indicate that surrogate sex-role models make a difference in masculine development in boys. A brother, uncle, grandfather, or male boarder may provide a boy with the appropriate role model for heightened self-esteem. Vess et al. (1983) reported that boys from divorced families with older brothers were more masculine than boys without older brothers. Boys with older brothers were also less dependent. If the mother encourages masculine behavior, the boys will behave in a more masculine way (Aldous, 1972; Biller, 1968, 1969, 1970, 1971).

Cognitive Changes in Father-Absent Boys

The general assumption in the literature of the effect of father absence on cognitive development has led to the conclusion that boys from single-parent families do less well academically. In an extensive review of the literature, Shinn (1978) noted that 12 of 54 studies looking at general measures of cognitive ability found deficits in quantitative performance and only one found improvement.

In one of the few studies done on infants, Pedersen, Rubenstein, and Yarrow (1979) looked at the cognitive development of 55 black infants aged 5 to 6 months living in lower socioeconomic circumstances. Of these, 27 were in father-absent homes. Male infants who had experienced minimal interaction with their fathers were significantly lower on the Mental Development Index on the Bayley Scales of Infant Development and in measures of social responsiveness, secondary circular reactions, and preferences for novel stimuli. Female infants seemed to be unaffected by the father loss.

Pederson et al. felt that alternative explanations, such as socioeconomic status, extended family in the household, and maternal behavior, were ruled out as factors. It is difficult, however, to develop sensitive measures of socioeconomic status that reflect quality of living. The numbers of adults in the households were the same for father-absent and father-present homes. No true test of maternal behavior was made to eliminate this alternative explanation, although the authors noted that substitute caregivers were common for both types of homes. On a very small subsample, direct observation was made of maternal behavior and no differences were found.

Blanchard and Biller (1971) found that, with respect to both grades and achievement test scores, early father-absent boys were underachievers. Late father-absent boys and low father-present boys usually obtained somewhat below grade level scores, whereas high father-present boys performed above grade level. The inclusion of low and high father presence as a control was a most helpful innovation. Too many investigators have treated father presence as if it were a unitary variable.

The reason for father absence also has an effect on cognitive functioning. Although father absence due to divorce, desertion, or separation was found to have its most negative effects for the initial 2 years of life for boys and girls, father absence due to death had the most negative cognitive effects when it occurred from 6 to 9 years of age for boys (Santrock, 1972). These findings suggest that the effect of father absence is not simply the absence of a role model. Anger, grief, and the reaction of the remaining parent all may play a role in the effect of father loss on academic achievement.

Several investigators have proposed that father absence results in a "feminine" pattern of skills and deficits in cognitive functioning, with relatively higher verbal skills and lower quantitative skills. In Shinn's (1978) review, 12 studies were found in which specific decrements in quantitative performance were obtained for father-absent children. Of 11 studies that reviewed verbal performance, 5 found improved verbal performance.

Lessing, Zagorin, and Nelson (1970, cited by Shinn, 1978) noted a socioeconomic effect of father absence. For "working class" families, father absence was associated with generally lower IQ scores on the Wechsler Intelligence Scale for Children (WISC). For middle class families, father-absent children had higher overall Verbal scores than father-present children, but lower scores on two performance subtests. These results suggest that father absence has its effect in several areas: role modeling, cultural values, and economics.

Shinn (1978) concluded that sex-role identification did not play an important role in academic performance. Financial hardship, high levels of anxiety, and low levels of parent–child interaction were seen as important causes of poor performance in children from single-parent households.

In a longitudinal study done in England of 17,000 children, including 418 children in father-absent homes (discussed in more detail in the later section on mother absence), Ferri (1976) found that there were no differences in amount of school absence for those in fatherless or two-parent families, either before or after demographic variables were controlled. Children raised in father-absent homes had lower arithmetic scores than children in intact families, but not as low as children in mother-absent homes. There was no sex difference in arithmetic ability. For reading ability, there was a negative effect of father absence, but this effect disappeared when the variable "free school meals" was controlled, suggesting that low income was a major contributing factor to low reading ability in father-absent homes.

One of the most carefully done studies controlling for sample selection and socioeconomic factors was that by Guidubaldi, Cleminshaw, Perry, and Mcloughlin (1983), who examined school performance for first, third, and fifth graders from divorced and intact homes. Children from intact families had higher Full Scale IQs, Wide Range Achievement Test scores, and higher spelling scores. When socioeconomic factors were statistically controlled (remember, a weak indicator of socioeconomics was the only one available), all of the academic differences between children of divorce and intact families dropped out, and only the Full Scale IQ difference remained in terms of cognitive factors.

Additional evidence for the effect of father absence comes from research of the effect of father surrogates on cognitive development. Shinn (1978) cited three studies in which father surrogates and stepfathers had a remedial effect on father-absent children. For example, Santrock (1972) found that remarriage of boys' mothers had a positive effect on academic performance. Guidubaldi et al. (1983) found that the presence of a stepfather for children with early father absence led to no deficits in cognitive functioning, whereas children with early father absence and no stepfather did have problems.

The research is relatively clear that boys experience deficits in cognitive functioning as a function of father absence. For middle class boys, father absence may result in improved verbal skills, but quantitative skills tend to be lower for father-absent boys regardless of socioeconomic level. Father surrogates and stepfathers, particularly if present during early childhood, may negate the effect of father absence. Given the evidence that a close relationship with a father or father surrogate makes a difference in academic functioning, mental health professionals who wish to help families optimize cognitive functioning, should encourage warm, frequent father contact. If father abandonment has occurred, it would be important to encourage the mother to seek the help of a Big Brother or an adult male relative or friend.

Emotional Adjustment and Father-Absent Boys

One 7-year-old boy was chronically afraid of trying new activities. He was afraid to swim, to be alone in a room in his house, to bicycle, and to play soccer. He had a warm relationship with both parents, who were divorced. It is possible that his fearfulness was related to specific parenting styles, modeling, or the fact that his parents had gotten a divorce.

There is evidence that emotional problems are more likely in single-parent families. Felner, Stolberg, and Cowen (1975) found that children from single-parent households were more likely to have school adjustment problems. If the parents were divorced, acting-out behavior was more common. If the father had died, the child was more likely to show moody withdrawal.

Santrock and Wohlford (1970) found that for father absence due to divorce (compared with father absence due to death), boys had more difficulty delaying gratification (e.g., waiting for a reward). Hoffman (1971) noted that father-absent boys consistently scored lower than father-present boys on a variety of indices of moral development. Socioeconomic status and reason for father absence were not controlled because the data were not collected for the purpose of this particular analysis. The inability to determine the effects of the reason for father absence is a problem in many of the earlier father-absent studies; thus, it is difficult to attribute the problems found to father absence per se.

FATHER ABSENCE AND DEVELOPMENT IN GIRLS

Some data suggest that girls are less affected by father absence than boys, but other research studies have indicated that girls are probably as much affected by father absence in terms of social development and heterosexual development.

Sex Role Identification

Marino and McCowan (1976) found that for girls, father absence seemed to lead to a closer identification with the female role. There was difficulty, however, in the development of male–female relationships after puberty. More negative attitudes toward males were likely in father-absent homes than in father-present homes. In families from divorce, college age girls with older brothers were less masculine than similar girls without older brothers (Vess et al., 1983). Girls with low father availability during childhood had less feminine self-concepts than those who reported high father availability (Fish, 1969). G. Jacobson and Ryder (1969) noted that many women who had father absence early in life had difficulties in achieving a satisfying sexual relationship with husbands. Hetherington (1972) found that father-absent girls in adolescence had greater mother dependency. Girls had the most difficulties in their heterosexual interactions if the father absence had begun before age 5. Vess et al. (1983) found no differences in sex-role identification for college students as a function of the earlier divorce of parents, so the effects of sex-role identification may diminish over time. Hainline and Feig (1978) also found no differences by college age for girls with father loss.

In her review of sex-typing research, Huston (1983) concluded that fathers play an important, but not irreplacable, role in girls' acquisition of heterosexual skills and sex-typed intellectual skills. Girls were given less emphasis in the father-absent literature since it was assumed that identification with the same-sex parent was crucial. Other theories have assumed a reciprocal interaction process between opposite-sex parent and child, which would explain why father absence should influence girls' sex-role development.

Ferri (1976) found no sex difference in adjustment as a function of father loss. Both boys and girls from fatherless homes were seen by teachers as less well adjusted (remember potential teacher bias) than children from intact families. When other variables were controlled (economics, number of schools attended, free school meals, family size, social class, sex of child independent of family type, foster care, and parental aspirations), the relationship of family type and adjustment disappeared, again indicating that economics plays a major role in the relationship of adjustment and single parenting. As might be expected, regardless of family type, girls were better adjusted than boys.

Cognitive Changes in Father-Absent Girls

Shinn (1978) noted that in 12 of the 21 reviewed studies that included girls, father absence had a detrimental effect on the girls' academic performance. This number of studies was about the same proportion of studies that found negative effects for boys. Marino and McCowan (1976) found that father absence enhanced verbal skills in girls and reduced quantitative skills. These effects were found for early, temporary, and permanent father absences. Lessing et al. (1970) found lower ability in perceptual-motor and manipulative spatial skills for both sexes as a function of father absence. In Ferri's (1976) study, low income was apparently a factor for poor reading skills for boys and girls, but poor ability in arithmetic remained statistically significant, even when "free lunch meals" was controlled.

MOTHER ABSENCE AND CHILD DEVELOPMENT

Research on mother absence is practically nonexistent, mainly because the frequency of mother absence is so low that to obtain samples that permit inferential statistics and generalization is almost impossible.

In a study already discussed for single fathers, Ferri (1976) reported on a British longitudinal study of 17,000 children born in Great Britain during 1 week in 1958. These children were followed up at 7 and 11 years of age. The study included a medical exam and interviews of the custodial parent (usually the mother) and a teacher. Although the original purpose of the study was a national perinatal mortality survey, the data provided an opportunity to study one-parent families. These data, however, come from a time that preceded the sharp increase in divorce rates in Western cultures, so that generalization to present-day results may be somewhat limited. Certainly, the degree of stigma or uniqueness may be less today.

The follow-up at 11 years of age included 11,385 children. Of these, 88 were in motherless homes, about half by divorce and half by death. (This number compares to 418 in fatherless homes.) This study is particularly important in that it is one of the few studies with a substantial number of mother-absent families. With more father custody being granted in modern courts, mother absence may be on the rise, permitting more research on the effect of mother absence. The results are discussed below.

Mother Absence and Development in Boys

School Performance

Ferri (1976) found that motherless boys had statistically significantly *better* overall school attendance than boys from intact homes. There was no difference as a function of the cause of the mother absence. For arithmetic performance, boys from motherless families, due to divorce or separation, obtained lower arithmetic scores than boys from intact families. For reading, the data were difficult to assess, but Ferri concluded that the mother-absent boys had significantly lower reading scores after other variables were controlled statistically. Economics, foster care, geographic mobility, parental aspirations, family size, and social class were all statistically significant variables. Although mother absence was significant, the amount of variance explained by mother absence was quite small compared with these other variables.

Social Adjustment

There was no evidence from Ferri's (1976) study that loss of a mother was in itself related to poorer overall adjustment. Loss of either parent through divorce was related to a child of either sex being less well adjusted than if the child was from a widowed or intact family. All statistical differences disappeared, however, when other demographic variables were controlled, findings similar to those discussed in Chapter 3.

Mother Absence and Development in Girls

The major concern for boys has been the effect of father absence and a lack of an adult male role model. The concern for development in girls should likewise focus on mother absence.

School Performance

In Ferri's (1976) study, girls in mother-absent homes (due to divorce or separation) had lower performance in arithmetic than those in intact homes. Foster care, family size, parental aspirations, and social class were more powerful predictors of arithmetic performance than mother absence regardless of the child's gender. The reason for mother absence may have had some influence on arithmetic performance. Mother-absent children of divorce had lower arithmetic scores than children who were without mothers due to other causes.

As observed in boys, mother-absent girls had lower performance in reading after other demographic variables were controlled, but the demographic variables accounted for more of the variance. The statistical analysis suffered from the small sample size.

Social Adjustment

Again, the results for girls in Ferri's (1976) study mirrored the results for boys. Girls from divorced families had poorer adjustment than girls who lost a parent by death (regardless of sex of parent) or girls from intact families. When demographic variables such as economics were controlled, the differences disappeared, suggesting that there was no evidence that the loss of mothers had any independent effect on girls' adjustment.

Santrock and Warshak's (1979) study on father custody found that father-custody girls were less feminine, less independent, and more demanding than mother-custody girls. This research suggests that girls may be less sex-role stereotyped and not as mature if in mother-absent homes, whereas boys do not seem to suffer.

Ferri (1976) noted that one reason why mother absence may have fewer apparent negative effects may be that mother-absent homes suffer much less from financial hardship than father-absent homes. Standard of living was lower, however, when either parent was absent.

EMOTIONAL ADJUSTMENT AND SINGLE PARENTING

Rubinstein, Shaver, and Peplau (1979) looked at the adjustment of adults who had experienced parental divorce when children. The earlier the divorce, the more likely the adults were to have low self-esteem and to experience loneliness as adults. They reported worry, despair, feelings of worthlessness, fearfulness, and general separation anxiety.

Mueller and Cooper (1986) surveyed 196 people aged 34 who were raised in single-parent or two-parent families. Adults raised by single parents had lower educational, occupational, and economic attainments. Although the authors proposed that the effect may be mediated by earlier marriage and children or lack of role modeling on problem solving, economics is also a likely mediator. Many fathers who pay child support stop such payments on the child's eighteenth birthday, and relatively few provide the costs for a college education.

A variety of clinicians have talked about the scapegoating that can occur in any family, intact or divorced, that may lead to one child's being identified as the problem. Anxiety and anger can be displaced toward one child.

In single-parent families, where loss and anger are common reactions to divorce (or loss by death), transference of feelings from the absent parent to the child is more likely to occur if the child is somehow reminiscent of that parent. Often, the basis of transference is toward the child of the same sex as the absent parent. This transference is even more likely if there is a strong physical resemblance. Several parents have reported difficulty in handling a particular behavior pattern in a child when that behavior pattern reminds them of the absent parent, particularly when that behavior pattern was a cause for the divorce. For example, one mother became incapacitated in the face of her son's lying because it reminded her of her ex-husband's lying. She had been unable to deal with her ex-husband's behavior and now could not deal with her son's.

A parent can become ineffective due to transference of reactions to a child, such that the parent identifies the child's behavior as "identical" to the unacceptable behavior of the absent parent. Although the child may indeed have picked up the unacceptable behavior through modeling, the parent needs to respond to a child in substantially different ways than to a spouse. The parent may need to be reminded that some problems in childhood are typical childhood problems (e.g., lying and stealing) and are not necessarily signs of inevitable undesirable adult outcomes. Family therapy may be needed to help the parent reassert the parenting role.

Blechman and Manning (1976) proposed that if the parent is persistently inefficient, the child may feel forced to take over that role, often in a maladaptive fashion. The child may take the role of the "identified patient" in order to help the family unite to deal with the unacceptable behavior. In my experience, this role is considerably more likely if the child learns that intrafamily tension is substantially reduced when everyone is angry at that child.

The problem of transference for the parent is similar to the problem of identification by the child. Kaseman (1974) noted that if the identification of the child is with the devalued self of the remaining parent, the child could come to loathe himself or herself. If the identification is with the absent parent, the child can carry unresolved feelings of pain.

Blechman (1982) argued that divorce or single parenting may result not in maladjustment, but in developmental lag. Santrock (1972), for example, found that although father-absent children had deficits in performance in the third grade, by the sixth grade there was only a nonsignificant trend. Vess et al. (1983) looked at the effects of early parental divorce on the sex-role development of college students. Of the sample, 84 had experienced parental divorce prior to the tenth birthday and 135 after the tenth birthday. There were no effects found of early divorce on sex role.

Blechman (1982) also noted that there have been suggestions that early parent loss may even lead to excellence among the highly gifted. Also, girls reared by single mothers may be better prepared in terms of preparation for employment, but suffer in preparation for traditional marriage. Blechman concluded that when multiple regression takes into account correlated variables, there is little relationship between adjustment and family type. Educational level, income, and quality of parenting are likely to be far more important variables.

There is evidence that single-parent families may struggle with problems not encountered by two-parent families. Zastowny and Lewis (1989) found that people from single-parent families saw their families as more disengaged, more inflexible, and higher in unresolved conflict than did people from intact families.

Huntley, Phelps, and Rehm (1986) investigated depression in 53 eldest children from mother-custody homes. Children were from 6 to 10 years old. Depression was measured by the child's self-report and by the mother's ratings. Boys reported themselves as more depressed than girls. Mother's level of depression was not related to self-report of the child's depression, but was related to the mother's perception of the child as depressed.

Huntley and Phelps (1990) investigated levels of depression in 76 oldest or only children of divorce who were from 6 to 10 years old. Children were of mixed race (unusual in such research) and were a mean of 4 years postseparation. On the measure of depression, 25% of the children were in the clinical range. In a series of multiple regressions, only child's gender predicted level of depression (probably more for girls, but the report was unclear). Contrary to what might have been expected, time since separation, age of child, income of parents, and frequency of contact with noncustodial parent were unrelated to levels of depression. When the type of person with whom the child had relationships was explored, only high-quality contact with adults other than family members predicted lower depression. Cause and effect remain undetermined: Although poor quality relationships may lead to depression, relating to a less depressed child is easier.

DELINQUENCY AND DIVORCE

The Cambridge-Somerville study (cited in Glueck & Glueck, 1950) was the historical antecedent to the assumption that "broken homes" cause delinquency. This study assumed that single-parent families were characterized by family disorganization and that this disorganization caused delinquency. Bowlby (1946) stated that broken homes caused delinquency. A subsequent analysis of the Cambridge-Somerville data (Craig & Glick, 1963) indicated that family conflict and parental criminal activity were better predictors of delinquency than were single-parent homes.

Nye (1958) concluded that children from single-parent homes committed only slightly more delinquent offenses than children from two-parent homes, but were twice as likely to be institutionalized for such offenses when caught than were children from two-parent homes. When children in two-parent homes were apprehended, the parents were more likely to seek psychotherapy as a solution for the problem and more likely to convince the courts to provide warnings or probation.

In a study of 3,700 high school students (Blechman, Berberian, & Thompson, 1977), self-reported drug use was not related to family type. However, peer drug use, age, parental occupation, remarriage, gender, and parental unemployment were all important predictors of drug use. As additional evidence that single parenting may not cause delinquency, Schulz and Wilson (1973) found that frequency of drug use by peers accounted for 75% of the variance in adolescent drug use, whereas family type accounted for a trivial amount of the variance. Maskin and Brookins (1974) noted that for 126 female delinquents in a girls' treatment center, recidivism was more likely to occur in two-parent families. Marital adjustment of two-parent families was a better predictor of successful treatment of the female delinquent than was coming from a divorced home.

In a review of the literature from 1970 to 1980, Cashion (1982) concluded that delinquency is not associated with a child's coming from a female-headed family, but is clearly related to poverty. Violence was highest for delinquent boys from two-parent families. Although delinquent girls had negative perceptions of fathers, they were not more likely to come from father-absent homes.

Finally, Blechman (1982) argued that cause and effect may be reversed. Temperamentally hard-to-handle children may increase the likelihood that parents will divorce by increasing stress on the family and may even encourage parents to divorce.

The evidence that single parenting plays a causative role in the development of delinquency is meager and probably an artifact of economics and bias.

HELP FOR SINGLE PARENTS

The journal *Family Relations* has published three very useful bibliographies. The first lists several organizations designed to help single parents, including those for men, women, the widowed, older mothers, and those concerned about children's rights, child snatching, child support, displaced homemakers, economics, child care, education, and the military ("Help for Single Parents," 1986). The second bibliography is a list of films useful to lay persons, teachers, and mental health interventionists on single parenting and custody (Kimmons & Gaston, 1986). Finally, Schlesinger (1986) provided a list of 80 annotated references from 1978 to 1985 on single parenting.

SUMMARY

Single-parent families are likely to have significant problems, with the consequences of single parenting, such as lower income, playing a major role.

Discipline is more difficult in single-parent households, particularly if enmeshment or disengagement is a problem. Sex-role behaviors are likely to be affected. School performance is also likely to be lower, although low income may play a major role in academic decline. With father absence, arithmetic skills may be lowered and adjustment in boys and girls affected. With mother absence, drawing conclusions is more difficult due to the limited number of studies, but reading skills may be affected and adjustment does seem to be poorer. Delinquency rates may not be greater in single-parent families, but court involvement is greater for children of single parents.

To be effective in working with children of divorce, the mental health professional needs to understand the impact of single parenting and the impact of predivorce conflict on the separation and postdivorce behaviors of parents and children. Some of the postdivorce stresses that children experience are related to the problems of the single-parent family.

CHAPTER 9

The Unique Problems of the Remarried Parent

> A 9-year-old boy refused to eat off a plate if his stepfather had washed it. If his stepfather was the last to take a bath, the boy would scour the tub before using it.
>
> A 7-year-old boy goes into a rage over his father's remarriage even though the boy is very fond of his new stepmother.
>
> A 12-year-old girl worries about a stepmother who seems to be jealous of the attention she gets from her father.

At the remarriage of a parent, a large number of children are referred for evaluation and treatment. The number of children who have to deal with the stress of the remarriage of one or more parents is quite large. Glick (1988, 1989a, 1989b) noted that in 1987, 8.3% of all married couples were part of stepfamilies (over 5.2 million families), and 40% of families today can expect to become stepfamilies before the youngest child is 18. Approximately 72% of recently divorced women are expected to remarry, ranging from a high of 81% for women with no children to a low of 57% for women with three or more children (Glick, 1989a, 1989b). Hernandez (1988) estimated that by 1990, only 56% of children would be living with two natural parents living together. Thus, treatment of children of divorce is more often than not the treatment of children of remarriage.

In Wallerstein and Blakeslee's (1989) 10-year follow-up report of the original Wallerstein and Kelly (1980c) sample, they reported that half the children in the study had experienced a second divorce of one parent. They noted that only 1 of 8 children in their sample felt that both parents had successful remarriages.

In the National Survey of Children for children from 7 to 11 years old and a follow-up 5 years later, Baydar (1988) found that remarriage was associated with an increase in emotional problems, with difficulty in concentration, withdrawal, and unhappiness for boys and girls and an increase in restlessness for boys. Thus, the clinician who wants to be effective working with children of divorce must address the dynamics of stress associated with remarriage. Although most parents expect difficulties with remarriage, many parents are surprised at how difficult the adjustment is (Messinger, 1976).

Indeed, the happiness of the new family may be more dependent on the stepparent–stepchild relationship than on the marital relationship. Crosbie-Burnett (1984) found that the stepfather–stepchild relationship of 87 Caucasians accounted for 59% of the variance in overall family happiness, whereas marital happiness accounted for only an additional 10%. Discipline and nurturance between the stepfather and stepchild correlated with family happiness .62 and .45, respectively, but added no additional variance in predicting family happiness.

It is not unusual for a new family to want to exclude the remaining parent and to wish for a new "nuclear" family. The realities of stepfamilies and nuclear families, however, makes them significantly different.

Because continued, warm, affectionate contact with both parents seem to be supportive for the best adjustment in children, remarriage usually works best for children if the biological parent and the stepparent do not try to exclude each other from the children's lives. If the biological parent is abandoning, the stepparent may take a more active parental role, particularly if the children are young.

Remarriage serves to precipitate children's problems for several reasons. First, the remarriage is a concrete statement that the parents are not going to reconcile. Given the frequency with which children harbor such fantasies, it is not surprising that children sometimes keep such fantasies alive for years. Any repressed anger at the parents comes forth at word of remarriage. In addition, the children may actively work toward breaking up the new marriage to make parental reconciliation possible.

The child may also have unresolved mourning of the previous relationship. Kleinman, Rosenberg, and Whiteside (1979) argued that prior to adolescence, children are developmentally unable to mourn a loss fully. Clearly, children do mourn, but their cognitive functioning may be limited in terms of understanding the loss until they reach adolescence. Thies (1977) argued that remarriage usually occurs before the children have had an opportunity to resolve the grief associated with the divorce. She felt that whether the divorce trauma is adequately resolved is the major determinant of whether the child will adjust to the remarriage.

The child is placed in a position of significant stress. Having previously lost a relationship, the child is again invited to attach and become vulnerable to the possibility of going through another divorce. Because second marriages have a higher divorce rate than first marriages, such concerns are quite realistic.

Children may resist accepting a new marriage because they wish reconciliation of biological parents, fail to fully mourn the loss of the previous family, or fear experiencing a new loss.

As discussed in the previous chapter, society is not developed for accepting single-parent families. Stepfamilies, however, develop somewhat greater superficial acceptance because they resemble nuclear families. The problem that stepfamilies have is that both they and society often wish to impose on them the same structure as that of the nuclear family, but such structure is malfunctional. This chapter outlines some of the dimensions that make it difficult for the stepfamily to function.

WHY DO STEPFAMILIES HAVE GREATER STRAIN THAN OTHER TYPES OF FAMILIES?

When a nuclear family begins, the bonding between the parents occurs prior to the bonding between each parent and subsequent child. The ability of this bond to continue to grow and strengthen over time allows for stronger leadership and a united front for the children. In dysfunctional intact families, one parent may permit a bond with a child to develop that excludes the other parent, but the nuclear family's structure tends to discourage such a move. Stepfamilies, however, are built on a structure that involves such a bond. Thus, in remarriage, reciprocal marital roles between husband and wife cannot be worked out prior to the parental roles (Fast & Cain, 1966).

Duberman (1973) noted that the parental role is learned gradually. Each parent brings to the marriage scripts based on that person's own childhood. When children are born, the parent decides either to apply that script spontaneously and usually without much consideration because "it feels natural," or to write a counterscript to do it better than was done for him or her. Such counterscripts are difficult to write and can never be done spontaneously.

In remarried families, the slow evolution and negotiation around new scripts do not have the opportunity to take place. There is no time for the parental bond to solidify before dealing with the children. Children often mount substantial resistance to any changes in parenting style. Messinger (1976) noted that for remarried families, money and child rearing are identified as the greatest problems.

In nuclear families, the more difficult developmental stages are sustained by the bonding that has occurred in previous stages. As H. S. Goldstein (1974) noted, a 2-year-old's tantrum is easier to tolerate if the parent can remember the holding and snuggling that occurred during infancy. The stepparent who marries a parent when the child is 2 or a beginning adolescent has less reason to stay attached than does the biological parent.

Developmental stages of each family member may be different in remarriage. Unless both the parent and the stepparent have children of approximately the same age, the developmental stages of the two parents are likely to be different. The demands of family life may be incompatible with one person's life cycle position (Sager, Steer, Crohn, Rodstein, & Walker, 1980).

For example, a stepfather with older children may find that he does not want to repeat the dependency of very young children.

In counseling remarried families, it is useful to help the family understand the resistance that may occur when parental figures are at different places in their life cycles. Parents who have already experienced a stage with their own children may resist having to go through the stage again with stepchildren. Also, a stepparent without children of his or her own may regret missing stages of development.

No matter how much the remarried family would like to pretend that the previous relationship did not exist, its presence is always there. Denying its existence creates pathology in the family. Often, the ghosts of the past haunt the remarried family. At least one marriage has already failed. Remarried families are always born out of loss, and expectations may be influenced by the hurt of the previous relationship (Whiteside & Auerbach, 1978). Seldom do people enter any marriage with the expectation that the marriage will not last. For second marriages, the fantasy that the couple can always work out the problems has already been shattered. The risk of a new divorce is always present.

Furstenberg (1987) found that the divorce rate of remarriages was only slightly higher than that of first marriages (56% vs. 49%). Marital adjustment has been found to be no poorer in remarriages than in first marriages (Hobart & Brown, 1988). Thus, the risk of another divorce is very real. Baydar (1988) noted that 42% of remarried couples break up within 5 years. Although second-marriage couples often get divorced because of problems with parenting (whereas in first marriages, parenting is much lower on the list of reasons for getting a divorce), childless remarried couples have about the same divorce rate as those with children. Therefore, the presence of children from prior marriages does not increase the risk of divorce for second marriages.

People have a strong tendency to avoid conflict in remarriages (Jones, 1978). Jones noted that jealousy is common in remarriages, particularly around feelings of being excluded and fear of loss. Couples often do not argue about significant issues because they are phobic about any disagreement, fearing it is a sign that another marriage is failing. H. S. Goldstein (1974), who referred to this tendency as "pseudomutuality," noted that there is often a denial of marital problems in remarriages, and the parents' referral of children's behavior problems is often a request for help.

Because remarried couples often have difficulty admitting to marital problems, they may use referral of the child for treatment as a method of seeking help. The clinician may want to change from child treatment or family therapy to marital counseling if this dynamic is recognized.

Concerns about previous relationships (e.g., "Just how attached is he to his former wife?") produce significant strain on this new relationship. Trying to get rid of reminders of that previous relationship may lead a stepparent to encourage a noncustodial parent to seek custody. Atwell, Moore, and Nowell (1982) noted several potentially negative motivations for such a move:

1. Minimizing contact between the spouse and the other parent
2. Reducing contact of the children with the other parent
3. Correcting perceived parenting errors made by the stepparent with the stepparent's own children.

Money may serve as a significant stress in remarriages. Messinger (1976) noted that financial problems often tie the remarriage to the first marriage. Mothers are sometimes embarrassed at the financial burden her children are to the stepfather. Child support payments are notoriously underpaid, increasing the burden on the stepfather. Messinger noted that remarried women were sometimes secretive about their financial resources with the new spouse, indicating a lack of trust in the new relationship and the need to protect themselves from exploitation.

Role definitions are not clear in remarried families. Although behavioral codes are well defined for nuclear families, society does not have a tradition of behavioral codes on how stepfamily members relate to one another (Fast & Cain, 1966; H. C. Johnson, 1980). People do not know how they are supposed to feel so they do not know if what they do feel is normal or acceptable. Naive expectations might develop, such as a parent's expecting a child to love a stepparent instantly or a child's expecting the stepmother to be wicked.

The complexity of stepfamily relationships also is substantially greater than that of nuclear families. With one or more adults with children, a remarriage can result in stepparents, stepchildren, biological parents, biological children, stepsiblings, half-siblings, stepgrandparents, and even exspouse and ex-step relations.

THE PROBLEM OF THE STEPFAMILY FOR THE UNREMARRIED PARENT

The biological parent who is not remarrying often has intense feelings about the remarriage of a former partner. Even when the remaining parent initiated the divorce, there are usually ambivalent feelings about the attachment to the former spouse. Thus, the remarriage can raise feelings of rejection: "She found someone else to love," or "He is giving her the affection he never gave me," or "It really is over." Competition is not unusual, particularly around affection from the children: "She may replace me as mother." The child may worry that giving affection to the stepparent will invite rejection (and indeed it can) from the biological parent of the same sex as the stepparent (Thies,

1977). Such competition is more likely for the mother, whose stereotyped role is nurturance. Fathers may feel relief because financial pressure may be lessened or guilt over inadequate financial support may be relieved.

THE PROBLEM OF THE STEPFAMILY FROM THE FAMILY'S POINT OF VIEW

Some of the stepfamily's problems are shared by the entire family. Not only does the entire stepfamily have to figure out how the sharply increased number of potential interactions can be handled, but other dynamics make adjustment difficult. Furstenberg (1987) found that the daily characteristics of stepfamilies are quite similar to those of first-marriage families. When remarried families do have problems, they tend to be around affection and discipline.

The Myth of Instant Love

The hope of a new start can lead to unrealistic expectations for remarried families. Everyone writing about stepfamily problems notes the difficulty families have believing that because the two adults love each other and a new family is being formed, everyone in the family should love one another (Visher & Visher, 1978). Parents and children are often shocked to discover that such instant love does not occur. Indeed, unless the stepparent and stepchild have had a long-term relationship where affection developed prior to the remarriage or the child is quite young, that affection may be a long time coming. Fast and Cain (1966) noted that some stepparents develop a hypersensitivity around whether they are accepted in the "parent" role. Such pressures make it difficult to have spontaneous interactions since all interactions are overinterpreted.

There are several reasons why affection is likely to be delayed, and appropriately so:

1. *The "burnt child."* The child has already lost contact with one parent due to divorce. The burnt child syndrome causes the child to be cautious about developing feelings of attachment to the new stepparent until trust in the stability of the new relationship develops.

Stepfamilies should be encouraged to allow children to develop affection at their own pace, without pressure. Trust develops slowly, particularly for a child who has already had an involuntary loss.

2. *Inverse relationship of child's age to time necessary for acceptance of the stepfamily.* The younger the child, the more quickly the child accepts a stepparent in a parenting role. Preschool age children often accept a stepparent's

affection with little or no anxiety. In particular, only children of preschool age adjust well to the remarriage of one or both parents (Benson-von der Ohe, 1987). Elementary age children are more cautious. By late elementary age, the evolution of trust may take up to 2 years.

In the 10-year follow-up of the original Wallerstein and Kelly (1980c) project, Wallerstein and Blakeslee (1989) found that the younger the child, the better the relationship with the stepfather. Of the younger children whose mothers had remarried, 90% felt that life had been better because of the stepfather. Of those well into elementary school at the time of the divorce, 90% did *not* feel that life had improved, and over half resented the stepfather. Many girls accepted the stepfather as a parent. Rarely did boys prefer the stepfather to the biological father. Although Wallerstein and Blakeslee felt that the stepfather had the most difficult role in the stepfamily, most research indicates that the stepmother struggles more. Less than 10% of children were close to a stepmother; however, the stepmothers were not seen as "wicked" stepmothers.

The adolescent's resistance to remarriage can be quite high for a variety of reasons. First, the adolescent often has a strong sense of loyalty to the nonremarried parent and sees the development of affection for a stepparent as disloyal. Second, the remarriage sexualizes the parent in a way that is often anxiety provoking to the teenager. Finally, because separation is the developmental task of the adolescent, asking adolescents to attach at the very time that they are working on psychological and physical separation places them in a difficult bind. Indeed, it is not unusual for the adolescent to never develop affectional bonds with a stepparent.

The stepfamily needs to be warned that the older the child, the more resistance to bonding. In particular, adolescents need to have permission to avoid bonding altogether.

3. *Loss of time and attention.* Another major source of resistance to bonding is the stepchild's possible resentment about the loss of time and attention from the biological parent. Blechman and Manning (1976) noted that the triad in nuclear families (mother, father, and child) tends to dilute the intensity of parent–child relationships. Because the marital bond predates the parental bond, it tends to be stronger. After divorce, the triad becomes a dyad with the parent and each child. That dyad does not include the relationship between parents; thus, the parent–child relationship intensifies. In fact, the bond can become so strong that it can be difficult for a stepparent to intervene. If the biological parent transfers primary allegiance to the new partner, the child may feel an enormous loss and resent the stepparent.

4. *The stepparent's trouble with affection.* Because the strong bond between the biological parent and child can be difficult to break into, the stepparent may resent the child's presence. Also, a stepchild's resistance to the new relationship can be very difficult to tolerate over a long period of time. It is difficult to love a child who does not want to be loved.

A stepchild's presence is a constant reminder to the stepparent that the remarried family is not a nuclear family. The child is a constant reminder of the previous relationship, particularly if the child is of the same sex as the absent parent, carries the same last name as the absent parent, or has a strong physical resemblance to the ex-spouse. Only when divorced spouses without children remarry can the existence of the prior marriage be forgotten on a daily basis.

5. *Sexuality.* Stepfamilies often can be characterized as having a weakened incest taboo. Familiarity within the developing intact family tends to provide protection from inappropriate sexual relationships. With stepfamilies, that taboo has not had a chance to develop, and parents and children can be distressed to discover inappropriate feelings.

It is extremely important that families entering remarriage discuss sexuality. What may have been a comfortable level of casual undress in the previous family may no longer be appropriate. The family needs to consider what may be provocative: a family member walking around nude or partially clothed, children bathing with parents, or children playing or sleeping in the parental bed. Especially for teenagers, the control of potentially stimulating behavior is important. Not only is it important to encourage stepfamilies to deal with this topic for stepparent–stepchild relationships, but also for the relationships between stepsiblings. It can be very stimulating for a teenage boy to suddenly find himself with a fully developed stepsister!

This increased sexuality can be another reason that family members may avoid affection within the stepfamily. Stepparent and stepchild may feel increased attraction to each other and may handle that anxiety with pseudo-hostility (H. S. Goldstein, 1974).

6. *Interrupted histories.* Visher and Visher (1979) noted that remarried families have difficulty recognizing the interrupted histories of the children. A child goes on a visitation with a noncustodial parent. Meanwhile, the family has gone on with its daily life. When the child returns, the family has difficulty remembering what the child does not know about events that have transpired since he or she left. Indeed, even when the family recognizes that the child needs to be reintegrated into the remarried family, the family members may be impatient and resentful of the need to habitually review events. When parent–child or stepparent–stepchild relationships are conflict filled, the interruptions are particularly destructive. For example, the child may leave on visitation in the middle of a fight. When the child returns several days later, the fight is forgotten. Thus, the likelihood of unresolved disagreement is increased.

Absent family members need to be updated on family history during absences.

7. *Crowding and the problem of territory.* Whiteside and Auerbach (1978) noted that remarriage often requires juggling of bedrooms and finding adequate space for everyone. Stepfamilies have to solve the problem of physical and role territories. With the blending of two families, space often becomes a problem. If two custodial parents marry, the need for space becomes critical as the family struggles to find room for all the children, often in a home designed to hold one set of children. Even when one parent is noncustodial, weekend visitations can create nightmares of space demands.

Family members who are asked to give up space because of the remarriage are likely to be resentful. Children who remain in the same home are likely to resent stepsiblings who move in and encroach on their territory. Families who are able to move to a new home at remarriage are likely to reduce feelings of encroachment for physical territory because both families are on equal footing.

8. *Changing roles.* Roles change with remarriage. The child who changes birth order is likely to be at risk for maladjustment after a remarriage, since the demands and privileges for that child are likely to change radically. The previously youngest child who finds that there is an even younger child is likely to feel significant loss at no longer being the baby of the family. The oldest child, who generally is given the greatest amount of responsibility, may find that responsibility disappearing as an even older child moves in or a stepparent takes over those roles.

Clinicians should help remarried families facilitate the integration of children whose birth orders change with the blending of families. Particularly, families should try to maintain as many rights and privileges as possible for each child so that psychological loss is reduced. A child who has had some caretaking responsibilities for a parent (cooking, cleaning, and other chores), should be asked to continue those responsibilities at some level (unless there is reason to believe that only relief would occur with relinquishment). The new stepparent may feel some irritation at not obtaining complete control over those roles, but integration of the children will be facilitated if the responsibilities are shared.

9. *Discipline.* Hetherington, Cox, and Cox (1979) vividly described the degree to which preschool children, particularly boys, may receive inadequate structure when in mother custody. Parents may feel sorry for a child after a divorce and mistakenly believe that leniency will "make up for the loss." Parents often are lenient after a divorce because their own lives are chaotic, and monitoring the children takes more energy than they have available. Mothers of young children may be ineffective in maintaining discipline and develop coercive, but chaotic styles of control. Hetherington, Arnett, and Hollier (1988) referred to this parenting style as ineffectively authoritarian. The

divorced mother gives more orders and focuses on negative behavior, and she is less playful, less affectionate, and less approving of the children than are mothers in intact families.

The lack of affectional bond and push for discipline with a stepparent may increase the likelihood of child abuse. Giles-Sims and Finkelhor (1984) indicated that stepparents may be overrepresented among child abusers and proposed a variety of theoretical explanations as to why.

10. *The lack of boundary definitions.* Ihinger-Tallman (1988) noted that interfamily and intrafamily boundaries are particularly confusing for remarried families. Children and stepparents may be confused about how to answer the question, "Who is in your family?" Relationships with stepgrandparents, particularly paternal (noncustodial father) grandparents, also are likely to be problematic.

The Shift from Single to Remarried Status

A common structure for remarried families is this: The mother has been ineffective in discipline and the children are out of control at some level. The mother has custody of the children and remarries a man who may have children of his own, but does not have custody. The stepfather has standards of behavior control that lead him to criticize the mother's parenting strategy. He makes the error of being too strict. He is rejected by the children as being unreasonable and depriving, and he is rejected by the mother as being cruel and rejecting of the children. He abrogates his parenting role in anger and hurt. The mother forms an unhealthy alliance with her biological children. The marriage continues in a cold war until the children are grown or the marriage ends in divorce.

This dynamic can be most unfortunate, particularly when the mother sees the remarriage as a rescue for out-of-control children and is therefore implicitly or explicitly asking the stepfather to immediately assume the disciplinary role. The stepfather who tries to move into a disciplinary role prior to the development of affection and trust will not be integrated into the family unit (Stern, 1978; Visher & Visher, 1979). Stern noted that the stepfather may need at times to take the child's side in the disagreement against the mother, provided it is an honest statement of beliefs.

Stern (1978) and Visher and Visher (1979) have estimated that it takes up to 1 ½ to 2 years for the stepparent–stepchild affectional bond to develop. Hetherington et al. (1988) felt that there are a series of adjustments that must occur over time, and most families are able to accomplish that process in 3 years.

The mother may be ambivalent about how much discipline she wants from the stepfather (Visher & Visher, 1978). She asks for discipline, but then is protective when the stepfather provides it. Stepfathers often feel that they receive double messages in this situation.

The stepfather should not try to assume a disciplinary role until affectional bonds have developed. The stepparent who gives new rules to stepfamilies prior to development of these affectional bonds will be hated. It does not help for the biological parent to introduce the new rules. Children know who caused the new rules to be developed. When the need is strong for the assertion of structure and limits, it may be appropriate for the divorced parent to consider family therapy to solve the problems prior to remarriage rather than asking the potential stepparent to solve them afterwards. Remarriage should not be used to solve discipline problems. The risk to the family is too great.

At the same time, the stepfather should not abrogate all parenting responsibilities. The development of an affectional bond and the assumption of disciplinary relationships both should be goals. Fast and Cain (1966) cautioned that the stepfather who behaves as a nonparent may not be helpful to a stepson who needs to have the intense mother–son bond weakened for adequate individuation.

H. C. Johnson (1980) noted that if there is active dislike between the child and stepparent, the biological parent must assume most of the parenting responsibility, including discipline. If the biological parent refuses to step in and assume this role, both the child and the stepparent are likely to feel resentful. Mills (1984) suggested that requests for limits by the stepparent go through the biological parent and that if the biological parent is to be temporarily absent, the biological parent should ask the stepparent to act like a babysitter and should provide explicit rules to the children and stepparent.

Clinicians should monitor the relationship between the stepparent and stepchild. If the relationship is poor, the stepparent needs to withdraw from primary parenting responsibilities and let the biological parent assume most of that responsibility.

Competition and Loyalty

As a part of the resentment and competition that a child may feel with a stepparent, the child may force the biological parent to choose between the stepparent and the child (Visher & Visher, 1978). A stepmother in this competitive bind will try to win the father over to her side. Visher and Visher noted that the stepmother usually succeeds. If the father sides with the children against the stepmother, the remarried family is in trouble.

In her longitudinal evaluation of stepfamily characteristics of latency age children, Hetherington (1987) found four patterns of parenting: permissive, disengaged, authoritarian, and authoritative. The authoritative style was characterized by high warmth, high involvement and monitoring, moderately high responsive control, and low conflict. All mothers except divorced mothers of boys had authoritative parenting. Divorced mothers of boys were more likely to be authoritarian. Stepfathers were more likely to be disengaged. Over time, stepfathers became more authoritative with stepsons and less authoritative and more disengaged with stepdaughters. With stepdaughters, the stepfather started off accepting, but found it difficult to gain acceptance and eventually disengaged.

Lifestyle

H. C. Johnson (1980) felt that a variety of issues have to be resolved when two families merge different lifestyles. Examples she gave were:

1. *Discipline.* This topic was discussed in the previous section.
2. *Eating habits.* Does the family eat together or separately? Can television be on during meals? Do children have to eat everything on the plate, taste everything, or pick and choose?
3. *Division of labor.* Who cooks, cleans, does the laundry, gets the car fixed, and balances the checkbook?
4. *Attitudes toward sex.* What is the appropriate level of dress around the house?
5. *Use of alcohol and drugs.* Is it acceptable for parents to use them? In front of the children? Are children allowed to use them?
6. *Attitudes toward obligations.* When do you pay bills? When do the children do homework?
7. *Manners.* What behaviors are required to facilitate polite interaction?
8. *Household rules.* What are the rules for the phone? Who cleans what?
9. *Expression of hostility, aggression, or disagreement.* How much is accepted? Is expressing anger a sign of disrespect?

Surnames

When remarriage was relatively uncommon, children were sometimes self-conscious about the fact that their last name differed from that of their custodial biological parent and stepparent. Today, people are so accustomed to remarried families that school districts as matter of course include last names of each family member on school records. Indeed, last names are also an issue for the remarried mother. She may choose to keep the previous married last name, to regain the family-of-origin name, to assume a hyphenated name with the new spouse, or to assume the traditional last name of the new spouse. Keeping the previous married name, even when the reason is professional identity, sometimes creates jealousy because the new spouse may see the move as an indication of attachment to the previous relationship.

One-third of adoptions in the United States are by stepparents. Particularly at the time of adoption, the question of names comes up. What shall the child be called? If abandonment by the noncustodial father has occurred, there may be little reason to keep the name of the father, and the child should be encouraged to move on to more appropriate identity.

The legal question of who can decide about the child's name change depends on the jurisdiction and whether the rules are prescribed by law. Some judges believe that the last name is the property of the father and will not permit adoption or name change without his permission. Some judges believe that the custodial parent has the right of control of the name and can make the decision without regard to the noncustodial parent's wishes. Nationwide, adoption usually requires the noncustodial parent's permission (Clingempeel, Shuwall, & Heiss, 1988). Although choice of names may seem trivial to some, the use of a last name can have powerful symbolic meaning to everyone involved.

Families should be cautious about instigating name changes for the children after remarriage. If the child has continued contact with the noncustodial father, name changes can serve as a widening hurt that reduces contact with the father. Generally, I recommend that name change not occur if there is any likelihood that the noncustodial father would withdraw and have less contact with the children after the name change. Certainly, the meaning of the change should be discussed with children old enough to express an opinion. If total abandonment has occurred with a noncustodial father, the name change can encourage a child to loosen an identification with a rejecting parent and to turn to a stepparent for those needs.

Even first names create problems for stepfamilies. Except for the very young, stepchildren typically call stepparents by their first names (Dahl, Cowgill, & Asmundsson, 1987). Very young children sometimes generate unique family names to designate differences (e.g., Daddy Bill and Daddy Mark).

It is not advisable to force children to use the same name for a parent and a stepparent. Such a move encourages competition between families, may generate guilt in the child for hurting a parent, and may increase communication problems.

STEPFATHERS

Stepfathers tend to have an easier time adjusting to the remarried family than do stepmothers. Duberman (1973) suggested that the stepmother may spend more time with the children because sex-role stereotypes require that behavior of her. The expectation is greater on the stepmother to provide for affectional needs. Given the cultural demands on fathers, the family may expect less of him in terms of energy and affection. This lack of expectations may be why there are no stepfather myths.

However, very young stepfathers are at risk for additional divorce. In Wallerstein and Blakeslee's (1989) 10-year follow-up report of divorcing families, all of the younger fathers had remarried (the number was not reported), most within 2 years. Ninety percent of these marriages failed. It should be noted that such use of percentiles without the numbers can be misleading as to how stable such results are.

The stepfather's prior marital status predicts how well the stepfather will get along with the children (Duberman, 1973). If the stepfathers were divorced, 54% had excellent relationships with the children; if widowed, 76% had excellent relationships; and if never married, 85% had excellent relationships. According to Duberman, the stepfather's feelings for the stepchildren were unrelated to the residence of his own children.

Perkins and Kahan (1979) examined the differences between 20 families with biological fathers and 20 with stepfathers. Family triads in which there were a husband, a wife, and a 12- to 15-year-old child were studied. If more than one child was in the designated age range, one was selected randomly. Typically, the custodial mothers in this study had initiated the divorce and had 3 years between marriages. All the children had maintained close contact with their natural fathers, seeing them on the average of twice a month. The fact that there was *no* abandonment suggests that the method of recruitment of participants did have some bias (although what the bias might be is unknown). These were college-level upper middle class families. Whether the stepfathers had other children was not stated in the report, so the data are summarized here rather than in the following sections.

Adjustment scores and satisfaction scores were higher for biological father families than for stepfather families for all three family members. Biological fathers were seen as better and more powerful than stepfathers. Perkins and Kahan felt that this result was counter to the prevailing belief that mothers tend to turn their children against the father after divorce.

Two years after remarriage, stepfathers rated themselves low on expressed affection to the stepchildren (Hetherington, 1987). There had been some extremely angry interchanges between stepfathers and stepdaughters. The stepdaughter generally saw the stepfather as hostile, punitive, and unreasonable on discipline. Stepdaughters in Hetherington's study were latency age girls.

Fischman (1988) noted that physical affection from the stepfather often created discomfort for girls, but that girls appreciated verbal praise and support from the stepfather.

For older stepdaughters, stepfathers should be verbally warm and supportive, but should be cautious about using physical contact (e.g., hugs) because such contact is frequently misunderstood or creates anxiety.

Benson-von der Ohe (1987), who looked at a longitudinal stratified sample over 4 years, found both positive and negative comments about the adjustment to the remarrriage. Three-fourths of the adults were satisfied at how well the stepchild and stepparent were getting along. Stepfathers, however, did not get closer over time. As many stepfathers had declines in relationships with stepchildren as had improvements. Amato (1987) reported that stepfathers were seen as providing less support, less control, and less punishment than biological fathers. Involvement with the child, however, grew considerably over time. Furstenberg (1988) noted that stepparent–stepchild relationships did not seem to be adversely affected by the child's contact with the noncustodial father when the child lived with a mother and stepfather.

Visher and Visher (1979) gave a useful discussion of the different constellations of stepparent as a function of who has children. Clearly, adjustment to remarriage is in part a function of the demands that different structures make. Each of these arrangements is described in the following sections.

Stepfather with No Children and Custodial Mother with Children

According to Visher and Visher, this dynamic produces the least difficulty for the stepfather. He has no guilt for having left behind other children who are not getting his time and energy. He does have difficulty with discipline because he has not had practice in doing it well and his expectations may be unrealistic. Also, he may have difficulty understanding the children because of his lack of contact with children in general.

Because the stepfather does not have his own children who behave differently from his stepchildren, the conflict in values may not be as apparent (Visher & Visher, 1979). When the children are on visitation with the biological father, the stepfather and mother may have time to develop their own relationship. Bowerman and Irish (1962) found that the level of affection toward stepfathers is markedly lower than toward biological fathers.

Brand and Clingempeel (1987) evaluated 40 white, middle income stepparent families (20 girls and 20 boys from 9 to 12 years old). All of the families involved a stepfather with no children of his own. The greater the positive behaviors by the biological mother toward the stepfather, the fewer positive feelings of affection by the stepson to the stepfather, perhaps due to feelings of competition or exclusion. However, if the biological mother treated the stepfather in a positive way, the stepfather was more positive in the way he treated the stepson, and the stepson was less aggressive and had a higher self-concept. For girls in stepfather families, positive behaviors tended to go together. If the mother was positive toward the stepfather, he and the stepdaughter were more positive with each other. Of course, because these results are correlational, it may be easier for the mother to be positive if she sees a positive relationship between her husband and her daughter.

In a study of the relationship of stepfathers and stepchildren and marital quality ($n = 60$), Orleans, Palisi, and Caddell (1989) found that negative acts and feelings between stepfather and stepchild were related (but only to a low degree) to poor marital adjustment. If the stepfather was involved with over-all family decisions, the marital adjustment and happiness tended to be high. Contrary to expectation, there was a low but positive relationship between the stepfather's making decisions about the children and marital adjustment. Time since remarriage was not included in the analyses. If 2 or more years had passed, such involvement may have occurred after stepfather–stepchild bonding had developed.

Noncustodial Stepfather with Children and Custodial Mother with Children

The difficulty in this family situation is the guilt that the father may feel about giving his stepchildren more attention than he gives his own children. These feelings may be increased by the jealousy that his own children may have. Sometimes, the father may feel so guilty about his abandonment that he is unable to establish relationships with his stepchildren (Visher & Visher, 1978).

This stepfather does have some understanding of children, but may be relatively nonunderstanding about the different parenting styles of his new wife, without awareness of the slow negotiations that developed the discipline pattern for his own children. Clingempeel, Ievoli, and Brand (1984), however, found that families of this type ($n = 16$) did not differ from families in which the stepfather had no children ($n = 16$) on measures of stepparent behavior, child behavior, and family problem solving. The small sample size does limit generalizability.

In a study of stepfathers (72% of whom had noncustodial children of their own) and mothers, J. Z. Anderson and White (1986) compared dysfunctional and functional intact families and stepfamilies. Dysfunctional families, regardless of marital type, had poorer marital adjustment than functional families. Dysfunctional stepfamilies had better marital adjustment than dysfunctional intact families and did not differ in marital adjustment from functional intact families. Dysfunctional intact families were particularly low in marital adjustment. Not surprisingly, stepchildren had a less positive relationship with stepfathers than children from intact families had with biological fathers.

As supporting evidence that the parent–child bond is a particular problem in remarried families, stepfamilies reported stronger parent–child coalitions than intact families and dysfunctional families reported such coalitions *more often* than functional families (J. Z. Anderson & White, 1986).

According to Hobart (1989), fathers with custody of children from a prior marriage had significantly lower marital adjustment scores than people in other types of remarried families. Clearly, these fathers and the marriages of these fathers are under greater stress.

Custodial Stepfather with Children and Custodial Stepmother with Children

Visher and Visher (1978) described this structure as being highly complex because there are many competing groups. Uninterrupted time between spouses may be limited, and territory may be a constant problem. Visher and Visher (1988) noted that this type of family would seem to have the greatest number of problems. In all stepfamilies, but particularly complex ones, Visher and Visher (1988) suggested encouraging dyadic relationships, including stepparent–stepchild relationships.

When two custodial parents marry, territory becomes a particularly serious problem.

STEPMOTHERS

The cruel or wicked stepmother is a ubiquitous figure in folklore around the world. The cruel stepmother myth exists in India, Hawaii, Chile, African countries, ninth century China, Indonesia, Iceland, the Apache tribe, eleventh century Ireland, and Greek mythology (Thomson, 1966). Of course, most Europeans and Americans have heard the Cinderella story. Given this overwhelming evidence for a common mythology, it is reasonable to assume that there is something about family dynamics across cultures that increases the likelihood that the stepmother will have a difficult time.

The wicked stepmother becomes a self-fulfilling prophecy. The stepmother tries to be very affectionate. The children reject the affection for what seem to them to be very good reasons, and the stepmother feels rejected and withdraws. The children then find that they were right to be cautious and feel justified in their caution.

Stepmothers should be encouraged to take time for affection and trust to develop. There should be explicit permission for stepchild and stepmother to not love one another. There should be a requirement for cordial, polite interaction, but love develops only if it is a choice.

Thomson (1966) said that the stepmother may be overeager to do a good job in parenting, by pushing too hard to teach the children to clean up or by "improving" their hairstyles or dress. Such behaviors can be interpreted by the children as mean rather than helpful. Thomson also noted that the extended family is likely to distrust the new parent, which can also set up that parent for failure. Another problem that stepmothers have is the wish to rescue the stepchildren, to make up for the upset caused by the original divorce (Kosinski, 1983).

Because stepmothers tend to spend more time with children than do stepfathers, there is more opportunity for conflict (Duberman, 1975). Stepmothers are often quite sensitive about the wicked stepmother role and work hard to avoid it. As McGoldrick and Carter (1980) pointed out, the alternative to the wicked stepmother myth is the myth depicted in "The Brady Bunch" television show, in which the integration and loving family is obtained with minimal difficulty. To avoid being the wicked stepmother and to try to be the Brady Bunch mother, the stepmother may provide enormous affection to the stepchild to hasten bonding. According to H. S. Goldstein (1974), children see this behavior as the stepmother's *competing* for the affection of the children with the biological mother. If the children allow themselves to accept the affection, they may feel disloyal to their biological mother. Thus, they suppress feelings of tenderness to avoid this disloyalty. Bernard (1971) and K. N. Walker, Rogers, and Messinger (1977) felt that stepmothering of teenagers is particularly difficult, because the disciplinary problems are greater at this age and conflict may be greater than with the children's own mother.

Numerous investigators have indicated that stepmothers have more trouble with adjustment to remarriage than do stepfathers (e.g., Kosinski, 1983). Remarried women with stepchildren (particularly stepdaughters) find that remarriage negatively affects their perception of the marital relationship more than is true for remarried women without stepchildren (Hobart & Brown, 1988).

Hetherington (1987) looked at 180 families for up to 6 years after the divorce. Of these, 42 were remarried families. In terms of parent adjustment, there were few differences between remarried mothers and nondivorced mothers. Mothers early in the remarriage had greater life and marital satisfactions. As found in other studies, nonremarried custodial mothers had lower general life satisfaction, less internal control, and higher level of loneliness and depression than remarried mothers.

Duberman (1973) also found that residence of her own children influenced how a stepmother felt about her stepchildren. If the mothers' own children resided with them, 67% had excellent relationships with their stepchildren. If the mothers' own children resided elsewhere, only 44% had excellent relationships with stepchildren. Stepmothers felt more anxiety, depression, and anger about the family than did biological mothers (Nadler, 1976). These stepmothers also had more interpersonal conflict in the family than did mothers not in a stepmother role.

Visher and Visher (1979) felt that unrealistic expectations drive the stepmother and create numerous problems: the myth of instant affection; the need to have a new, close-knit, nuclear family; and the need to keep the family happy. Even an apparently simple task such as cooking meals can cause a battle. One 6-year-old complained to me that his father's promise that the new stepmother was a terrific cook was not true. Reingold (1976) noted that it was axiomatic that children would not like their stepmother's cooking. Nothing tastes right. Even peanut butter and jelly sandwiches will invariably have the wrong amount of peanut butter or too much jelly. Indeed, acceptance of a stepmother's cooking may be a sensitive thermostat of how the relationship is developing.

Santrock and Sitterle (1987) evaluated 18 children aged 7 to 11 in remarried father-custody homes, 26 in remarried mother-custody homes, and 25 from intact families. Data collection included observation of the child interacting with each parent separately. Never-divorced mothers tended to discipline girls more than did stepmothers, but stepmothers tended to discipline boys more than did mothers. A remarried mother was more likely than a stepfather to be involved in stepchild discipline, to take the stepchild along on errands, to discuss problems, and to provide more comfort and sympathy. Children felt that a noncustodial mother was more involved than a noncustodial father.

Draughon (1975) identified three roles that a stepmother can have in the new family: (1) primary mother, (2) other mother, and (3) friend. Draughon felt that the other mother role was not a good model. The primary mother role can be used only if the biological mother has abandoned the children *and* the mourning is complete. If there is a strong bond between biological mother and child, the friend role could be the most useful model for a stepmother to follow.

Klee, Schmidt, and Johnson (1988/1989) had a somewhat more optimistic view of how stepmothers would do. Ninety percent of children over 10 years of age felt related to a stepfather, and 75% felt related to a stepmother. Thus, stepmothers were less accepted, but still accepted as a member of the family at a high level.

Stepmother with No Children and Father with Children

Duberman (1973) indicated that stepmothers with no children of their own tend to have a more difficult time than mothers, stepmothers with children of their own, fathers, and stepfathers. They have no experience to aid them in the tasks of being a stepmother.

Jones (1978) noted that the stepmother–stepdaughter relationship was the most difficult. If the stepdaughter gets into a power play, it is important that the biological father communicate clearly and consistently the guidelines for appropriate behavior.

Brand and Clingempeel (1987) evaluated 22 white, middle income stepmother families (where the stepmother had no children of her own). The 11 boys and 11 girls were from 9 to 12 years old. The small number of subjects limits generalizability, but similar studies are rare so this one is important to review. There were dramatic differences between how stepsons and stepdaughters related to stepmothers. The more positive the marriage, the less positive the stepmother–stepdaughter relationship and the poorer the stepdaughter self-concept. The authors noted that girls in father-custody families often had especially problematic relations with their biological mothers, or the father would not have custody. These girls also may have had a higher status position in the single-parent family as confidant and household manager for their fathers. Thus, there may be difficulty with mothers or with the loss of the special relationship with the fathers.

If the stepdaughter had a poorer relationship with the stepmother, she was more likely to visit frequently with the noncustodial mother. The longer the stepdaughter had lived with the father and stepmother, the more positive the stepdaughter–stepmother relationship became and the less the aggression and inhibition on the part of the stepdaughter (Clingempeel and Segal, 1986).

OTHER RESEARCH ON THE STEPCHILD'S GENDER

Bray (1988) found that children aged 6 to 9 in stepfamilies did not suffer from lower self-esteem than age-matched children from intact families. Boys and girls in stepfamilies had more behavior problems than children in nondivorced families. Boys had higher levels of intellectual performance and lower life stress if they had a stepfather than did girls, even though the boys had more behavioral problems. Boys did better when there was more cohesion and emotional bonding with mothers and stepfathers. Girls did better with less emotional bonding with mothers.

STEPSIBLING RELATIONSHIPS

Duberman (1973) found that 24% of stepsibling relationships were rated as excellent, 38% as good, and 38% as poor. Cross-sex stepsibling relationships seemed to be better than same-sex stepsibling relationships. In those families in which there was a child as a product of the new marriage, 44% of the stepsibling relationships were excellent, compared with only 19% in which the remarriage was childless. Thus, the presence of a new baby would seem to benefit stepsibling relationships.

In a later study, Duberman (1975) found that when the remarried couple had a child together, the children from former marriages were *more* likely to have harmonious relations within the family. In addition, Duberman found that 78% of remarried families in which the couple had a child together rated the stepparent–stepchild relationship as excellent, whereas 53% of families who had had no children together rated the stepparent–stepchild relationship as excellent. Perhaps the new baby is a symbol to the stepchild that this relationship has developed a commitment. Certainly, the birth provides a shared identity with the stepparent: "You are the parent of my half-brother."

Although the birth of a child from the new family may be helpful to the stepchildren, Santrock and Sitterle (1987) found that a new child had a negative effect on the ability of the stepparent and custodial parent to work together to parent the other children.

The birth of a new child may improve feelings on the part of stepchildren. Perhaps the children relax somewhat with the (incorrect) expectation that this marriage is now more likely to last, given the commitment that a new child implies. In addition, the half-brother or half-sister is now a shared link with the stepparent. The stepmother is no longer simply a stepmother, but a mother of a half-sibling. In contrast, the parent and stepparent seem to have great difficulties working together to parent the other children after the birth of a new child.

In contrast, Ganong and Coleman (1988) found no effect of a mutual child on marital adjustment, family affect, conflict and parent-child closeness. Older children, however, did not distinguish between half siblings and full siblings and saw themselves as belonging to the same family.

Duberman (1975) also found that stepsiblings have a better relationship if their primary residence is in the same house. When the relationship is based on visitation times, the stepsiblings have less opportunity to interact and develop a relationship. In addition, visiting stepsiblings often are treated differently because they are not present as often (e.g., they may be exempt from household chores). Special preferences for visiting stepsiblings can create barriers that make it more difficult for relationships to develop.

To facilitate effective integration of stepsiblings, parents should review problems of preferential treatment.

CHILD ADJUSTMENT AND REMARRIAGE

The research is not clear concerning the effect of remarriage on adjustment of children. Langner and Michael (1963) found that children living in a remarried family were less well adjusted than either children living in a family that had experienced bereavement of a parent or children living in a family of divorce without remarriage. They also found that remarriage appeared to be most stressful for children of lower socioeconomic status. For middle class families, the older the child at the time of the remarriage, the more the stress.

In a large-scale study of 2,145 stepchildren, Bowerman and Irish (1962) found that children residing with both biological parents least often felt rejected by either or both of them. In a stepparent home, the children were more likely to feel rejected by their biological parents and much more rejected by the stepparent. Boys were less likely to feel rejected than girls, regardless of the type of home. When asked whether they wished that they lived in a different home, children living with both biological parents together were least likely to wish for a different home. That wish was somewhat more likely for children in a mother–stepfather home, and most likely for children in a father–stepmother home.

Wilson, Zurcher, MacAdams, and Curtis (1975) found that stepfamilies did not differ from nuclear families in crime and delinquency, child abuse, self-esteem, or independence. Compared with adults raised in nuclear families, adults who grew up in stepfamilies obtained lower educational levels (perhaps due to lower income as a child), had lower family income as adults, and were less inclined to feel that most people were helpful and fair. Adults raised in stepfamilies were also less satisfied with their own married lives than adults raised in nuclear families.

In a review of 38 empirical studies, Ganong and Coleman (1984) argued that more studies supported stepchildren liking stepfamilies than disliking them. In their own research, Coleman and Ganong (1984) compared intact, single-parent, and stepfamily structures and family integration and their effects on attitudes toward marriage and divorce for high school and college students. Children from mother–stepfather and mother-only families were more positive about divorce than were children from intact families. High family integration (compared with low family integration) was related to positive attitudes toward marriage, regardless of type of family. Length of time in a stepfamily was unrelated to attitudes.

Ganong and Coleman (1984) reported that a majority of studies found no differences in self-image for children in nuclear or single-parent families, and only one found clear lower self-esteem in stepfamily children. Two studies found some lower self-concept as a function of remarriage when the children were adolescents or adults. For mental health, stepfathers seemed to mitigate the effects of father absence. The frequency of psychosomatic complaints was no different for stepchildren than for children from other types of families.

Clingempeel, Ievoli, and Brand (1984) reported that girls in mother–stepfather families gave fewer positive verbal and more negative problem solving behaviors toward stepfathers than did boys, whereas the stepfathers did not differ in the types of communications to stepsons and stepdaughters. In another study, Clingempeel, Brand, and Ievoli (1984) looked at 16 step-mothers and 16 stepfathers (it is not clear whether the stepfathers were the same as in the previously described study). Based on 3½-hour home interviews with stepchildren, stepparents, and biological parents, the authors reported that stepparent–stepdaughter relationships were more problematic than other relationships. Love was lower and detachment was higher for these relationships compared with all the others.

Hodges and Bloom (1984) found that 18 months after the separation, children living in divorced homes were better adjusted than children living in still separated homes, who in turn were better adjusted than children living in remarriage homes. Because this study evaluated adjustment so soon after the separation, the lower adjustment levels (as described by the parents) may have been due to the quick remarriage, rather than the remarriage per se.

Santrock and Sitterle (1987) found that children in simple stepmother families (with children from one family only) had more positive self-worth than children in complex stepmother families. As in other research mentioned in this book, economics made a difference. The higher the combined income of the custodial father and stepmother, the greater the positive self-worth of the children and the more competent the social interactions between stepmother and stepchildren. The more children in the family, the higher the level of conflict (Santrock & Sitterle, 1987). The happiest remarriage families seemed to involve adolescent girls who were in joint custody (Crosbie-Burnett, 1989).

In one of the more carefully matched, longitudinal studies of remarriage, Hetherington, Cox, and Cox (1985) obtained data from a 6-year follow-up of 124 middle class white children, half from divorce and half from intact families. Of the 60 originally divorced mothers, only 18 remained single. Two of the parents had redivorced, and there were six changes of custody. Of the 64 originally intact families, 53 were still intact. By adding additional subjects, the authors were able to compare 30 sons and 30 daughters in each of three groups: remarried mother/stepfather, divorced mother with sole custody, and intact family. Boys and girls with recently (2 years or less) remarried mothers had more externalizing problems than children from intact families as rated by themselves and their parents. Two years after remarriage, boys did not see themselves as different from boys from intact families, although the stepfathers viewed them as more externalizing. Girls who were stepdaughters continued to view themselves as having more problems than girls from intact families, and the stepfathers agreed.

Amato and Ochiltree (1987) investigated the academic records of stepchildren. In a study of 402 Australian families, they found that children in remarried families had lower reading ability than children from intact families. The poor reading ability of children from one-parent families was accounted for largely by lower standard of living. Economics did not explain the poorer reading ability of children in remarriage. Indeed, for adolescent children in stepfamilies, the greater the time since the separation, the poorer the reading ability.

Although remarriage can lead to maladjustment in stepchildren, it is difficult to untangle why. As noted earlier in this chapter, a couple may identify a child as a problem to avoid working on the troubled marriage. The remarriage may present particular problems of adjustment to the child. Just because a child has problems and lives in a remarried family, however, does not imply a cause-and-effect relationship. As in the discussion on divorce and adjustment (see Chapters 2 and 3), it should not be assumed that all problems flow from remarriage.

The clinician needs to help families untangle stepfamily problems from normal developmental problems (Nichols, 1980). Recognizing that a problem is typical of adolescents and not "caused" by the remarriage may lead to a more relaxed level of problem solving.

It is clear from the research that the older the child, the more resistant the child is to the remarriage (Benson-von der Ohe, 1987). Teenagers have difficulty with the remarriage for a variety of reasons. First, with the remarriage, the adolescent often loses status, as well as responsibilities and freedoms that were previously available. Second, the stepfamily is asking the adolescent to bond at just the time in his or her life that he or she is trying to separate. Thus, the stepfamily's expectation conflicts with the developmental needs. Third, it has been suggested that separating from two families may be more difficult than separating from one. Finally, the sexuality of remarriage and problems of mutual attraction discussed previously are more potent for the adolescent. Indeed, hostility can serve as a defense against such unacceptable feelings. The stepmother's role with adolescents may be particularly difficult (K. N. Walker et al., 1977). She is more likely to spend time with the teenagers and may face more disciplinary problems.

Adolescents in their struggle for autonomy may use blackmail for getting what they want. The threat of moving to the other family if not given what he or she wants can lead an insecure stepfamily to give in to unreasonable demands (Whiteside & Auerbach, 1978).

Although it may be reasonable for an adolescent to change residences, the clinician should encourage the two families to band together to prevent an adolescent from using the threat of moving from one family to the other as a ploy for manipulating reduced structure. Both families should be helped to provide a united front (if possible) concerning the conditions under which a change is appropriate.

Jones (1978) noted that the adolescent can also turn a younger sibling against the stepparent. The adolescent may view the affection that the younger sibling is likely to feel toward a stepparent as traitorous to the absent parent and the adolescent. Punishment of the adolescent for this provocative behavior can be particularly problematic. Each punishment is treated as an attack, and the vicious cycle of provocation, punishment, and retaliation begins (Fast & Cain, 1966; Jones, 1978). I have worked with some teenagers who bind the parents in such a way that no response is likely to reduce the level of anger. The provocation is so strong that parents cannot ignore it. Attempts to put the relationship on a more positive attitude is met with disdain. No attempts at giving are accepted. Attempts at ignoring the behavior escalate the battle. Family therapy may be helpful, but it may be difficult to get the teenager (particularly boys) to participate. Individual therapy is sometimes more palatable, but again resistance can be high.

REMARRIAGE AND VISITATION

D. S. Jacobson (1987) evaluated several family types in terms of who had custody, the mother or father, and which parent(s) had remarried. She then related the types of family with the child's behavior problems and the probability of visitation with a noncustodial parent. She found four common types: custodial single mother with remarried father, custodial remarried mother with remarried father, custodial remarried mother with single father, and custodial remarried father with single mother. Of these four types, the highest level of child behavior problems were in the families with custodial remarried father and single mother. The greatest amount of visitation occurred for custodial mother and both parents remarried. The custodial remarried father with single mother had the least visitation. Generally, the younger the child (children in this study were 8 to 17 years of age), the more the visitation. The exception was when both parents had remarried and there was high visitation regardless of the child's age. Visitation levels were high for all groups, ranging from 27 hours for the least visiting group to 41 hours for the most visiting group for a 2-week period.

BIBLIOTHERAPY TO HELP CHILDREN OF REMARRIAGE

Coleman and Ganong (1989) provided a useful, annotated review of 50 self-help books for stepparents. They noted that a third of the men and almost half of the women in stepfamilies sought information and advice from self-help books.

DEATH OF A DIVORCED PARENT AND STEPFAMILIES

When a divorced parent dies, the children have more difficulty with the grieving process than if the parents are not divorced. The children usually recognize the ambivalence or clear anger of the remaining parent and often do not feel that the remaining parent is available to aid in the mourning process. Particularly, when it is the custodial parent who dies, the remaining stepfamily comes under increased pressure. With the remarriage of the remaining parent, the child is particularly likely to see that parent as having changed allegiances (as indeed that parent has), and has difficulty talking to the parent about the grieving.

For the stepmother or stepfather married to the noncustodial parent, a problem of particular poignancy develops when the custodial parent dies. Typically, with the death of the biological custodial parent, the noncustodial biological parent obtains guardianship of the children. The stepparent who was quite comfortable (or more likely, somewhat comfortable) with the visitation, suddenly finds himself or herself with custody and full-time parenting.

When a divorced parent dies, the need for therapy for the children may be quite high. Because the remaining parent is often seen as unavailable for mourning, a neutral person can facilitate that process. When the parent who died was custodial and the remaining parent has remarried, the stepparent may need support for the stress of obtaining full custody when that arrangement was not the original understanding.

I have worked with several stepparents who have shown impressive forbearance for this unexpected situation. This family dynamic is clearly at risk for problems. In one family, several issues were raised by the death of the custodial mother. The family needed help in integrating the son into a family with stepmother and stepsister. The father, who had remarried some years before, needed help in facilitating mourning for the son. The father had created resentment in the family by being so concerned about the son's loss that he had been quite permissive with the son while maintaining strict rules for the stepdaughter. Indeed, some of the son's behavior problems were not in response to the mother's death and incomplete mourning, but to inadequate structure in the home. Once the rules were made uniform in the family, resentment was reduced and the son became better behaved. In another case, a boy had experienced a series of deaths in the family, including the custodial mother, and had to be helped with mourning and fear of death itself. Chronic depression is also a common outcome of this family dynamic.

WHEN REMARRIAGE SHOULD OCCUR

The median number of years for a custodial mother to remarry is 6.3 years. About 30% remarry in 3 years, increasing to 50% at the end of 5 years, and 60% by 8 years (Baydar, 1988). Remarriage seems to work best in terms of child adjustment if it occurs between 2 and 4 years after the breakup of the previous marriage. If the remarriage is too soon, the children are not given an opportunity to grieve the loss of the previous relationship. If remarriage occurs much later, habits of interaction become more difficult to break. The child has become more used to the attention and roles assigned and resents the stepparent's intrusion to a greater degree.

RELATIONSHIPS WITH STEPGRANDPARENTS

One problem that can arise in remarried families is the difference in the relationships of grandparents to their biological grandchildren and to stepgrandchildren. It is only natural for grandparents to have a greater bond with a biological grandchild than with a stepgrandchild because there has been more time and contact (often from birth) to develop bonding and because the biological relationship may lead to stronger identification. Particularly in families with both stepchildren and biological children, differential treatment of the biological grandchild (e.g., on birthdays and holidays) can unintentionally create feelings of rejection and abandonment by the stepchild.

If the grandparent is willing, it may be helpful for family unity and reduction of territorial feelings to request that the grandparent provide similar gifts and time to biological and stepgrandchildren.

BIBLIOGRAPHIES ON STEPFAMILIES

Several bibliographies on stepfamilies are available for those who wish to systematically review the literature (Bergquist, 1984; Ihinger-Tallman, 1988; J. J. Miller & Soper, 1982; L. Walker et al., 1979). The best overviews of working with remarried families are by Visher and Visher (1979, 1988).

THE PREDICTION OF DIFFICULTIES FOR REMARRIED FAMILIES

McGoldrick and Carter (1980) proposed nine warning signs for troubles for remarried families:

1. A wide discrepancy between family life cycle stages for the two families. When one parent has older children and the other has either no children or very young children, the discrepancy creates new problems of adjustment. One parent has to recycle over a previously accomplished stage, sometimes with strong reluctance.
2. Denial of prior loss or quick remarriage.
3. Failure to resolve the intense relationship issues of the first family.
4. Expectations that remarriage will be easily accepted by the children.
5. Inability to give up the ideal of the intact first family.
6. Forcing primary loyalty to the new family.
7. Exclusion of other parent or grandparents.
8. Denial of differences of a remarried family.
9. Shift in custody of children at time of remarriage.

THE PREDICTION OF SUCCESS IN REMARRIAGE

Based on the previous discussion, it is possible to be so discouraged about the ability of remarried families to survive as to recommend against remarriage in any case where there are children, particularly older children. Although the remarried family does have vulnerabilities that are unique to that family structure, by no means are all remarried families doomed. Numerous adults have reported strong feelings of affection for a stepparent, as well as parent–stepparent marriages that are strong and loving. Some research supports the belief that stepfamilies can do very well.

Bernard (1971) looked at census data, case material, and questionnaires filled out by close acquaintances of 2,009 remarried families. Although some people went through serial marriages, one right after another, most people were as successful in remarriages as first marriages. Bernard noted that the strengths in remarriages include age, maturity, a new environmental situation, and greater motivation to reduce marital difficulties. She felt that the variables associated with remarriage success were:

1. The partners were over 20 years of age in the first marriage.
2. The partners had good first marriages.
3. The spouses have college-level education.
4. Either no children were born in the first marriage or the wife has sole custody of her children.
5. Both sets of parents are favorable to the remarriage.
6. The community is favorable to the wife's remarriage.
7. An optimal time lapse has occurred between marriages.

COHABITING "STEPPARTNERS"

With the sharp increase in cohabiting relationships in the United States over the last decade, more and more children are being exposed to a live-in relationship between one of their parents and a significant other. Some of these relationships represent serial monogamy, others only a series of short-term relationships. Children who attach to such "parenting" figures tend to give up trying to attach because the repeated sense of loss is too painful. Relatively stable, enduring relationships in which the cohabiting partner is in a relationship similar to marriage are more common, but these lack the community sanctions for validity.

If the role of the stepparent is vague and ill defined, the role of the cohabiting pseudo-stepparent, or *steppartner,* is even more so. Because the relationship lacks community legitimacy, it is not unusual for the steppartner to be significantly snubbed. In one family with which I worked, the father had joint custody and his steppartner played a significant role in child care, including feeding and babysitting the 3-, 4-, and 6-year-olds. Although the steppartner became quite attached to the children, the community gave no legitimacy to her role. Other parents expressed disapproval when she showed up at school functions and they snubbed her socially. She had to work significantly hard to define what kind of parenting role was appropriate. In communities in which cohabiting is common, the cohabiting steppartner may have an easier time. In most communities, however, the problems of the stepparents are compounded by the lack of definition of this new role.

The cohabiting steppartner is likely to need significant help in defining his or her role. Although many of the issues around parenting are the same as for stepparents, the lack of legitimacy may require more negotiations within the family to clarify and negotiate expectations. Family-oriented therapy is likely to be helpful in this process.

SUMMARY

Clinicians working with families of divorce are often working with remarried families. Effective interventions can be facilitated by knowledge of development; potential problems in the area of affection, discipline, territory, loyalties, and interrupted history; and the typical problems of each family member.

CHAPTER 10

Group Therapy Strategies for Children in School and Community

Group therapy approaches can be powerful interventions for children of divorce. In a group setting, children can find that their experiences are shared by others, that their fears are not unique, and that others have solved some of the problems about parental divorce. Each child also has the opportunity to be in a helpful, supportive role with other children, a process that enhances self-esteem and competence.

SCHOOL-BASED INTERVENTIONS

School provides an important setting for group interventions. All children are accessible, and prevention or early detection of problems is possible. Because children of divorce are more likely to have academic and behavior problems in the classroom, helping them is consistent with the educational mandate of the school.

This section focuses on group therapy and instructional approaches to interventions in the schools. Carlson (1987) felt that school-based interventions are likely to be inadequate if the child is experiencing chronic school problems, particularly if the problems began before the marital separation, if the child has serious psychopathology, or if the child is from a chronically dysfunctional or conflictual family.

School-based interventions are less likely to be effective if the child has severe problems or a severely dysfunctional family.

Interventions are generally broken down into the following age groups to take into account the different cognitive abilities of the children:

- Preschool children
- Early elementary school, grades 1 to 3
- Late elementary school or early middle school, grades 4 to 6
- Junior high school or later middle school, grades 7 to 8

- High school, grades 9 to 12 (may be broken up into grades 9 to 10 and grades 11 to 12).

As discussed in the following sections, preplanning for school-based programs requires covering some basic issues regardless of the age of the children.

Administrative Support

The mental health professional should start by meeting with the administration and staff of the school in which the intervention will be based. If the school feels that there is a need and is willing to devote some resources to providing a program, several questions need to be resolved prior to offering the program. These questions involve parental permission, timing, classroom teacher involvement, parental involvement, and identifying therapists and participants.

Getting Parental Permission

Is parental permission required for children to participate? Although school districts vary in policy regarding parental permission, particularly when counselors in the school are providing the service and when the service is provided during school hours, protection of the school from upset parents suggests that permission usually should be obtained, and perhaps be legally required. For high school students, the ability to make a decision about participation in services without parental permission may be more appropriate, again depending on school administrative policy. School districts are enormously vulnerable to angry parents, and any upset from parents is likely to hurt the program.

Parents may be reluctant to provide permission out of concern that the child will reveal family secrets. Because no child is required to talk in the group and the focus of many such groups is educational, it is often possible to reassure the parent that the purpose of the groups is not to discuss highly personal issues, but to help the child think about the various aspects of the divorce experience, to explore feelings that may be held in common with children in the group, and to work on solving day-to-day problems. For programs based on topic-oriented units, describing some of the units may reduce parental anxiety about the child's participation. For example, parents may be informed that the program includes units on building self-esteem, understanding feelings about the self, understanding other people's feelings, and general problem solving. These topics sound less "loaded" than discussing why parents got divorced.

Some parents are reluctant to have their children participate because of concern that participation is an admission that the divorce was harmful to the children. Information sheets that depathologize the children are likely to be helpful. Parents who feel grievously harmed by the divorce and who want to prove that it was harmful to their children are often eager to have their child participate.

One surprise for me when I worked with school guidance counselors in junior high school groups was that the level of problems of the children who participated was often significantly higher than that of the children whom I was seeing in my practice. Upon reflection, it was easy to explain. Parents who show sufficient concern to take their children to a therapist are already demonstrating several resources (i.e., sufficient sensitivity to potential or actual problems that the child is having, financial ability, and the willingness to invest time and energy in seeking therapy for the child). Parents of children in school programs are often willing to have a child participate because it involves no time, energy, or money. Therefore, children with less support than those who end up in private therapy may participate in school-based programs.

Timing

The issue of when the intervention will be provided raises questions: Will the intervention be provided during school hours, or before or after school? If the program is provided during school hours, how will the disruption to the school time be handled? Some schools use a nonacademic activity time for the groups, such as lunch hour (students bring their own lunches), and others have rotated the hour of the school day in which the groups meet to minimize the amount of time that the child misses a particular academic activity.

Many participants feel special getting out of class during school hours to attend a program. In fact, the opportunity to miss class can be so powerful a special consideration that it may produce a placebo effect. Recently, I served on a dissertation committee in which the faculty requested that in a study of the effectiveness of an elementary school-based intervention program, the control group should be children getting out of class for another special activity. The control setup (a very expensive control) was a program of career planning; children either went to the divorce group or to the career planning group. With this elimination of a powerful attention placebo, no benefits were found in the behavior of children who participated (Boren, 1982).

Before-school or after-school group programs lose some of the special treatment for the children (an advantage if the children tend to feel stigmatized), but pose other problems. In schools in which a significant number of children arrive by school bus, extracurricular programs will make it impossible for some children to participate. In addition, if the parent has to provide transportation, defensive parents and those who work (a likely occurrence in families of divorce) may be unwilling or unable to bring the child in early or pick the child up after school.

Teaching staff may express some concerns about the effects of missing class for these children, some of whom may already be having academic problems. It does not help the child of divorce to antagonize the classroom teacher by participating in the program. If the time is rotated, however, the child should not miss more than two classes at a particular time of day for the entire program, which for most children is not likely to be a serious problem. Also, at test times, flexibility can be exercised so that the child can take a make-up test or miss the group during a test, depending on the feelings of each classroom teacher.

If the teaching staff are willing to tolerate the disruption to the teaching schedule, providing groups during school time will increase the likelihood of participation by children most needing the group support.

Classroom Teacher Involvement

Should the classroom teacher be involved in identifying the children who should be invited to participate? This question can best be answered by the teaching staff. Do they want to participate? Would they be willing to participate in a program evaluation? What problems in the classroom concern them the most? Would they like a report back to the teaching staff about how well the groups work? This latter question raises the issue of confidentiality and how it will be handled in the school. I believe that confidentiality of individual children should be protected, so that specific feedback about individuals should be avoided.

Schools often feel that any information about a child should be shared with the staff. In a therapeutic situation, however, the limits of confidentiality should be made clear. If the teachers are going to receive feedback about individual children, parents and children should be informed at the time that informed consent is acquired. Trust is basic to the therapeutic process, and school-based groups are more effective if the children are informed (truthfully) that all information is to be kept within the group. It may be useful to indicate that information about abuse cannot be kept a secret and should not be. Parents should also be told that individual feedback about their child will not be available.

Parental Involvement

Should pre- and posttreatment meetings be held for the parents? Certainly, if parents show enough concern to be willing to come into the school to discuss what the groups will do and what the issues of divorce are for children, the intervention is likely to be more powerful. Parents who want help understanding their children, want suggestions about child-rearing strategies, and want to support their children getting help, are likely to support the groups.

Requiring parental participation will increase the impact on children who participate, but will prevent participation of some children, perhaps those who are in the greatest need.

Sonnenshein-Schneider and Baird (1980) recommended obtaining basic information from parents of elementary age children. This information builds a communication channel with the parents and provides a realistic assessment of each child's situation. As they noted, children can introduce fantasy as reality, and the counselor can help the child separate these issues.

Number of Therapists

If possible, it is extremely helpful to have two therapists, rather than one, particularly if they are of each gender. Although two therapists are expensive, it is helpful to have one therapist focusing on the child speaking and the other watching for reactions among the other children. It is possible to draw out relatively quiet children by noting that they seem to be reacting to what another child is saying. If the group has trouble settling down, control is also easier if the two therapists sit apart. Two leaders also make it possible to model adults interacting without conflict and to role play for the adults around issues of the divorce.

Identifying Potential Participants

Drake (1981) suggested several criteria for identifying which children need additional help. The first criterion is identifying which children are having unusual adjustment problems. Are the problems typical reactions for a child of that age and gender? Can the child be expected to recover from this reaction using his or her natural coping skills? A second criterion is length of time for crisis resolution. Has the child manifested the problems for more than 1 or 2 years? A third criterion is the degree of the problems, particularly depression and explosiveness. Drake noted that comments about self-harming behaviors should be given special notice. Additional assessments that follow Kelly and Wallerstein's (1976) model include obtaining a brief history indicating the child's understanding of the divorce and the available support systems.

INTERVENTION STRATEGIES

The following sections are summaries of several school-based and other group interventions. Presented in some detail are those programs that are unique, those that have served as model programs, and those for which evaluations of effectiveness have been obtained. Other programs are described in terms of new contributions. Reference to the original publication should be made if elaboration is desired.

Preschool Interventions

Preschool-based programs are rare. Rossiter (1988) described a six-session group program, in which two therapists and no more than five children participate per group. Because children this young are reassured with a routine, the structure of the sessions follows the same format every week: a snack, an activity, a film or story, art work, and nondirected play. The six sessions are as follows:

1. The therapists use a toy porcupine that talks about being afraid of being in the group. Children are asked how to help the porcupine. The topic of divorce is introduced, and each child is encouraged to tell about that child's situation. A metaphorical story of five sticks floating down a river and overcoming an obstacle is used. The children talk about their feelings. They then begin to create individual books by drawing a picture of their family and dictating a story to the therapist, who writes it down.

2. The focus of the second session is on abandonment. Using the porcupine and a maple tree seed (with two pods that can be separated and both grow), the therapists tell a story about the seed. The children then act in a play about the seed. A short film on feeling sad is presented, and the children are asked to draw a picture about when they have felt sad. The children then dictate a narrative for the developing book.

3. The purpose of the third session is to explore reconciliation fantasies. Using the inability of oil and colored water to mix, the therapists present the difference between wishes and reality. Children are asked to draw an important wish and dictate a narrative. A story on an impossible wish is read.

4. The discussion in the fourth session is on transitions between parents. The therapists use the porcupine to introduce feelings of missing the absent parent and to ask the children to problem solve for the porcupine. If participants visit overnight, children are asked to use a suitcase, clothing, and other articles to pack what they take with them when they visit. A 10-foot-long plastic tunnel is used to represent transition, and an animal family play is used to work on transitions. The children draw a picture of the tunnel for the book. A story on visitation is read.

5. The focus on the fifth session is on happy times. The stick story is used, but each stick is given one of the children's names. The children draw a picture of the stick overcoming obstacles for the book. A "divorce box" is constructed, with pictures of good and bad things about divorce pasted on it.

6. The focus of the final session is on saying good-bye. The porcupine talks about feeling good and bad about saying good-bye. The stick story is continued with the sticks making their goal. Using painted blocks, children make a city for children whose parents do not live together. Each child draws a picture on good-byes for the book, and a story on saying good-bye is read.

Elementary School Interventions

Early Elementary School Interventions

Generally, it is recommended to have a somewhat smaller group for early elementary age children than for later elementary age children because their need for attention may be higher, their need for structure may be greater, and their ability to wait for attention may be less. Groups of 6 or 7 may be adequate. Sonnenshein-Schneider and Baird (1980) recommended that sessions be limited to 15 or 20 minutes for younger primary groups. Children need to have group rules explained, including the concept of confidentiality (i.e., that no one talks to anyone else about what the group talks about).

Elementary school age children are low on empathy for each other. The cruelty of teasing at this age can be extraordinary. There must be strong control by the leader or leaders to prevent the teasing that is common among children in primary school (and up to 15 years of age).

Keeping secrets must be emphasized. The leaders must explain rules to prevent teasing and attacking statements and must exert control over the group to stop such statements should they occur.

Sonnenshein-Schneider and Baird (1980) noted that a common part of the egocentrism of this age is the competition for attention by telling war stories. Almost every child had at least one traumatic story that was told and retold to the group. The child expects the story to have the same shock value for all the other children. With the retelling, however, the story begins to lose its tragic power, and the child gets the message that the event was not that bad and was survivable.

Early elementary school programs often focus initially on interventions that are not specific to divorce. Group building techniques, affective training, and general problem solving may all precede any discussion of divorce per se. Later, the program may involve divorce-specific discussions.

The following suggestions are examples for group building by Joan Levine and Norman Dewhurst of a Mental Health Team in the Cherry Creek School District in Colorado:

1. *The name game.* Have each child add something to his or her name that says something about himself or herself. Then the child repeats what the previous person said about himself or herself.
2. *Car wash.* Have the children form two lines. Each child goes down a line and looks at a person and says something positive (a potentially difficult exercise). The child being complimented can only say, "Thank you."

More divorce-specific exercises include:

1. *Reverse fantasies.* Have the children draw four pictures: a happy time with the family, a sad time with the family, what the child would like to have happen now, and what the child would like to have happen in 2 years. The pictures are used for discussion.

2. *Group murals.* Every child draws on a large sheet of paper something important happening in the family.

3. *A family tree.* Each child draws his or her family tree.

4. *Children sit in a circle.* Provide a topic and each child draws a part of the picture and passes it on. For example, children may draw a composite picture of the day the family split up.

5. *Bibliotherapy.* Read from books about children going through divorce.

6. *Discuss pictures relevant to divorce.*

To help children understand their family situation in a way consistent with their concrete operational thinking, Sonnenshein-Schneider and Baird (1980) suggested drawing family pictures with a separate picture of the absent parent. They also suggested brainstorming in conjunction with role playing and role rehearsal. When a group member expresses a problem, the group brainstorms possible solutions. When a possible solution is found, the children role play and rehearse the act of asking for what they want. Early brainstorming may have a funny, wild feeling that is part of the group cohesion. Wild solutions decline, and the counselor can direct the discussion to form functional solutions. Sonnenshein-Schneider and Baird also used storybooks, slide-tape programs, and movies. Puppets were used to act out feelings and situations.

For younger elementary school children, Drake (1981) suggested play involving family changes, using "dress up" adult-like clothes, doll houses and furniture, and household items as props for common household scenes. For sublimating aggression, Drake suggested using an inflated plastic clown for punching, toy percussion musical instruments, and banging tools such as hammers. Sports can also provide aggression outlets. Creative opportunities, using clay, cutting and pasting, or finger painting, can provide outlets for feelings. These suggestions are similar to those that would be used by a play therapist in an individual setting, but clearly can be used in the school setting, either by a counselor in individual or group therapy or by the classroom teacher.

Drake also focused on helping the young child communicate feelings, particularly to release feelings of depression. She provided a list of 48 feelings that a person might have when parents separate or divorce. The teacher or counselor might read these to the child and ask the child to choose the ones that he or she feels. Other feeling-eliciting activities include drawing pictures of feelings, teaching empathic assertion (Kessler & Bostwick, 1977), and role playing.

Drake suggested pairing a child experiencing shame associated with the separation and divorce with a child who is openly accepting of the parent's divorce. Group work for children of divorce can also help a child accept the divorce without shame.

Many of Drake's (1981) suggestions can also be used for the later elementary school children.

Later Elementary School Interventions

It is easier to provide interventions for fourth, fifth, and sixth graders than for younger children because the increased verbal skills make it easier for the older children to talk about the divorce. They are also significantly less egocentric and can recognize both similarities and differences between their experiences and the experiences of other children in the group. Because these children's attention span is significantly longer, discussion can last for longer periods of time, perhaps 30 to 45 minutes rather than 20. Groups can be slightly larger (7 to 10) since children are more likely to have some self-control.

Levine and Dewhurst suggested the following activities for this age:

1. Have each child say three things about himself or herself. One thing should be false. The group must guess which one. (I particularly like this exercise because it taps the game playing preference of this age group.)
2. Role play the courtroom divorce scene. Children who were at court often have strong memories of the event, whereas children who were not have strong fantasies. Reenactment can help the child think about and work through the feelings about the divorce.
3. Write a book about the divorce. One chapter is written for each session. The therapist suggests a topic for each session. Topics might include divorce, parental dating, family secrets, family spying, remarriage, money, or visitation. A variation on this approach includes having the children give advice to other children going through divorce or advice to parents on how to help children.
4. Use sentence stems to encourage verbalization of feelings. Stems might include such statements as "My mother gets angry at me when . . ." or "I get sad about . . ." Children write down their answers in private and can keep them private if they wish. The therapist then brings up a stem and invites children to read their answers aloud. Putting it in writing reduces anxiety about saying it aloud and increases the chances that the children can discuss the issue raised.
5. Role play. The therapists (particularly if male and female) role play a divorcing couple. The children write the script for the problem. The therapists can role play appropriate problem solving or have the children suggest solutions to the problem with which the parents are struggling.

Cantor's Groups

In her program for third through sixth graders, Cantor (1977) included many of the topics discussed later for secondary school students, including eavesdropping, spying, being used by a parent, not liking to have to choose between parents, the loss of a parent, relationships with stepparents, visitation, and court battles. Cantor also used parts of *The Boys and Girls Book About Divorce* (Gardner, 1970) as a basis for stimulating discussion. One group wrote a play, including scenes on fighting, separating, going to court, and developing new relationships.

Wilkinson and Bleck's Groups

Wilkinson and Bleck's (1977) program for children's divorce groups includes the following exercises:

1. Naming each other.
2. Keeping secrets.
3. An animal like you. Have each child draw a picture of an animal that the child feels is most like himself or herself. For example, a child might draw a lion because the child roars at people when he or she is angry.
4. Pleasant and unpleasant feeling words. Have the children list as many feeling words as they can think of. Have them make two lists, one for pleasant feelings and one for unpleasant feelings.
5. Filmstrip entitled "Understanding Changes in the Family: Not Together Anymore" (Guidance Associates, 1973).
6. Personal shield. Have each child draw a shield with four separate parts. The children draw a picture in each part: (1) a good time they had with their family, (2) an unpleasant time they had with their family, why they think their parents got divorced, and something they would like to see happen to the family next year.
7. Role playing the problems of divorce. Have the children list as many problems of divorce as possible, and select the two or three most important by group vote and role play them. Then discuss the solutions.
8. Puppet plays. Use puppets to dramatize the problems. One member is the director of the play. The counselor leads a group discussion of the feelings, behaviors, and consequences of the characters. Children then discuss alternate ways to solve the problems.
9. Positive aspects of divorce. The children cut out pictures from magazines or draw pictures that might stand for pleasant things that happened as a result of the divorce. They then share the experiences.
10. Positive feedback. One person sits in a chair and the rest of the group says positive things to that person.
11. Each person relates what has been learned in the group.

The Helping Children of Divorce Groups

B. J. Green (1978) developed the HELPING Children of Divorce program. HELPING is an acronym for Health, nonjudgmental Environment, becoming aware of the Learning process, establishing Positive relationships, Images for happy lives, Need to know, and Guidance of behaviors, actions, and consequences. For each of these areas, Green included basic treatment strategies to help children.

The program is based on eight sessions, each having three components: (1) an icebreaker, (2) a stimulus activity, and (3) closing time.

The following are examples of icebreakers:

1. Each child makes a name tag with name, favorite thing, favorite television show and star, three favorite foods, favorite color, and one word that describes him or her. After pairing children in dyads to discuss name tags, each dyad introduces themselves to the group.

2. The children participate in either–or forced choice, a value clarifications exercise (Simon, Howe, & Kirschenbaum, 1972). Each child divides a paper into four spaces and draws or writes something that child likes to do alone, with a friend/friends, with the family, and with one parent. Each child then shares the answers with the group.

3. On the back of self-portraits, the children list positive, rational statements that describe themselves. Other children add to each child's list.

4. Each child draws a family portrait, labels members, and discusses it.

5. Each child is given a design (a star with a central circle) and asked to fill the spaces with pictures, words, or symbols. The center of the design is self-image, and the outside points are learning, friends, family, feelings, a positive thought kept all the time, and a behavior that is enjoyable or has gotten under control.

Stimulus activities include the following:

1. Each child is given a copy of *The Boys and Girls Book about Divorce* (Gardner, 1970) and parts are discussed over several sessions.

2. The group works on a poster that depicts feelings that come with divorce. The children then complete a personal set of "feeling gauges," indicating the intensity of several divorce-related feelings.

3. The group brainstorms problems that children see about divorce and possible solutions.

4. The children play the Acting, Feeling, Choosing Game (Keat, 1978).

5. The children watch the filmstrip, "Understanding Changes in the Family: Not Together Anymore (Guidance Associates, 1973). The children divide into dyads and role play the child in the film and the child's friend.

6. The group watches the television program "Breakup" (National Instructional Television Center, 1973).

Closing activities include the following:

1. The group discusses privacy, confidentiality, rules for discussion, and future sessions.
2. The children's homework is to finish reading the book.
3. The children write down feelings that they have during the week.
4. Children tell themselves and another person how they feel once each day for the next week.
5. Children are to increase their lists of positive self-statements, and tell someone what they like about him or her once each day.
6. Each child talks to a close friend about the divorce and reports back to the group about the experience.
7. Each child talks to one family member about the divorce and reports back about the experience.
8. The group has a party.

Crosbie-Burnett and Newcomer (1989) used a modification of Green's HELPING modes, borrowing also from Hammond's (1981c) and Wilkinson and Bleck's (1977) programs. They added an activity based on the movie "Tender Places" (Films for Humanity, 1987), with a discussion about the feelings of the 10-year-old boy whose parents had divorced. They also added a quiz of 11 commonly held beliefs about divorce as a basis for discussion.

Bowker's Groups

Bowker (1982) developed an intervention program in which elementary school children created and produced a sound filmstrip that told the story of separation and divorce from the child's point of view. Two groups of fifth-grade children met weekly for one academic year (an unusually long time for such groups) to discuss issues and feelings about the family breakup. Unlike most groups described above, these children were grouped by sex. Each child was interviewed individually, told about the group, and invited to participate. Bibliotherapy, which was used more heavily than in other described programs, included *How Does It Feel When Your Parents Are Divorced?* (Berger, 1977) and *What's Going to Happen to Me? When Parents Separate or Divorce* (LeShan, 1978). The children then developed a story line and prepared graphics. They worked on crayon and ink drawings to depict feelings. Using magazines, they created word and picture collages. They selected background music, wrote dialogue, and taped the story. Classrooms were invited to see the film and enter into discussion. A special viewing for parents was made available.

The Children of Family Change Groups

The Children of Family Change program (Holdahl & Caspersen, 1977) was developed for children from 8 to 12 years of age. The children met for 5 consecutive days for 1 hour per session. The program was designed to be therapeutic through education rather than through counseling. The program used a model of training that led the children to identify life events that require readjustment, to personalize the events to their own lives, to integrate feelings with their knowledge and interpretation of stressful events, to apply skills to solve problems, and to practice those skills. During the program, the children read five books on divorce (e.g. *Rosie and Michael,* Viorst, 1975a; *The tenth good thing about Michael,* Viorst, 1975b; *Where is daddy?* Goff, 1969; *Gaston,* Saroyan, 1972), family conflict, and relationships.

Kalter, Pickar, and Lesowitz's Groups

Kalter, Pickar, and Lesowitz (1984) described a school-based program for fifth and sixth graders. Children met for 1 hour per week at school for 8 weeks. Group leaders were one male and one female. The group was given four rules: (1) members would talk one at a time so everyone could be heard, (2) feelings would be respected, (3) a member who did not want to talk could pass, and (4) everything said was private. During the sessions, the children created a group-generated story, role played, performed skits, and made a group newspaper on how children think about divorce.

Kalter et al. noted that several themes were common: anxiety over parental battles, conflict over loyalties, anxiety over possible change in custody, sadness over the loss of the original family and less contact with the father, excitement and anxiety about the mother's dating, and anger at the mother's boyfriend or new husband over discipline.

Stolberg and Cullen's Groups

Stolberg and Cullen (1983) developed a primary prevention program for children from 8 to 13 years of age with three components. The Children's Support Group was a school-based educational program designed to help children with a supportive group experience. The intervention involved 12 weekly 1-hour sessions led by one or two mental health professionals. The group experience included impulse control training, communication skills training, anger control skills, and relaxation techniques. Discussion, modeling, and role playing were used to teach children new ways of handling divorce-related situations. Children were selected who were not having significant behavioral or emotional problems.

Each 1-hour session was divided into two sections (Stolberg & Garrison, 1985). Part I included a discussion of a specific session-linked topic, such as "Whose fault is it?" What do I do on vacation?" and "Do I worry about my dad?" Part II of each session involved the teaching, modeling, and rehearsal of specific cognitive-behavioral skills.

Gwynn and Brantley's Educational Support Groups

Gwynn and Brantley (1987) presented a program for 9- to 11-year-olds whose parents had been separated for a year. The program comprised the following eight sessions:

1. Introduction. Children made puppets to facilitate role playing later. Each child was encouraged to tell something about himself or herself and something that had happened since the divorce.
2. Children learned how to talk about the divorce to friends and teachers, using a filmstrip and role playing.
3-4. Children learned how to handle situations and feelings during visitation. They discussed divorce-related vocabulary, and made drawings about visitation.
5. Children were asked to identify feelings that parents and children share and how they are shown. A filmstrip and role playing followed up on the discussion. Stepfamily problems were introduced.
6. Children were asked to share problems regarding parent and sibling conflicts.
7. Children were taught problem solving techniques using a modification of the Talking, Feeling, and Doing Game (Gardner, 1973).
8. Children discussed the new skills and information that the sessions had provided. Good-bye pictures were drawn. Children were asked to draw possible future events that would be positive.

Tedder, Scherman, and Wantz's Support Groups

Using some exercises not mentioned in the above studies, Tedder, Scherman, and Wantz (1987) developed a group support approach for 10- and 11-year-olds. The new activities were the following:

1. Each child was given eight circles of construction paper representing segments of a caterpillar. The children filled in the circles by writing or drawing the following on segments 1 through 8: (1) a head with an expressive face, (2) three words that describe themselves, (3) two hobbies, (4) three current feelings, (5) birthplace, (6) where they would like to be, (7) an activity they would like to do, and (8) a quality that makes them special.
2. A bingo-type feeling game.
3. An interview with a judge.

Other exercises for the 11 sessions overlapped with previously described programs.

Evaluations were done before and after the program (without a control group). The parents rated the children as being less distractible, having fewer behavior problems, and having improved peer relations and maturity. The absence of a control group meant that any observed changes could have been due to the passage of time. Teachers did not report any changes in the classroom.

Other Groups

Two additional interventions were developed for parents. The Beyond Divorce program, developed by Kessler (1977), involved a 10-session adult education program. Parenting Alone Together was a 10-session educational program developed for the Beyond Divorce program. This program provided single parents with support, information about divorce, and strategies for increasing family cooperation, family communication skills, and child management skills. Discussion of the effectiveness of these programs is presented later in the chapter.

Secondary School Interventions

Techniques for junior and senior high school students do not necessarily vary, although the psychological mindedness and maturity of the participants certainly do. Anxiety and self-consciousness may make junior high kids more reluctant to participate. Empathy is lower because the shift from concrete operational thinking to formal operational thinking means that the child has lost the concrete empathy of late latency but is not yet able to use the abstract ability of adolescence. Boys may show an increasing concern about participating because sex role is a central issue for adolescent boys, and talking about problems is often not accepted by boys as a way of handling upset. We found that seventh-grade boys were somewhat willing to participate, but that ninth-grade boys were often reluctant.

Group Composition

It is useful to build the group with teenagers at different levels of psychological mindedness. Teenagers with good coping skills and relatively little upset about the divorce may provide good role models for the rest of the group. It also is useful to invite some teenagers who are relatively verbal and comfortable with the adult leaders. Too many highly verbal members may lead to competition for center stage rather than providing some potential leaders for discussion. Highly aggressive, negativistic members should be avoided or limited to one. More than one may feed off each other in a synergistic way that would be destructive to the group process.

Group Strategies

Barbara Kulton, Barbara Stiltner, and I led junior high school groups that met for one period (40 minutes) each week. The techniques we used were developed by Kulton and Stiltner. We rotated class times for the group. In one group, we tried to have two consecutive periods at times, but the 80-minute sessions seemed too long for junior high students.

In these groups, the teenagers drew life lines representing the major events in their lives, that is, when they were born, where they lived, and what things happened to them in their lives up to the present time. The line could be straight, jagged, or curved. Students typically marked moves, births, deaths, and accidents (e.g., "When I was 6, I broke my arm"). This exercise gave them an opportunity to tell the group when the divorce happened and with whom they were presently living. In one group with whom I worked, several members became so upset telling the group about when the divorce occurred that they had trouble continuing the discussion. Later, these same adolescents indicated that telling the group was the most useful experience they had had, as it was the first time they had ever told anyone what had happened. The advantage of revealing this information early is to reduce secrets about living situations and to help the entire group know the living situation of each member.

Several problems are more likely in junior high groups than in younger groups. Teasing can be vicious and must be prevented. Confidentiality has to be stressed, given children's tendency to gossip at this age. Although students who dominate the group should be given their chance to have their say, they should be controlled. Competition between participants should be discouraged. A child who says, "You think you have problems!" should be encouraged to first listen and then talk about his or her situation. Also, the leader must control tangential responses that either reduce tension or gain attention. Leaders should not worry about teens who seldom talk, but who are monitoring the process. The quiet ones seem to watch and learn even if they do not feel comfortable speaking.

Even when they do not contribute, nonverbal junior and senior high students may obtain significant benefits from group membership by observing and modeling.

Empathy training is important with early adolescents because of their egocentrism. Asking the group to paraphrase what a participant has said is helpful training.

Ventilation of feelings can increase self-esteem, but continued griping is not therapeutic. Focusing on problem solving after ventilation is more useful, as is helping a child to discover when to give up on a particular problem and look elsewhere to get those particular needs satisfied.

Junior and senior high school groups require less structure than elementary school groups. Because this age group can be more reflective, it is possible to use short vignettes to start the group, and then let group discussion carry the therapy. For example, a 5- or 10-minute narrative might describe problems of divorce that some children feel. Such a presentation can make it easier for the group to agree or disagree based on their own experience. Topics we have used include the following:

1. How did you hear about the divorce? How did your parents tell you? Could they have done it better? Did you know what was going to happen? Was it hard or easy to ask questions? What questions did you have?

2. What would you like to say to your parents about the divorce? Do you think it was a good idea? Would you like them to get back together? Any advantages? Any disadvantages?

3. How do you talk with parents? How is anger handled? Is there a more constructive way to communicate anger?

4. Is there enough money? Is there child support? Is it predictable? Do parents fight over money?

5. What do you do about parents dating?

6. What are the problems of having a single parent?

7. What are the problems of remarriage?

8. How are holidays handled? (These children often have significant concerns about where they will be on holidays. Parents often avoid discussing this issue until late and do not know that the teenager is worried. Teens should be encouraged to ask their parents about holiday visitation.)

9. How do you feel about the future? Do you want to marry?

10. Do your parents want you to spy? How can you get out of the middle?

11. How do you look at both sides of options for solving problems? (One major strategy for use with adolescents is training them to look at both sides of an issue and to tolerate ambivalence about a problem. If the teen is able to list all the good and bad about a person or all the good and bad about the various alternatives for solving problems, splitting is reduced and better problem solving results.)

12. How much control do you want? How much control do you need? Do parents take your feelings into account enough? Too much?

The groups I worked with met for 10 weeks and celebrated the last session by going out to eat as a group. Group solidarity was strong. Some friendships continued beyond the termination of the groups. We got numerous requests for continuing the groups, which we had to turn down in order to give other children in the school an opportunity to participate.

High School Groups

As might be expected, high school programs tend to be less structured than junior high programs. A core idea is presented to initiate the discussion. Coffman and Roark (1988) described a group counseling program for groups of 5 to 10 students. In the initial session, information about the effect of divorce was presented. Facilitation primarily involved encouraging expression of feelings or providing support. "I" and "we" interactions were emphasized, using reflection, clarification, linking between students, and redirection (from negative aspects or from a dominant member). If a member was unable to move from "I" to "we" in focus, that person was offered individual psychotherapy.

BIBLIOTHERAPY WITH CHILDREN

Several of the group programs use popular books as a core for discussion about the problems of divorce. Clearly, the vicarious experience of another child's coping with similar issues can be helpful for children. Bibliotherapy using books that might be helpful to the child and to the parent can be provided. (Reading lists are provided by Bernstein, 1977; Cantor & Drake, 1983; J. Fassler, 1978; Freeman, 1985; McKay, Rogers, Blades, & Gosse, 1984.)

INTERVENTIONS WITH PARENTS

Drake (1981) suggested that school-based programs for parents can also be helpful. Programs on helping children with separation and divorce can be the basis of parent–teacher meetings. Information presented in Chapters 2 and 3 on typical reactions and concerns of children at different ages can be used. Chapter 11 provides specific suggestions for information and strategies that can also be used when talking with parents. Parents can be encouraged to use the books suggested in the previous section on bibliotherapy.

INTERVENTIONS WITH TEACHERS

Classroom teachers sometimes have a substantial bias that children of divorce are always maladjusted. Workshops for the classroom teacher can reduce these stereotypes. In addition, it is useful to train the classroom teacher to provide help to parents undergoing marital separation. The classroom teacher can also evaluate when additional understanding and structure are indicated. A broader intervention and prevention program at the classroom level may involve classroom reading and discussion on how different families work.

INTERVENTIONS AT THE SCHOOL SYSTEM LEVEL

School policy can have a significant impact on children of divorce. For example, does the school have a policy of providing information about the child to both biological parents, regardless of custody? Personal information about the child may have to be provided only to the custodial parent, unless a permission form is obtained from the custodial parent.

It is important for the schools to do what they can to keep both parents involved with the child and to provide support for the child in the school setting. According to the Federal Educational Rights and Privacy Act, non-custodial parents have access to a child's school records unless there is a court ruling prohibiting it (Drake, 1981). Schools can usually send newsletters about school activities, concerts, talent shows, and parent–teacher nights to noncustodial parents without permission of the custodial parent.

Forms

Drake (1981) noted that restructuring the information requested on forms is important for children of divorce. If an emergency form does not indicate the special family circumstances for the child, the child may feel left out or ashamed. Providing more than one line for parents' names and providing for the child and the custodial mother to have different last names are two examples. It also may be useful to the school to know the type of custody if the parents are divorced and whether there are any restrictions on access to information, to school announcements, or to the child.

Parent–Teacher Conferencing

Parent–teacher conference nights can be particularly difficult for divorced parents. Although it is an extra burden for teachers, it is likely to pay off if divorced parents are given the option of two separate appointments (particularly if either has remarried or is cohabiting). In addition, it may be difficult for either parent to come if the parent cannot arrange for a sitter for the child and the child's siblings. Burns and Brassard (1982) noted that single parents often have limited income to hire a sitter. If the noncustodial parent has remarried, that family also may need a sitter.

The teacher should try to have both parents involved in parent conferencing. If a parent–teacher organization or the school provides free babysitting for parent conferences, single-parent participation is likely to increase.

In a survey of 1,237 single parents, Clay (1981, cited in Carlson, 1987) noted that single parents feel that their school involvement is discouraged by the school schedule. In addition, the parents felt that most school–home communications were negative.

Classroom teachers should be sensitive to single parents' vulnerabilities around predominantly negative communications about their child. It is important to establish a sense of support and of liking the child (if the teacher does like the child) so that communication places negative behavior in the context of competencies.

Burns and Brassard (1982) noted that single parents may need additional structure to help with homework supervision and may not have the resources to help the child every day. They also suggested that fatherless children may benefit from assignment to male teachers.

Prevention of Child Snatching

Burns and Brassard (1982) provided useful suggestions on how the school can build protections against child snatching:

1. Ask parents to inform the school when custody issues are being contested.
2. Ask sole custody parents to provide the school with copies of legal documents.
3. Inform teachers.
4. Have a list or file of children of divorce and indicate who can pick them up. This information is particularly helpful if an unknown parent or other adult asks to remove a child in the middle of the school day.

Curriculum

Schools should review their curricula for bias against children of divorce. As Clay (1981, cited in Carlson, 1987) noted, although curriculum defines the intact family as the norm, many families have alternative structures. Fiction and nonfiction reading should include single-parent families, remarriage, children living with grandparents, and, in communities where it is common, never-married couples. The use of literature with never-married couples should be sensitive, however, to the moral values of each school's community. Even word problems in mathematics could include problems describing all kinds of families. History could focus on how families have changed over time. Such literature can lead children from alternative family structures to feel less different and may encourage affective expression and effective problem solving.

GROUPS FOR PARENTS

Cantor and Drake (1983) described in some detail why a group approach can be helpful to parents. They noted that a group approach is particularly helpful to parents because separation and divorce tend to generate loneliness and isolation. Working with other parents who have shared similar life experiences with divorce, visitation, and single parenting provides an opportunity to express feelings, share experiences, reduce feelings of uniqueness and incompetence, and support mutual problem solving. It is important in such groups to keep the focus on parenting, not on the adults' other concerns. As noted by Cantor and Drake, the purpose of *parenting* groups is to benefit the children by helping the parents. Financial concerns, the adult's sexuality, work and career concerns, and dating (except as it affects the children) are for discussion in divorce groups, rather than parenting groups.

Divorced parent groups have the advantage of keeping the topics focused on common experiences with children. Divorce groups, which are not limited to parenting, are unlikely to be as beneficial to the children, since not all group members are parents and the focus is broader.

Cantor and Drake (1983) noted several reasons why groups are a useful strategy: opportunity for mutual support, reduced costs, and reduction in threat. They cautioned that some factors are counterproductive for effective groups. For example, group members with severe pathology, such as depression or psychotic thinking, are unlikely to benefit from a group experience and may have a negative impact on the group itself. Cantor and Drake recommended that such individuals seek individual therapy instead. They also noted that the group may not be an appropriate place to air special child concerns, such as adoption or major handicaps.

Cantor and Drake (1983) described a structured group program for divorced parents. The intent of the program was to prevent, reduce, or correct the problems that children might experience postdivorce. The sessions focused attention on divorce-related issues, such as custody, visitation, and adaptation of parenting skills to the divorce situation. The program consisted of eight 1 1/2-hour sessions with 8 to 12 participants. All ages of children were considered.

Each lesson consisted of educational materials, an opportunity for parents to identify examples from their own experience, and small group exercises, consisting of vignettes with incomplete endings. Parents were asked to complete the stories by answering the questions, "What was the child communicating by that behavior?" or "What should the parent do now?" The subgroups then reconvened into a larger group and shared the discussion. Other sessions focused on good parenting, helping children with their reactions to divorce, handling custody and visitation, dating, remarriage, and helping the parents with their own feelings about these topics.

PROGRAMS FOR CHILDREN IN OTHER SETTINGS

Kessler and Bostwick (1977) developed a small group experience for 10- to 17-year-olds. About 10 children met for one 6-hour session on a Saturday. The program was limited to a single session because some adolescents came from as far away as 150 miles to participate. The program included exercises on identification and communication of feelings, empathy, and divorce-specific concerns.

A court-mandated workshop for adolescents was described by Young (1980). A family relations court required 12- to 17-year-olds whose parents had filed for divorce to attend one of seven workshops on divorce. At the beginning of each workshop, participants answered a questionnaire composed of four sections: demographic background, expectations and feelings about the workshop, concerns about the divorce, and assessment of "blame" for the divorce. Activities included discussion of attitudes and feelings about divorce.

PROGRAMS FOR PARENTS AND CHILDREN

Magid's Children Facing Divorce Program

Magid (1977) described an innovative program for children of divorce that used role playing and videotapes of vignettes of common divorce situations. Members of several families met once a week for 6 weeks. Seven vignettes showing common family scenes were used as the basis for stimulating discussion. All the vignettes used children of divorced families. Some of the vignettes were "Remember When," "Momma's New Boy Friend," and "Who's to Blame?" Other topics, which varied from group to group depending on need, included "Divorce and the Variability of Human Perception," "Children Facing Guilt and Loneliness," "Children Facing New Step Relations," "Looking Ahead," and "Why Are We Here?"

Children and parents were separated and saw the same vignettes in separate groups. The children watched part of the tape. The leader froze the tape and asked questions, such as what the child in the story might be feeling. After some discussion, the story continued. The purpose of the tapes was to help the children to see the divorce as terminating the relationship between parents, to see their own roles in the divorce, to accept their feelings, and to begin talking about these feelings with their parents. Later, the children were encouraged to develop their own vignettes.

Parents were shown the same vignettes with a focus on what the children might be feeling. Both parents were encouraged to attend unless the anger or hurt was so high as to interfere with their ability to focus on the program. For the first 5 weeks, the parent sessions were separate from the children's. The final meeting was a joint session for the parents and children to share their experiences.

Bornstein, Bornstein, and Walter's Group Psychotherapy

In a report of group therapy for 6- to 12-year-olds, Bornstein, Bornstein, and Walters (1985) described a program of 1 1/2-hour sessions provided over 6 consecutive weeks. The children met alone for the first five sessions and with their parents for the final session. The sessions were described in some detail. A male and a female therapist participated, and 5 to 10 children were in each group. Exercises included discussions about divorce, role playing on communication, practicing communication skills, problem solving, and anger control. At the final session, parents and children discussed three videotapes.

Single-Parent Project

Cebollero, Cruise, and Stollak (1986) described a pilot project of concurrent groups for mothers and children, aged 4 to 12, who were experiencing the long-term effects of divorce. The adult activities included group discussion, homework, written summaries, and training of the mothers to be cotherapists for the children's groups. The children participated in group activities and free play. Family drawings, puppet shows, and games were used. Use of the mothers as cotherapists was considered very successful.

Groups for Remarried Families

Mowatt (1972) described a program of group therapy with stepfathers and their wives. The couples had sought help with their children's behavior problems. The group consisted of three stepfathers and their wives which met for an hour and a half a week for six months. The children involved ranged from 10 to 17. As explained in the chapter on stepfamilies, older children tend to have more trouble with remarriage and this study's target group was consistent with that view. Problems included truancy, vandalism, underachievement and running away from home for boys and sexual promiscuity in the case of the one girl. Children were seen once at intake.

The purpose of the group was to provide peer group and identification models. As might be expected from the literature on problems of remarriage, the stepfathers were not clear about how far to go in assuming the role of father. All the fathers (all three, remember) had moved from a "pal" relationship prior to marriage to a parent after the marriage. How much affection to show was another question and the fathers were uncomfortable about expressing affection. Disciplining and enforcing rules was the major focus of attention. All the children resented the mother showing attention to the stepfather. Mothers tended to blame the stepfathers since the problems tended to start after the marriage. Mothers criticized the fathers for not being rescuers while the fathers criticized the mothers for poor management of the children. The stepfather often seemed rivalrous of stepsons and potentially attracted to the stepdaughters. Part of the rivalry with the stepsons may have been the physical resemblance with the biological father. As part of the group process the mothers started to realize that they were pushing the stepfathers away from the children.

Nadler (1983) described a group program for stepfamilies that involved a six-week didactic and discussion group to help families understand the problems of remarriage, stepchildren, childrearing and discipline and difficulties with the ex-spouse and visitation. The program involved six, one-and-a-half hour sessions, each focused on a separate problem. Groups were generally 8 to 10 people. The structure of the program was as follows:

Session 1. Introduction: Exploration of the commonality of stepfamily problems. All the stepparents were having trouble coping and many blamed the children for the problems. The myth of instant love was explained.

Session 2. Roles and conflicting loyalties. The second session tried to help families understand how conflicting loyalties generate problems. Alignments based on biological lines threatened family integration.

Session 3. Communication skills. This session stressed the open expression of feelings. There was discussion of the "stepparent disavowal syndrome" which occurs when the stepparent initially invests in the child and then is hurt by the rejection and finally feels rage and avoidance.

Session 4. Problems concerning the stepchild. Focussing on the stepchild situation and how to deal with childrearing and discipline was the theme of the fourth session. Hostility toward the stepparent was explained to be a function of feelings of abandonment, loss of security, resentment over the divorce, rivalry for affection, and feelings of disloyalty.

Session 5. Problems in marital interaction. Stepparents often feel the least cared for in the family. The natural parent does not tend to support the stepparent. Sometimes the problem is the demand from the stepparent to have the biological parent always confirm their point of view.

Session 6. Problems of visitation and the ex-spouse.

Mandell and Birenzweig (1990) reported on a group pilot project for remarried families. The project involved three families with seven children from 6 to 12 years of age. The children were divided into two groups based on age. There were six sessions over 6 weeks. The children met for 1 1/2-hour meetings, whereas the parents met for 2 hours. For five sessions, the parents met separately from the children. For the final 2-hour session, everyone met together. Themes for the six sessions were getting to know each other, the child's perspective, roles and expectations, parent–stepchild relationships (or for the adults, marital relationships), planning for the future, and sharing. The last session presented a guide developed by the children on "do's and don'ts."

WORKBOOKS FOR GROUPS

Group Counseling for Children of Divorce. Hammond (1979, 1981b, 1981c) developed a workbook for children of divorce that provides structured activities for group counselors working with these children. As in other approaches, this one included warm-up activities and group rules. Suggested activities included:

1. Getting to know others. Children use cards to indicate name, favorite animal, and dream vacation spot.
2. Four pictures of families of divorce are used to stimulate discussion about divorce.
3. Family coat of arms. The coat of arms is similar to Wilkinson and Bleck's (1977) personal shield, but children add three words to describe the family.

4. Discussion of the Book *My Dad Lives in a Downtown Hotel* (Mann, 1973). This book is appropriate for fourth-grade reading level. Hammond's book provides discussion questions for the group process.

Other exercises in the workbook are on value clarification, role playing of six situations related to divorce, and discussions about the perfect marriage, stepparenting, peer pressure, assertiveness, problem solving, and saying good-bye.

Divorce Group Counseling for Secondary Students

Hammond (1981a) also developed a workbook for secondary school children. Similar exercises were used as for elementary school children, but adapted for older children. The process for group treatment for older children included:

1. Introduction and group goals. Children used a card to describe themselves, their favorite animal, and the place they would like to go on vacation.
2. Value clarification sheet. Thirteen value-laden divorce statements were used for discussion.
3. Bibliotherapy. For older children, Hammond recommended *How to Get It Together When Your Parents Are Coming Apart* (A. Richards & Willis, 1976). Discussion questions are provided in Hammond's book.
4. Family closeness and goal setting. The children drew a family relationship chart.
5. Challenge Process. This exercise was similar to Sonnenshein-Schneider and Baird's (1980) brainstorm, but included a contract to work toward a solution.
6. Review goals and music. Using an exercise that probably is very popular with teenagers, Hammond suggested three popular songs to be played. After each one, the group discussed the message.

Parting: A Counselor's Guide for Children of Separated Parents

Bradford et al. (1982) developed a counselor's guide for children of separation and divorce for the South Carolina Department of Education. The workbook incudes sample forms, a simple evaluation form, a student bibliography, a film and filmstrip guide, and references. Although the workbook was designed for children from kindergarten to twelfth grade, the exercises seem best suited for children in late elementary school and junior high.

Warm-up activities include:

1. *Houses my family live in.* The children draw pictures of their families' houses, including figures (stick figures are acceptable) of

family members. Bradford et al. cautioned about protecting children who do not know where family members are or who have a parent in a jail or hospital. They provided discussion questions about the different families.

2. *Scrambled feelings.* The children unscramble letters of feeling-oriented words. There is a discussion afterward.

3. *Coping with feelings.* Children are helped to think about how to cope with different feelings in ways that do not cause problems or hurt anyone. The exercise involves providing each child with a paper cut in the shape of a cloud in which the child is to list ideas. The authors suggested constructive coping and discussion.

Group activities include:

1. *Getting to know you.* Find someone in the group who fits each of 13 categories (e.g., "Loves to eat vegetables"). Have that person sign the sheet. No person can sign the sheet for more than two categories.

2. *Changes.* Children list changes in the family and self, as well as feelings about those changes.

3. *Things that bother me.* Each child is given a list of 30 potentially bothersome problems. The child is asked to check those that bother him or her and circle the check for the three that are most bothersome. One problem is then selected to discuss how to solve it.

4. *Communication.* This exercise includes a list of nine questions about divorce, such as whether parents divorce children, why divorce occurs, whether the child could get the parents back together, and whether the child gets caught in the middle.

5. *Make believe.* This exercise provides 10 short vignettes in which the children are asked to role play the situation and imagine how each person feels and acts.

Other Workbooks

DIVORCE IS . . . A KIDS COLORING BOOK.   Magid and Schreibman (1980) created a useful coloring book that presents each of 25 problems of divorce on the left page and a solution to that problem on the right page. Some group therapists may find the coloring book a useful adjunct to group work.

KIDS' STEPFAMILY KIT.   Magid (1990) created a second coloring book on stepfamilies. Themes include feelings about the divorce, parents' dating, remarriage, territory, sharing, names, holidays, a new baby, and shared love.

THE DIVORCE WORKBOOK: A GUIDE FOR KIDS AND FAMILIES.   Ives, Fassler, and Lash (1985) developed a wonderful workbook that attempts to help children aged 4 to 12 with information and feelings about divorce. Chapters, which are written in a mixture of children's (authentic) handwriting and adult print, give information on marriage, separation, divorce, legalities, feelings, and self-help. Children respond to workbook exercises.

CHANGING FAMILIES: A GUIDE FOR KIDS AND GROWN-UPS. A follow-up workbook by Fassler, Lash, and Ives (1988) covers remarriage for the same age group. Topics include families, separation, divorce, new families, feelings, and helping yourself. The book can be used by parents, teachers, or counselors. Younger children need to be read to and need help with some vocabulary.

RESEARCH ON SCHOOL-BASED AND NON-SCHOOL-BASED INTERVENTION PROGRAMS

Using modifications of Wilkinson and Bleck's (1977) approach, Omizo and Omizo (1987) evaluated the effectiveness of school-based groups. They randomly assigned 30 children of divorce to intervention groups and 30 children of divorce to a control condition. The control participants were also taken out of the classroom but viewed films not related to divorce. Groups had 10 children each and met for 1 hour for 10 consecutive weeks. At the end of the study, children in the group counseling felt better about themselves, felt more in control of their lives, had higher aspirations and lower anxiety, and felt more accepted than children in the control group.

Roseby and Deutsch (1985) reported on a school-based program for fourth and fifth graders designed to provide training in cognitive social role taking and assertive communication. Rare for this type of study, they included a placebo control group that simply discussed feelings about the divorce (a tough comparison indeed in that such a group also should have positive effects). The social role taking group had statistically significantly more positive changes in beliefs and attitudes about the divorce than did the discussion control group. Depression and school behavior were not affected by the cognitive therapy, leading the authors to speculate as to whether a period of consolidation of changed attitudes might be needed. It is also possible that such generalization might not occur, or that the two groups would be equally effective in inducing change.

Gwynn and Brantley (1987) evaluated the Educational Support Group intervention program discussed previously in this chapter. They compared children in the intervention group with children paired in a nontreatment control group. Children in the intervention group showed greater decreases in depression, anxiety, and negative feelings about the divorce and higher scores on divorce information than children in the control. Gwynn and Brantley noted that although the results suggested that a short program of eight sessions might be useful, some of the gains (but not all) may also have been due to the extra attention that the children in the intervention groups received.

R. F. Anderson, Kinney, and Gerler (1984) compared the effects of divorce counseling groups for third to sixth graders with a randomly assigned control group. Activities overlapped with many already presented. Children in the treatment groups showed improved attitudes toward divorce and improved classroom conduct compared with the control group. Academic grades were not affected.

Bornstein, Bornstein, and Walters (1988) evaluated the effects of a group-based program for 31 children aged 7 to 14 whose parents were recently divorced. Children were randomly assigned to treatment or waiting list controls. A short, six-session group program based on Bornstein et al.'s (1985) program (described previously) was evaluated. The investigators used a large number of measures, including child's self-concept; child's ratings of parent–parent conflict and parent–child conflict; parents' ratings of child behavior, parent–parent conflict, and dissatisfaction with the child; and teacher's ratings of the child. Conflict was reported by parents to decline over time for both the treatment and control groups; however, the teacher-rated Behavior Problem Checklist showed a significant decline for the treatment group and a slight increase for the control group. The small number of subjects led to a low statistical power and may have masked true effects.

Pedro-Carroll (1983; Pedro-Carroll & Cowen, 1985) evaluated extensively the effectiveness of a school-based intervention program for 72 third- through sixth-grade children in four elementary schools. Of these children, 40 were assigned to an intervention group and 32 to a matched, delayed treatment, control group. Groups were similar in location, grade, gender, and length of time since parental separation. Extensive evaluation materials were obtained, including teacher's ratings of competencies and problem behaviors; children's perceived competence and trait-anxiety, attitudes about divorce, and experiences in the group; parents' ratings; and group leaders' ratings.

The intervention program followed Stolberg and Cullen's (1983) 12-week Children's Support Group program, described in detail earlier in this chapter. The focus of this group was to provide support for feelings and thoughts about the divorce and to teach specific coping skills around personal problem solving, anger self-control, and communication.

Teachers reported positive changes in adjustment for children who participated in the intervention group, compared with those in the delayed treatment control group. These changes included reductions in moody-anxious behavior, in learning problems, and on the overall school problem index. Teachers also rated the intervention children as having greater increases in total school competence scores and specific competencies of better peer sociability, frustration tolerance, compliance with rules, and adaptive assertiveness. Children in the intervention group rated themselves as less anxious after the intervention than did children in the delayed treatment control, and their parents also rated them as better adjusted. Group leaders also rated the children in the intervention group as better adjusted at the end of treatment than those in the control group, with higher scores on total competence, total problems, and total ratings. Child-reported self-competence and self-esteem were not significantly different for the two groups.

Although Pedro-Carroll's project presented an optimistic view of the effectiveness of school-based intervention for children of divorce, the study had some problems (as is true for most studies). Pedro-Carroll was careful to acknowledge these problems. First, the raters were not blind to the category in which the child belonged. It took a tremendous amount of energy to perform this study. Teachers, therapists, and parents all knew which children were being treated and which were not. This problem is potentially major because the social demands of the study could have produced the positive results. Second, the sample was limited to a small, homogeneous sample of predominantly white, middle class, suburban children. Finally, not mentioned by Pedro-Carroll, the participants' willingness to be in the study may have produced unknown biases in the sample obtained.

This research project plays a particularly important role in the evaluation of interventions for children of divorce because it is the first of a series of replications. In the first replication (Pedro-Carroll, Cowen, Hightower, & Guare, 1986), 54 children of divorce (fourth to sixth graders) participated in the 11-session program and were compared to 78 demographically matched children from intact families. Although less well adjusted than the children from intact families prior to the intervention, children of divorce showed significant improvement in shy-anxious, frustration tolerance, and adaptive assertiveness as rated by the teacher; trait anxiety as rated by the child; and total teacher and parent ratings. Such results could be explained by regression toward the mean effects (children who are worse off tend to improve), although the mean time since separation was long (a 48-month average). Such a long time since separation would tend to rule out regression effects, but not eliminate them as alternative explanations.

In a third extension of this research (Alpert-Gillis, Pedro-Carroll, & Cowen, 1989), the effectiveness of the program was evaluated for 52 second and third graders who were an average of 3¾ years postseparation. The prevention/intervention program was expanded to serve younger children in a more urban setting and from low-income homes. These children were given a similar intervention program as in the previous studies, with more emphasis on low-income settings, extended families, and use of materials (books, pictures, and puppets) representing diverse ethnic backgrounds. Common law and cohabiting relationships were accepted as functionally equivalent to marriage in defining children who had experienced a parental separation. Child feelings, parent ratings, teacher ratings, and group leader ratings were used to evaluate the effectiveness of the program. There were 52 children of divorce in the control group and 81 children from intact families in a second comparison group.

Even almost 4 years postseparation, children of divorce (preintervention) were not as well adjusted as children from intact families, demonstrating long-term negative effects of the separation or its correlates. In evaluating the effectiveness of the intervention groups, children in the groups expressed greater improvement in feelings about the divorce, self-concept, and coping ability. Teachers saw improvement in school-based competencies, but not behavior problems. Parents felt that the children improved in dealing with feelings, appropriate behavior, and problem solving.

The study did not control for the general effect of adult attention, children were not assigned randomly, and parents and teachers were aware of whether the child was in the intervention group. The findings, however, were consistent with the previous studies, and this study used better controls than the previous studies. For example, regression toward the mean effects were eliminated as an alternative explanation.

Kalter et al. (1984) evaluated their intervention program that was summarized earlier in this chapter. Four of the six groups that received the school-based intervention were evaluated using a postintervention evaluation, but there was no control group. The evaluation used parent reports, child questionnaires, and pre-post comparison on the Self-Competency Scales, the AML (Aggressive-outgoing; Moody-internalization; Learning disability) (Cowen et al., 1973), and the Divorce Perception Test (Plunkett & Kalter, 1984). Parents were generally favorable, and half reported specific changes that they had observed. Interviews with the children suggested that the children experienced the groups as positive. Pre-post comparison on the Self-Competency Sales and the AML did not produce significant findings. On the Divorce Perception Test, 4 of the 25 items were significant, including a reduction in wishes for reconciliation, feelings of confusion about the divorce, and feelings that the divorce was their fault, as well as a wish to perform better at school. In the absence of a control group of children who had experienced parental divorce but who had not had the interventions, the data are impossible to interpret. Negative feelings may decline over time as a natural process of working through the divorce. In addition, one might expect two items to significantly change just by chance.

Stolberg and Garrison (1985) summarized the evaluation of their group interventions for children of divorce. The four groups in their study were the children's support group, the single-parents' support group, a combined condition, and a no-treatment control. A description of the single-parents' group was presented by Garrison, Stolberg, Mallonnee, Carpenter, and Antrim (1983). Data were collected preintervention, postintervention, and 5 months later. Measures included The Fisher Divorce Adjustment Scale, the Single Parenting Questionnaire, the Life Experiences Survey, the Piers-Harris Children's Self-Concept Scale, and the Child Behavior Checklist.

Self-concept improvement was significantly higher for children in the children's support group condition than for the children in the combined intervention group and no-treatment control. Parents' improvement on the

Fisher Divorce Adjustment Scale was significantly greater in the single parent support group condition than for parents in the combined intervention. Improved social skills in children for the children's support group condition were not significant statistically until the 5-month follow-up. The combined intervention was not more powerful than the separate interventions for the children and the parents. These groups reported only two areas of improvement over the controls: fewer increases in negatively evaluated change events and greater reductions in positively evaluated events. The surprising ineffectiveness of the combined interventions group may have been due to demographic differences between this group and the others. Mothers in this group had been separated longer, had a lower employment status, and reported less visitation time for the child with the noncustodial father than was true for the other groups. Stolberg and Garrison (1985) noted that there was no random assignment of people to groups. In addition, the reliance on self-report instruments limited the interpretation of data. Despite these problems, this study and the Pedro-Carroll studies are important beginnings that seem to demonstrate that school-based interventions are useful to children.

In a study of an elementary school approach, Burke and Van de Streek (1989) evaluated an 8-week abbreviated form of Hammond's (1981c) group approach. They found statistically significant improvements in self-concept for children in the treatment group compared with children in a nontreated control.

In one of the few studies that evaluated the effectiveness of interventions for junior high students, Sheridan, Baker, and de Lissovoy (1984) compared (1) structured groups, (2) bibliotherapy, and (3) a nontreatment control. They found no difference in attendance, grade point average, self-concept, or behavior at home even though the teenagers in both types of therapy felt that they were helped.

In a study involving elementary and early junior high children, Bornstein et al. (1988) compared a six-session group approach of 7 children with a control of 16 children matched for age, gender, and parent ratings of parental conflict. The small numbers limit generalizability, but such studies are sufficiently rare that this one is worthy of comment. The first five sessions were oriented toward identification of feelings, communication skills, and anger management. The final meeting included parents and children. There was no measurable effect for parent ratings of child behavior or conflict. There was no group effect on the children's self-ratings on anxiety, attitudes toward the separation, or self-conflict. Children in both groups reported an increase in parent–child conflict over time. The only measure that was related to the group was a significant improvement for children in the intervention group over the children in the control on teacher-rated behavior problems.

Reports of the effectiveness of group-based interventions have mixed results. Generally, participants' feelings of anxiety and sadness seem to be reduced and self-esteem seems to be increased. Behavior ratings by teachers and parents present mixed results.

SUMMARY

Group approaches for parents and for children of divorce would seem to be powerful intervention strategies. Intervention in the schools is particularly likely to reach children in need of help who are unlikely to receive help in other ways. Group therapy approaches typically involve exercises on awareness of feelings, effective communication, problem solving, and shared experiences associated with the divorce, single parenting, and remarriage of parents. Research clearly documents that children report feeling better following group interventions. Whether behavior improves at home and school is less clear.

CHAPTER 11

Advising Parents:
The Parent as Consultee

Parents worry about the effects of divorce on their children. They seek advice on how best to help their children. They read self-help books on what to expect and how to be helpful. If self-help books were sufficient, consultation with parents would seldom be necessary. However, the number of variables, the personal involvement, and the uniqueness of each situation make it difficult for a self-help book to fit sufficiently well to be more than general help.

Consultation is far more than providing parents with information about children's needs during and after divorce. Certainly, that information is useful and should be provided. Parents, however, are often unable to utilize such information initially because of emotional involvement with the situation. In addition, they are not asking for psychotherapy and would be offended if the contact led to the suggestion that they needed treatment. A consultation strategy is usually more appropriate to fill their need to provide adequate care for the children. Particularly useful are contacts with parents who are seeking advice prior to telling the children and prior to the separation. There are no models in the literature for working specifically with parents around their concerns for their children. Thus, I have adapted a model from mental health consultation, an area that has not been traditionally applied to parent work.

Parents do not want to be told that they are doing things wrong. They do not want to add to the burden of guilt around the separation and divorce. They may want to scapegoat the child, and thus may be defensive about any interpretation of their role in the problem. A family therapy model (see Chapter 13) tends to be more powerful than parent consultation because the family dynamics can be observed and the clinician can intervene in an ongoing process. Often, however, one or two consultations are all that are needed or available. Although some families are maladaptive or malfunctioning, others simply need information and can utilize that information well.

This chapter is based on a mental health model that Saul Cooper and I developed, which is discussed in considerable detail in our edited book *The Mental Health Consultation Field* (Cooper & Hodges, 1983). That book does not deal with parenting consultation or with divorce, but the principles of intervention are the same. In addition, many concepts in this chapter were influenced by the thinking of the most influential theorist in mental health consultation, Gerald Caplan (1970). No empirical research is cited in this chapter because, to my knowledge, the consultation model has not been previously applied to working with divorced parents. The specific advice suggested for divorcing parents draws on my own experience and the literature.

Cooper and Hodges (1983) conceptualized consultation as focusing on the underlying reason why the consultee (in this chapter, the parent) could not solve the problem of the child's behavior. The first model, the *educational model,* assumes that the failure to solve the problem results from lack of knowledge or skill. Mental health professionals who prefer this model are often oriented toward behavior modification. The second model, the *individual process model,* assumes that the parent's difficulty in solving the child's problems is due to the parent's attitudes, motivation, intrapsychic conflicts, or personal style. Dynamically and humanistically oriented therapists are more likely to favor this model for helping the parent. Theme interference (G. Caplan, 1970) and stereotyping (Heller & Monahan, 1983) are examples of concepts in this model. The final model is the *system model* in which the parent's problems are embedded in the characteristics of the family or the community in which the family belongs. Intervention in this model may focus around changing channels of communication, power, support, and influence. Although a systems-oriented therapist may work with the parents alone, the therapist is likely to want to work with the whole system and see at least the family and maybe related figures who belong to the system (e.g., grandparents, neighbors, and friends).

To develop an intervention strategy, professionals need to consider every problem brought to them by parents at each level of conceptualization. Professionals must consider to what degree this problem can be considered a lack of knowledge or skill, an intrapsychic or personality problem, or a family or community systems problem.

As intervention moves from education to process to systems, the intervention tends to become more powerful, long lasting, and difficult. This chapter covers the first two models. Family therapy is covered in Chapter 13.

GENERAL PRINCIPLES OF CONSULTATION

Consultation is not teaching. It is an interactive model in which the consultant helps parents learn to cope with the problems that they cannot solve with their present skills. It is not therapy. The function of consultation is to provide a supportive, noninterpretative environment in which parents can take the risk to change. Parents are not blamed for the difficulties. Such blame tends to increase guilt and withdrawal rather than constructive problem solving. Advice giving and education occur in the context of understanding the dynamics of parenting, interpersonal anxiety and defenses, and intrapersonal interactions.

The following are basic principles for use in consultation:

1. The primary principle in any consultation is to start with the perceived needs of the parent (G. Caplan, 1970). Too frequently, mental health professionals identify an area in which work needs to be done and jump in to work on that topic. As stated in the previous chapters, parents often use the acting out of the child as the basis for avoiding their own issues. The child obliges by maintaining the misbehavior in order to reduce family anxiety.

Consultation should begin by addressing the perceived needs of the parents. By responding to the perceived needs, mental health professionals can help parents feel empowered, experience increased self-esteem, and feel more optimistic about the possibility of other changes.

Once perceived needs have been responded to, parents are more willing to permit professionals to raise an issue of concern, such as the parent–parent relationship.

2. The consultant's responsibility is to work with the parents to find a strategy of intervention that works for them. Mental health consultants should not present their favorite intervention, expecting the parents to adopt that strategy. The solution must fit the personality style. The parents must feel free to reject the professional's advice for whatever reason. When the parents feel pressured to try a particular intervention, they might make it fail. I have had parents quote back to me things I know I never said. Such a process told me that the solution did not fit the dynamics of the parents. It was then my responsibility to (1) diagnose why that intervention was inappropriate for those parents and (2) help the parents find a solution.

3. Consultants demonstrate their competence by the questions they ask, not the answers they give (G. Caplan, 1970). The purpose of the intervention is to increase the parents' competence in parenting, not to demonstrate the magical powers of the consultant. Through answering questions, the parents are trained in how to think about their child's problems. In addition, the use of questions involves the parents more actively, requiring them to engage in the issues, rather than allowing them to passively tune out the consultant.

4. The consultant must respect the parent's competence. The consultant needs to find areas of competence and use those areas as bases for developing solutions.

5. The consultant must do follow-up. Even a 5-minute phone call after a single consultation session can uncover a reluctant or embarrassed parent who has not used the intervention or found that it did not work.

Follow-up enhances diagnoses of problems, fine tunes an intervention, and communicates caring.

6. The consultant must not assume that the "bag of tricks" he or she has developed over time will work in every instance. I try to prepare parents for the possibility that a particular intervention will not work for a particular child. Temperament (in the child or parent), history, poor implementation, or other unknown factors can invalidate a seemingly effective intervention. In consultation, the consultant should set up the intervention as a trial strategy to gather more information, rather than as the only possible solution. This attitude enables the parents to return for more information, permitting a diagnosis as to whether the intervention plan was inappropriate or the parents were ineffective (or the suggestions were inappropriate *for these parents*).

7. The consultant must prepare parents for the difficulty in implementing a plan. Not only does it take tremendous energy to treat a child differently from what feels natural and spontaneous, but the child is often disoriented by finding that the rules have changed.

Consultants need to warn parents that when they are trying a new intervention for handling behavior, often the behavior gets worse for a while rather than better. Children do what they know how to do best. When a parent changes the rules, the child has an investment in keeping the same pattern of interaction going. Tantrums become worse when parents change the script. The child tries to go back to the old script. Parents who are not warned of this intensification will prematurely abandon an intervention.

Tremendous social support for the parents may be needed during this time. Short, 5-minute phone calls to encourage parents to stay with the intervention and to reward them for the investment in helping their children can be very helpful in maintaining the parents' behavior.

8. The consultant must listen to how the parents symbolize the problem. Such a diagnosis can help in determining what kinds of intervention are likely to be effective. Using the same symbolic language is likely to increase a sense of being understood and accepted (G. Caplan, 1970). The consultant should ask the parents to describe the behavior and sequence of behaviors rather than use labels. When a parent describes a child as aggressive, ask the parent to describe some typical episodes, the parent's handling of the behavior, and the child's response to that handling. Parents tend to be better at describing behavior than at diagnosing.

9. Consultation with parents provides a strong primary prevention opportunity. The two ways in which consultation can efficiently help a family are to reduce stress and to immunize the parent or child from the stress. Helping the parents anticipate the problems that might occur as a function of separation (or even the intervention) can be very helpful in preventing

maladaptive responses by the parents. For example, suggesting to parents that they provide the child with explanations of the separation and clear information about the structure of access in the future will allow parents to reduce the child's anxiety.

10. Trust builds extensively over time rather than intensively in one sitting. It is better to have four ½-hour consultations with parents spread over 2 months than a 2-hour marathon session. Although extensive contact is not always available to the professional, particularly when the child has problems in several areas or skill training is involved, it is useful to encourage parents to come back on a regular basis for several sessions.

WHO SHOULD BE INVOLVED IN CONSULTATION?

Often, one parent is more psychologically minded and wants help in parenting while the other is unwilling to participate. Refusal by a noncooperative parent sometimes comes as a message to the other parent: "It is your inadequate parenting that is causing the problem and I don't need help." Usually, the custodial parent asks for help because the almost constant child care responsibility makes that parent the target of the child's maladaptive behavior. Because the custodial parent is more likely to be placed in a position of enforcing discipline, requiring homework, insisting on a clean bedroom, and being involved in child rearing during the work week (when the parent is also tired from work and housekeeping), more conflict with child rearing occurs with that parent.

When the consultation request occurs at the point of separation, the initiator of the divorce and the noninitiator (the person who involuntarily lost the marital relationship) are equally likely to request help. The initiator asks for help because of guilt that the decision to separate is harmful for the children or because the problem that led to the decision to leave is, from that person's point of view, also damaging to the children. The noninitiator asks for help because, in addition to feelings of abandonment, that person also has to deal with the emotional responses of the children. Sometimes, the request for help exaggerates the harm to the children as "proof" that the leaving damaged everyone. Such guilt induction toward the initiator leads to investments in maintaining the child's disruptive behavior, thus making consultation very difficult.

When the above factors are combined, it is more likely that if only one parent asks for help, it is the mother. The mother is twice as likely as the father to be the initiator (Bloom, Hodges, & Caldwell, 1982). Not only is the mother much more likely to be the custodial parent, but women are also more likely to seek professional help and see talking to a professional as helpful.

The consultant who is asked by one parent for parent consultation should request whether it would be acceptable to have both parents present.

Diagnostic information is more informative with both parents present, and interventions tend to be more powerful.

Asking for Help or Ammunition?

The single parent asking for help presents a problem for consultation. It is easy for that parent to blame the absent parent for the problems with the child and to avoid changing behavior. The report of the absent parent's behavior is affected by the feelings of a hurt or angry person. Also important is the frequency with which this combination is used to set up the mental health professional for custody disputes or relitigation.

When asked for advice by a single parent, particularly just after separation or just prior to litigation, the consultant must avoid answering direct questions about the appropriateness of certain behaviors. The consultant needs to find out who is perceived as having those behaviors to determine whether the person is asking for personal help or looking for ammunition against the absent parent.

This type of judgmental error can result in a subpoena for the consultant to repeat his or her statement to a judge. Although the consultant may be willing to make general statements about parenting, quotes out of context can misrepresent the consultant's view. Descriptions of the other parent's behavior are merely hearsay and may be substantially distorted. Because families are systems and not simply a collection of unconnected behaviors, there are often substantial omissions about the behavior of the complaining parent.

Both Parents

Unless one parent has remarried, consulting with both parents together is preferred. It is extremely important that the parents be required to put aside their ongoing battle to focus on the child's behavior. If the consultant is not strict in demanding control of the session, the parents' battle can erupt into rage. When the rage response is high, consultation can be used to help the parents accept the divorce and then focus on helping the child. Under such conditions, it is difficult to tell when the intervention is consultation and when it is family therapy.

Once a consultant has seen both parents in consultation, he or she should try to avoid seeing either parent alone in subsequent meetings. If the therapeutic position is to help both families, single meetings can undermine trust. If one parent wants a consultation alone, the consultant should request that the parent get permission from the other parent for an individual meeting and offer a similar visit for that other parent. Refuse confidentiality with the other parent. Obtaining secrets can bind the consultant from being effective.

Both Parents and One Cohabiting or Remarried Partner

When one parent has remarried or developed a long-term, stable cohabiting relationship, the consultant needs to carefully consider with the parents whether to include the new partner. Excluding that person denies his or her parenting role. With several couples with whom I have worked, the willingness to involve the new partner has been a symbolic admission that the marriage was over.

Discussions of how the child interacts with everyone involved can be very useful. It is also helpful to have clear guidelines about how the child is to deal with a stepparent role. Information in Chapter 9 can be helpful in defining problems for the stepparent.

Both Parents and Both Stepparents

Seeing both parents and both stepparents in a single group is a potentially powerful and problematic combination. Meetings should be brief. The stepparents (or cohabiting partners) often harbor chronic and intense rage at the other spouse motivated by jealousy or care for their partner who was hurt by this other person and a wish to maintain distance between the two families. The ex-spouses may have their rages mitigated by affectional ties (which may or may not be threatening). I often start consultation with separate meetings for each of the two households, to help each couple decide what issues need to be negotiated with the other family. Those meetings can be followed after several sessions with a joint meeting of everyone.

THE EDUCATION MODEL

Mental health professionals often overlook the power of education in helping others. It is presumptuous to assume that every problem is due to unresolved childhood conflict. Well-meaning parents often do not know what else to do and are quite willing to assume a new intervention as soon as it is presented to them. Even if an intervention is only 50% effective (a level I have found to be true for parents handling a child's aggression with aggressive punishments), its efficiency would suggest that the educational model might be tried first.

The degree to which some mental health professionals forget what they have learned about learning principles in teaching parents how to deal with their children is surprising. Most mental health professionals know that lecture formats are not very useful in therapy. When working with parents in an educational mode rather than therapy, however, some mental health professionals give a long list of advice that the parent is supposed to follow.

Parents' habitual ways of handling the child's problems are difficult to break. New learning follows well-established patterns of behavior modification, reinforcement, and modeling. In addition, a significant part of parent–child interactions is skill (knowing how to do something) rather than knowledge (knowing what needs to be done). Parents who do not know how to express affection, or to be sensitive to feelings, or to reward appropriate behaviors need to develop these skills slowly and with successive approximations to the desired behavior. Such new learning takes tremendous energy, and parents need significant social support to maintain that energy until the new behaviors become habitual.

Because the mental health professional is being asked to be the expert, there is a tendency to give advice too soon. By asking questions, the professional can assess the parents' various needs, their repertoire of skills, and the degree to which lack of knowledge or skill is involved. By careful assessment, the professional also models problem solving behavior for the parent. When a skill deficit is involved, there must be a careful plan of acquisition and support. I recommended that one parent, who had come from a family in which no one ever touched and affection was seldom expressed, touch the shoulder or back of her daughter for 1 second, several times a day. I judged that any longer would be difficult for the mother to tolerate. With successive meetings spread out over several months, we increased the time to 2 or 3 seconds.

In an excellent summary of educational model strategies, Kuehnel and Kuehnel (1983) focused on behavioral approaches for helping consultees (e.g., parents) to develop knowledge or skills. They looked at instructions, modeling, shaping, behavioral rehearsal with structured feedback, and homework assignments.

The next section describes the basic principles for providing information to parents.

Advice for Parents

Specific Advice

Parents can be provided information about how children typically react to divorce that can be potentially useful for them. Given the age of the children, gender, amount of family conflict, developmental history, finances, temperaments, reasons for the divorce, presence or absence of significant others, and psychological mindedness, the professional can develop ideas about what information and advice would be useful to the parents. Chapters 2 and 3 of this book have information that could serve as a base.

When parents seek consultation prior to telling the children of an intended separation, the opportunity to help parents anticipate, listen, and facilitate discussion around concerns of the children is good. The fact that the parents are so concerned about their children's welfare that they seek professional help prior to the separation indicates strengths in the family that are likely to work in favor of good outcomes. Caplan (1970) called this provision of information prior to the stressful event "anticipatory guidance."

The following are specific suggestions for parents of divorce who request advice:

1. Provide predictability for the children. Children are very upset by having their world views destroyed. Parents are often insensitive to children's needs to understand what happens next. Where will the noncustodial parent live? How often will there be visits? How predictable will visits be? How will the family handle the old home? Will there be a move? The more children feel that they know what will happen, the lower the level of anxiety, particularly as the parents' predictions unfold. According to Wallerstein and Kelly (1980c), 80% of parents do not provide the children with assurance of continuity of care.

2. Tell children that a separation or divorce is pending, taking into account the child's developmental abilities and needs. Children gradually develop the ability to understand the future (see Chapter 7), which is the gauge for deciding how early to tell the children. When the separation occurs after a blowup, however, no warning is possible. For very young children, a week to 10 days may be all that the child can handle. Excessive time beyond the child's ability to comprehend could increase anxiety. For an adolescent, 4 to 6 weeks can be helpful for integrating and anticipating the event.

If parents are discussing the possibility of a separation, children should not be told of the possibility until the decision is made. Once the decision is made, when the child is told should be related to the child's time perspective.

Parents have difficulty telling the children about the divorce. The parents are already upset, and sometimes it is difficult to tolerate the child's anxiety and anger. According to D. S. Jacobson (1978c), it is usually the mother who tells the child.

3. Be truthful about why the separation is occurring, but do not burden the children with details (Magid, 1977). Cantor and Drake (1983) noted that excessive disclosure is confusing to children and indicated that it is not good parenting to provide children with information that would lead them to turn against the other parent. Cantor and Drake suggested that extramarital affairs, homosexuality, and impotence are best omitted from information given to children. They also recommended that the older the child, the more complete the explanation for the separation needs to be.

Although attacks on the other parent are harmful (see item 11 below), overconcern with protecting the image of the other parent can lead to confusion. When a parent only praises the absent parent, a reasonable question for the child to ask is, "If he's so great, why did you want him out?"

4. Decide whether to tell the teachers that the child is going through a family divorce. This issue is tricky. As mentioned in Chapters 2 and 8, there is reason to believe that teachers may stigmatize children of divorce. At

the same time, a teacher is likely to be significantly more tolerant of a child's acting out when the behavior is put in context. Although tolerance and understanding are desirable, however, permissiveness is not. Children need firm structure in the school setting, with support and understanding when coping becomes difficult. In general, I recommend that the schools be told.

Magid (1977) gave additional useful advice:

5. Reassure the child that he or she is not alone.

6. Use resources. Books for parents and for children can help in understanding divorce (Bernstein, 1977). Also, a variety of organizations in many communities can serve to provide information and social support.

7. Do not allow the children to become messengers between families. Do not allow the children to become small adults.

8. Do not isolate siblings.

9. Do not allow children to become counselors to your problems. (See Chapter 2 on parentification of children.)

10. Do not make promises to children and then not fulfill them. Children need predictability. Parents who easily promise outings or gifts and then forget can produce profound hurt and uncertainty about the future.

11. Do not attack or denigrate the ex-spouse in front of the children. The child typically identifies with both parents. When the children are invited to join with a parent in attacking the other parent, self-esteem necessarily suffers. Although it is quite appropriate for a parent to tell a child that the parent is angry at the ex-spouse, details as to why or frequent exposure to that anger hurts the child. The parent should avoid labels in particular. Comments such as "I don't know why your father did not show up for visitation—I know it hurt your feelings" are preferred over generalizations such as "Your father is irresponsible."

12. Do not argue about financial matters in front of the children. Magid's advice to specifically mention finances was wise, because this area is one in which the intensity of anger is great and parents feel particularly justified in enlisting the child's loyalty (e.g., "We could buy you a new coat if your father were not so irresponsible").

13. Keep interparental hostility in check (Cantor & Drake, 1983). The parent should communicate respect for the child's feelings about the other parent.

14. Do not allow your own guilt to interfere with parental responsibility. Do not be overprotective or underprotective.

The following advice can also be useful:

15. Protect the attachments of the children. Do not move unless you have to. Try to make it possible for the child to continue to see playmates.

16. Tell the children that it is not their fault that the divorce is occurring. Inform the children that they are still loved even though the parents no longer love each other. Cantor and Drake (1983) indicated that young children need to have their specific concerns dealt with. Young children cannot understand that they are not responsible for the divorce or parental conflict unless this information is specifically structured around their own fantasy. Older children are able to separate out their own responsibility if they are given adequate information about why the divorce occurred.

For young children, it is useful to check back about their understanding of why the divorce occurred. If the child harbors a fantasy about causing the divorce, the child needs to have that fantasy disconfirmed.

17. Tell the children that they will not be abandoned. (Provide this promise only if it is true that neither parent will abandon.) The children may need information about family or friends who will serve as backups if parents are unavailable.

18. Inform the children that parents can make mistakes. Children can learn from parents' mistakes.

19. Tell the children how their lives will change (Cantor & Drake, 1983) in terms of family structure, a change in residence, a mother going to work, less money, and their need to help with chores.

20. Inform the children several times that there is nothing they can do to change the situation (Cantor & Drake, 1983). Children need to be discouraged from trying to reunite the parents. The desire for reconciliation can be so strong that this message usually has to be repeated several times.

21. Encourage the child to talk about feelings and to ask questions. D. S. Jacobson (1978a) found that the more the child is encouraged to talk about the divorce, the better the adjustment. If the child has difficulty expressing feelings, use the techniques Hiam Ginott (1965) and Virginia Axline (1969) presented below to open up trust and self-confidence through expression of feelings.

The following technique for helping parents to help the child talk about feelings is outlined in Cooper and Hodges (1983, p. 31):

a. Tell the child how he or she appears to be feeling several times a day. Try to focus on both positive and negative feelings. Try to make some of the comments in passing, on the way to another room or while the child is watching television or playing.

b. Make the comments short. Simply say, "You look bored," or "You enjoyed playing with your sister," or "I made you angry when I said that you had to go to bed now."

c. Do not use judgmental phrases, such as ". . . and if you felt that way more often you would get along better with your brother" or ". . . and if you weren't so angry, we would have more fun." It is surprising how often parents criticize children for having a good time by reminding them of all the bad feelings. Parents have a great deal of difficulty accepting feelings without judgments.

d. Do not pause. Children become so accustomed to judgmental statements that if a parent leaves an expectant pause, a child will automatically fill in the judgmental phrase. By making the simple statement of feedback about feelings without a pause, the parent communicates acceptance without pressuring the child to feel differently.

Experience with this technique indicates that the child initially shows no change in behavior (expect the child to show surprise at the change in the parent's behavior). After about 3 weeks, the child will spontaneously elaborate on a feeling without any request from the parent. After 6 weeks, the child will talk about feelings prior to any reflection from the parents.

22. Help the child understand the difference between destructive and constructive anger. Tantrums are destructive. They invite retaliation or withdrawal. The purpose of communicating angry feelings is to encourage effective problem solving around the problem that led to the anger in the first place. This approach implies encouraging children to control their anger rather than being overwhelmed by it.

Gordon (1970) talked about anger as an emotion that is secondary to feelings of hurt, rejection, and fear. He suggested that communication around those feelings tends to be more effective than around the anger. Particularly for younger children, anger and aggression are a common response to separation and divorce. It is useful to help parents cope with these responses.

Information Process

When giving parents advice about how to deal with children, particularly when specific intervention strategies are being suggested, the mental health professional should remember basic principles of learning. Behaviors should be broken into small units, and behavior shaping used to help parents move toward the correct behavior.

The professional should work on only a limited number of problems at a time, starting with the most intrusive problem. Once a problem is moving toward solution and the related parental problem solving behavior is becoming more habitual, the next problem can be attacked. Mental health professionals who try to give multiple solutions to problems are increasing the likelihood of failure. Parents, like other people, have a limited ability to remember a large number of interventions.

The mental health professional should work on solving only a limited number of child behavior problems at one time. Parents become overwhelmed with too many solutions and will not implement any of them. The professional should begin with the parent's perceived needs and then move to other problem areas as the parent becomes more successful.

Try to provide support to the parents for the intervention effort. I suggested to a teacher that she call the parents daily to report on the stealing and lying behavior of the parents' two children and to provide support for the consistency with which the parents were following through. Five-minute phone calls several times during the first few weeks gave the parents an opportunity to ask questions, to fine tune an intervention, and to receive emotional support for the effort in changing behavior. To further build in support, I called the teacher once a week to support *her* support of the parents.

Skills Training for Parents

Kuehnel and Kuehnel (1983) suggested several techniques for facilitating skills learning.

1. *Role playing.* It is helpful for the parent to practice the desired parenting behaviors in a role playing situation with feedback from the consultant. Behavior shaping can be used.
2. *Modeling.* Modeling can be a powerful technique for helping parents understand how to perform a particular behavior. In this case, the parent can play the child and the consultant play the parent. By demonstrating the behavior in a role playing situation, the parent may feel less stress and see the exact behavior that is being discussed.
3. *Homework assignments.* The parent is asked to try out the behaviors in real life. It is important that the parent has sufficient skills to carry out the behavior successfully. The consultant should choose a single problem behavior that is clearly observed and help the parent solve that problem before moving on to another problem.
4. *Dependency.* The parent should be encouraged to maintain the behaviors without the constant support of the professional. To reduce dependency, meetings should become shorter and shorter and the time between meetings should be increased.

INDIVIDUAL PROCESS CONSULTATION

The professional may utilize individual process consultation when he or she determines that the parent cannot solve the child's problem because of intrapsychic dynamics, unconscious motivation, or problems in objectivity. This strategy of consultation is similar to G. Caplan's (1970) consultee-centered case consultation.

Caplan proposed *theme interference* as a category of individual process problems. In theme interference, the parent has a syllogism in which if a child belongs to an initial category, an inevitable undesirable outcome is expected. Parents carry with them many themes around the topic of divorce. Examples include, "A child from a broken home is doomed to become delinquent," "A child of divorce will inevitably hate his or her parents," and "Children cannot be angry at parents after divorce or they will grow up warped in terms of their identity."

Caplan proposed that a major error in handling this problem is *unlinking*, in which the consultant indicates that the child does not actually belong to the parent's initial category. An example of unlinking in this situation would be a comment such as, "This child isn't really like a child of divorce, because there is frequent contact with both parents." Although such a removal from the initial category may temporarily solve this problem, the theme has not been touched and remains to affect other behaviors. In addition, if the parent receives other information suggesting that the child *is* a child of divorce, the theme interference immediately takes over.

Caplan proposed that the consultant's role is to invalidate the theme by breaking the inevitable link between the initial category and outcome. To simply disagree with the parent is ineffective. The parent "knows" the theme at an emotional level and is likely to disqualify the expert if such a simple solution is tried.

Because such "stereotypes" can rarely be changed by direct confrontation, Caplan proposed that the professional agree that the outcome feared (or wished for in the case of the angry parent) is indeed a possible outcome, but that other outcomes are possible and indeed might be facilitated. Heller and Monahan (1983) also suggested focusing on unrecognized assets in the child as a way of helping the parent open up other, more desirable outcomes.

Stereotypes or theme interferences by parents of divorce can be invalidated by demonstrating that other desirable outcomes are possible and that a change in behavior can facilitate those outcomes.

Reframing by Focusing on the Child

Another technique for handling theme interferences is to reframe the problem as one that the child has rather than one that the parent has. Because the parent is likely to be defensive in response to direct confrontations regarding what he or she is doing wrong, a parent can listen more easily to suggestions that his or her reaction is a natural response to the child's behavior (which from a systems analysis is perfectly true). By reframing the problem as a problem of the child, other individual process problems, such as overinvolvement or underinvolvement, explosive anger at the child, and chronic anxiety in the parent, can all be addressed without attacking the defenses. For example:

1. *Chronic anger at the child.* The clinician can say, "The problem your child has is that she is going around making people angry all the time. How can we help her not do that?" The focus is now on helping the child, rather than on the chronic anger of the parent.

2. *Disinterest.* The consultant might say, "This child's problem is that he pushes people away from him so that they don't want to interact with him. We need to help him with his need to have distance from others." Again, the parent can look at withdrawal in the child, but does not get labeled as having that problem except as a reasonable response to the child's behavior.

3. *Dependency.* The consultant can say, "She is constantly giving messages for people to take care of her, even when she doesn't need the help. We need to help her be more independent."

Reframing a parent's problem as a natural response to the child's problem can be helpful in getting a parent to consider behaving differently in order to help the child. The technique avoids direct confrontation with the parent's defensive process and permits movement. Consultants should not use this technique (for that matter, any technique) dishonestly. This reframing technique should be used only for those problems in which a true interaction between the parent's behavior and the child's behavior is likely to be maintaining the problem. Given the frequency of this dynamic, such a caveat is not much of a restriction.

Reframing by Focusing on a Different, Underlying Problem

Another reframing technique is to translate what is seen as a motivational problem into a skill problem. Parents often are immobilized by a belief system that indicates that a child should want to behave well. A child who does not behave well is flawed, and therefore the parent can do nothing effective. Reframing the problem as one that the child does not know how to do, rather than being too lazy to do, helps the parent think about how to help the child develop a more adaptive position. This technique has been helpful in working with such problems as attention span ("She doesn't know how to attend for long periods of time"), self-control ("He hasn't the skill to control himself"), study habits ("She hasn't learned good study skills and how to work for long periods of time"), aggression ("He needs to learn how to control his anger and use it effectively"), and trust ("She needs to learn to trust the world again").

Parental Support

A procedure that is helpful in working with parents is *role enhancement.* Anything that the consultant does that aids the parents in having more motivation and energy for working with the child is likely to help the child. Helping the parents be more effective in one particular area is likely to help generalization to other parenting areas. G. Caplan (1970) suggested that using the same symbolism as the consultee (in this case, a parent) is useful in helping the parent hear the intervention. For example, if a parent frequently uses the word "respect," the clinical intervention will likely work better if the same word is used in the solution.

G. Caplan (1970) identified several cues that an intrapsychic problem may be present. Generalizing inappropriately from previous experience is a cue. Omitting key facts in presenting the child's situation, facts that are discovered much later or only by accident, are also cues of interpersonal interferences. Other cues include overidentification with the child, transference, and characterological distortions. Omitting key figures in the child's life is a cue. A grandparent with whom the child has frequent contact, but who is not mentioned, may be the source of conflict.

THE SYSTEMS INTERVENTION MODEL

When working with parents in consultation, there are two systems to keep in mind, the family as a system and the broader community in which the family exists. When the family as a system is the target of intervention, the system approach is basically family therapy (see Chapter 13). Whereas a system approach may be used to interpret to the parents why the child may be behaving in a particular way, a systems intervention is more likely to be effective if the child's entire family, or two sets of families, are seen in therapy. In terms of a broader community intervention, the consultant can have contact with a variety of individuals in the family's life, including significant others, teachers, grandparents, child care workers, medical professionals, and any others who affect how the family responds to the stress of divorce.

Broadly speaking, a systems intervention may include increasing community tolerance and support for single parents, reducing stigma, increasing legal structures to provide a stable financial basis for families, increasing mediational services, and reducing adversarial divorce procedures. Big Brother and Big Sister programs in the community, recreational facilities for families, and increasing coping skills in children and parents may also play a general role in helping families. Informational services for marriage, marital counseling, divorce counseling, single-parent family support, and remarriage have also been used to respond to a community's need at the systems level.

SUMMARY

In conclusion, working with parents can be facilitated by using a consultation model. Parents are likely to provide less resistance when defenses are protected, rather than challenged. Parents can be helped with developing effective interventions by the use of an educational model, an individual process model, or a systems model. All consultation problems should be reviewed at all three levels of intervention prior to the professional's making a decision as to how to intervene.

CHAPTER 12

Individual Psychotherapy: Play, Work, and Talking with Children

Most children have a limited capacity to talk for any length of time about their feelings and problems. The capacity to be introspective about internal experience is almost nonexistent in preschoolers, grows during elementary school as the child learns to differentiate internal experience from the experience of others, and becomes a useful skill by middle adolescence. As the child nears 11 or 12 years of age, the ability to think and talk about feelings becomes more developed.

Prior to developing the cognitive ability to think about feelings, children demonstrate their construction of the world and their reaction to it in their behavior in the context of family, friends, and school, and more specifically in their play. The clinician has several choices of modalities for working with distressed or misbehaving children. These modalities, which reflect the contexts of child development, include play therapy, family therapy, and group therapy.

SELECTING TYPE OF INTERVENTION FOR CHILDREN

Individual child therapy would likely be the treatment of choice in the following conditions:

- The parents are psychologically unavailable for family therapy.
- The child's maladaptive behavior is related to past misinterpretations of events and not to ongoing stress.
- The child needs to learn to separate his or her identity and problems from those of the parents.
- The child could benefit from a consistent, predictable therapist in the midst of a chaotic family life.
- The child needs someone who does not have divided loyalties to provide a unique advocacy.

Work with the parents is always necessary with therapy with young children. With adolescents, it is better to have a separate mental health professional provide parent consultation (if needed), so that the adolescent can trust that the psychotherapist will keep the material confidential. Adolescents often need to separate from parents, making parent involvement less necessary or useful.

Family therapy (discussed in Chapter 13) would seem to be the treatment of choice when:

1. The child's problems appear to develop from continued family conflict or family avoidance of problems (Cantor & Drake, 1983).
2. The child is solving a problem of conflict within the family by acting out and focusing the attention on the child rather than on the conflict between parents.
3. Boundaries of authority and affection are violated. The child may have too little or too much structure. The family may be participating in the parentification of the child (see Chapter 2). Family therapy can be very useful in reestablishing appropriate roles. Negotiated rules and consequences for rule breaking can be a powerful intervention in family work.

Group therapy (discussed in Chapter 10) is the treatment of choice when peer issues predominate or when the child may benefit from modeling by peers for talking about problems (Cantor & Drake, 1983). Group therapy is also of benefit when prevention of future problems is the goal, as the child can see other children solving problems that that child has not yet faced.

The first part of this chapter describes play therapy strategies for young children. The second section summarizes other programs designed to help children of divorce.

PLAY THERAPY

Erikson (1963) said that children find self-cure in the activity of playing. There is ample clinical evidence (although it is difficult to demonstrate empirically) that children express their preoccupation, concerns, and competencies in play. When the child is faced with unpleasant stressful situations over which mastery is incomplete, play provides an opportunity for the child to rework the meaning of the stress and to practice solutions. Numerous clinicians have remarked about how restricted problem solving is in a child who does not have play or fantasy available as a problem solving tool.

The young child is limited in perspective taking (i.e., the ability to see the world from various points of view) that would be helpful in gaining alternative ways of coping with the stress of the divorce. Introspection is difficult for school age children and very limited in preschool age children. It is the rare child who can talk for long about the separation and divorce or the upset over the chronic battling of the parents. Even the child who can talk about it at all is likely to exhaust the range of cognitions in a very short time. When a child is able to talk about the divorce and maintain the anxiety about the topic at manageable levels, the therapist should encourage the discussion of feelings and problem solving. I had one extremely bright 8-year-old who was able to talk extensively about his unhappy feelings about the divorce. Even with him, play became an adjunct for exploring alternatives without undue stress.

For the average child, play provides an avenue for communication in a safe, trusting environment. Some child therapists believe that the Rogerian qualities of accurate empathy, nonpossessive warmth, and genuineness are necessary and sufficient for change to occur for children as well as for adults. An example of such noninterpretative therapy is that of Axline (1969).

The relationship with the therapist is crucial, particularly with children undergoing the stress of marital separation, instability of postseparation lifestyles, and chronic upset between parents.

The therapist is often the only significant adult in the child's life who is constant, accepting, and consistently caring. That stability alone is likely to be therapeutic. The caring from the therapist is also likely to help the child experience himself or herself as worthwhile.

The Effects of a Stable, Caring Relationship

My private practice is in Boulder, Colorado, which is a relatively small town. Clinicians in small towns recognize that it is difficult to keep one's personal life and professional life completely separate. One day a 10-year-old girl whom I was seeing in play therapy happened to see me in a store with one of my daughters. At the next therapy session, I expected some reaction about finding out something personal about me and perhaps jealousy about my having a daughter. I didn't expect the reaction I got: "I can't get over the fact that you are a father." When asked whether she had noticed that I wore a wedding ring, she said, "Yes." I then asked why it had never occurred to her that I might be a father, and she said, "Because *you* enjoy playing with me." Even if the content of the play had not been useful to her, the awareness of having an adult enjoy being with her was an important experience.

Does the Therapist's Gender Make a Difference?

The example just given raises the question of whether the therapist's gender should be taken into account. Generally, the answer is no; children will work on whatever they need to work on. The only exception to that rule is when the child has had no close experience with an adult member of a specific gender.

If the noncustodial parent is abandoning and the child has had no experience with an adult of that parent's gender, there is a decided advantage in selecting a therapist of that gender. This gender match would give the child the potential experience of having a warm relationship with a person of that gender. In other cases, the therapist's gender is not relevant.

One mother suggested that she get a female therapist for her daughter since she felt that the primary conflict was with the mother. I indicated to her that I felt that the child would likely work on whatever she needed to work on, regardless of the therapist's gender. Indeed within three sessions, I was playing a a female role in our play, suggesting that the mother was correct in her perception of the conflict.

The Play Therapist's Role

Play therapy is much more difficult than adult therapy. In fact, some evidence indicates that burnout is relatively high among play therapists. By mixing adult, couple, family, and play therapy, the therapist can avoid the exhaustion that can occur in working intensively with children. There are several primary reasons why play therapy presents difficult work:

1. Play therapy is much like thinking in one language and talking in another. The child expresses a conflict or stress in symbolic language through play. The therapist must translate that play into a conceptual understanding of the underlying conflict. The therapist must then decide whether to provide a direct or metaphorical response that the child can understand. This response has to be done while the child is still expressing that theme and has not moved to another. I discuss more about interpretation later.

2. Feedback as to whether the interpretation was useful is often delayed. Adults will give the therapist clues as to how useful a particular interpretation is by either accepting and using it, demonstrating a variety of defensive responses to it, or directly indicating why it is not useful. Although children sometimes indicate that an interpretation is useful, it is not unusual for the therapist to have to wait several sessions to see whether a particular interpretation resulted in changes in the child's perceptions of the world.

3. The therapist needs to be loose, playful, able to laugh and enjoy the child, and able to provide energy. Therapists who had a restricted range of emotional experiences in their own childhoods may have difficulty loosening up with a child in a way that helps the child experience life in a new way. The ability to have a range of emotional experience is important to all therapy regardless of the client's age, but many therapists-in-training who are relatively effective with adult clients find it difficult to make the transition to child therapy.

4. Because the child usually is not the person to make the decision to seek therapy, the child often does not understand the purpose of therapy and

will not help in providing the focus. The child may resist therapy out of fear that the therapist is an agent for the parents rather than an advocate for the child. In addition, the child is usually incapable of understanding the link between having personal problems and playing with a therapist. The child who does not want to play may create special problems for the therapist. The therapist must be creative about encouraging play and in providing play settings that can help support change.

5. The therapist must be supportive to parents as well as the child in therapy. Some child therapists maintain chronic anger at parents, seeing them as the enemy who "damaged" the child in therapy. When the therapist identifies with the child and sees the parent as the enemy, the therapeutic stance is lost and the therapist is likely to be less effective.

6. The system with which the therapist interacts is far more complex than is typical in adult therapy. Working with a child should always involve at least one parent, and optimally both. It may involve working with two families, perhaps both with stepparents. Classroom teachers, day care providers, and even grandparents may be involved. Seldom is play therapy limited to one contact a week with only the child.

Goals of Play Therapy

All play therapies have the same goals:

1. *Increase recognition and acceptance of feelings.* Almost all therapy for children places value in helping the child understand what the feelings are. Axline (1969), Ginott (1965), and Gordon (1970) focused on acceptance as a major goal of therapy. There is an apparent paradox in child psychology around the acceptance of feelings. It is clear that sometimes acceptance of feelings helps a child to feel more accepted, increases self-esteem, and improves problem solving. At other times, acceptance seems to reinforce the the expression of negative feelings so that the child who is sympathetically responded to for angry expression of feelings may increase that expression. Learning theory suggests that sometimes attention can reinforce the expression of negative feelings, and experience suggests that sometimes parents reinforce whining or anger by responding to it. It is my personal experience that although recognition and expression of feelings are necessary for therapy, they are not sufficient.

The child must experience the therapist as warm and accepting of the child (but not necessarily of the behavior). Helping the child understand what feelings are being experienced and that those feelings are acceptable is a basic prerequisite to therapy. With very bright children, this acceptance may be sufficient for change to occur, but most children need additional help to understand what the implications of having those feelings are.

2. *Change from acting out to talking out.* One major function of therapy is to help the child learn to use verbal symbols for problem solving. Helping the child think about the conflicts in life rather than behaving automatically to them can improve the child's adjustment. Thus, one function of play therapy is to give identification to feelings of play figures, that is, to talk about how they feel and why they feel that way rather than simply letting the figures continue to be destructive, withdrawn, or scared.

When one child started hitting a large punching doll, I started hitting the doll too. After a while, I started to tell the doll why I was angry at it, using themes that I understood from the child or the parents to likely be the ones that the child had some concern about. Later, I talked to the doll directly with little aggression. Such a sequence also demonstrates the ally role discussed later in this chapter.

3. *Improve problem solving.* I believe that all feelings are perfectly logical. The feelings are logically connected to the underlying perceptions of the world. There are only incorrect premises about the nature of the world. Helping the child see that there are alternative ways of perceiving the world and that there are alternative ways of coping with those problems will improve problem solving.

4. *Direct the child toward getting needs met.* Erikson (1963) noted that cultures are designed to protect the family and the family is designed to protect the child. Every family is expected to provide nurturance and protection to children. When, for whatever reason, the family or environment does not perform that function, the child may have to solve the problem normally solved by the family.

5. *Increase discrimination so that problem solving and getting needs met are more appropriate.* If a child feels attacked, he or she needs to learn that he or she is not being attacked by everyone. If the child feels abandoned, he or she needs to understand that there are people who are willing to stand by him or her. For example, one 10-year-old boy came in very angry and refused to interact with me. I said, "When you come in here angry with me, I feel that you are angry at grown-ups and I am one more grown-up." Although such a comment may not always work, in this case, the child immediately calmed down and began to play. The play, of course, had themes related to his anger at adults.

Diagnosis in Play Therapy

The Initial Parent Interview

Prior to the therapist's seeing the child for the first time, a meeting with both parents (if available) is essential. Whether it is better to meet with the parents together or separately may depend on the quality of the relationship between them. Because one very important issue is the quality of the relationship between the parents, the therapist should always request a joint appointment initially. If the requesting parent indicates that such a meeting would be extremely difficult, the therapist should readily agree to separate meetings.

If the noncustodial parent has regular contact with the child, meeting with that parent might be considered as a condition of accepting a therapeutic contract. If the parent rarely sees the child or is an abandoning parent, such a requirement may not be necessary. However, if it is possible for a therapist to reengage an abandoning parent with support for adequate parenting, such a strategy should be considered.

In that first session, the concerns of the parent(s) are elicited, and a developmental history is taken, covering conception, pregnancy, delivery, infancy, and development. Informed consent for contact with the schools should be obtained if appropriate. It is best, however, not to contact the schools until after the diagnostic play therapy sessions. I am particularly interested in areas in which each parent sees the facts as different. Because retrospective reports are notoriously inaccurate, *both* parents may be wrong and such reports should be taken with a grain of salt and considered tentative.

At the initial contact with the parents, the therapist also explains how play therapy works and what the next steps are. The parents should be given an explanation to tell the child about why they are coming (a surprising number of parents take children to therapy with no explanation of why they are going to see this strange person). Instructing the parents what to tell the child about therapy indicates the importance of providing explanations to the child. In addition, it enables assessment of the degree to which the parents are able to follow up on such suggestions.

The parents should be told the rules of confidentiality, that is, that the child will be told that the sessions are confidential and that parents will not be informed of anything that the child tells the therapist or of the content of the play. Exceptions to this rule involve abuse or situations in which the child may be potentially harmful to self or others. The therapist should provide information about the general problem areas that the child is having and whether the therapy is able to provide help in those areas. It should be noted that many child therapists do not maintain such a confidentiality orientation and believe that parents should be informed of the ongoing therapy content.

Parents should be seen on a regular basis, depending on an assessment of how much they need to change their behavior in order to facilitate the therapy and how resistive they are likely to be to the changes in the child. To reduce competition between the parents and therapist, the parents should be informed that the reasons a therapist can often be helpful when it is difficult for parents are twofold:

1. The therapist is not important enough. Children can afford to take chances with the therapist because they do not care very much how the

therapist feels. Children can have difficulty talking to parents because they care very much about how the parents feel.

2. The therapist only has the responsibility of understanding and being helpful. The major responsibility for physical protection and providing structure for the child's emotional and physical well-being belongs to the parents. Therefore, the therapist does not have to say "no" as often.

Play Therapy Evaluation

The first few sessions in play therapy provide the therapist with an opportunity to understand what symbols the child uses, how much fantasy is available as a problem solving tool (or escape), and where the child is developmentally. The playroom should have eliciting materials that encourage the child to enter play. Appropriate materials include a doll house with family figures, puppets, play clothes, balls, blocks, crayons, paper, and a wide range of toys. Age-appropriate toys should be selected, as well as toys that may be too young and too old for the child (to evaluate developmental level). Toys should also be appropriate and inappropriate from a sex-role stereotypic perspective. It is important to have materials that elicit a range of emotionally oriented behaviors. Because aggression is a common problem, materials that elicit aggression are especially important. Punch dolls (which must be quite durable) that are similar in height to the child are useful. Foam rubber bats and pretend swords and knives can also be helpful. Avoid materials that can cause harm, such as darts, plastic swords, and hard plastic toys.

Children should be told that there are five rues in the playroom:

1. They may not hurt themselves.
2. They may not hurt the therapist.
3. They may not damage the room or toys.
4. They must end play on time.
5. The room must in order at the end of the session so that other children can use it.

Other eliciting materials include dolls and family figures with a house. Younger children often prefer more fanciful houses, such as castles. Some people have argued that if the therapist is working with children of divorce, it is appropriate to have *two* doll houses, on the grounds that two are more likely to reflect the reality of the child. Although two doll houses are available to the children I work with, children rarely provide a fantasy involving two homes. Children often identify one home as primary or are manifesting the wish for reconciliation by using a single home. With the recent increase in joint residential custody, however, this dynamic may change.

If the child is reluctant to separate from the parent in the waiting room, the parent may accompany the therapist and child to the playroom and stay for a few minutes. If the child shows any anxiety about separation, the therapist can tell the child that the parent will remain in the waiting room and that the child can see the parent any time during the session. (The therapist should warn parents to stay in the waiting room for the first few sessions.) The ability to return to the parent usually is enough reassurance, and few children check out the presence of the parent (although a request to go to the rest room may serve the function of checking on the parent's presence).

During the first session, the therapist should spend some time with the child explaining who the therapist is and why the child is there. Because parents frequently do not provide any explanation to the child as to why the child is suddenly seeing this strange person in this strange setting, it is important to provide a truthful (although not necessarily exhaustive) explanation. For very young children, an appropriate explanation is that a therapist is like a "worry" doctor and that worry doctors talk about worries and do not use medicine or shots. The child could be told that someone in the family is worried. The parents may be worried about the child, or they may see the child as worried about stresses in life.

Older children should be told that everything that they say is secret and that parents will not be told about play or discussions unless the child might hurt himself or herself. Other people will be told if the child is being hurt. The children should be informed that parents are very curious about what happens in play therapy. They should be given permission to tell their parents if the children wish. The therapist should also say, however, that it is appropriate to tell the parents, "The therapist said I do not have to tell."

Experience indicates that children who choose to keep the content of the therapy secret from parents are often more serious about using the time effectively. Although nothing may have happened in therapy that could remotely affect the parents, the wish to keep the content secret has two functions: (1) it reflects individuation from the parents, and is a healthy statement of growth, and (2) it can indicate a recognition that future sessions may move into meaningful material.

During the first session or two, the therapist plays a more passive role to see how the child handles the therapist's presence and the new room, and which toys he or she prefers. Fantasy play is encouraged by having the therapist participate in the fantasy. No interpretation is made during the diagnostic phase, and only elaborations based on the child's leads are used. Children are sometimes reluctant to enter into play either because they do not have fantasy as a resource (indicating fewer problem solving skills in a child) or because they are self-conscious about letting an adult into the play. The degree of enjoyment that most children experience once joint play occurs is profound and aids the development of the therapeutic alliance.

Generally, therapists who enter into and participate in play rather than remaining passive observers facilitate the therapeutic alliance. Only therapists capable of genuine playfulness should try this strategy, however. A stilted participation will be experienced by the child as rejection.

Play Interpretation

There are two stages in the creative aspect of play therapy. The first stage is to propose a series of hypotheses about the symbolic meaning of the play. The following questions are useful in proposing hypotheses:

1. What is the child's cognitive understanding of the world? From Piaget's theory come the questions about object permanence, time perspective, egocentrism, and cause–effect thinking. From Erikson come questions about basic trust, autonomy, and industry. From Freudian developmental theory come questions of psychosexual development, and from object relations theory come questions about attachment, individuation, and separation.

2. How is the child's view of the world distorted and how is it accurate? The context of the developmental history is important in making initial estimates of the accuracy of the world view. How dangerous is it? If parents report child or spousal abuse or severe battles with yelling and screaming, the child's view of the world as a violent place is understandable.

Assessment of play therapy candidates may require two or three sessions. Toward the latter part of this time, the therapist may see the degree to which the child can tolerate mild changes in the play through interpretation. The second or third session may begin with an invitation to talk about the child's life, and whether the child has any worries. Later, interpretations that encourage the child to change the cognitive and affective understanding and develop new coping strategies should be provided.

The Role of Interpretation

Based on the dynamic and cognitive approaches that serve as a theoretical base of this book, the role of interpretation is central to play therapy. How is the therapist helping the child change his or her cognitive understanding of the nature of the world? Once hypotheses are developed concerning what the child's cognitive understanding of the world is and how it is distorted or accurate, two additional questions are required in order to develop effective interpretation:

1. What would be adequate coping for this child? The therapist has to determine what world view would be more helpful than the one the child has.

2. How can that change in cognitive understanding be presented to the child within the context of play? One major dimension on which interpretative play therapists differ is the degree to which they give interpretations

within or outside the metaphor. The therapist can have another character in the fantasy present alternatives (within the metaphor). The therapist can comment on the feelings or options of the protagonist in the play (again, within the metaphor). Finally, the therapist can note the similarities of play characters with real events in the child's world (out of the metaphor).

The more the symbols are disguised, the greater the child's defensive structure. Some defensiveness is healthy. The child with no defenses is likely to be quickly overwhelmed by stress. Some children draw a parallel between their lives and the characters in the play. I took the role of a hated gym teacher with one child, and he proceeded to joyously attack me. Older children who take nonhuman figures or highly developed fantasy figures may be expressing the need to have greater distance from the emotionality of the play.

The more the child is able to tolerate the anxiety associated with an interpretation, the better able the child is to develop adequate coping strategies for the problem at hand. It is generally useful to provide as direct an interpretation as the child is able to utilize. For example, talking to the child about real events, if tolerated, may be more useful than talking about characters in a fantasy. If not tolerated, talking about the fantasy is useful.

Sometimes, the child will begin talking about a problem, but cut off discussion because the anxiety level is too high. The child may be able to deal with the issues involved by disguising the anxiety-provoking elements to a greater degree, thereby reducing the associated anxiety.

For example, a divorced mother informed a therapist that her 6-year-old son had gotten into a fight with a girl in his class at school. When the therapist asked the child what had happened, the child was unwilling or unable to discuss it. The therapist then asked whether the child could demonstrate what had happened using the dolls. By using the dolls (and only slightly disguising the figures since the child was indicating that he was reporting on a factual event), the child was able to depict what had happened. The enactment was abbreviated, but complete. Later in the same session, the child gave a rich story of a boy who had been attacked by a girl and had to defend himself. That story was not presented as factual, but gave details about how the child had experienced and justified his behavior.

Greater abstraction in symbolization in an interpretation can be helpful if the child is still overwhelmed by anxiety.

When a child is overwhelmed with anxiety, the symbolization can be expressed with animals rather than people as actors in the play. Even greater distance can occur when more primitive symbols such as bombs, explosions, or other inanimate objects express feelings.

When the child is incapable of discussing a particular issue, the therapist can give permission for a range of emotions and cognitions by discussing what "some children" feel in similar circumstances and asking whether this child has similar experiences.

The therapist should be concerned when a child does not maintain some distance. The child who uses real names of family members for actors in a play may not be establishing enough distance to effectively manipulate the symbols for useful problem solving. If a therapist feels that a child is not learning to cognitively manipulate symbols and learn symbolic problem solving, the therapist should encourage the child to distance the symbols.

The therapist should monitor the level of abstraction in the symbols that the child uses in play therapy to optimize the level of problem solving. As therapy progresses, a child often lowers the levels of anxiety associated with symbols as problem solving becomes more effective. The therapist may then be able to be more direct in the interpretations given to the child. Effective therapy can be obtained, however, without ever directly interpreting the meaning of the symbols to the child.

To do effective play therapy, a play therapist must watch the favorite movies and television shows of children, at least once. Some therapists find this viewing a onerous chore, but others like an excuse to see some movies that they would otherwise not see. After the *Star Wars* movies came out, numerous children in play therapy introduced star wars themes. When the movie *Willie Wonka and the Chocolate Factory* appeared on television, I had two children introduce chocolate factory stories in therapy. Not only is it important to know what stories "hook" the child, but it is also very important to spot changes in the story that fit the child's needs. Popular television shows including superpowers are often incorporated into the fantasy.

Generally, the older and more adjusted the child, the greater the ability to use interpretations that draw parallels with the child's life. Often, later therapy sessions will include more direct interpretation.

How to Tell When an Interpretation Is Helpful

Because the therapist is dealing with symbolic imagery, there is no procedure to determine whether the hypothesis concerning a symbol's meaning is correct. Interpretations can only be useful or not useful to the child. For an interpretation to be useful, it minimally must be at a level of cognitive complexity that the child is capable of utilizing. In addition, to utilize the information, the child must not be overwhelmed with anxiety.

There are several indicators that the interpretation is helpful:

1. The child incorporates the comment into the context of play. If the child is willing to use the suggestion with the characters in the play, the interpretation *may* have been useful. If the child spontaneously incorporates the suggestion in future play sessions, the interpretation has been

demonstrated as useful. Children will sometimes indulge an adult without developing cognitive schemas associated with the interpretation. The failure to incorporate an interpretation in future play is likely to be an indication that the interpretation was not useful at the present time, because either the hypothesis or the timing was wrong.

When an interpretation is very reasonable, but is ineffective in changing the content of play, it is useful to turn around the potential way in which the symbols are being used. For example, it may be useful to propose that the symbol is a defense rather than a wish. A 9-year-old boy created a fantasy using building blocks and toy trucks in which a building caught on fire and a fire truck had to come and rescue the boy off the burning building. Although the boy accepted the therapist's low-level interpretations about an out-of-control world and the need to be rescued, and even metaphorical suggestions that it was nice to have a rescuer around (the therapist) when things were not going well, his play did not change over several weeks. Assuming that these interpretations were not useful, the therapist reinterpreted the play to mean that the person was setting the fire in order to force the firemen to prove that they still cared. This interpretation resulted in changed play. Ultimately, the boy's theme of having problems as a way of getting people to care was a recurrent symbol.

2. A child refuses to include a suggestion in the play. Clearly, the interpretation is not useful.

3. The child stops the play and requests to play something else. Play disruptions are errors in therapy and are usually responses to intense anxiety. Such disruptions are extremely useful, however, since they indicate clearly what symbols are being used. The therapist should permit the disruption, and use a less direct method of introducing the interpretation in the future or determine the smaller steps that the child needs to be able to accept the interpretation.

Process Themes in Play Therapy

A variety of content themes have been observed in working with children of divorce and are useful to anticipate. Knowing specific symbolic content areas for children of divorce can be useful in forming initial hypotheses about the meaning of specific fantasy material. Because children form idiosyncratic meanings, the therapist must be ready to abandon a hypothesis if the data indicate that interpretations based on that hypothesis are not useful.

The sequence of themes provides a useful indicator of the psychological development of the child. One child built forts that were immediately destroyed by the enemy. The inability to protect himself was a recurrent theme. The therapist and child explored both why the enemy was so powerful and how to build a stronger fort: Can the child negotiate with the enemy? Can he talk to them about why they want to destroy him? Can he get help to make him stronger?

When the play therapist enters play with the child, it is better to play the child's ally, rather than the enemy, for two reasons. First, the child is more willing to let an ally have alternative solutions to the problem than an enemy. Second, the child will often object when the enemy behaves less like an enemy. The child will then try to exert greater control over the script. With the role of ally, the therapist can raise questions about the enemy's motives and possible alternative ways of handling the enemy that model more effective problem solving.

An example of sequencing is a child who began by building laser beams that would destroy the galaxy. This child had major problems with aggression in school. Indeed, the hypothesis was developed that this child felt the need to destroy everything before it destroyed him. As we worked together to destroy the galaxy, the anger gradually became more circumscribed from destroying the solar system, to demolishing the world, to attacking aliens, and finally to providing protection so that attack was not necessary. We raised questions about why they were out to get us and whether perhaps they were scared of us. Finally, we developed ways of protecting ourselves without attack. The child experienced a similar reduction in the use of aggression outside therapy.

Common Themes of the Play Therapy of Children of Divorce

The following are common themes in play therapy of children of divorce:

1. *Anger.* The angry child is more intrusive than a grieving, withdrawn one. Acting out anger in school or at home (or both) is a common impetus for parents to seek therapy for the child.
   Because acting out of anger is a common response of preschool and early elementary school age children, helping the child to deal with the expression of anger is important. First, linking the aggression to feelings of abandonment, unfairness, being attacked, deprivation, and not feeling loved is helpful to the child. Then, the process is to help the child see that tantrum behavior evokes attack or withdrawal, but not negotiation. Talk and negotiation are likely to be more helpful. If negotiation is not helpful, the child must then turn to others to get needs met. Constructive anger addresses the cause of the anger and negotiates reduction in that cause. The child must learn self-control as part of that negotiation.

2. *Abandonment.* The child must decide whether true abandonment has occurred, how to ask for more support, how to gain reassurance that remaining people will not abandon, and how to get needs partially met.

3. *Loss.* Toomin (1974) proposed that loss is a basic issue for the child. She felt that the process of coping with loss is the same, whether the loss is due

to death, divorce, or a widening of psychosocial distance. Losses must be mourned in order for the child to separate from the absent person and develop new relationships.

Toomin's therapeutic approaches (either by working with parents or with the child) all involve working with the child around mourning, that is, helping the child over and over again to express feelings of sadness and anger. Defenses against loss must be dealt with, including premature detachment and excessively close relationship with the other parent, or internalization of the lost person as a way of avoiding loss. Toomin felt that internalization of negative qualities occurs when the absent parent is feared. Identification with the aggressor is a common defense against overwhelming anxiety. Toomin noted that it was more common to internalize an idealized positive image of a separated father, even when the father was cruel.

Although conceptualizing loss as an underlying construct for divorce is consistent with Bowlby's (1969) theoretical view of grief in childhood, there is some question about whether the child responds to all losses with the need for mourning. Mourning is significantly more difficult when the absent parent is either partially absent or completely absent, but alive. Whether children conceptualize loss of a relationship as a loss requiring mourning is an empirical question. Children's egocentrism may lead to internalized feelings of rejection, but not grieving. The research discussed in Chapters 2 and 3 indicates that prior losses do not predispose a child of divorce to greater distress to parental separation and divorce.

Gardner (1976) also noted that grief and depression were common thematic issues for children of divorce, but listed several other common themes as well:

4. *Denial.* All therapists of children of divorce note that denial of the underlying feelings around the divorce process is a common response of children who have difficulty and are in need of psychotherapeutic help.

5. *Blame and guilt.* Blame and guilt are discussed in detail in Chapter 2.

6. *Immaturity.* Regression can be a response to overwhelming stress or can be an attempt to draw attention away from parental conflict to the child as the identified patient. Children can wish to be younger to return the family to the predivorce stage of development.

7. *Hypermaturity.* Pseudomaturity was discussed in detail in Chapter 2.

8. *Reconciliation preoccupation.*

9. *Self-esteem.*

10 *Sex-role identification and sexual identity.* For children dealing with oedipal issues (and unlike classical analytic theory, I do not believe in the inevitability of the Oedipus complex), the separation of parents can be either the winning of the conflict, producing overwhelming anxiety in the child, or the losing of the conflict, causing the child to feel rejected. As noted in

Chapter 2, parents can feed these fantasies by allowing the child into the parental bed. In a similar fashion, older children, at late latency and adolescence, can be identified as the "man" or "woman" of the house and become overburdened. It is important that parent consultation strongly deal with these problems.

11. *The quest for the wanted person.* Tessman (1978), in her book on therapy with children of divorce, mentioned an additional theme for children of divorce: the quest for the wanted person. Tessman was struck by the frequency with which children of divorce develop a quest for the lost parent. This quest may be a wish to merge with the wanted person or to be like that person, or it may be a way of dealing with loss. This quest obviously prevents mourning and development of new attachments. This theme has also been addressed in other parts of this text.

12. *Cinderella.* My own experience in play therapy has indicated that the Cinderella theme is common. Children often feel a sense of deprivation "while others are allowed to go to the ball." If played out in its entirety, the Cinderella theme offers hope to the child of being rescued, of being loved, and of having the rejecting family members rejected themselves. Other ways in which this deprivation theme gets played out includes stealing and starving. Concern with lack of nurturance is developmentally more advanced than another common theme I have observed, that is, annihilation.

13. *Annihilation.* One of the most primitive themes is the total destruction of self. Repeated themes of self-destruction give a clear picture of the panic that the separation has created for the child. Indeed, as noted in the examples in the previous section, rage may be a defense against this fear of self-destruction (i.e., kill before being killed).

14. *Feelings of guilt, responsibility of fear of retribution* (Derdeyn, 1977).

15. *Feelings of devaluation* (Derdeyn, 1977).

Techniques for Encouraging Fantasy Play

Some children are quite resistant to fantasy play because they either do not use fantasy in their lives or are afraid of the implications of sharing their fantasies. Late latency boys have particular difficulty getting into fantasy play. Gardner (1976) developed numerous games to entice the child into trying fantasy. These are discussed in some detail later in this chapter.

One technique that I have found useful for children who are resistant to fantasy play is playing radio announcer. When a child is shooting foam basketballs, I will pick up a block or racket and pretend that it is a microphone and start announcing the shots as a sports announcer. Then I try to interview the basketball player about how he feels about winning or losing or what happens when he misses a shot.

A resistant 11-year-old girl and I played news and weather reporters. I made up headlines that fit her problems, for example, "A guru is found in cave up in mountains. He doesn't want to interact with anyone. He says that no one can hurt him up there." The weather report she gave was revealing about the turmoil she felt: "The weather in Alaska is most unusual today. There is a line down the middle of the state. On one side it is 50° below zero and on the other 110°. Down the middle, there are earthquakes and wind storms." With another child, I played fortune teller, in which I told the fortune including stress lines and coping.

I use any available technique. One child was unwilling to stay in the play therapy room. We roamed around the building. He asked if he could learn the keypunch machines. I let him use the keypunch machines to encourage him to deal with me in the playrooms. We made a deal: If he would go into the playroom with me and play, we could spend 10 minutes on the machine. While he punched "secret" codes, I punched interpretations.

Another useful strategy for involving children in fantasy is Winicott's (1971) Squiggles game. This technique involves drawing a random (and rather simple) set of lines on a piece of paper. The therapist shuts his or her eyes and makes a mark on the paper, and the child is to turn it into something. Then the child is asked to do the same thing, and the therapist turns it into something. The therapist and child continue to take turns. The therapist continues the theme introduced by the child, usually with little elaboration, and avoids interpretation until he or she feels that the child and therapist are talking about the same theme and that the child is able to use the interpretation. Examples Winicott gave in his book indicate that interpretation was given both within and outside of the metaphor. The Squiggles game has been used successfully for children of ages 6 to 12.

I used the Squiggles game with a child who kept drawing themes of danger. My drawing had a big fish chasing a little fish that was swimming into a hole too small for the big fish. My message to the child was that there were ways in which a little fish could be safe from danger. If the drawing had occurred at another point in therapy, I might have drawn another big fish to help the little fish from danger (representing an alliance with either a supportive parent or the therapist).

Termination of Play Therapy

As the degree of conflict in the play imagery becomes significantly less, the therapist can tell when termination is near. Acting out behavior becomes significantly reduced in the nontherapy world, and self-control and higher self-esteem become more stable. Sometimes, the imagery itself tells the therapist (T) that it is time for the child (C) to stop therapy:

C: Pretend we are in a domed city.
T: OK.
C: We are looking out a round window.

(A pretend window opens up. The therapist makes science fiction-like sounds to indicate the opening of the round window.)

T: What do we see? (A reasonable question, because the therapist does not know where this fantasy is going.)

C: What we see is poisonous gas. You know, I used to think that poisonous gas was miles and miles thick. But I recently discovered that it is only a foot thick and on the other side there are birds, and trees and flowers.

Clearly this child was telling the therapist that he was ready to stop therapy.

Termination in play therapy with children of divorce is particularly problematic. It is important that the termination not reinstate a sense of parental loss and rejection that the child has already experienced. The termination should not result in the child's feeling one more adult abandonment.

Several strategies are useful to aid in termination. The therapist can give the child some control over quitting time. The therapist may indicate that life is going so well now that it is close to time to stop. The child could be allowed to decide the exact date, given a small range of times in the near future. Children who have completely finished and show high levels of adjustment often pick the earliest time. Also, children who find attending therapy painful because of their concern about the stigma often terminate as soon as possible. Children who select the middle date are often showing the ability to compromise between their wants and their needs. Finally, children who hang on to therapy as long as possible may still be expressing dependency needs or strong attachment to the therapist. Regardless of when the child chooses, this choice is one termination of a relationship in life over which the child has some control.

The therapist can indicate to the child that although the relationship will end, the therapist will continue to care and will remember the child forever. This communication fosters object permanence in a Piagetian and object relations sense. "Forever?" one 11-year-old girl asked me. "I will never forget you," I said. Three years later she wrote me a letter that began, "Did you forget?" Since that case, another girl, who moved out of state, also wrote to me, essentially asking the same question.

The therapist wants to do everything possible to encourage object permanence, that is, to ensure the child that the therapist still exists, that the therapist still cares, and that the child can still care about the therapist. An 11-year-old boy whom I had terminated a month previously knocked on my office door. Although I was in conference with students and could not spend time with him, I stopped what I was doing for 5 minutes to express pleasure at seeing him. He seemed enormously relieved that I still cared, smiled happily, and ran off satisfied. He never again contacted me. I believe that

that 5-minute contact was reassurance that I meant it when I said that I still cared after the therapy was over.

Such reassurance is particularly important when children have experienced abandonment by a noncustodial parent or death of a parent. Establishing a belief that caring continues beyond the contact gives them the opportunity to hold on to the gains received from the therapy and use the identifications and bondings that they have not only with the therapist, but with other, more important people in their lives.

GARDNER'S MUTUAL STORYTELLING TECHNIQUE

In his book, *Psychotherapy with Children of Divorce,* Richard Gardner (1976) described a therapeutic technique for many children in therapy. His therapeutic technique is not used for borderline or psychotic children or for any child in which elaboration of fantasy is contraindicated. He focused on individual child therapy with parental observation and intermittent participation. The younger the child, the more parental involvement might occur.

Gardner's mutual storytelling technique involves having the child tell a made-up story with a moral. The therapist then tells the same story with similar settings and the same characters, but with healthier adaptations and resolutions. He or she uses humor and drama to encourage a therapeutic alliance. The technique is a more structured form of play therapy. Gardner's technique is completely compatible with my own view of what children need and the prior discussion in this chapter. By using fantasy, the therapist allows children to talk indirectly about what is bothering them and provides new cognitions about the perception of the world and what would be better strategies for coping with that stress.

The technique requires the same tasks of the therapist as does play therapy. The therapist must answer the following questions: What theme is the child presenting in the story? Which figures in the story represent the child, and which represent significant others? What retelling of the story would provide the child with a different view of the world and better ways of coping with it?

Gardner demonstrated both how the therapist retells a story and the cognitive reorientation provided the child about a more realistic coping with the reality of the child's life. The therapist does not give the child unrealistic expectations about the reduction in stress or how much parents may be able to give. Such a technique obviously works only to the degree that the therapist has a clear picture of family dynamics in order to determine what would be more effective coping.

Gardner's book is particularly useful in describing the cognitive reorientations that such children tend to need. Examples of such changes in world view include:

1. If the theme of the story is to keep secrets, the child is given the message that children are better off when information is not kept secret.

2. If the child gives a story of being alone, the message is that life is easier with help.

3. If the story is that the child is fragile, the countermessage is that the child is not so fragile.

4. The child's acting out needs to be changed to talking out. (Note that this message is common to all interpretative and existential child therapies.)

5. Children need to learn to get needs met where appropriate, from other family members or friends. They should not keep asking for needs to be met from a parent who cannot meet them.

6. Children need to learn that partial solutions are better than no solutions, and to accept partial happiness and partial meeting of needs.

7. An important message is that everyone is both good and bad. As previously noted in this book, children often split as a way of handling their ambivalence about their parents. The child who chooses one parent over the other is engaging in maladaptive problem solving and inviting self-rejection through the identification with one parent.

8. They must reduce identification with acting out parents.

9. Children need to reduce fantasy of reconciliation and get on with life.

10. Children must avoid becoming parent surrogates.

11. Children must not win the oedipal conflict.

Much of Gardner's book on therapy with children of divorce presented techniques for helping children get into fantasy material. The child of divorce who has fantasy available is more likely to do effective problem solving. Examples on how to help children get into storytelling include making up a story television program and playing a variety of games, such as bag games in which objects and words are drawn and a story is made up about them, word games for stories, the alphabet soup game, and the Talking, Feeling, Doing Game (an excellent game designed by Gardner).

TESSMAN'S ANALYTICALLY ORIENTED THERAPY

Tessman's (1978) book, *Children of Parting Parents,* provides another major description of therapy. This book is rich with case histories of children dealing with parental separation and divorce. From Tessman's point of view, the purpose of therapy is to help the child make peace with the loss so as not to lose the capacity for loving. When the child cannot share the sense of loss with others and substitutes symptoms for grieving, then psychotherapy is indicated.

The quest for the absent person is one way in which the child avoids dealing with the loss. As previously mentioned, the quest may be a searching for the rejecting or abandoning parent with a wish to merge or identify with that parent. The child may search for faces at shopping centers, looking for the parent, even when the abandonment was so long ago that the child no longer knows what the parent looks like. The quest prevents grieving of the lost relationship and prevents further growth.

Tessman cautioned that the child should not be asked to separate from a therapist in too few sessions. If an intake evaluation is being done prior to starting therapy, she recommended that no more than two evaluation sessions be done if transfer to another professional might follow.

For services provided in an agency or institutional setting, the evaluation procedure should not risk an increase in feelings of abandonment. A child can quickly attach to a person doing assessment and feel a loss when transferred to another therapist.

Tessman also warned the therapist to avoid countertransference issues of wanting to be the person to fill the void for the child. The loss is real, and substitution of the therapist as a pseudo-parent is not adaptive. The child must experience the loss of the therapist at some time in the future. The therapist's role is to help the child deal with that loss. Therapy provides a reliable relationship with sufficient support to allow the child to risk sadness.

Tessman felt that confrontation in therapy has two purposes. First, confrontation is used as an "effort to unmask denial." This reason for confrontation is less often needed because the child's problem is less often denial of inner impulses than it is denial of the reality of the loss of love of the absent parent. The child must give up an omnipotent self-image or parent image that could make everything come out all right.,

The second purpose of confrontation is to eliminate depression around abandoning the quest for the absent, wanted person. Anger toward the therapist is a likely dynamic in this stage. Tessman viewed giving up such wishes for having the pleasure of the intact family as similar to giving up all infantile wishes. Being able to make choices for himself or herself can be enormously freeing up to the child, who no longer behaves in such a way as to bring back the absent parent.

Tessman cautioned the therapist not to become so intrigued with the imaginative nature of play therapy as to lose sight of the goal of utilizing the material for ego building. Ego building occurs when the therapist supports the child's interest in sublimation and gratifying realities and does not interpret the underlying libidinal significance. When Tessman discussed interpretation at this stage, she was describing a process of problem solving very similar to my own cognitive orientation and totally consistent with Gardner's ego-supportive reorientation toward reality.

Tessman also noted that rapid "transference cure" based on the positive relationship with the therapist is common with neurotic children. I have received reports from parents of sudden improvement of a child's behavior long before I have provided reinterpretations of the child's cognitive orientation. Although Tessman feel that some children gain enough inner freedom from such transference cure to be able to continue growth, my experience indicates that the child usually needs continued help with working through the experience of the divorce and what it meant.

Transference cure can occur only with the neurotic child. (The impulse-ridden child cannot develop such identification with the therapist.) Anxiety about wishing restitution of a deserting or depriving parent and fear of abandonment can lead a neurotic child to act out the fear by breaking appointments, stealing, and being unresponsive or avoiding involvement. Countertransference issues with such a child are particularly dangerous to the therapy. The therapist may be led to overpunitive or overpermissive reactions. The therapist may have fantasies of rescuing the child from rejecting parents. Given the rejection by the child of this fantasy, the therapist can then become disenchanted and be either depressed or angry about the treatment.

HOSMAN AND FROILAND'S LOSS MODEL

Hozman and Froiland (1976) developed a theory of therapy based on the assumption that children of divorce must grieve loss of the parental relationship in the same way that children of parental death must grieve that loss. Using the concept of loss developed by Kubler-Ross, they proposed that children had to go through the following five stages:

1. *Denial.* Children try to eliminate thinking about the separation and divorce and associated loss. Manifestations include withdrawal and isolation from peers, teachers, and the environment. Tantrum behavior can be designed to push others away. The therapist needs to directly confront this behavior and legitimize the child's feelings by helping the child come to express feelings as an acceptable part of the personality. Role playing can be used to help the child accept feelings. Play therapy encourages children to express their reality. The authors also suggested providing role models to help the child observe people who have experienced a divorce and accepted the reality with appropriate behaviors. Bibliotherapy, records, or tape recordings can have that releasing effect.

2. *Anger.* The child responds at the anger stage by striking out at anyone involved in the separation and divorce or against parent surrogates, such as teachers. Hozman and Froiland assumed that the underlying dynamic was a feeling of guilt for causing the divorce. (As mentioned in Chapter 2, the apparent frequency of the guilt response to divorce is age specific. There is some

doubt about how common the guilt response is.) The first therapeutic move is to help the child recognize and focus the anger and understand its origins. The child is given unconditional positive regard while experiencing the anger so that the child can accept that emotion as part of the self. The second move is to channel the anger, to limit the expression to appropriate ways. The therapy may have a releasing effect on the aggression, by using displacement or symbolic expression (e.g., by hitting a stuffed animal or blowing up a balloon). The authors recommended the kit, *Developing Understanding of Self and Others* (1970). Hozman and Froiland noted that owning feelings is not an end in itself, but a prerequisite to better functioning.

Substantial evidence from learning theory research suggests that catharsis is not adequate therapy. Encouraging a child to express angry feelings without providing the training for self-control and better negotiation may encourage tantrum behavior rather than better functioning. Although Hozman and Froiland gave recognition to that process, they did not indicate how to support that next step.

3. *Bargaining.* The child at the bargaining stage attempts to reunite the parents. The child may try to be particularly good if he or she perceives that the parent left because of the child's bad behavior. The therapist's role is to help the child see the lack of personal responsibility for and control of the situation. The basic therapy strategy is to initiate interactions in which the child is responsible for his or her own behavior and not for the behavior of others. The authors recommended problem solving games and puzzles and construction toys as promoting that self-concept.

Although a provocative idea, it would be difficult to determine whether the symbolic content was in the mind of the therapist or the child. There is substantial reason to believe that constructive interactions with a stable, caring therapist may help the child, independent of the process of interpretation or constructive reconceptualization. My own preference is to gain evidence for how the child symbolizes and to use that symbolism for communicating more effective ideas to the child.

4. *Depression.* When the child realizes that bargaining will not work to reunite the parents, the child may feel badly about past behaviors or missed opportunities. Mourning may occur. The child needs help in owning the feeling of depression. Allowing the child to cry and otherwise express emotion may be helpful. The child should then be encouraged to reinitiate activities. Peers may be used to draw the child back into social activity.

5. *Acceptance.* The final stage of mourning the loss of the intact family is acceptance with a lack of despair. Individual worth is intrinsic, and not determined by the divorce. The child is able to accept ambivalence toward parents.

Hozman and Froiland noted that not every child goes through all of these stages and that the order is not invariate. Given that view, the question can be raised as to how helpful such a model is. Clearly, the feelings addressed are more or less common for children of divorce, but many other responses also occur. Although Hozman and Froiland suggested some potentially useful strategies for helping children cope with the loss, their guiding theoretical bases are not clear.

DERDEYN'S CRISIS INTERVENTION MODEL

Derdeyn's (1977) model of therapy for children from 3 to 8 years of age is basically a description of therapy for the mother, father, and child, given in general terms rather than as specific techniques. Assistance for the child included play therapy with interpretations to the child's feelings about the divorce, family group therapy, and individual work with the father and mother. Derdeyn discussed the blurring of generational boundaries, the need for structure and authority, a parent's identification of the child with the absent parent, and depression due to unresolved loss. Themes of concern that could impede the therapy included sensitivity to parental anger, feelings of guilt, responsibility and fear of retribution, feelings of devaluation, guilt as a defense against existential anxiety, fear of abandonment, and the wish to reunite the parents.

THE DIVORCE AND MOURNING PROJECT OF MARIN COUNTY, CALIFORNIA

Given the extensive publications by Wallerstein and Kelly about the 131 children of divorce whom they studied, it is easy to overlook the fact that the study occurred in the context of therapy services. Three reviews summarized that service (American Institutes for Research, 1980; Wallerstein & Kelly, 1977, 1980c).

The direct services involved providing counseling for the family members affected by the divorce, with an emphasis on short-term crisis intervention. Family members were generally seen for individual sessions, although family therapy occasionally was performed.

Stages of Assessment

Three stages of assessment were used to determine the child's needs to be addressed in the short-term treatment:

1. *Developmental assessment* involved a detailed history from the parents, detailed information from the school, and direct observation of the child for several hours.

2. *Divorce-specific assessment* focused on the child's response to the divorce or separation situation. Thoughts, fantasies, affect, and behavioral

responses to the divorce were explored. The degree to which pain and anxiety were consciously experienced and the defensive mechanisms were evaluated, as was the degree to which these responses were influenced by conscious or unconscious pressure from the parents. The child's understanding of the divorce and what the child had been told were also determined. Wallerstein and Kelly found that the children, particularly preschool children, were very confused about the meaning of divorce and the reasons for the divorce.

As noted in Chapter 2, many preschool children had been given no explanation for the divorce. When affective reactions were assessed, the following questions were evaluated: How much pain was being experience? Were irritability and aggressive behavior present? Were overt or underlying depressive reactions present? Defensive mechanisms to cope with the pain of divorce were evaluated: How contained was the response to the divorce? Finally, an inquiry into the appearance of new symptoms was made.

3. *Social system assessment* included parent–child relationships, siblings, extended family, school, peers, and other activities. Lack of support was a particular concern.

The Intervention

The first question of intervention was with whom will the intervention take place? First, the mother was usually seen, followed perhaps by the father. Then the children were seen individually. Most clients were seen for 3 months or longer, rather than 6 weeks as suggested in the original crisis model. Three intervention types were included:

1. *Child centered.* Both parents were encouraged to provide explanations to the child about the divorce. Children needed assurance of continued contact and support. The noncustodial parent was encouraged to continue contact. Specific advice was given to parents about handling children's age-appropriate responses to the divorce and understanding children's anger and the common responses to divorce.

2. *Child–parent relationship intervention.* This intervention was to help parents with their capacity to respond effectively to the children. This approach helped the parents understand the children's dynamics and themselves, as well as why it was difficult to perform parental functions. Parents were helped to regain parental control.

3. *Adult centered.* These interventions were designed to help parents with needs beyond the parental ones.

Children were seen for varying amounts of individual therapy. Children under 8 were generally seen only once or twice. Children from 9 to 12 were usually seen three or four times. Teenagers often were hesitant to come in. Not surprisingly, girls were more willing to talk about their problems than boys, particularly teenagers. At-risk children were seen as those who felt responsible, who strongly reminded a parent of the other spouse, and who were caught up in a custody battle.

Wallerstein and Kelly's Intervention Models

Wallerstein and Kelly (1980c) did not feel that there was an observable progression of defined stages in the child's response to the divorce, an observation at odds with Hozman and Froiland's (1976) grief model. Wallerstein and Kelly felt that the response to the divorce was more related to the developmental stage, environment, and parent–child relationship than to predictable stages of response to divorce.

One model in working with the children involved utilizing the divorce-specific assessment. This approach usually involved three to four 1-hour sessions, centering on exploration, clarification, and some education and was combined with intensive work with parents. Although Wallerstein and Kelly did not provide information about the format of the intervention with the children, examples they provided suggest that interpretative play therapy and direct discussion about the divorce issues were used with the children. The play therapy, which included doll house play and drawing, was used with very young children and with children unable or unwilling to use the therapist to explore their feelings.

Because preschool children needed repeated explanations about the meaning of the divorce over a long time period, parents were in a better place than the therapist for making these explanations. Wallerstein and Kelly (1977) felt that the interventions with the preschool children were not particularly useful. Intervention with the parents seemed to be far more effective for these children.

The second model was an extended, focused crisis intervention, which was more commonly used with school age children. For early latency children, denial was not as available as for younger children. These children had a great deal of difficulty talking about the divorce. Indeed, talking about the divorce seemed to sharply increase the pain, sometimes almost unbearably. Wallerstein and Kelly (1977) found a "divorce monologue" useful, in which the therapist discussed typical responses of other children without asking the child to discuss his or her own experience. A format such as "many kids your age whose parents are divorcing, feel . . ." permits the child to listen without revealing personal pain. When appropriate, details of the child's own situation were included in the monologue. In the example given by Wallerstein and Kelly (1977a), the purpose seemed to be to permit the release of feelings, reduce the sense of loneliness (other kids have felt the same way), and open opportunities for further exploration. Clearly, this technique could be used to suggest different ways of responding to the stressors, providing alternative solutions similar to Gardner's mutual storytelling technique. For children able to discuss their feelings, such techniques were not needed.

For later latency and preadolescent children, the brief intervention model was particularly helpful. Three or four sessions were usually sufficient for the therapist to (1) help the child to see the realities of the situation and to avoid situations that were not for the child to solve and (2) give specific advice related to that child's situation. Longer interventions were needed for severe guilt over causing the divorce, guilt over being the favored child, and intense loyalty alignment between the child and one parent against the other parent.

Goals of both models and across all ages included reduction of suffering and of cognitive confusion, increase in psychological distance from the divorce, and successful resolution of various idiosyncratic issues (e.g., a mentally disturbed parent or the dilemma of choosing between parents).

Although little of the effectiveness of the Marin County project is mentioned in the publications, Wallerstein and Kelly (1980c) noted that, of the children who were damaged by the conflicts of the unhappy marriage or the neglect of unhappy parents, 75% improved at 5 years and that one-half of those accomplished that improvement with the help of therapy. How this improvement was assessed was not discussed. Of the parents who received counseling, 40% of the men and a higher percentage (unspecified) of the women felt that the counseling was very useful and were still following suggestions 5 years later.

Given that the publications from this project focused on typical responses of children shortly after the separation, and at 1, 5, and 10 years later, it is not clear to what extent the therapy changed those views. The impression is clear that some children perceived the therapy as useful. Without a control group, it is difficult, if not impossible, to determine whether the therapy was helpful in a long-term sense. However, the same can be said for all the therapies discussed in this chapter.

DLUGOKINSKI'S DEVELOPMENT APPROACH

Dlugokinski (1977) proposed an engagement–disengagement process for children of divorce. The children must go through a three-step process of orientation, integration, and consolidation.

1. *Orientation.* The divorce is a shock to the child's lifestyle. The child may be overwhelmed, and blocking of some of that stress may occur. Anxiety is disowned. Sad feelings are not actually experienced or grieved over. The counselor's demonstration of concern is essential.

2. *Integration.* A few weeks or months after the divorce, feelings about the divorce become personalized, and the child responds with anger, sad-

ness, excitement, and some degree of disorientation. Fusion of parent and child identities may be a way of denying the new reality. Depression may blunt the anxiety and lead the child to avoid establishing a new identity. The therapist must help the child experience and accept the self. The therapist must tolerate the child's strong emotions without rejecting so that the child can also accept them and avoid self-escaping alternatives.

3. *Consolidation.* Tools for effective daily living are incorporated. At this point, regular sessions can cease.

LATE LATENCY THERAPY

No individual therapies are designed specifically for late latency (10- to 12-year-old) children of divorce. Children of this age who began therapy at a younger age are quite willing to continue fantasy work. Children beginning therapy at this age are often reluctant to participate in fantasy material.

Whether the child is willing to participate in fantasy material or able to maintain a discussion of feelings and problems in life may depend in part on the child's developmental level.

Some children of this age are more interested in games, which can be used to strengthen the therapeutic alliance. Therapy can be successful with some game playing and some talking about problems. Games with discussion of feelings as a theme can be mixed with games of chance or skill. Because it is important to give the child some chance of winning, if the child is not particularly good at games, the therapist should encourage some games that involve elements of chance so that the child can experience success.

It is usually not useful to let the children win, although I have usually permitted the children to make up rules that give them an advantage. When a child cheats to win, the therapist might permit the cheating, but comment on the importance to the child of his or her winning. The child should be encouraged to see the game as a sharing experience rather than a competition.

Some children can talk about their problems while engaged in playing games. I was able to carry on a long discussion with one child while playing checkers. As soon as the game was over, the discussion stopped. Eye contact and the absence of a distractor were simply too anxiety provoking.

ADOLESCENT THERAPY

Work with adolescents in individual therapy is particularly taxing. The testing of limits, negativism, lack of trust, and need to individuate even at the cost of adaptive functioning make the adolescent a particularly difficult client.

Adolescent Resistance to Therapy

Because the adolescent is likely to see the therapist as an agent of the parent and be highly resistive to treatment, it is important to return the control to the adolescent. I inform adolescents that I will see them three times at the requirement of their parents. After that time, I will not see them unless they are willing to continue. Whether the parents require the adolescent to continue with treatment is between the adolescent and the parents, but the adolescent has complete control after three sessions as to whether *I* am the therapist.

Teenagers are more likely to accept a therapeutic alliance if given some control as to who the therapist is. Letting the teenager decide whether to continue with the therapist after three sessions gives some control back to the teenager and reduces resistance to treatment. If a therapeutic alliance cannot be established in three sessions, the likelihood of ever establishing one is lower. For very disturbed teenagers, inpatient treatment without choice may be required. If the teenager refuses to accept anyone, the parent must decide with consultation whether to continue the child in therapy with a low probability of being helpful.

The success rate for resistant children is likely to be quite low. Using the above strategy, the ability to develop a therapeutic alliance increases substantially. However, the strategy does mean accepting the "no" from some teenagers. About 90% of the adolescents given this choice decide to continue.

Avoiding the Parent Role and Accepting Feelings

A major focus of working with adolescents is to increase their sense of being understood, both in terms or what their feelings are and why those feelings exist. As for younger children, the strategy is then to increase the quality of problem solving for the adolescents. The therapist must not provide answers to problems, because that move reinstates for the adolescents a parental role that they are likely to be already fighting.

Attitudes toward the therapy indicate to some degree where the teenager is developmentally. Seventh and eighth graders are often humiliated at the idea of seeing a "shrink," even in Boulder, Colorado, where the use of therapy is quite common. These teenagers are preoccupied with belonging and not being different from the cliques to which they belong. Fear of being seen and of someone from school finding out may haunt early adolescents. Older teenagers may feel ambivalent. Mature teenagers are more likely to accept the idea that they have problems for which they need help and to acknowledge that need with peers. One teenager went out of her way to be with a group of peers just before treatment so that she could say it was time to go to see her "shrink." Having someone there to listen to her was a source of prestige, not shame. Obviously, that attitude was a good predictor of her openness to being helped.

It is important for the adolescent's therapist to avoid the parental role.

I tell teenagers that I am there to help them, not to force them to become what their parents want. I explain the limits of confidentiality. I inform them that I must see the parents from time to time (unless the adolescent has already separated from the parents). I promise to tell the adolescent everything from therapy that I will tell the parents and give him or her veto power over what I say (except for those categories of things I *must* tell the parents for the physical protection of the client or the parents). Even when I am required to break confidentiality (e.g., for child abuse), I will tell the adolescent first that I have to inform authorities.

The amount of testing with adolescents can be trying. Some adolescents have wanted to smoke in my presence (I do not permit it, but make it clear that I cannot have anyone smoke during therapy because I am allergic to smoke). Some teenagers use curse words to see if I will admonish them. One 14-year-old girl told me an incoherent, rambling, upset story of drinking beer over the weekend and losing her virginity. Working hard all through the session, I tried to help her to understand why she did it and what coping she wanted to do in the future. I was quite concerned, but did not contact the parents. At the next session, I learned that she had made up the whole story (and very convincingly, I might add) to see if I would tell her parents. She was in a position to prove that it had not happened. Because her parents did not hear from me about the story, she then decided to trust me with a discussion of some concern to her, but in a much less stressful and loaded area. Another teenager took me for my word that the time was hers to use as she wished, and she spoke not one word to me for three sessions (I learned to bring a book to read). After three sessions, she began to talk about her anger. Exhausting therapy!

Because teenagers use resistance and negativism as part of their strategy to accomplish separation and individuation, getting an alliance that is helpful in the working of problems can be particularly difficult. Use of the therapeutic double bind or paradoxical intervention can be useful in breaking up that resistance. In this technique, the adolescent is encouraged to increase the resistance. One girl I was seeing was cursing me in detail in every session, expressing her anger at being in therapy and exclaiming how much she hated all adults. At the beginning of the next session, I encouraged her to tell me to go to hell in as vivid and colorful language as she could, to really give it to me. This paradoxical intervention places a client in a bind. To refuse to fight me would be to cooperate. To tell me to go to hell would be to go along with my suggestion and cooperate. Her response was, "Why would I want to do that?"

SUMMARY

Most forms of individual psychotherapy with children of divorce involve acceptance and clarification of feelings, assessment of cognitions, and support for more effective problem solving. For young children, fantasy is particularly helpful in providing a low-anxiety forum for exploring ideas. For adolescents, trust and problem solving seem to be helpful.

CHAPTER 13

Interventions with Families

Family therapy is frequently the treatment of choice in helping children with the problems of divorce. The intervention is with the context in which the family disruption occurred. Intervention with the child alone often does not change the system that encouraged that child's adaptation. Often, the family has an investment in keeping the adaptation unchanged and will resist a child's movement toward more healthy functioning. In family therapy, more helpful behaviors can be encouraged and practiced.

The family may need for the child to have the symptoms to avoid resolving other anxiety-provoking issues. As the child learns new means of coping through individual or group therapy, the family becomes threatened and works to reinstate the homeostasis that was present prior to the therapy. For example, a mother took her 14-year-old son to therapy because he was immature and dependent. As he worked through his dependency and became more autonomous, she complained vigorously that he now stood up to her (interpreted as disrespectful and obstinate). She was very unhappy with the new set of problems she now had. Family therapy, then, makes the assumption that symptoms have functions within the family and that the child with the problem and the family have an investment in keeping the very behavior that they are asking to get rid of.

Family therapy should be avoided when custody is in question; when one parent is unavailable because of abandonment, prison, or heavy substance abuse; and when the danger of family violence exists (Cantor & Drake, 1983). Family therapy can be useful when only one parent and the children are involved, but the therapist should be careful to assess the degree to which the absent parent plays a major role in maintaining the dynamic. Family therapy for the two families (each parent with all the children) can be effective.

FAMILY THERAPY SYSTEMS

There are many types of family therapy systems. For the purpose of this chapter, however, four primary ones will be reviewed:

1. Psychoanalytically oriented family therapy with strong interests in multigenerational lines was founded by Bowen (1976). The purpose of this

therapy is to help people understand family themes that influence behavior over generations.

2. Strategic intervention is based on the paradoxical methods of Milton Erickson and Jay Haley (Haley, 1963). Paradoxical treatment involves encouraging the symptom as a way of handling the defensive style. Asking someone to resist has the effect of forcing cooperation regardless of what the person is doing.

3. The structural therapy of Minuchin (1974) may be the most useful of the family therapy approaches for families undergoing divorce or remarriage. The focus is on determining the boundaries, rules, and hierarchies that exist in the family.

Minuchin was interested in how the family uses space and the degree to which the family members are enmeshed or disengaged from one another. The two styles sometimes occur in alternation. The only way some people can leave an enmeshed family is to completely disengage.

Minuchin recommended disrupting the process by redefining sick or maladaptive behavior as positive or as serving a positive function. In this way, destructive motives are eliminated. For example, a therapist might say, "You are asking her to protect you" when the complaint is overcontrol. He also focused on complementarity of behavior. One person is encouraged to behave in a certain way by the behavior of the other. In addition, Minuchin phrased motivations in a positive way: "You protect him even when he doesn't need it."

4. Behaviorist family therapy has as its focus reciprocity and exchange of benefits, as opposed to coercion. This form of therapy encourages communication with "I" messages and avoids labeling the feelings of the other person (a central focus in most family therapies), providing an atmosphere of support and understanding, problem solving, and behavior exchange. Contracts and homework are common techniques.

All forms of family therapy, regardless of orientation, seem to be concerned with boundaries. Are parents playing a parental role? Are the children allowed to continue to be children, and are they provided proper guidance and support? The structural approach refers to boundaries, and the behavioral approach refers to executive subsystems.

Several problems are presented when working with divorced families that make them more complex than nuclear families (Cantor & Drake, 1983). Confidentiality is a particularly difficult problem. In addition to the legal problem, if there are separate sessions with individual subsets of the family system, it is important that secrets not be permitted.

Therapists should not permit family members to share secrets that cannot be discussed with other family members. Such secrets can result in collusion of the therapist with one or more of the family members, which can sabotage the therapy.

On more than one occasion, I have seen a family member who felt grievously hurt that a previous therapist knew all along that there was an extramarital relationship, while that family member was operating on the assumption that chances of reconciliation were possible.

Therapists should be cautious in indicating agreement with any family member. The therapist should support process and communication. Family members should be encouraged to ask questions, not to have the therapist ask the questions. Asking questions and indicating agreement can also result in apparent alliances between the therapist and family members that can be destructive to the process.

Some states give legal confidentiality to family therapy, but others do not. When future litigation occurs, having established the limits of confidentiality initially will avoid hurt and outraged feelings.

FAMILY THERAPY WITH DIVORCING FAMILIES

Cantor and Drake (1983) gave the following list of issues to be addressed with parents in family therapy:

1. Transition to single-parent status
2. Child care and discipline
3. Dating, remarriage, and stepchildren
4. Loneliness
5. Different relationship with former spouse, relatives, and children
6. Finances
7. Housing
8. Anger and other unresolved feelings
9. Child-napping
10. Grieving
11. Employment
12. Custody
13. Communication problems
14. Loss of generational boundaries.

They also gave a list of issues to be addressed with children:

1. Change of status
2. Adjustment to visitation
3. Loss of family life and contact with parent

4. Stepparents, stepsiblings, and half-siblings
5. Moving
6. Change of schools and friends
7. Loyalty
8. Involvement with custody issues.

Kaplan's Family Therapy

Kaplan (1977) provided some excellent examples of the use of structural family therapy for children of divorce. He suggested working with the subgroups of the family that seem the most stressful for the child. His case histories give examples of diagram analysis of boundaries, illustrating excessive closeness or distance. Kaplan gave useful examples of a mother who becomes a child with her child and her own parents, and another example of a helpless and neglectful mother. In one case history, Kaplan outlined the interaction in a family with an overprotective custodial mother and her child. He diagramed the interaction initially as in Figure 1.

In Figure 1, the dotted line indicates excessive closeness and the vertical lines indicate excessive distance. As can be seen in the figure, the mother has inadequate separation from the child, a 9-year-old girl, and the father is excluded from both. The child was having trouble in the classroom, with daydreaming, thumb sucking, and poor school work. She did not interact with her peers. The mother was overprotective, not allowing the child to go to the store a few yards from her home or to play on the sidewalk in front of the house. The child was not allowed to see the father. In an individual session with the child, bizarre behavior was apparent and the child repeatedly requested to see the mother. For 20 sessions, the mother and child were seen together. Initially, the child played as if the therapist was not in the room.

During this time, the therapist met with the father alone and had some sessions with the mother and father together. After 4 months of treatment, the child and the father had a session. The child and father had a long talk in the presence of the therapist, and the child complained about a variety of appropriate issues.

After the father–daughter sessions, the child was able to tolerate being with the male therapist. Then the therapist and child played while the mother read

Figure 1. A mother (M) and child (C) in an enmeshed relationship in which the noncustodial father (F) is excluded. (From Kaplan, S. L. (1977). Structural family therapy for children of divorce: Case reports, *Family process, 16,* 75–83. Reprinted with permission of S. L. Kaplan and Berkshire Medical Center.)

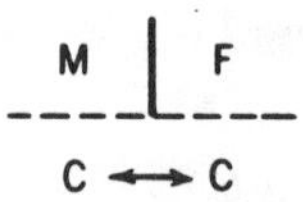

$$M \quad | \quad F$$
$$----\underline{\quad}----$$
$$C \longleftrightarrow C$$

Figure 2. Theoretical goal for therapy for the families of the custodial mother (M), noncustodial father (F) and nine-year-old daughter (C). (From Kaplan, S. L. (1977). Structural family therapy for children of divorce: Case reports. *Family Process, 16,* 75–83. Reprinted with permission of S. L. Kaplan and Berkshire Medical Center.)

in another part of the room. Finally, the mother was able to leave the therapist and child together. During this time, the child's behavior at home and school was significantly better.

Figure 2 illustrates the goal for therapy. In the figure, the barrier between mother and father is maintained, as is appropriate for divorced parents. The boundary between the child and each parent is of an appropriate closeness, with the child moving back and forth between parents.

In any family therapy approach, it is recommended that the therapist graph the dynamic of boundaries, hierarchy, and disengagement that may exist in the family. The therapist should then graph the theoretical ideal relationship, which takes into account healthy family functioning and appropriate distance between the divorcing spouses and protects the relationship of the child with each parent, if possible.

Goldman and Coane's Family Therapy

Goldman and Coane (1977) also discussed strategies in working with families of divorce. Their model of intervention involved four parts:

1. Redefining the family as including both parents, regardless of the divorce. They cautioned about families talking of the absent parent as if he or she were dead. Once both parents are included, the therapists then work on the difficult process of clarifying generational boundaries.

Similar advice about including the absent parent was given by Leader (1973) for many of the same reasons. Peck (1975) also insisted that every family remnant member come to the interviews. According to Peck, the mother–child "marriage" can have extraordinary homeostasis that is difficult to change. When parents move into the roles of appropriate parental responsibilities, it tends to reduce the acting out of the children. As the generational boundaries are established, each parent can then work on relational ties with each child. The child is then given the opportunity to separate and individuate in a safe environment.

Goldman and Coane noted that the family suffers from "the guilt of omnipotence." The divorce is everyone's fault. Each parent feels threatened by the other parent, and the children feel it is their responsibility to promote reconciliation.

2. Providing structure for firm generational boundaries to reduce parentification of the children, and encouraging the parents to fight battles without involving the children.

3. Providing an opportunity for the family to experience a "replay of the history of the marriage." This replay permits a correction of the distortions of the marriage.

4. Helping the parents divorce emotionally. The therapist may need to help the parents do their own separation and individuation.

Peck's Family Therapy

Peck (1975) recommended using a cotherapist to reduce the loneliness of working alone. From his theoretical position, the cotherapists work best if of opposite genders. The therapist couple serves as a surrogate marital dyad that "adopts" the mother and children. The transference is reduced, and the single parent is less likely to look to two therapists as a potential marital partner or rescuer.

Peck's position was that the mother–child family is having trouble because of the incompleteness of the divorce. The therapists refuse to solve the battle between the parents, and they use child's play to get the children to be just children. They model moving in and out of child's play without losing respect. The therapists support the mother as she separates from the children and gives up her love–hate battle with her former husband.

Isaacs's Family Therapy

Like Peck, Isaacs (1981) believed that families may get stuck because one or more of the family members cannot leave the experiences of the old family and are unwilling or unable to develop new arrangements and life patterns in the new family. She also pointed out that other strategies, needs, and desires may influence the difficulty in resolving the divorce process. Isaacs's theory of intervention is to assess the individual strategies, determine how these strategies block the divorce process, and develop a counterstrategy to help the family develop a more productive future. As with other therapies, the counterstrategy is to encourage the parents to abandon retaliation and secret agendas (e.g., covert strategies to force reconciliation) and have as a primary goal the protection of the children.

Interventions given in case histories focused on such problems as acting helpless as a strategy for keeping the other parent involved with the family and recreating a "phantom" family of the past; tolerating tantrums to maintain love; reducing guilt; setting poor boundaries about time, space, and control; protecting a parent from angry or avoidant feelings; and maintaining a family in which everyone was inappropriately disengaging from each other.

Isaacs, Montalvo, and Abelsohn (1986) described in detail a very useful structure for working with difficult divorced families. The family therapists used controlled encounter with various subsystems of the family to strengthen weak coalitions, to increase appropriate boundaries, to work on hierarchical reorganization, and to restore the parents' executive functions. They provided numerous illustrations to demonstrate these processes. Particularly useful were examples of working with preseparation families, sporadic and scared fighters, chronic fighters, and violent-prone families.

For preseparation families, the therapists refocused each family on the needs of the children. The parents were required to reshape their relationships with their lawyers and make the parents, not the lawyers or the therapists, responsible for decisions concerning themselves and the children. The family therapists worked to prepare the children for the separation and encouraged the parents to support the children with routines and favorite activities.

Parents going through separation can increase security in the children by maintaining (or reinstating) favorite activities and familiar routines for family play, eating, bedtime, and reading times.

Isaacs et al. (1986) noted that some people will, with uncanny skill, select a lawyer who will act on their wishes. Then the parents can blame the lawyer for their acting out.

Postdivorce Family Therapy of Moreland, Schwebel, Fine, and Vess

The postdivorce family therapy of Moreland, Schwebel, Fine, and Vess (1982) is oriented toward helping both parents stay involved with the children. Based on a review of the literature, they concluded that postdivorce therapy should have the following goals: (1) to increase ex-spouse cooperation in parenting, (2) to improve the quality and effectiveness of parent–child communication, and (3) to train the mother and father in behavioral management techniques.

They noted that ex-spouses ideally should develop "circumscribed mutuality" around parenting. The avenue to such mutuality involves helping the parents express feelings; explore competencies, choices, and opportunities for growth; relate current hurts and angers to past rejections; recognize their own contributions to the conflict; and learn from past mistakes. Each parent is encouraged to initiate discussion with the other parent.

If one parent has severe pathology, it may be difficult to obtain the circumscribed mutuality. The addition of a new emotional relationship will also place limits on the ability to coparent.

Family Therapy with Very Young Children

In a very different kind of family therapy, P. A. Rosenthal (1979) reported on therapy with families of divorce with 2- to 4-year-old children. The child is given an explanation as to why the child and family need help. The therapist tells the child that the parent and therapist will help the child with play and with talking about his or her upsetting feelings. The therapist sees the family in a large playroom. Interpretative play therapy then is accomplished both in the presence of the parent and with the parent joining in.

Conjoint Mother–Daughter Therapy

Kalter (1984) described a conjoint mother–daughter treatment program for working with adolescent girls. These girls frequently presented a sexualized, pseudomature quality. Although they seemed to be demanding greater independence, Kalter felt that their actions were in fact indicating a wish for greater supervision. These girls viewed their mothers as unfair and tyrannical and were quite resistive to beginning treatment. The girls had intense separation conflicts and would have been quite resistive to individual treatment. Self-esteem problems were intense, and individual treatment was seen as stigmatizing and derogative. Kalter felt that the two developmental issues that had to be addressed were (1) separation from the mother and (2) the damaged sense of femininity. Although highly sexualized, these girls did not feel worthwhile as women. They felt unattractive, but longed to be loved. The daughter experienced the loss of the father as personal rejection around being lovable and feminine.

Adolescents are often particularly resistant to individual therapy. They see the move into therapy as defining them as the ones with the problem, which is a put-down. Although adolescents are also quite resistant to family therapy, they often will accept a family approach more readily than individual work.

Strategic Family Therapy with Adolescents

Nicholson (1987) described a strategic family therapy approach for separated families. In this therapy, problems are seen as adaptations by the family to solve a present difficulty. Once the therapist identifies the maladaptive behavioral sequence in the family, the therapist gives tasks and directives within the framework of the family's belief system that are designed to interrupt that sequence. By reframing the maladaptive behavior as helpful, the family is encouraged to comply.

A Multiple Impact Therapy Approach

Multiple impact therapy has been used with divorced families in treating adolescents (Ritchie & Serrano, 1974). The technique uses two therapists with team–family sessions, individual sessions, and various combinations. The different structures for therapy were seen by the authors as providing the opportunity for improving communication and for assessing, clarifying, and redefining goals. The adolescent is seen as fixated in ego development because of the family's inability to facilitate growth.

The theory proposed four functional roles in the family: aggressive (leadership), passive-aggressive (criticism), emotional unstable (spontaneity), and passive-dependent (passivity-cooperation). When a family functions well, these roles work with cooperation and flexibility. Maladaptive families choose roles that are inconsistent with their personality or stage of development.

The initial strategy in the therapy is to shift the parents from fighting with each other to being concerned with the child's welfare. The past is defined as secondary, while the here-and-now and future are given primary importance. Then, mutually agreed-upon goals are developed. The goal of the therapy is to provide some consistency and security for the child.

The adolescent is encouraged to understand his or her role in the parental conflict and to mourn the loss of the relationships. The adolescent is also encouraged to give up any omnipotent fantasies and manipulations about reconciliation or retaliation. The authors presented a fairly detailed case history, illustrating the analysis of family dynamics and changing structures of meetings. Different configurations of family meetings were used, with the inclusion of a stepparent and a future stepparent.

FAMILY THERAPY WITH SINGLE-PARENT FAMILIES

Most therapies for families of divorce focus on the divorcing and recently divorced family and attempt to include both parents. It may be difficult to decide what to do about families in which the absent parent is unavailable, because of geographic distance, uninvolvement, or a wish to be excluded.

Bray and Anderson (1984) described case histories of working with single-parent families in therapy. Their therapy was based on strategic intervention. As noted in Chapter 8 on single-parent families, Bray and Anderson assumed that role overload, economic hardships, isolation, and loss and grief are common problems of single-parent families. The parenting role of the noncustodial parent also must be resolved.

Bray and Anderson used reframing to have the family view the symptoms of the child (a suicide attempt in one case history) as a wish to help the family. In another case, they complimented a mother on her unconscious knowledge of the danger of getting a divorce. In another family in which a 3 1/2-year-old's tantrums were the presenting problem, the therapist congratulated the mother for doing such a fine job in such difficult circumstances and for helping her child to be strong willed and independent. The reframing was to help the child express this strong-willed personality appropriately.

They supported the mother in learning how to handle tantrums. They also reframed the child's tantrum behavior as the child's expression of the mother's anger at the father for leaving. The child was also presented as interfering with dates because the child knew that the mother was not yet ready to date. Such an interpretation would encourage the mother to see the child's behavior as positively motivated and encourage her to assume responsibility for her own behavior.

FAMILY THERAPY WITH STEPFAMILIES

After providing a detailed model of stepfamily dynamics, McGoldrick and Carter (1980) presented models of family therapy with remarriages. The three key emotional issues that they felt required resolution were (1) ending the emotional attachment to the ex-spouse, (2) giving up attachment to the nuclear family concept and accepting a different model, and (3) accepting the time, space, ambivalence, and problems of remarried families.

Similar to Bowen (1978), they recommended going back several generations to evaluate the parental marriage. Rather than the classic triangle in nuclear families with the parents and children, McGoldrick and Carter felt that there were six common triangles in remarried families. They coached the adults to differentiate from families of origin. They worked on nuclear family problems if the clients were motivated to do so.

In this model, the previously divorced spouse may be coached in the presence of the new spouse to work out the relationship with the ex-spouse. In cases where the new couple get along well, a severely misbehaving child may be engaged in a conflict with the other parent. The authors proposed that under these conditions, it is important that the stepparent retain a neutral position rather than be against the child. The biological parent is put in charge of managing the child's behavior. This technique was frequently used in the examples given. McGoldrick and Carter noted that such a technique was difficult to implement if the biological parent worked long hours and the stepparent was home with the children.

The authors listed the following as general goals of therapy:

1. Forming an open coparenting relationship between the biological parents
2. Working out the emotional divorce
3. Firming up parental boundaries and not giving children the power of deciding on remarriage, custody, or visitation
4. Accepting divided loyalties.

McGoldrick and Carter (1980) prepared a three-generational genogram. They tried to be particularly sensitive to family members in different life cycle stages. Helping the child handle the loss of any exceptionally close relationship with a single parent was also emphasized.

Kaplan's (1977) description of structural family therapy, described previously, also gave case histories of remarried families. In a case in which a 7-year-old boy was having severe temper tantrums, the therapist first worked on an excessive boundary and disengagement problem of the biological mother with the child. The therapist then worked on reducing the boundary with the stepfather.

Crohn et al. (1981), from the Remarried Consultation Service of the Jewish Board of Family and Children's Services in New York City, discussed the clinical experience with a program specifically designed to help remarried families. From 1977 to 1979, the service treated 213 remarried families with 367 children. Children were characterized by impulse control problems (38%), school problems (36%), and psuedo-independence (23%). A large group (83%) were described as having dysfunctional relations with a parent or stepparent. Only 9% were considered free of problems; however, these were families that by definition were having some problems or were not likely to seek the services of the clinic.

In the initial contact, the therapists (usually two) worked to stay neutral and not to be allied with any part of the family system. Family members from both households were invited to the first session. The evaluation sessions took from one to four visits and lasted from 1½ to 2 hours each.

Similar to Ritchie and Serrano (1974), Crohn et al. (1980) utilized multiple impact family therapy based on McGregor, Ritchie, and Serrano (1964). Multiple impact therapy implies that different family members may be seen in different combinations as the therapist identifies areas that need work. Crohn et al. recommended against seeing the child alone in individual treatment early in the process, because the child may then be scapegoated as the problem and the parents may withdraw from the treatment process. Later in treatment, child work is more appropriate and more likely to be successful.

Avoid beginning treatment of a family by seeing the child in individual therapy with the intent of moving to family therapy later. Always start with the entire family or with the parents. Often, the family would prefer that the child be seen as the problem and want the child to be seen first. In addition, the child who forms a therapeutic alliance with the therapist can feel betrayed by the move to family therapy, both by the experienced reduction in support and concerns of confidentiality.

During evaluation, the therapist had the family draw a genogram of the family, a process that is relatively nonthreatening and permits even very young children to participate. Issues such as unresolved mourning, fights, secrets, illness, divorce, and remarriage were revealed. This genogram allowed the therapist to understand the family dynamics. The genogram was left on the table during each session and added to as new information was gathered.

The genogram was central to assessment because history is central in working with remarried families. Crohn et al. (1980) argued that history is even more vital in treating remarried families than in treating nuclear families. Specifically, cross-generational alliances are major blocks to shifting relationships to a more appropriate level of interaction.

Because unresolved mourning is a major blockage in many remarried families, the therapist should focus on the mourning process and the symptoms in the family that indicate that unfinished work needs to be done. Exposing myths is also a part of the work with remarried families (myths were discussed in some detail in Chapter 9). Myths of the wicked stepmother, instant love, the perfect mate, the idealized (or monster) absent parent, and the perfect family are all problems with which a therapist must deal. Thus, one major focus is to redefine the child's problems as problems of the family. Then the family is helped to understand the system. Stressing differences between family members rather than similarities seems to facilitate growth.

H. C. Johnson (1980) proposed several areas that clinicians should evaluate as part of working with stepfamilies:

1. Unclear expectations
2. Losses and gains
3. Questions of physical and emotional turf
4. Differences in lifestyle
   a. Discipline
   b. Eating habits
   c. Division of labor
   d. Attitudes toward sex
   e. Use of alcohol and drugs
   f. Attitudes toward obligations
   g. Manners
   h. Household rules
   i. Expression of hostility, aggression, or disagreement
5. Benefits, including relief from child care, sharing stepsibling relationships, harmonious family life, an increase in emotional giving, and the extended circle of friendly, giving adults.

In stepfamilies, the development of boundaries may include a greater distance in the boundary between the stepparent and child than between the biological parent and child. Particularly for children who are of school age, the stepparent needs to wait for the affectional bond to develop before assuming a disciplinary role (see the extended discussion of this issue in Chapter 9).

H. C. Johnson (1980) noted that when there is active dislike between the stepparent and child, the biological parent should assume most of the parenting responsibilities, particularly discipline. If the biological parent avoids this responsibility, both the child and stepparent are likely to feel angry and abandoned.

Given the enormous contribution that Emily and John Visher have made in helping stepfamilies, it is not surprising that they have also made insightful comments concerning therapy with stepfamilies (Visher & Visher, 1988, 1989). They listed typical obstacles to developing postdivorce parenting coalitions (in which parent and stepparent form a united front of care and control of the children):

1. Parents may have inadequate psychological separations.
2. Parents may have chronic hostility.
3. Parents may lack commitment to the children.
4. Stepparents may be excluded from the coalition.
5. Parents may fear more loss as the children attach to stepparents.
6. Anxiety can be generated by a family system in which two households are linked only through the children.

Using parent–stepparent couples and joint sessions between two families, the therapist can work on these problems. This strategy may involve strengthening the new couple's alliance. Particularly important is to include the stepparent in the coalition. In the process, the stepparent's role can be clarified. It is important for the therapist, not one of the parents, to contact both families and to define narrowly the focus of the joint meeting as on the children. Visher and Visher recommended that if only one parent is remarried, he or she should include a friend, relative, or live-in partner to balance the power of the sessions.

N. D. Brown and Samis (1986/1987) applied a structural family therapy analysis to both the understanding of structural problems in a remarriage and the implications for intervention. Examples included an overinvolved stepparent, a triangulated child, parallel dysfunctional families, dysfunctional intact families, and dysfunctional binuclear families in which the child was the stabilizer of the original marriage. In each case, Brown and Samis felt that the intervention involved having the parents set appropriate, functional boundaries and place the needs of the children above their own. They used techniques such as reframing, heightening, and intensifying, and involved in the therapy the concepts of complementarity and unbalancing power.

Sometimes the therapist has a problem deciding which family system to treat. For example, in a residential treatment setting, Weisfeld and Laser (1977) focused on the original parents in treating the child and felt that inclusion of stepparents at times could hinder the therapeutic process. The advantage of multiple impact therapy is that the therapist can consider working with each separate system that may be disordered.

In family therapy with remarried families, the therapist should consider care-fully the effect of establishing therapy based on the original nuclear family and excluding stepparents. The stepparent may already be significantly excluded. Multiple impact therapy strategies permit working on each system, and also have the advantage of treating the systems as separate systems.

Crohn et al. (1981) described several problems that a therapist for families of remarriage tends to have. Countertransference and burnout are frequent problems. Therapists can have unrealistic expectations about how a remarried family should work, with either the nuclear family or the "Brady Bunch" as models (remarried families get into trouble when they have the same expectations that they did in first marriages). Therapists sometimes join the denial system of the family and avoid taboo topics. Some therapists have not paid sufficient attention to protecting positive images of both biological parents. The therapist can be drawn into wanting to be the "good" parent for children, particularly when the absent parent has abandoned the children. Therapists who are overwhelmed by the complexity of stepfamilies sometimes move toward overcontrol. Joining with a cotherapist is one way to guard against some of the problems described above.

SUMMARY

Family therapy with divorcing families, single-parent families, and remarried families provides a powerful way to restructure self-defeating interactions. Clinicians should have a clear understanding of the dynamics of family therapy and of each type of family before intervening in this manner.

CHAPTER 14

A Final Word

Clearly, interventions for children of divorce involve far more than providing psychotherapy for a distressed child. The reasons why dysfunctional families, separation, divorce, single parenting, and remarriage are difficult for children are multilayered and complex. Society needs to restructure the *context* of child development to reduce the stress associated with the painful process of marital dissolution.

Social change, education, and intervention can provide important and enduring benefits for children of divorce. When mental health professionals, lawyers, and judges are more aware of the developmental needs of children of divorce and their families, the original process of divorce may be more humane and the subsequent structure supportive of all family members. Mediation as an alternative to adversarial court battles is an excellent example, and early evidence suggests that it might be a major preventive procedure. Joint legal custody and joint physical custody are other examples of structure that seem to facilitate continued contact and bonding between the children and each parent in some families. Earlier social changes that became important in reducing conflict and harm to the family were the development of no-fault divorce and conciliation court counseling. More subtle are attitude changes in the community by school teachers, the clergy, and other important key social support figures, who can reduce stigma and improve coping. Another important strategy for supporting the family through divorce is educating divorcing parents and children concerning the family's needs around divorce and ways of providing support, information, and adequate coping, as well as maintaining the dignity and integrity of each family member.

Primary prevention in which anticipated problems are eliminated before they start should become important for the future. Changes to increase financial support to children and to maintain as much as possible the predivorce quality of life for children are likely to lower subsequent maladjustment. Early detection of problems and effective intervention techniques can serve as remediation when the structure of society fails to provide adequate support to children to prevent the problems from occurring.

This book provides a large number of recommendations. Many are based on solid research and extensive clinical experience. Others are more tentative, and hopefully clearly identified as such. If the quality of life for divorcing couples is to improve, the state of the art must improve. Then some of the recommendations in this book will likely undergo modification.

WHAT ARE THE INCREASES IN KNOWLEDGE IN RECENT YEARS?

Progress has been made in learning how to help children of divorce since the publication of the first edition of this book 5 years ago. The effect of parental conflict on children is now clearly documented. The need to reduce frequency of changes of parental access for these children is clear. The importance of protecting the economic well-being of children continues to be replicated in research. Father custody is now more clearly understood. Joint physical custody is not indicated where parents are engaged in severe conflict.

WHAT IS NOT YET KNOWN ABOUT HELPING CHILDREN OF DIVORCE?

The list of what has not yet been empirically determined that would be of vital importance in helping children of divorce is surprisingly basic. Few changes have been made in these basic questions since the first edition of this book. The following is a nondefinitive list of important questions that have yet to be answered:

1. How effective are custody and access assessments? Is there a basis for deciding what the standards for assessment should be?
2. What is the best visitation pattern based on the child's age? (Although there is more agreement that young children present special problems of parent access, the most appropriate combinations for various conditions have yet to be established.)
3. In joint residential custody, what is the optimal timing of the residence switch as a function of the child's age? Is there a destructive pattern that should be avoided?
4. How should society handle geographic moves for joint physical custody? In such cases, should the best interests of the child determine which parent gets primary physical care? Should the moving parent be penalized for the move by not being given one-half of shared access? (Some of these questions are clearly value laden rather than empirical.)
5. What is the best way to handle long-distance visitations with low frequency and long duration?
6. Under what conditions is joint legal custody or joint physical custody not in the child's best interests? (It is clearly understood that high parental conflict is incompatible with joint custody.)

7. How can joint physical custody work well with infants and toddlers? (There is a risk of anxious attachment, but the research has not been done to determine what conditions increase the risk of anxious attachment.)

8. Does mediation help child adjustment? Are there situations in which mediation does not help the family?

9. Should the courts limit access under adverse situations, such as psychopathological noncustodial parents, abusive noncustodial parents, psychopathological reactions to visitation by the custodial parents, and severe conflict between parents?

10. How much risk for negative outcomes is acceptable? (In terms of determining the child's best interests, the court is asked to guess what will happen. Some jurisdictions are willing to accept relatively low probabilities of negative outcomes, whereas others are more concerned about avoiding harm.)

Despite this long list of unknowns, mental health professionals working with children of divorce continue to use theory, some research, and their best judgment based on clinical experience to try to help the family adjust to the stressful life events involved in separation, divorce, and remarriage.

References

Abarbanel, A. (1979). Shared parenting after separation: A study of joint custody. *American Journal of Orthopsychiatry, 49,* 320–329.

Adam, K. S., Lohrenz, J. G., & Harper, D. (1973). Suicidal ideation and parental loss: A preliminary research report. *Canadian Psychiatric Association Journal, 18,* 95–100.

Adams, M. (1984, December 20). Kids and divorce: No long-term harm. *USA Today,* p. 1, 5D.

Ahrons, C. R. (1979). The binuclear family: Two households, one family. *Alternative Lifestyles, 2,* 499–515.

Aldous, J. (1972). Children's perceptions of adult role assignment: Father absence, class, race, and sex influences. *Journal of Marriage and the Family, 9,* 55–65.

Allison, P. D., & Furstenberg, F. F., Jr. (1989). How marital dissolution affects children: Variations by age and sex. *Developmental Psychology, 25,* 540–549.

Alpert-Gillis, L. J., Pedro-Carroll, J. L., & Cowen, E. L. (1989). The children of divorce intervention program: Development, implementation, and evaluation of a program for young urban children. *Journal of Consulting and Clinical Psychology, 57,* 583–589.

Amato, P. R. (1987). Family processes in one-parent, stepparent, and intact families: The child's point of view. *Journal of Marriage and the Family, 49,* 327–337.

Amato, P. R., & Ochiltree, G. (1987). Child and adolescent competence in intact, one-parent and step-families: An Australian study. *Journal of Divorce, 10*(3/4), 75–96.

American Institutes for Research. (1980). *Helping youth and families of separation, divorce and remarriage* (DHHS Publication No. OHDS 80-32010). Washington, DC: U.S. Department of Health and Human Services.

Anderson, J. Z., & White, G. D. (1986). An empirical investigation of interaction and relationship patterns in functional and dysfunctional nuclear families and stepfamilies. *Family Process, 25,* 407–422.

Anderson, R. F., Kinney, J., & Gerler, E. R., Jr. (1984). The effects of divorce groups on children's classroom behavior and attitudes toward divorce. *Elementary School Guidance and Counseling, 19*(1), 70–76.

Armstrong, L. (1985, March/April). Daddy dearest wins the day. *New Directions for Women, 1,* 11.

Association of Family and Conciliation Courts. (1988). *The sexual abuse allegations project: Final report.* AFCC, 1720 Emerson St., Denver, CO 80218.

Atwell, A. E., Moore, U.S., Nielsen, E., Levite, Z. (1984). Effects of joint custody on children. *Bulletin of the American Academy of Psychiatry and the Law, 12*(2), 149-157.

Atwell, A. E., Moore, U. S., & Nowell, C. S. (1982). The role of stepparents in child custody disputes. *Bulletin of the American Academy of Psychiatry and the Law, 10*(3), 211–217.

Ault, R. L. (1977). *Children's cognitive development: Piaget's theory and the process approach.* New York: Oxford University Press.

Awad, G. A. (1978). Basic principles in custody assessments. *Canadian Psychiatric Association Journal, 23*(7), 441–447.

Awad, G. A., & Parry, R. (1980). Access following marital separation. *Canadian Journal of Psychiatry, 25*(5), 357–365.

Axline, V. M. (1969). *Play therapy* (rev. ed.). New York: Ballantine Books.

Bahr, S. J. (1981). An evaluation of court mediation: A comparison in divorce cases with children. *Journal of Family Issues, 2*(1), 39–60.

Barnard, C. & Jenson G. (1984). Child custody evaluation manual precedents and practices, Midwest Custody Evaluation and Psychological Services. As cited in P. Bushard, J. Gifford, K. M. Jefford, B. Morgan-Sandoz, K. Raiford & E. Rudd. *Guidelines for court connected child custody evaluations.* Portland, OR: Association of Family and Conciliation Courts.

Baydar, N. (1988). Effects of parental separation and reentry into union on the emotional well-being of children. *Journal of Marriage and the Family, 50,* 967–981.

Beaber, R. J. (1982). Custody quagmire: Some psycholegal dilemmas. *The Journal of Psychiatry and Law, 10,* 309–326.

Benedek, R. S., & Benedek, E. P. (1977). Post-divorce visitation. *Journal of the American Academy of Child Psychiatry, 16,* 256–271.

Benjamin, M., & Irving, H. H. (1990). Comparison of the experience of satisfied and dissatisfied shared parents. *Journal of Divorce and Remarriage, 14*(1), 43–61.

Benson-von der Ohe, E. (1987). *First and second marriages.* New York: Praeger.

Bentovim, A., & Gilmour, L. (1981). A family therapy interactional approach to decision making in child care, access and custody cases. *Journal of Family Therapy, 3,* 65–77.

Berger, T. (1977). *How does it feel when your parents get divorced?* New York: Julian Messner.

Bernard, J. (1971). *Remarriage: A study of marriage* (2nd ed.). New York: Russell and Russell.

Bernstein, J. E. (1977). *Books to help children cope with separation and loss.* New York: R. R. Bowker.

Bergquist, B. (1984). The remarried family: An annotated bibliography, 1979–1982. *Family Process, 18,* 107–119.

Biller, H. B. (1968). A note on father absence and masculine development in lower-class Negro and white boys. *Child Development, 39,* 1003–1006.

Biller, H. B. (1969). Father absence, maternal encouragement and sex role develop-ment in kindergarten-age boys. *Child Development, 40,* 539–546.

Biller, H. B. (1970). Father absence and the personality development of the male child. *Developmental Psychology, 2,* 181–201.

Biller, H. B. (1971). The mother–child relationship and the father-absent boy's per-sonality development. *Merrill-Palmer Quarterly, 17,* 227–241.

Biller, H. B. (1981). Father absence, divorce, and personality development. In M. E. Lamb (Ed.), *The role of the father in child development* (2nd ed., pp. 489–552). New York: Wiley.

Black, J. C., & Cantor, D. J. (1989). *Child custody.* New York: Columbia University Press.

Blanchard, R. W., & Biller, H. B. (1971). Father availability and academic perform-ance among third-grade boys. *Developmental Psychology, 4,* 301–305.

Blechman, E. A. (1982). Are children with one parent at psychological risk? A methodological review. *Journal of Marriage and the Family, 44,* 179–195.

Blechman, E. A. Berberian, R. M., & Thompson, W. D. (1977). How well does number of parents explain unique variance in self-reported drug use? *Journal of Child Clinical Psychology, 45,* 1182–1183.

Blechman, E. A., & Manning, M. (1976). A reward–cost analysis of the single-parent family. In E. J. Mash, L. A. Hamerlynck, & L. C. Handy (Eds.), *Behavior modifica-tion and families* (pp. 61–90). New York: Brunner/Mazel.

Block, J. H., Block, J., & Gjerde, P. F. (1986). The personality of children prior to divorce: A prospective study. *Child Development, 57,* 827–840.

Bloom, B. L., Asher, S. J., & White, S. W. (1978). Marital disruption as a stressor: A review and analysis. *Psychological Bulletin, 85,* 867–899.

Bloom, B. L., & Hodges, W. F. (1988). The Colorado separation and divorce program: A preventative intervention program for newly separated persons. In R. H. Price, E. L. Cowen, R. P. Lorion, & J. Ramos–McKay (Eds.), *14 ounces of prevention: A casebook for practitioners* (pp. 153–164). Washington, DC: American Psychologi-cal Association.

Bloom, B. L., Hodges, W. F., & Caldwell, R. (1982). A preventive intervention pro-gram for the newly separated: Initial evaluation. *American Journal of Community Psychology, 10,* 251–264.

Bloom, B. L., Hodges, W. F., & Caldwell, R. A. (1983). Marital separation: The first eight months. In E. J. Callahan & K. A. McKluskey (Eds.), *Life-span developmental psychology: Non-normative events* (pp. 218–239). New York: Academic Press.

Bloom, B. L., Hodges, W. F., Caldwell, R. A., Systra, L., & Cedrone, A. R. (1977). Marital separation: A community survey. *Journal of Divorce, 1,* 7–19.

Bloom, B. L., Hodges, W. F., Kern, M. B., & McFaddin, S. C. (1985). A preventive intervention program for the newly separated: Final evaluations. *American Journal of Orthopsychiatry, 55,* 9–26.

Blush, G. J., & Ross, K. L. (1987). Sexual allegations in divorce: The SAID syndrome. *Conciliation Courts Review, 25,* 1–11.

Booth, A., Brinkerhoff, D. B., & White, L. K. (1984). The impact of parental divorce on courtship. *Journal of Marriage and the Family, 65*(4), 85–94.

Boren, R. (1982). *The therapeutic effects of a school-based intervention program of the divorced.* Unpublished doctoral dissertation, School of Education, University of Colorado, Boulder.

Bornstein, M. T., Bornstein, P. H., & Walters, H. A. (1985). Children of divorce: A group treatment manual for research and application. *Journal of Child and Adolescent Psychotherapy, 2*(4), 267–273.

Bornstein, M. T., Bornstein, P. H., & Walters, H. A. (1988). Children of divorce: Empirical evaluation of a group-treatment program. *Journal of Clinical Child Psychology, 17,* 248–254.

Bowen, M. (1976). Principles and techniques of multiple family therapy. In P. Guerin (Ed.), *Family therapy.* New York: Gardner Press.

Bowen, M. (1978). *Family therapy in clinical practice.* New York: Jason Aronson.

Bowerman, C. E., & Irish, D. P. (1962). Some relationships of stepchildren to their parents. *Marriage and the Family, 24,* 113–121.

Bowlby, J. (1946). *Forty four juvenile thieves: Their characters and home life.* London: Ballice, Tindall, & Cox.

Bowlby, J. (1969). *Attachment and loss: Vol. 1. Attachment.* London: Hogart.

Bowser, K. A. (1982). Divesting grandparents of statutory grandchild visitation rights by stepparent adoption. *University of Missouri, Kansas City Law Review, 50,* 231–240.

Bowser, M. A. (1982). Children and divorce: Being in between. *Elementary School Guidance and Counseling, 17,* 126–130.

Bradford, A., Moore, R. S., Enwall, B., Taylor, J., Cooper, S. B., & Williams, C. G. (1982). *Parting: A counselor's guide for children of separated parents.* (EDRS No. ED 227391) Columbia, SC: South Carolina Department of Education.

Brady, C. P., Bray, J. H., & Zeeb, L. (1986). Behavior problems of clinic children: Relation to parental marital status, age and sex of the child. *American Journal of Orthopsychiatry, 56,* 399–412.

Brand, E., & Clingempeel, W. G. (1987). Interdependencies of marital and stepparent–stepchild relationships and children's psychological adjustment: Research findings and clinical implications. *Family Relations, 36,* 140–145.

Brand, E., Clingempeel, W. G., & Bowen-Woodward, K. (1988). Family relationships and children's psychological adjustment in stepmother and stepfather families. In E. M. Hetherington & J. D. Arasteh (Eds.), *Impact of divorce, single parenting, and stepparenting on children* (pp. 299–324). Hillsdale, NJ: Erlbaum.

Brandwein, R. A., Brown, C. A., & Fox, E. M. (1974). Women and children last: The social situation of divorced mothers and their families. *Journal of Marriage and the Family, 36,* 498–514.

Braver, S. L., Gonzalez, N., Wolchik, S. A., & Sandler, I. N. (1989). Economic hardship and psychological distress in custodial mothers. *Journal of Divorce, 12*(4), 19–34.

Braver, S. L., Wolchik, S. A., Sandler, I. N., Fogas, B. S., & Zvetina, D. (1987, August). *Parental reports of noncustodial parent visitation: Some recent findings.* Paper presented at the symposium, Parent–Child Contact after Divorce: Causes and Consequences, at the American Psychological Association Convention, New York.

Bray, J. H. (1988). Children's development during early remarriage. In E. M. Hetherington & J. D. Arasteh (Eds.), *Impact of divorce, single parenting, and stepparenting on children* (pp. 279–298). Hillsdale, NJ: Erlbaum.

Bray, J. H., & Anderson, H. (1984). Strategic interventions with single parent families. *Psychotherapy: Theory, Research and Practice, 21*(1), 101–109.

Bresee, P., Stearns, G. B., Bess, B. H., & Packer, L. S. (1986). Allegations of child sexual abuse in child custody disputes: A therapeutic assessment model. *American Journal of Orthopsychiatry, 56,* 560–569.

Bronson, G. W. (1972). Infants: Reactions to unfamiliar persons and novel objects. *Monographs of the Society for Research in Child Development, 37*(3).

Brown, D. G. (1982). Divorce and family mediation: History, review, future directions. *Conciliation Courts Review, 20*(2), 1–44.

Brown, N. D., & Samis, M. D. C. (1986/1987). The application of structural family therapy in developing the binuclear family. *Mediation Quarterly, 14/15,* 51–69.

Burchinal, L. G. (1964). Characteristics of adolescents from unbroken, broken and reconstituted families. *Journal of Marriage and the Family, 26,* 44–51.

Burden, D. S. (1986). Single parents and the work setting: The impact of multiple job and homelife responsibilities. *Family Relations, 35,* 37–43.

Bureau of the Census. (1989). *Statistical abstractions of the United States* (109th ed). Washington, DC: U.S. Government Printing Office.

Burke, D. M., & Van de Streek, L. (1989). Children of divorce: An application of Hammond's groups counseling for children. *Elementary School Guidance and Counseling, 24,* 112–118.

Burns, C. W., & Brassard, M. R. (1982). A look at the single parent family: Implications for the school psychologist. *Psychology in the Schools, 19,* 487–494.

Caldwell, R. A., & Bloom, B. L. (1982). Social support: Its structure and impact on marital disruption. *American Journal of Community Psychology, 10,* 647–667.

Caldwell, R. A., Bloom, B. L., & Hodges, W. F. (1984). Sex differences in separation and divorce: A longitudinal perspective. In A. U. Rickel, M. Gerrard, & I. Iscoe (Eds.), *Social and psychological problems of women: Prevention and crisis intervention* (pp. 103–120). Washington, DC: Hemisphere.

Camara, K. A., & Resnick, G. (1988). Interparental conflict and cooperation: Factors moderating children's post-divorce adjustment. In E. M. Hetherington & J. D. Arasteh (Eds.), *Impact of divorce, single parenting, and stepparenting on children* (pp. 169–196). Hillsdale, NJ: Erlbaum.

Campbell, L. E. G., & Johnston, J. R. (1986/1987). Multifamily mediation: The use of groups to resolve child custody disputes. *Mediation Quarterly, 14/15,* 137–162.

Cantor, D. W. (1977). School-based groups for children of divorce. *Journal of Divorce, 1,* 183–187.

Cantor, D. W., & Drake, E. A. (1983). *Divorced parents and their children: A guide for mental health professionals.* New York: Springer.

Caplan, G. (1970). *The theory and practice of mental health consultation.* New York: Basic Books.

Carlson, C. I. (1987). Helping students deal with divorce-related issues. *Special Service in the Schools, 3*(3/4), 121–138.

Cashion, B. G. (1982). Female-headed families: Effects on children and clinical implications. *Journal of Marital and Family Therapy, 8*(2), 77–85.

Cebollero, A. N., Cruise, K., & Stollak, G. (1986). The long-term effects of divorce: Mothers and children in concurrent support groups. *Journal of Divorce, 10*(1/2), 219–228.

Chasin, R., & Grunebaum, H. (1981). A model for evaluation in child custody disputes. *American Journal of Family Therapy, 9*(1), 43–49.

Chesler, P. (1986). *Mothers on trial.* New York: McGraw-Hill.

Chess, S., Thomas, A., Korn, S., Mittelman, M., & Cohen, J. (1983). Early parental attitudes, divorce and separation, and young adult outcome: Findings of a longitudinal study. *Journal of the American Academy of Child Psychiatry, 22,* 47–51.

Clawar, S. S. (1984). How to determine whether a family report is scientific. *Conciliation Courts Review, 22*(2), 71–76.

Clingempeel, W. G., Brand, E., & Ievoli, R. (1984). Stepparent–stepchild relationships in stepmother and stepfather families: A multimethod study. *Family Relations, 33,* 465–473.

Clingempeel, W. G., Ievoli, R., & Brand, E. (1984). Structural complexity and the quality of stepfather–stepchild relationships. *Family Process, 23,* 547–560.

Clingempeel, W. G., & Reppucci, N. D. (1982). Joint custody after divorce: Major issues and goals for research. *Psychological Bulletin, 91*(1), 102–127.

Clingempeel, W. G., & Segal, S. (1986). Stepparent–stepchild relationships and the psychological adjustment of children in stepmother and stepfather families. *Child Development, 57,* 474–484.

Clingempeel, W. G., Shuwall, M. A., & Heiss, E. (1988). Divorce and remarriage: Perspectives on the effects of custody arrangements on children. In S. A. Wolchik & P. Karoly (Eds.), *Children of divorce: Empirical perspectives on adjustment,* pp. 145–181. New York: Gardner Press.

Coffman, S. G., & Roark, A. E. (1988). Likely candidates for group counseling: Adolescents with divorced parents. *The School Counselor, 35*(4), 246–252.

Coleman, M., & Ganong, L. H. (1984). Effect of family structure on family attitudes and expectations. *Family Relations, 33,* 425–432.

Coleman, M., & Ganong, L. (1989). Stepfamily self-help books: Brief annotations and ratings. *Family Relations, 38,* 91–96.

Coller, D. R. (1988). Joint custody: Research, theory, and policy. *Family Process, 27,* 459–469.

Conger, J. J., & Petersen, A. (1984). *Adolescence and youth: Psychological development in a changing world* (3rd ed.). New York: Harper & Row.

Coogler, O. J. (1978). *Structured mediation in divorce settlement: A handbook for marital mediators.* Lexington, MA: Lexington Books.

Coogler, O. J., Weber, R. E., & McKenry, P. C. (1979). Divorce mediation: A means of facilitating divorce and adjustment. *The Family Coordinator, 28,* 255–259.

Cooney, T. M., Smyer, M. A., Hagestad, G. O., & Klock, R. (1986). Parental divorce in young adulthood: Some preliminary findings. *American Journal of Orthopsychiatry, 56,* 470–477.

Cooper, S., & Hodges, W. F. (1983). *The mental health consultation field*. New York: Human Sciences Press.

Copeland, A. P. (1985). Individual differences in children's reactions to divorce. *Journal of Clinical Child Psychology, 14*(1), 11–19.

Corwin, D. L., Berliner, L., Goodman, G., Goodwin, J. & White, S. (1987). Child sexual abuse and custody disputes: No easy answers. *Journal of Interpersonal Violence, 2*(1), 91–105.

Cowen, E. L., Dorr, D., Clarfield, S., Kreling, B., McWilliams, S. A., Pokrachi, F., Pratt, D. M., Terrell, D., & Wilson, A. (1973). The AML: A quick screening device for early identification of school maladaptation. *American Journal of Community Psychology, 1,* 12–35.

Craig, M. M., & Glick, S. J. (1963). *Ten years experience with the Glueck Social Prediction Table*. New York: New York City Youth Board.

Crohn, H., Sager, C. J., Rodstein, E., Brown, H. S., Walker, L., & Beir, J. (1981). Understanding and treating the child in the remarried family. In I. R. Stuart & L. E. Abt (Eds.), *Children of separation and divorce: Management and treatment* (293–317). New York: Van Nostrand Reinhold.

Crook, T., & Raskin, A. (1975). Association of childhood parental loss with attempted suicide and depression. *Journal of Consulting and Clinical Psychology, 43,* 277.

Crosbie-Burnett, M. (1984). The centrality of the step relationship: A challenge to family theory and practice. *Family Relations, 33,* 459–463.

Crosbie-Burnett, M. (1989). Impact of custody arrangement and family structure on remarriage. *Journal of Divorce, 13*(1), 1–16.

Crosbie-Burnett, M., & Newcomer, L. L. (1989). A multimodal intervention for group counseling with children of divorce. *Elementary School Guidance and Counseling, 23,* 155–166.

Cummings, E. M. (1987). Coping with background anger in early childhood. *Child Development, 58,* 976–984.

Cummings, E. M., Zahn-Waxler, C., & Radke-Yarrow, M. (1981). Young children's responses to expressions of anger and affection by others in the family. *Child Development, 56,* 1274–1282.

Cummings, E. M., Zahn-Waxler, C., & Radke-Yarrow, M. (1984). Developmental changes in children's reactions to anger in the home. *Journal of Child Psychology and Psychiatry, 25,* 63–74.

Dahl, A. S., Cowgill, K. M., & Asmundsson, R. (1987). Life in remarriage families. *Social Work, 32*(1), 40–44.

D'Andrea, A. (1983). Joint custody as related to paternal involvement and paternal self-esteem. *Conciliation Courts Review, 21*(2), 81–87.

Derdeyn, A. P. (1975). Child custody consultation. *American Journal of Orthopsychiatry, 45,* 791–801.

Dredeyn, A. P. (1977). Children in divorce: Intervention in the phase of separation. *Pediatrics, 60*(1), 20–27.

Derdeyn, A. P. (1985). Grandparent visitation rights: Rendering family dissension more pronounced? *American Journal of Orthopsychiatry, 55,* 277–287.

Derdeyn, A. P., & Scott, E. (1984). Joint custody: A critical analysis and appraisal. *American Journal of Orthopsychiatry, 54,* 199–209.

Developing understanding of self and others. (1970). Circle Pines, MN: American Guidance Service.

Dishon, M. (1985). Psychological aspects and factors in planning visitation. *Family Law News, 8*(3), 36–39.

Dlugokinski, E. (1977). A developmental approach to coping with divorce. *Journal of Clinical Child Psychology, 6*(2), 27–30.

Dorpat, T. L., Jackson, J. K., & Ripley, H. S. (1965). Broken homes and attempted and completed suicide. *Archives of General Psychiatry, 12,* 213–216.

Drake, E. A. (1981). Helping children cope with divorce: The role of the school. In I. R. Stuart & L. E. Abt (Eds.), *Children of separation and divorce: Management and treatment* (pp. 147–172). New York: Van Nostrand Reinhold.

Drapkin, R., & Bienenfeld, F. (1985). The power of including children in custody mediation. *Journal of Divorce, 8*(3/4), 63–95.

Draughon, M. (1975). Stepmother's model of identification in relation to mourning in the child. *Psychological Reports, 36,* 183–189.

Drill, R. L. (1986). Young adult children of divorced parents: Depression and the perception of loss. *Journal of Divorce, 10*(1/2), 169–187.

Duberman, L. (1973). Step-kin relationships. *Journal of Marriage and the Family, 35,* 283–292.

Duberman, L. (1975). *The reconstituted family: A study of remarried couples and their children.* Chicago: Nelson-Hall.

Eagle, R. S., & Sheaffer, S. (1989). Clinican's recommendations in access disputes involving initiation or renewal of access. *Journal of Divorce, 12*(4), 49–67.

Emery, R. E. (1982). Interparental conflict and the children of discord and divorce. *Psychological Bulletin, 92,* 310–330.

Emery, R. E. (1988). Mediation and the settlement of divorce disputes. In E. M. Hetherington & J. D. Arasteh (Eds.), *Impact of divorce, single parenting, and stepparenting on children* (pp. 53–71). Hillsdale, NJ: Erlbaum.

Emery, R. E. (1989). Family violence. *American Psychologist, 44,* 321–340.

Emery, R. E., & Jackson, J. A. (1989). The Charlottesville mediation project: Mediated and litigated child custody disputes. *Mediation Quarterly, 24,* 3–18.

Emery, R. E., & Wyer, M. M. (1987a). Child custody mediation and litigation: An experimental evaluation of the experience of parents. *Journal of Consulting and Clinical Psychology, 55,* 179–186.

Emery, R. E., & Wyer, M. M. (1987b). Divorce mediation. *American Psychologist, 42,* 472–480.

Erickson, S. K., & Erickson, M. S. Mc. (1988). *Family mediation casebook: Theory and process.* New York: Brunner/Mazel.

Erickson, E. (1963). *Childhood and society.* New York: W. W. Norton.

Evans, A., & Neel, J. (1980). School behaviors of children from one-parent and two-parent homes. *Principal, 60*(1), 38–39.

Everett, C. A. (Ed.). (1987). Minority and ethnic issues in the divorce process [special issue]. *Journal of Divorce, 11*(2).

Faller, K. C. (1991). Possible explanations for child sexual abuse allegations in divorce. *American Journal of Orthopsychiatry, 61,* 86–91.

Farber, S. S., Felner, R. D., & Primavera, J. (1985). Parental separation/divorce and adolescents: An examination of factors mediating adaptation. *American Journal of Community Psychology, 13,* 171–185.

Fassler, D., Lash, M., & Ives, S. B. (1988). *Changing families: A guide for kids and grown-ups.* Burlington, VT: Waterfront Books.

Fassler, J. (1978). *Helping children cope: Mastering stress through books and stories.* New York: The Free Press.

Fast, I., & Cain, A. C. (1966). The stepparent role: Potential for disturbances in family functioning. *American Journal of Orthopsychiatry, 36,* 485–491.

Fay, R. E. (1985). Joint custody of infants and toddlers. *Medical Aspects of Human Sexuality, 19*(8), 134–139.

Federico, J. (1979). The marital termination period of the Divorce Adjustment Process. *Journal of Divorce, 3*(2), 93–106.

Felner, R. D., Stolberg, A., & Cowen, E. L. (1975). Crisis events and school mental health referral patterns of young children. *Journal of Consulting and Clinical Psychology, 43,* 305–310.

Felner, R. D., Terre, L., Farber, S. S., Primavera, J., & Bishop, T. A. (1985). Child custody: Practices and perspectives of legal professionals. *Journal of Clinical Child Psychology, 14*(1), 27–34.

Felner, R. D., Terre, L., Goldfarb, A., Farber, S. S., Primavera, J., Bishop, T. A., & Aber, M. S. (1985). Party status of children during marital dissolution: Child preference and legal representation in custody decisions. *Journal of Clinical Child Psychology, 14*(1), 42–48.

Felner, R. D., Terre, L., & Rowlinson, R. T. (1988). A life transition framework for understanding marital dissolution and family reorganization. In S. A. Wolchik & P. Karoly (Eds.), *Children of divorce: Empirical perspectives on adjustment,* pp. 35–65, New York: Gardner Press.

Ferri, E. (1976). *Growing up in a one-parent family: A long-term study of child development,* Windsor, England: NFER.

Films for Humanity. (1987). *Tender places* [Film]. New York: Films for Humanity.

Fine, S. (1980). Children in divorce, custody and access situations: The contribution of the mental health professional. *Journal of Child Psychology and Psychiatry, 21,* 353–361.

Fine, M. A., Moreland, J. R., & Schwebel, A. I. (1983). Long-term effects of divorce on parent–child relationships. *Developmental Psychology, 19,* 703–713.

Fine, M. A., & Schwebel, A. I. (1987). An emergent explanation of differing racial reactions to single parenthood. *Journal of Divorce, 11*(2), 1–15.

Fischer, J. L. (1983). Mothers living apart from their children. *Family Relations, 32,* 351–357.

Fischer, J. L., & Cardea, J. M. (1981). Mothers living apart from their children: A study in stress and coping. *Alternative Lifestyles, 4,* 218–227.

Fischman, J. (1988). Stepdaughter wars. *Psychology Today, 22*(11), 38–41.

Fish, K. D. (1969). Paternal availability, family role structure, maternal employment, and personality development in late adolescent females. *Dissertation Abstracts International, 30*(9-B), 4369.

Fletcher, C. N. (1989). A comparison of incomes and expenditures of male-headed households paying child support and female-headed households receiving child support. *Family Relations, 38,* 412–417.

Flynn, T. (1984, March 25). Single parenthood. *The Sunday Denver Post,* "Contemporary," p. 2.

Folberg, H. J. (Ed.). (1985). *Joint custody and shared parenting. A handbook for judges, lawyers, counselors and parents.* Portland, OR: Association of Family and Conciliation Courts.

Forehand, R., Brody, G. H., Long, N., Slotkin, J., & Fauber, R. (1986). Divorce, divorce potential, and interparental conflict: The relationship to early adolescent social and cognitive functioning. *Journal of Adolescent Research, 1,* 389–397.

Forgatch, M. S., Patterson, G. R., & Skinner, M. L. (1988). A mediational model for the effect of divorce on antisocial behavior in boys. In E. M. Hetherington & J. D. Arasteh (Eds.), *Impact of divorce, single parenting, and stepparenting on children* (pp. 135–154). Hillsdale, NJ: Erlbaum.

Foster, H. H. (1973). Divorce reform and the Uniform Act. *Family Law Quarterly, 7,* 170–210.

Foster, H. H., & Freed, D. J. (1978). Life with father: 1978. *Family Law Quarterly, 11,* 321–342.

Franklin, R. L., & Hibbs, "B" (1980). Child custody in transition. *Journal of Marital and Family Therapy, 6,* 285–291.

Freeman, E. B. (1985). When children face divorce: Issues and implications of research. *Childhood Education, 62,* 130–136.

Frey, R. G. (1986). Being a divorced father as primary parent: A phenomenological investigation. *Conciliation Courts Review, 24*(1), 71–78.

Fulton, J. A. (1979). Parental reports of children's post-divorce adjustment. *Journal of Social Issues, 35*(4), 126–139.

Funder, K. (1989). Grandparents in children's post-divorce families. *Family Matters, 25,* 47–49.

Furstenberg, F. F. (1987). The new extended family: The experience of parents and children after remarriage. In K. Pasley & M. Ihinger-Tallman (Eds.), *Remarriage and stepparenting: Current research and theory* (pp. 42–61). New York: Guilford Press.

Furstenberg, F. F., Jr. (1988). Child care after divorce and remarriage. In E. M. Hetherington & J. D. Arasteh (Eds.), *Impact of divorce, single parenting, and stepparenting on children* (pp. 279–298). Hillsdale, NJ: Erlbaum.

Furstenberg, F. F., & Nord, C. W. (1985). Parenting apart: Patterns of childrearing after marital disruption. *Journal of Marriage and the Family, 47,* 893–904.

Furstenberg, F. F., Peterson, J. L., Nord, C. W., & Zill, N. (1983). The life course of children of divorce: Marital disruption and parental contact. *American Sociological Review, 48,* 656–668.

Galper, M. (1978). *Co-parenting: Sharing your child equally.* Philadelphia: Running Press.

Ganong, L. H., & Coleman, M. (1984). The effects of remarriage on children: A review of the empirical literature. *Family Relations, 33,* 389–406.

Ganong, L. H., & Coleman, M. (1988). Do mutual children cement bonds in step-families? *Journal of Marriage and the Family, 50,* 687–698.

Ganong, L. H., & Coleman, M. (1989). Preparing for remarriage: Anticipating the issues, seeking solutions. *Family Relations, 38,* 28–33.

Gardner, R. A. (1970). *The boys and girls book about divorce.* New York: Bantam Books.

Gardner, R. A. (1973). *The talking, feeling, and doing game* [Game]. Cresskill, NJ: Creative Therapeutics.

Gardner, R. A. (1976). *Psychotherapy with children of divorce.* New York: Jason Aronson.

Gardner, R. A. (1987). *The parental alienation syndrome and the differentiation between fabricated and genuine child sex abuse.* Cresskill, NJ: Creative Therapeutics.

Gardner, R. A. (1989). Differentiating between bona fide and fabricated allegations of sexual abuse of children. *Journal of the American Academy of Matrimonial Lawyers, 5,* 1–25.

Garrison, K. M., Stolberg, A. L., Mallonnee, D., Carpenter, J., & Antrim, Z. (1983). *The single parents' support group: A procedures manual.* Unpublished manual, Divorce Adjustment Project, Virginia Commonwealth University, Richmond.

Gelles, R. J. (1989). Child abuse and violence in single-parent families: Parent absence and economic deprivation. *American Journal of Orthopsychiatry, 59,* 492–501.

Gersick, K. (1979). Fathers by choice: Divorced men who receive custody of their children. In G. Levinger & O. C. Moles (Eds.), *Divorce and separation: Context, causes and consequences* (pp. 307–323). New York: Basic Books.

Ginott, H. G. (1965). *Between parent and child.* New York: Macmillan.

Giles-Sims, J., & Finkelhor, D. (1984). Child abuse in stepfamilies. *Family Relations, 33,* 407–413.

Girdner, L. K. (1979, August). *On some contradictory aspects of child custody policy (with emphasis on the expert witness).* Paper presented at the Annual Meeting of the National Council on Family Relations, Boston, MA.

Girdner, L. K. (1985a). Adjudication and mediation: A comparison of custody decision-making processes involving third parties. *Journal of Divorce, 8*(3/4), 33–47.

Girdner, L. K. (1985b). Strategies of conflict: Custody litigation in the United States. *Journal of Divorce, 9*(1), 1–15.

Gladstone, J. W. (1987). Factors associated with changes in visiting between grandmothers and grandchildren following an adult child's marriage breakdown. *Canadian Journal on Aging, 6*(2), 117–127.

Glenn, N. D., & Shelton, B. A. (1983). Pre-adult background variables and divorce: A note of caution about overreliance on explained variance. *Journal of Marriage and the Family, 45,* 405–410.

Glick, P. C. (1988). The role of divorce in the changing family structure: Trends and variations. In S. A. Wolchik & P. Karoly (Eds.), *Children of divorce: Empirical perspectives on adjustment,* pp. 3–34, New York: Gardner Press.

Glick, P. C. (1989a). Remarried families, stepfamilies, and stepchildren: A brief demographic profile. *Family Relations, 38,* 24–27.

Glick, P. C. (1989b). The family life cycle and social change. *Family Relations, 38,* 123–129.

Glueck, S., & Glueck, E. (1950). *Unraveling juvenile delinquency.* Boston: Harvard University Press.

Goff, B. (1969). *Where is daddy? The story of a divorce.* Boston: Beacon.

Goldman, J., & Coane, J. (1977). Family therapy after the divorce: Developing a strategy. *Family Process, 16,* 357–362.

Goldstein, H. S. (1974). Reconstituted families: The second marriage and its children. *Psychiatric Quarterly, 48,* 433–440.

Goldstein, J., Freud, A., & Solnit, A. (1973). *Beyond the best interests of the child.* New York: Free Press.

Goldstein, S., & Solnit, A. J. (1984). *Divorce and your child.* New Haven, CT: Yale University Press.

Goldzband, M. G. (1982). *Consulting in child custody: An introduction to the ugliest litigation for mental-health professionals.* Lexington, MA: Lexington Books.

Golombos, S., Spencer, A., & Rutter, M. (1983). Children in lesbian and single-parent households: Psychosexual and psychiatric appraisal. *Journal of Child Psychology and Psychiatry and Allied Disciplines, 24,* 551–572.

Gordon, T. (1970). *P.E.T.: Parent Effectiveness Training.* New York: Van Rees Press.

Grebe, S. C. (1988). Structured mediation and its variants: What makes it unique. In J. Folberg & A. Milne (Eds.), *Divorce mediation: Theory and practice.* New York: Guilford Press.

Green, A. H. (1986). True and false allegations of sexual abuse in child custody disputes. *Journal of the American Academy of Child Psychiatry, 25,* 449–456.

Green, B. J. (1978). HELPING children of divorce: A multimodal approach. *Elementary School Guidance and Counseling, 13*(1), 31–45.

Green, R. (1982). The best interests of the child with a lesbian mother. *Bulletin of the AAPL, 10*(1), 7–15.

Greene, R. M., & Leslie, L. A. (1988/1989). Mothers' behavior and sons' adjustment following divorce. *Journal of Divorce, 12*(2/3), 235–251.

Gregory, I. (1966). Retrospective data concerning childhood loss of a parent. *Archives of General Psychiatry, 15,* 362–367.

Greif, G. L. (1987). A longitudinal examination of single custodial fathers: Implications for treatment. *The American Journal of Family Therapy, 15,* 253–260.

Greif, G. L. (1990). Split custody: A beginning understanding. *Journal of Divorce, 13*(3), 15–26.

Greif, J. B. (1979). Fathers, children and joint custody. *American Journal of Orthopsychiatry, 49,* 311–319.

Greif, J. B., & Simring, S. K. (1982). Remarriage and joint custody. *Conciliation Courts Review, 20*(1), 9–14.

Grossman, S. M., Shea, J. A., & Adams, G. R. (1980). Effects of parental divorce during early childhood on ego development and identity formation of college students. *Journal of Divorce, 3*(3), 263–272.

Group for the Advancement of Psychiatry. (1981). *Divorce, child custody, and the family.* San Francisco: Jossey-Bass.

Guidance Associates. (1973). *Understanding changes in the family. Not together anymore* [Film]. Pleasantville, NY: Guidance Associates.

Guidubaldi, J., Cleminshaw, H. K., Perry, J. D., & Mcloughlin, C. S. (1983). The impact of parental divorce on children: Report of the nationwide NASP study. *School Psychology Review, 12,* 300–323.

Guidubaldi, J., Cleminshaw, H. K., Perry, J. D., Nastasi, B. K., & Lightel, J. (1986). The role of selected family environment factors in children's post-divorce adjustment. *Family Relations, 35,* 141–151.

Guidubaldi, J., & Perry, J. D. (1984). Divorce, socioeconomic status, and children's cognitive–social competence at school entry. *American Journal of Orthopsychiatry, 54,* 459–468.

Guidubaldi, J., & Perry, J. D. (1985). Divorce and mental health sequelae for children: A two-year follow-up of a nationwide sample. *Journal of the American Academy of Child Psychiatry, 24,* 531–537.

Guttman, J., & Broudo, M. (1988/1989). The effect of children's family type on teachers' stereotypes. *Journal of Divorce, 12*(2/3), 315–328.

Gwynn, C. A., & Brantley, H. T. (1987). Effects of a divorce group intervention for elementary school children. *Psychology in the Schools, 24,* 161–164.

Hainline, L., & Feig, E. (1978). The correlates of childhood father absence in college-aged women. *Child Development, 49,* 37–42.

Haley, J. (1963). *Strategies of psychotherapy.* New York: Grune & Stratton.

Hall, M. (1978). Lesbian families: Cultural and clinical issues. *Social Work, 23,* 380–385.

Hammond, J. M. (1979). Children of divorce: Implications for counselors. *School Counselor, 27*(1), 7–14.

Hammond, J. M. (1981a). *Divorce group counseling for secondary students.* Ann Arbor, MI: Cranbrook.

Hammond, J. M. (1981b). *Group counseling for children of divorce.* Ann Arbor, MI: Cranbrook.

Hammond, J. M. (1981c). Loss of the family unit: Counseling groups to help kids. *Personnel and Guidance Journal, 59,* 392–394.

Hansen, C. M. (1982). *The effects of interparental conflict on the adjustment of the preschool child to divorce.* Unpublished doctoral dissertation, University of Colorado, Boulder.

Hare-Mustin, R. T. (1976). The biased professional in divorce litigation. *Psychology of Women Quarterly, 1*(2), 216–222.

Harris, B. S. (1977). Lesbian mother child custody: Legal and psychiatric aspects. *Bulletin of the American Academy of Psychiatry and the Law, 5*(1), 75–89.

Hauser, B. B. (1985). Custody in dispute: Legal and psychological profiles of contesting families. *Journal of the American Academy of Child Psychiatry, 24,* 575–582.

Haynes, J. M. (1981). *Divorce mediation: A practical guide for therapists and counselors.* New York: Springer.

Haynes, J. (1988). Power balancing. In J. Folberg & A. Milne (Eds.), *Divorce mediation: Theory and practice*. New York: Guilford Press.

Heath, P. A., & Lynch, S. (1988). A reconceptualization of the time since parental separation variable as a predictor of children's outcomes following divorce. *Journal of Divorce, 11*(3/4), 67–85.

Heath, P. A., & MacKinnon, C. (1988). Factors related to the social competence of children in single-parent families. *Journal of Divorce, 11*(3/4), 49–66.

Heller, K., & Monahan, J. (1983). Individual process consultation. In S. Cooper & W. F. Hodges (Eds.), *The field of mental health consultation* (pp. 57–69). New York: Human Science Press.

Help for single parents: Agencies and organizations. (1986). *Family Relations, 35,* 213–214.

Hepworth, J., Ryder, R. G., & Dreyer, A. S. (1984). The effects of parental loss on the formation of intimate relationships. *Journal of Marital and Family Therapy, 10*(1), 73–82.

Hernandez, D. J. (1988). Demographic trends and the living arrangements of children. In E. M. Hetherington & J. D. Arasteh (Eds.), *Impact of divorce, single parenting, and stepparenting on children* (pp. 3–22). Hillsdale, NJ: Erlbaum.

Herzog, E., & Sudia, C. E. (1973). Children in fatherless families. In B. M. Caldwell & H. N. Ricciuti (Eds.), *Review of child development research: Volume three. Child development and social policy*. Chicago: University of Chicago Press.

Herzog, J. M. (1980). Sleep disturbance and father hunger in 18- to 28-month-old boys: The Erlkoenig syndrome. *Psychoanalytic Study of the Child, 35,* 219–233.

Hess, R. D., & Camara, K. A. (1979). Post-divorce family relationships as mediating factors in the consequences of divorce for children. *Journal of Social Issues, 35*(4), 79–96.

Hetherington, E. M. (1966). Effects of parental absence on sex typed behaviors in Negro and white preadolescent males. *Journal of Personality and Social Psychology, 4,* 87–91.

Hetherington, E. M. (1972). Effects of paternal absence on personality development in adolescent daughters. *Developmental Pathology, 7,* 313–326.

Hetherington, E. M. (1987). Family relations six years after divorce. In K. Pasley & M. Ihinger-Tallman (Eds.), *Remarriage and stepparenting: Current research and theory* (pp. 185–205). New York: Guilford Press.

Hetherington, E. M., Arnett, J. D., & Hollier, E. A. (1988). Adjustment of parents and children to remarriage. In S. A. Wolchik & P. Karoly (Eds.), *Children of divorce: Empirical perspectives on adjustment* (pp. 67–101). New York: Gardner Press.

Hetherington, E. M., Cox, M., & Cox, R. (1979) Beyond father absence: Conceptualization of effects of divorce. In E. M. Hetherington & R. D. Parke (Eds.), *Contemporary readings in child psychology*. New York: McGraw-Hill.

Hetherington, E. M., Cox, M., & Cox, R. (1985). Long-term effects of divorce and remarriage on the adjustment of children. *Journal of the American Academy of Child Psychiatry, 24,* 518–530.

Hirst, S. R., & Smiley, G. W. (1984). The access dilemma—A study of access patterns following marriage breakdown. *Conciliation Courts Review, 22*(1), 41–52.

Hitchens, D. (1979/1980). Social attitudes, legal standards and personal trauma in child custody cases. *Journal of Homosexuality, 5*(1/2), 89–95.

Hobart, C. (1989). Experiences of remarried families. *Journal of Divorce, 13*(2), 121–144.

Hobart, C., & Brown, D. (1988). Effects of prior marriage children on adjustment in remarriage: A Canadian study. *Journal of Comparative Family Studies, 19,* 381–396.

Hodges, W. F., & Bloom, B. L. (1984). Parent's report of children's adjustment to marital separation: A longitudinal study. *Journal of Divorce, 8*(1), 33–50.

Hodges, W. F., & Bloom, B. L. (1986). Preventive intervention for newly separated adults: One year later. *Journal of Preventive Psychiatry, 3*(1), 35–49.

Hodges, W. F., Buchsbaum, H. K., & Tierney, C. W. (1983). Parent–child relationships and adjustment in preschool children in divorced and intact families. *Journal of Divorce, 7*(2), 43–58.

Hodges, W. F., Landis, T., Day, E., & Oderberg, N. (in press). Infants and toddlers and post divorce parental access. *Journal of Divorce and Remarriage.*

Hodges, W. F., London, J., & Colwell, J. B. (1990). Stress in parents and late elementary age children in divorced and intact families and child adjustment. *Journal of Divorce and Remarriage, 14*(1), 63–79.

Hodges, W. F., Tierney, C. W., & Buchsbaum, H. K. (1984). The cumulative effect of stress on preschool children of divorced and intact families. *Journal of Marriage and the Family, 46,* 611–617.

Hodges, W. F., Wechsler, R. C., & Ballantine, C. (1979). Divorce and the preschool child. *Journal of Divorce, 3,* 55–69.

Hoeffer, B. (1981). Children's acquisition of sex-role behavior in lesbian-mother families. *American Journal of Orthopsychiatry, 51,* 536–544.

Hoffman, M. L. (1971). Father absence and conscience development. *Developmental Psychology, 4,* 400–406.

Holdahl, S., & Caspersen, P. (1977). Children of family change: Who's helping them now? *The Family Coordinator, 26,* 472–477.

Hoorwitz, A. N. (1982). "Extraordinary circumstances" in custody contests between parent and non-parent. *The Journal of Psychiatry and Law, 10,* 351–361.

Hoorwitz, A. N. (1983). The visitation dilemma in court consultation. *Social Casework, 64*(4), 231–237.

Hozman, T. L., & Froiland, D. J. (1976). Families in divorce: A proposed model for counseling the children. *The Family Coordinator, 25*(3), 271–276.

Huntley, D. K., & Phelps, R. E. (1990). Depression and social contacts of children from one-parent families. *Journal of Community Psychology, 18*(1), 66–73.

Huntley, D. K., Phelps, R. E., & Rehm, L. P. (1986). Depression in children from single-parent families. *Journal of Divorce, 10*(1/2), 153–161.

Huston, A. C. (1983). Sex-typing. In E. M. Hetherington (Ed.), *Handbook of child psychology* (pp. 387–467). New York: Wiley.

Ihinger-Tallman, M. (1988). Research on stepfamilies. *Annual Review of Sociology, 14,* 25–48.

Ilfeld, F. W., Ilfeld, H. Z., & Alexander, J. R. (1982). Does joint custody work? A first look at outcome data of relitigation. *American Journal of Psychiatry, 139*(1), 62–66.

Irving, H. H. (1980). *Divorce mediation: The rational alternative.* Toronto: Personal Library.

Irving, H. H., Benjamin, M., & Trocme, N. (1984). Shared parenting: An empirical analysis using a large data base. *Family Process, 23,* 561–569.

Irving, H. H., Bohm, P., MacDonald, G., & Benjamin, M. (1979). *A comparative analysis of two family court services: An exploratory study of conciliation counseling.* Toronto: Welfare Grants Directorate, Department of National Health and Welfare and the Ontario Ministry of the Attorney General.

Isaacs, M. B. (1981). Treatment for families of divorce: A systems model of prevention. In I. R. Stuart & L. E. Abt (Eds.), *Children of separation and divorce: Management and treatment* (pp. 242–262). New York: Van Nostrand Reinhold.

Isaacs, M. B. (1988). The visitation schedule and child adjustment: A three year study. *Family Process, 27,* 251–256.

Isaacs, M. B., & Leon, G. H. (1987). Race, marital dissolution and visitation: An examination of adaptive family strategies. *Journal of Divorce, 11*(2), 17–31.

Isaacs, M. B., Montalvo, B., & Abelsohn, D. (1986). *The difficult divorce: Therapy for children and families.* New York: Basic Books.

Ives, S. B., Fassler, D., & Lash, M. (1985). *The divorce workbook: A guide for kids and families.* Burlington, VT: Waterfront Books.

Jacobs, N. L., Guidubaldi, J., & Nastasi, B. (1986). Adjustment of divorced-family day care children. *Early Childhood Research Quarterly, 1,* 361–378.

Jacobson, D. S. (1978a). The impact of marital separation/divorce on children: I. Parent–child separation and child adjustment. *Journal of Divorce, 1,* 341–360.

Jacobson, D. S. (1978b). The impact of marital separation/divorce on children: II. Interparent hostility and child adjustment. *Journal of Divorce, 2,* 3–19.

Jacobson, D. S. (1978c). The impact of divorce/separation on children: III. Parent–child communication and child adjustment and regression analysis of findings from overall study. *Journal of Divorce, 2,* 175–194.

Jacobson, D. S. (1979). Stepfamilies: Myths and realities. *Social Work, 24,* 202–207.

Jacobson, D. S. (1987). Family type, visiting patterns, and children's behavior in the stepfamily: A linked family system. In K. Pasley & M. Ihinger-Tallman (Eds.), *Remarriage and stepparenting: Current research and theory* (pp. 257–272). New York: Guilford Press.

Jacobson, G., & Ryder, R. G. (1969). Parental loss and some characteristics of the early marriage relationship. *American Journal of Orthopsychiatry, 39,* 779–787.

Jauch, C. (1977). The one-parent family. *Journal of Clinical Child Psychology, 6*(2), 30–32.

Johnson, B. (1985). Gender identification among fathers with custody. *Conciliation Courts Review, 23*(2), 75–78.

Johnson, C. L. (1988). Postdivorce reorganization of relationships between divorcing children and their parents. *Journal of Marriage and the Family, 50,* 221–231.

Johnson, H. C. (1980). Working with stepfamilies: Principles of practice. *Social Work, 25,* 304–308.

Johnson, M. K., & Hutchinson, R. L. (1988/1989). Effects of family structure on children's self-concepts. *Journal of Divorce, 12*(2/3), 129–138.

Johnston, J. R., Campbell, L. E. G., & Mayes, S. S. (1985). Latency children in post-separation and divorce disputes. *Journal of the American Academy of Child Psychiatry, 24,* 563–574.

Johnston, J. R., Campbell, L. E. G., & Tall, M. C. (1985). Impasses to the resolution of custody and visitation disputes. *American Journal of Orthopsychiatry, 55,* 112–129.

Johnston, J. R., Gonzalez, R., & Campbell, L. E. G. (1985, August). *Ongoing post-divorce conflict as predictor of child disturbance.* Paper presented at the Annual Meeting of the American Psychological Association, Los Angeles.

Johnston, J. R., Gonzalez, R., & Campbell, L. E. G. (1987). Ongoing post-divorce conflict and child disturbance. *Journal of Abnormal Child Psychology, 15,* 493–509.

Johnston, J. R., Kline, M., & Tschann, J. M. (1989). Ongoing postdivorce conflict: Effects on children of joint custody and frequent access. *American Journal of Orthopsychiatry, 59,* 576–592.

Jones, S. M. (1978). Divorce and remarriage: A new beginning, a new set of problems. *Journal of Divorce, 2*(2), 217–227.

Jouriles, E. N., Barling, J., & O'Leary, K. D. (1987). Predicting child behavior problems in maritally violent families. *Journal of Abnormal Child Psychology, 15,* 165–173.

Kagan, J., Kearsley, R., & Zelazo, P. (1978). *Infancy: Its place in human development.* Cambridge, MA: Harvard University Press.

Kalter, N. (1977). Children of divorce in an outpatient psychiatric population. *American Journal of Orthopsychiatry, 47,* 40–51.

Kalter, N. (1984). Conjoint mother–daughter treatment: A beginning phase of psychotherapy with adolescent daughters of divorce. *American Journal of Orthopsychiatry, 54,* 490–497.

Kalter, N. (1987). Long-term effects of divorce on children: A developmental vulnerability model. *American Journal of Orthopsychiatry, 57,* 587–600.

Kalter, N., Pickar, J., & Lesowitz, M. (1984). School-based developmental facilitation groups for children of divorce: A preventive intervention. *American Journal of Orthopsychiatry, 54,* 613–623.

Kalter, N., & Rembar, J. (1981). The significance of a child's age at the time of parental divorce. *American Journal of Orthopsychiatry, 46,* 20–32.

Kaplan, S. L. (1977). Structural family therapy for children of divorce: Case reports. *Family Process, 16,* 75–83.

Kaseman, C. M. (1974). The single-parent family. *Perspectives in Psychiatric Care, 12,* 113–118.

Kaye, S. H. (1988/1989). The impact of divorce on children's academic performance. *Journal of Divorce, 12*(2/3), 283–298.

Keat, D. B. (1974). *Fundamentals of child counseling.* Boston: Houghton Mifflin.

Keat, D. B. (1978). *The acting, feeling, choosing game: A multimodal game for children* [Game]. Harrisburg, PA: Professional Associates.

Keilin, W. G., & Bloom, L. J. (1986). Child custody evaluation practices: A survey of experienced professionals. *Professional Psychology: Research and Practice, 17,* 338–346.

Kellam, S. G., Ensminger, M. E., & Turner, R. J. (1977). Family structure and the mental health of children: Concurrent and longitudinal community-wide studies. *Archives of General Psychiatry, 34,* 1012–1022.

Kelly, J. B. (1981). The visiting relationship after divorce: Research findings and clinical implications. In I. R. Stuart & L. E. Abt (Eds.), *Children of separation and divorce: Management and treatment* (pp. 338–361). New York: Van Nostrand Reinhold.

Kelly, J. B. (1989). Mediated and adversarial divorce: Respondents' perceptions of their processes and outcomes. *Mediation Quarterly, 24,* 71–88.

Kelly, J. B., Gigy, L., & Hausman, S. (1988). Mediated and adversarial divorce: Initial findings from a longitudinal study. In J. Folberg & A. Milne (Eds.), *Divorce mediation: Theory and practice.* New York: Guilford Press.

Kelly, J. B., & Wallerstein, J. S. (1976). The effects of parental divorce: Experiences of the child in early latency. *American Journal of Orthopsychiatry, 46,* 20–32.

Kelly, J. B., & Wallerstein, J. S. (1977a). Brief interventions with children in divorcing families. *American Journal of Orthopsychiatry, 47,* 23–39.

Kelly, J. B. & Wallerstein, J. S. (1977b). Part-time parent, part-time child: Visiting after divorce. *Journal of Clinical Child Psychology, 6*(2), 51–54.

Kennedy, J. F., & Keeney, V. T. (1988). The extended family revisited: Grandparents rearing grandchildren. *Child Psychiatry and Human Development, 19*(1), 26–35.

Keshet, H. F., & Rosenthal, K. M. (1978). Fathering after marital separation. *Social Work, 23,* 11–18.

Kessler, S. (1977). *Beyond divorce: A divorce primer.* Atlanta: National Institute of Professional Training.

Kessler, S., & Bostwick, K. S. (1977). Beyond divorce: Coping skills for children. *Journal of Clinical Child Psychology, 6,* 38–41.

Kimmons, L., & Gaston, J. A. (1986). Single parenting: A filmography. *Family Relations, 35,* 205–211.

Kinard, E. M., & Reinherz, H. (1984). Marital disruption: Effects on behavioral and emotional functioning in children. *Journal of Family Issues, 5*(1), 90–115.

Kinard, E. M., & Reinherz, H. (1986). Effects of marital disruption on children's school aptitude and achievement. *Journal of Marriage and the Family, 48,* 285–293.

Kirkpatrick, M., Smith, C., & Roy, R. (1981). Lesbian mothers and their children: A comprehensive survey. *American Journal of Orthopsychiatry, 51,* 85–100.

Kitson, G. C., & Langlie, J. K. (1984). Couples who file for divorce but change their minds. *American Journal of Orthopsychiatry, 54,* 469–489.

Klee, L., Schmidt, C., & Johnson, C. (1988/1989). Children's definition of family following divorce of their parents. *Journal of Divorce, 12*(2/3), 109–127.

Kleinman, J., Rosenberg, E., & Whiteside, M. (1979). Common developmental tasks in forming reconstituted families. *Journal of Marital and Family Therapy, 5,* 79–86.

Kline, M., Tschann, J. M., Johnston, J. R., & Wallerstein, J. S. (1989). Children's adjustment in joint and sole physical custody families. *Developmental Psychology, 25,* 430–438.

Knight, R. G. (1983). Female homosexuality and the custody of children. *New Zealand Journal of Psychology, 12,* 23–27.

Koel, A., Clark, S. C., Phear, W. P. C., & Hauser, B. B. (1988). A comparison of joint and sole legal custody agreements. In E. M. Heatherington & J. D. Arasteh (Eds.), *Impact of divorce, single parenting, and stepparenting on children* (pp. 73–90). Hillsdale, NJ: Erlbaum.

Koopman, E. J., Hunt, E. J., & Stafford, V. (1984). Child related agreements in mediated and non-mediated divorce settlements: A preliminary examination and discussion of implications. *Conciliation Courts Review, 22*(1), 65–70.

Kosinski, F. A. (1983). Improving relationships in stepfamilies. *Elementary School Guidance and Counseling, 17,* 200–207.

Krantz, S. E., Clark, J., Pruyn, J. P., & Usher, M. (1985). Cognition and adjustment among children of separated or divorced parents. *Cognitive Therapy and Research, 9*(1), 61–77.

Kressel, K., Butler-DeFreitas, F., Forlenza, S. G., & Wilcox, C. (1989). Research in contested custody mediations: An illustration of the case study method. *Mediation Quarterly, 24,* 55–70.

Kuehnel, T. G., & Kuehnel, J. M. (1983). Mental health consultation: An educational approach. In S. Cooper & W. F. Hodges (Eds.), *The mental health consultation field* (pp. 39–55). New York: Human Sciences Press.

Kulka, R., & Weingarten, H. (1979). The long-term effects of parental divorce in childhood on adult adjustment. *Journal of Social Issues, 35,* 50–78.

Kurdek, L. A. (1986). Custodial mothers' perceptions of visitation and payment of child support by noncustodial fathers in families with low and high levels of pre-separation interparent conflict. *Journal of Applied Developmental Psychology, 7,* 307–323.

Kurdek, L. A., & Berg, B. (1983). Correlates of children's adjustment to their parents' divorces. In L. A. Kurdek (Ed.), *Children and divorce: New directions for child development* (pp. 47–60) (No. 19). San Francisco: Jossey-Bass.

Kurdek, L. A., & Berg, B. (1987). Children's beliefs about parental divorce scale: Psychometric characteristics and concurrent validity. *Journal of Consulting and Clinical Psychology, 55,* 712–718.

Kurdek, L. A., Blisk, D., & Siesky, A. E. (1981). Correlates of children's long-term adjustment to their parents' divorce. *Developmental Psychology, 17,* 565–579.

Lahey, B. B., Hartdagen, S. E., Frick, P. J., McBurnett, K., Connor, R., & Hynd, G. W. (1988). Conduct disorder: Parsing the confounded relation to parental divorce and antisocial personality. *Journal of Abnormal Psychology, 97,* 334–337.

Lamb, M. (1981). The development of father–infant relationships. In M. Lamb (Ed.), *The role of the father in child development* (2nd ed., pp. 459–488). New York: Wiley.

Landis, J. T. (1960). The trauma of children when parents divorce. *Marriage and Family Living, 22,* 7–12.

Langner, T. S., & Michael, S. T. (1963). *Life stress and mental health.* New York: Free Press of Glencoe.

Laosa, L. M. (1988). Ethnicity and single parenting in the United States. In E. M. Hetherington & J. D. Arasteh (Eds.), *Impact of divorce, single parenting, and stepparenting on children* (pp. 23–49). Hillsdale, NJ: Erlbaum.

Leader, A. L. (1973). Family therapy for divorced fathers and others out of home. *Social Casework, 54,* 13–19.

LeShan, E. (1978). *What's going to happen to me? When parents separate or divorce.* New York: Scholastic.

Levin, M. L. (1988/1989). Sequelae to marital disruption in children. *Journal of Divorce, 12*(2/3), 25–80.

Lewin, E. (1981). Lesbianism and motherhood: Implications for child custody. *Human Organization, 40*(1), 6–14.

Lewis, M. (1974). The latency child in a custody conflict. *Journal of the American Academy of Child Psychiatry, 13,* 635–647.

Lewis, M., Feiring, C., & Weinraub, M. (1981). The father as a member of the child's social network. In M. E. Lamb (Ed.), *The role of the father in child development* (pp. 259–294). New York: Wiley.

London, J. (1989). *Parental marital status and parentification: A study of childhood family environment and intimacy in young adulthood.* Unpublished doctoral dissertation, University of Colorado, Boulder.

Long, N., & Forehand, R. (1987). The effects of parental divorce and parental conflict on children: An overview. *Developmental and Behavioral Pediatrics, 8,* 292–296.

Long, N., Forehand, R., Fauber, R., & Brody, G. H. (1987). Self-perceived and independently observed competence of young adolescents as a function of parental marital conflict and recent divorce. *Journal of Abnormal Child Psychology, 15,* 15–27.

Long, N., Slater, E., Forehand, R., & Fauber, R. (1988). Continued high or reduced interparental conflict following divorce: Relation to young adolescent adjustment. *Journal of Consulting and Clinical Psychology, 56,* 467–469.

Longfellow, C. (1979). Divorce in context: Its impact on children. In G. Levinger & O. C. Moles (Eds.), *Divorce and separation: Context, causes, and consequences* (pp. 287–306). New York: Basic Books.

Lopez, F. G., Campbell, V. L., & Watkins, C. E. (1988). The relation of parental divorce to college student development. *Journal of Divorce, 12*(1), 83–98.

Lowenstein, J. S., & Koopman, E. J. (1978). A comparison of the self-esteem between boys living with single-parent mothers and single-parent fathers. *Journal of Divorce, 2*(2), 195–208.

Lowery, C. R. (1985). Child custody in divorce: Parents' decisions and perception. *Family Relations, 34,* 241–249.

Lyons, T. A. (1983). Lesbian mother's fears. *Women and Therapy, 2*(2–3), 231–240.

Luepnitz, D. A. (1982). *Child custody: A study of families after divorce.* Lexington, MA: Lexington Books.

Luepnitz, D. A. (1986). A comparison of maternal, paternal and joint custody: Understanding the varieties of post-divorce family life. *Journal of Divorce, 9*(3), 1–12.

Maccoby, E. E., Depner, C. E., & Mnookin, R. H. (1988). Custody of children following divorce. In E. M. Hetherington & J. D. Arasteh (Eds.), *Impact of divorce, single parenting, and stepparenting on children* (pp. 91–114). Hillsdale, NJ: Erlbaum.

MacFarlane, K. (1988). Child sexual abuse allegations in divorce proceedings. In K. MacFarlane & J. Waterman (Eds.), *Sexual abuse in young children: Evaluation and treatment* (pp. 121–150). New York: Guilford Press.

MacGregor, R., Ritchie, A. M., Serrano, A. C., & Schuster, F. P. (1964). *Multiple impact therapy with families.* New York: McGraw-Hill.

MacKinnon, C. E., Brody, G. H., & Stoneman, Z. (1986). The longitudinal effects of divorce and maternal employment on the home environments of preschool children. *Journal of Divorce, 9*(4), 65–78.

Magid, K. M. (1977). Children facing divorce: A treatment program. *Personnel and Guidance Journal, 55,* 534–536.

Magid, K. (1990). *Kid's stepfamily kit.* Denver, CO: K. M. Productions.

Magid, K. M., & Schreibman, W. (1980). *Divorce is . . . A kids' coloring book.* Gretna, LA: Pelican Publishing.

Mahler, M. S., Pine, F., & Bergman, A. (1975). *The psychological birth of the human infant.* New York: Basic Books.

Mandell, D., & Birenzweig, E. (1990). Stepfamilies: A model for group work with remarried couples and their children. *Journal of Divorce and Remarriage, 14*(1), 29–42.

Mann, P. (1973). *My dad lives in a downtown hotel,* New York: Scholastic Press.

Marino, C. D., & McCowan, R. J. (1976). The effects of parent absence on children. *Child Study Journal, 6,* 165–182.

Maskin, M. B., & Brookins, E. (1974). The effects of parental composition on recidivism rates in delinquent girls. *Journal of Clinical Psychology, 30,* 341–342.

McDermott, J. F. (1968). Parental divorce in early childhood. *American Journal of Psychiatry, 124,* 1424–1432.

McDermott, J. F. (1970). Divorce and its psychiatric sequelae in children. *Archives of General Psychiatry, 23,* 421–427.

McDermott, J.F., Tseng, W., Char, W. F., & Fukunaga, C. S. (1978). Child custody decision making. *Journal of the American Academy of Child Psychiatry, 17,* 104–116.

McGoldrick, M., & Carter, E. A. (1980). Forming a remarried family. In E. A. Carter & M. McGoldrick (Eds.), *The family life cycle: A framework for family therapy.* New York: Gardner Press.

McKay, M., Rogers, P. D., Blades, J., & Gosse, R. (1984). *The divorce book.* Oakland, CA: New Harbinger.

McKinnon, R., & Wallerstein, J. S. (1986). Joint custody and the preschool child. *Behavioral Sciences and the Law, 4*(2), 169–183.

McKinnon, R., & Wallerstein, J. S. (1988). A preventive intervention program for parents and young children in joint custody arrangements. *American Journal of Orthopsychiatry, 58,* 168–178.

McLoughlin, D., & Whitfield, R. (1984). Adolescents and their experience of parental divorce. *Journal of Adolescence, 7,* 155–170.

Mednick, B., Reznick, C., Hocevar, D., & Baker, R. (1987). Long-term effects of parental divorce on young adult crime. *Journal of Youth and Adolescence, 16*(1), 31–45.

Mendes, H. A. (1979). Single-parent families: A typology of life-styles. *Social Work, 4*(1), 37–48.

Messinger, L. (1976). Remarriage between divorced people with children from a previous marriage. *Journal of Marriage and Family Counseling, 2,* 193–200.

Mian, M., Wehrspann, W., Kaljner-Diamond, H., LeBaron, D., & Winder, C. (1986). Review of 125 children 6 years of age and under who were sexually abused. *Child Abuse and Neglect, 10,* 223–229.

Miller, B. (1979). Gay fathers and their children. *The Family Coordinator, 28,* 544–552.

Miller, J. J., & Soper, B. (1982). An emerging contingency, the stepfamily: Review of the literature. *Psychological Reports, 50,* 715–722.

Miller, T. W., & Veltkamp, L. J. (1986). Use of fables in clinical assessment of contested child custody. *Child Psychiatry and Human Development, 16*(4), 274–284.

Mills, D. M. (1984). A model for stepfamily development. *Family Relations, 33,* 365–372.

Milne, A. L. (Ed.). (1979). *Joint custody: A handbook for judges, lawyers and counselors.* Portland, OR: Association of Family & Conciliation Courts.

Minuchin, S. (1974). *Families and family therapy,* Cambridge, MA: Harvard University Press.

Moore, C. W. (1988). Techniques to break impasse. In J. Folberg & A. Milne (Eds.), *Divorce mediation: Theory and practice.* New York: Guilford Press.

Moreland, J., Schwebel, A. I., Fine, M. A., & Vess, J. D. (1982). Postdivorce family therapy: Suggestions for professionals. *Professional Psychology, 13,* 639–646.

Morley, I., & Stephenson, G. (1977). *The social psychology of bargaining.* London: Allen & Unwin.

Morris, S. J. (1989). Sexually abused children of divorce. *Journal of the American Academy of Matrimonial Lawyers, 5,* 27–46.

Morrison, J. R. (1974). Parental divorce as a factor in childhood psychiatric illness. *Comprehensive Psychiatry, 15,* 95–102.

Mowatt, M. H. (1972). Group psychotherapy for stepfathers and their wives. *Psychotherapy: Theory, Research and Practice, 9,* 328–331.

Mueller, D. P., & Cooper, P. W. (1986). Children of single parent families: How they fare as young adults. *Family Relations, 35,* 169–176.

Musetto, A. P. (1980). Evaluating families with custody or visitation problems. *Advances in Family Psychiatry, 2,* 523–531.

Mussen, P. H., Conger, J. J., & Kagan, J. (1979). *Child development and personality* (5th ed.). New York: Harper & Row.

Nadler, J. H. (1976). *The psychological stress of the stepmother.* Unpublished doctoral dissertation, California School of Professional Psychology, Los Angeles.

Nadler, J. H. (1983). Effecting change in stepfamilies: A psychodynamic/behavioral group approach. *American Journal of Psychotherapy, 37*(1), 100–112.

National Association of Elementary School Principals. (1980). One-parent families and their children. *Principal, 60*(1), 31–37.

National Center for Health Statistics. (1990). Advanced report of final divorce statistics, 1987. *Monthly Vital Statistics Report, 38*(12, Suppl. 2). Hyattsville, MD: Public Health Service.

National Instructional Television Center. (1973). *Breakup* [Television program]. Bloomington, IN: Author.

Nelson, R. (1989). Parental hostility, conflict and communication in joint and sole custody families. *Journal of Divorce, 13*(2), 145–157.

Neugebauer, R. (1988/1989). Divorce, custody and visitation: The child's point of view. *Journal of Divorce, 12*(2/3), 153–168.

Newman, G. (1981). *101 Ways to Be a Long Distance Super-Dad.* Mountain View, CA: Blossom Valley Press.

Nichols, W. C. (1980). Stepfamilies: A growing family therapy challenge. In L. R. Wolberg & M. L. Aronson (Eds.), *Group and Family Therapy, 1980.* New York: Brunner/Mazel.

Nicholson, S. (1987). The go-between: Strategic therapy with teenagers in separated families. *Australian and New Zealand Journal of Family Therapy, 8*(1), 6–12.

Norton, A. J., & Glick, P. C. (1986). One parent families: A social and economic profile. *Family Relations, 35,* 9–17.

Nungesser, L. G. (1980). Theoretical bases for research on the acquisition of social sex-roles by children of lesbian mothers. *Journal of Homosexuality, 5*(3), 177–187.

Nye, F. I. (1978). Child adjustment in broken and in unhappy unbroken homes. *Marriage and Family Living, 19,* 356–361.

Omizo, M. M., & Omizo, S. A. (1987). Group counseling with children of divorce: New findings. *Elementary School Guidance and Counseling, 22*(1), 46–52.

Orleans, M., Palisi, B. J., & Caddell, D. (1989). Marriage adjustment and satisfaction of stepfathers: Their feelings and perceptions of decision making and stepchildren relations. *Family Relations, 38,* 371–377.

Paquin, G. W. (1988). The child's input in the mediation process: Promoting the best interests of the child. *Mediation Quarterly, 22,* 69–81.

Parry, R. S., Broder, E. A., Schmitt, E. A. G., Saunders, E. B., & Hood, E. (1986). *Custody disputes: Evaluation and intervention.* Lexington, MA: Lexington Books.

Pearson, J. (1981). Child custody: Why not let the parents decide? *The Judges Journal, 20*(1), 4–12.

Pearson, J., Munson, P., & Thoennes, N. (1983). Children's rights and child custody proceedings. *Journal of Divorce, 7*(2), 1–21.

Pearson, J., & Thoennes, N. (1982). Mediation and divorce: The benefits outweigh the costs. *Family Advocate, 4*(3), 26–32.

Pearson, J., & Thoennes, N. (1985). Research report: Mediation versus the courts in child custody cases. *Negotiation Journal, 1*(3), 235–244.

Pearson, J., & Thoennes, N. (1988). Divorce mediation research results. In J. Folberg & A. Milne (Eds.), *Divorce mediation: Theory and practice*. New York: Guilford Press.

Peck, B. B. (1975). Psychotherapy with disrupted families. *Journal of Contemporary Psychotherapy, 7*(1), 60–66.

Pedersen, F. A. (1981). Father influences viewed in a family context. In M. Lamb (Ed.), *The role of the father in child development* (2nd ed., pp. 295–317). New York: Wiley.

Pedersen, F. A., & Robson, K. S. (1969). Father participation in infancy. *American Journal of Orthopsychiatry, 39,* 466–472.

Pedersen, F. A., Rubenstein, J. L., & Yarrow, L. J. (1979). Infant development in father-absent families. *Journal of Genetic Psychology, 135,* 51–61.

Pedro-Carroll, J. (1983). *The children of divorce intervention project: An investigation of the efficacy of a school-based prevention program.* Unpublished doctoral dissertation, University of Rochester, Rochester, New York.

Pedro-Carroll, J., & Cowen, E. L. (1985). The Children of Divorce Intervention Project: An investigation of the efficacy of a school-based prevention program. *Journal of Consulting and Clinical Psychology, 53,* 603–611.

Pedro-Carroll, J. L., Cowen, E. L., Hightower, A. D., & Guare, J. C. (1986). Preventive intervention with latency-aged children of divorce: A replication study. *American Journal of Community Psychology, 14,* 277–289.

Perkins, T. F., & Kahan, J. P. (1979). An empirical comparison of natural-father and stepfather systems. *Family Process, 18,* 175–183.

Peterson, J. L., & Zill, N. (1986). Marital disruption, parent–child relationships, and behavior problems in children. *Journal of Marriage and the Family, 48,* 295–307.

Petronio, S. (1988). Communication and the visiting parent. *Journal of Divorce, 11*(3/4), 103–110.

Pitts, F. N., Meyer, J., Brooks, M., & Winokur, G. (1965). Adult psychiatric illness in family members: A study of 748 patients and 250 controls. *American Journal of Psychiatry, 121* (suppl.), i–x.

Plunkett, J., & Kalter, N. (1984). Children's beliefs about reactions to parental divorce. *Journal of the American Academy of Child Psychiatry, 23,* 616–621.

Polikoff, N. D. (1982). Why are mothers losing: A brief analysis of criteria used in child custody determinations. *Women's Rights Law Reporter, 7,* 235–243.

Porter, B., & O'Leary, K. D. (1980). Marital discord and childhood behavior problems. *Journal of Abnormal Child Psychology, 8,* 287–295.

Quinn, P., & Allen, K. R. (1989). Facing challenges and making compromises: How single mothers endure. *Family Relations, 38,* 390–395.

Ramos, S. (1979). *The complete book of child custody.* New York: G. P. Putnam's Sons.

Raschke, H. J., & Raschke, V. J. (1979). Family conflict and children's self-concepts. *Journal of Marriage and the Family, 41,* 367–374.

Raskin, D. C., & Esplin, P. W. (in press). Assessment of children's statements of sexual abuse. In J. Doris (Ed.), *The suggestibility of children's memory (with special reference to the child witness).* Washington, DC: American Psychological Association.

Rebelsky, F., & Hanks, C. (1971). Fathers' verbal interaction with infants in the first three months of life. *Child Development, 42*(1), 63–68.

Reingold, C. B. (1976). *Remarriage.* New York: Harper & Row.

Reinhard, D. W. (1977). The reaction of adolescent boys and girls to the divorce of their parents. *Journal of Clinical Child Psychology, 6,* 15–20.

Reppucci, N. D. (1984). The wisdom of Solomon: Issues in child custody determination. In N. D. Reppucci, L. A. Weithorn, E. P. Mulvey, & J. Monahan (Eds.), *Children, mental health, and the law* (pp. 59–78), Beverly Hills, CA: Sage.

Ricci, I. (1985). Mediator's notebook: Reflections on promoting equal empowerment and entitlements for women. *Journal of Divorce, 8*(3/4), 49–61.

Richards, A., & Willis, I. (1976). *How to get it together when your parents are coming apart.* New York: Bantam Books.

Richards, C. A., & Goldenberg, I. (1985). Joint custody: Current issues and implications for treatment. *The American Journal of Family Therapy, 13*(4), 33–40.

Richards, C. A., & Goldenberg, I. (1986). Fathers with joint physical custody of young children: A preliminary look. *American Journal of Family Therapy, 14,* 154–162.

Rickel, A. U., & Langner, T. S. (1985). Short-and long-term effects of marital disruption on children. *American Journal of Community Psychology, 13,* 599–611.

Ricks, S. S. (1984). Determining child custody: Trends, factors, and alternatives. *Conciliation Courts Review, 22*(1), 65–70.

Ringler-White, M. (1982, May). *Supervised visitation: Working with the most difficult parents.* Paper presented at the Child Custody Conference (Visitation: From Chaos to Cooperation), The Interdisciplinary Committee on Child Custody and the Continuing Legal Education in Colorado, Inc., Boulder.

Risman, B. J. (1986). Can men "mother"? Life as a single father. *Family Relations, 35,* 95–102.

Risman, B. J. (1987). Intimate relationships from a microstructural perspective: Men who mother. *Gender and Society, 1*(1), 6–32.

Risman, B. J., & Park, K. (1988). Just the two of us: Parent–child relationships in single-parent homes. *Journal of Marriage and the Family, 50,* 1049–1062.

Ritchie, A. M., & Serrano, A. C. (1974). Family therapy in the treatment of adolescents with divorced parents. In R. E. Hardy & J. G. Cull (Eds.), *Therapeutic needs of the family: Problems, descriptions and therapeutic approaches* (pp. 91–99). Springfield, IL: C. C. Thomas.

Robinson, B. G. (1985). Family services. Victoria, British Columbia: British Columbia Services Branch.

Rohrlich, J. A., Ranier, R., Berg-Cross, L., & Berg-Cross, G. (1977). The effects of divorce: A research review with a developmental perspective. *Journal of Clinical Child Psychology, 6,* 15–20.

Roseby, V., & Deutsch, R. (1985). Children of separation and divorce: Effects of a social role-taking group intervention on fourth and fifth graders. *Journal of Clinical Child Psychology, 14*(1), 55–60.

Rosenblum, K. E. (1986). Leaving as a wife, leaving as a mother. *Journal of Family Issues, 7,* 197–213.

Rosenthal, D., Leigh, G. R., & Elardo, R. (1985/86). Home environment of three- to six-year-old children from father-absent and two-parent families. *Journal of Divorce, 9*(2), 41–48.

Rosenthal, P. A. (1979). Sudden disappearance of one parent with separation and divorce: The grief and treatment of preschool children. *Journal of Divorce, 3*(1), 43–54.

Rossiter, A. B. (1988). A model for group intervention with preschool children experiencing separation and divorce. *American Journal of Orthopsychiatry, 58*, 387–396.

Rubenstein, C., Shaver, P., & Peplau, L. A. (1979). Loneliness. *Human Nature, 2*, 58–65.

Sack, W. H., Mason, R., & Higgins, J. E. (1985). The single-parent family and abusive child punishment. *American Journal of Orthopsychiatry, 55*, 252–259.

Sager, C. J., Steer, H., Crohn, H., Rodstein, E., & Walker, E. (1980). Remarriage revisited. *Family and Mental Health Journal, 6*, 19–33.

Sandler, I. N., Wolchik, S. A., & Braver, S. L. (1988). The stressors of children's postdivorce environments. In S. A. Wolchik & P. Karoly (Eds.), *Children of divorce: Empirical perspectives on adjustment* pp. 111–143. New York: Gardner Press.

Sanik, M. M., & Mauldin, T. (1986). Single versus two parent families: A comparison of mothers' time. *Family Relations, 35*, 53–56.

Santilli, L. E., & Roberts, M. C. (in press). Custody decisions in Alabama before and after the abolition of the tender years doctrine. *Law and Human Behavior.*

Santrock, J. W. (1970). Influence of onset and type of paternal absence on the first four Eriksonian crises. *Developmental Psychology, 3*, 273–274.

Santrock, J. W. (1972). Relation of type and onset of father absence on cognitive development. *Child Development, 43*, 455–469.

Santrock, J. W. (1975). Father absence, perceived maternal behavior and moral development in boys. *Child Development, 46*, 753–757.

Santrock, J. W., & Sitterle, K. A. (1987). Parent–child relationships in stepmother families. In K. Pasley & M. Ihinger-Tallman (Eds.), *Remarriage and stepparenting: Current research and theory* (pp. 273–299). New York: Guilford Press.

Santrock, J. W., & Tracy, R. L. (1978). The effects of children's family structure status on the development of stereotypes by teachers. *Journal of Educational Psychology, 70*, 754–757.

Santrock, J. W., & Warshak, R. A. (1979). Father custody and social development in boys and girls. *Journal of Social Issues, 35*, 112–125.

Santrock, J. W., & Wohlford, P. (1970). Effects of father absence: Influence of the reason for and the onset of the absence [Summary]. *Proceedings of the 78th Annual Convention of the American Psychological Association, 5*, 265–266.

Sarnoff, C. (1976). *Latency.* New York: Jason Aronson.

Saroyan, W. (1972). Gaston. In E. D. Landau, S. L. Epstein, & A. Platt-Stone (Eds.), *Child development through literature.* Englewood Cliffs, NJ: Prentice-Hall.

Satir, V. (1972). *Peoplemaking.* Palo Alto, CA: Science and Behavior Books.

Schachere, K. (1990). Attachment between working mothers and their infants: The influence of family process. *American Journal of Orthopsychiatry, 60*, 19–34.

Schaefer, E. (1965). Children's reports of parental behavior: An inventory. *Child Development, 36,* 413–424.

Schlesinger, B. (1982). Children's viewpoints of living in a one-parent family. *Journal of Divorce, 5,* 1–23.

Schlesinger, B. (1986). Single parent families: A bookshelf: 1978–1985. *Family Relations, 35,* 199–204.

Schnayer, R., & Orr, R. R. (1988/1989). A comparison of children living in single-mother and single-father families. *Journal of Divorce, 12*(2/3), 171–184.

Schulz, D. A., & Wilson, R. A. (1973). Some traditional family variables and their correlates with drug use among high school students. *Journal of Marriage and the Family, 35,* 628–631.

Sears, R. R., Maccoby, E. E., & Levin, H. (1957). *Patterns of child rearing.* Evanston, IL: Row, Peterson.

Sheridan, J. T., Baker, S. B., & de Lissovoy, V. (1984). Structured group counseling and explicit bibliotherapy as in-school strategies for preventing problems in youth of changing families. *The School Counselor, 32,* 134–141.

Shiller, V. M. (1986). Loyalty conflicts and family relationship in latency age boys: A comparison of joint and maternal custody. *Journal of Divorce, 9*(4), 17–38.

Shinn, M. (1978). Father absence and children's cognitive development. *Psychological Bulletin, 85,* 295–324.

Simmons, R. C., Rosenberg, F., & Rosenberg, M. (1973). Disturbance in the self-image at adolescence. *American Sociological Review, 38,* 553–568.

Simon, S. B., Howe, L. W., & Kirschenbaum, H. (1972). *Values clarification.* New York: Hart.

Skafte, D. (1985). *Child custody evaluations.* Beverly Hills, CA: Sage.

Slater, E. J., Stewart, K. J., & Linn, M. W. (1983). The effects of family disruption on adolescent males and females. *Adolescence, 18,* 931–942.

Smith, R. M. (1976). The impact of fathers on delinquent males. *Dissertation Abstracts International, 35*(10-A), 6487–6488.

Sonnenshein-Schneider, M., & Baird, K. L. (1980). Group counseling children of divorce in the elementary schools: Understanding process and technique. *Personnel and Guidance Journal, 59*(2), 88–91.

Sorensen, E., & Goldman, J. (1989). Judicial perception in determining primary physical residence. *Journal of Divorce, 12*(4), 69–87.

Sorosky, A. D. (1977). The psychological effect of divorce on adolescents. *Adolescence, 12,* 123–136.

Southworth, S., & Schwarz, J. C. (1987). Post-divorce contact, relationship with father, and heterosexual trust in female college students. *American Journal of Orthopsychiatry, 57,* 371–382.

Springer, C., & Wallerstein, J. S. (1983). Young adolescents' responses to their parents' divorces. In L. A. Kurdek (Ed.), *Children and divorce: New directions in child development* (pp. 15–27) (no. 19). San Francisco: Jossey-Bass.

Sroufe, L. A. (1979). The coherence of individual development. *American Psychologist, 34,* 834–841.

Staff. (1980, September 4). One-parent kids troubled. *APGA Guidepost.*

Stahl, P. M. (1986). Attitudes and beliefs about joint custody: Findings of a study. *Conciliation Courts Review, 24*(2), 41–45.

Steinman, S. (1981). The experience of children in a joint-custody arrangement: A report of a study. *American Journal of Orthopsychiatry, 51,* 403–414.

Steinman, S. B., Zemmelman, S. E., & Knoblauch, T. M. (1985). A study of parents who sought joint custody following divorce: Who reaches agreement and sustains joint custody and who returns to court. *Journal of the American Academy of Child Psychiatry, 24,* 554–562.

Steller, M., & Koehnken, G. (1989). Criteria-based statement analysis. In D. C. Raskin (Ed.), *Psychological methods in criminal investigation and evidence* (pp. 217–245). New York: Springer.

Stern, P. N. (1978). Stepfather families: Integration around child discipline. *Issues in Mental Health Nursing, 1*(2), 50–56.

Stewart, J. R., Schwebel, A. I., & Fine, M. A. (1986). The impact of custodial arrangement on the adjustment of recently divorced fathers. *Journal of Divorce, 9*(3), 55–65.

Stolberg, A. L., & Bush, J. P. (1985). A path analysis of factors predicting children's divorce adjustment. *Journal of Clinical Child Psychology, 14*(1), 49–54.

Stolberg, A. L., Camplair, C., Currier, K., & Wells, M. J. (1987). Individual, familial and environmental determinants of children's post-divorce adjustment and maladjustment. *Journal of Divorce, 11*(1), 51–70.

Stolberg, A. L., & Cullen, P. M. (1983). Preventive interventions for families of divorce: The divorce adjustment project. In L. A. Kurdek (Ed.), *Children and divorce: New directions for child development* (pp. 71–82). San Francisco: Jossey-Bass.

Stolberg, A. L., & Garrison, K. M. (1985). Evaluating a primary prevention program for children of divorce. *American Journal of Community Psychology, 13*(2), 111–124.

Stott, M. W. R., Gaier, E. L., & Thomas, K. B. (1984). Supervised access: A judicial alternative to noncompliance with visitation arrangements following divorce. *Children and Youth Services, 6,* 207–217.

Stuart, R. B., & Jacobson, B. (1986/1987). Principles of divorce mediation: A social learning theory approach. *Mediation Quarterly, 14/15,* 71–85.

Stull, D. E., & Kaplan, N. M. (1987). The positive impact of divorce mediation on children's behavior. *Mediation Quarterly, 18,* 53–59.

Suarez, J. M., Weston, N. L., & Hartstein, N. B. (1978). Mental health interventions in divorce proceedings. *American Journal of Orthopsychiatry, 48,* 273–283.

Tedder, S. L., Scherman, A., & Wantz, R. A. (1987). Effectiveness of a support group for children of divorce. *Elementary School Guidance and Counseling, 22*(2), 102–109.

Tessman, L. (1978). *Children of parting parents.* New York: Aronson.

Teyber, E., & Hoffman, C. D. (1987). Missing fathers. *Psychology Today, 21*(4), 36–43.

Thies, J. M. (1977). Beyond divorce: The impact of remarriage on children. *Journal of Clinical Child Psychology, 6*(2), 59–61.

Thomas, A., & Chess, S. (1984). Genesis and evolution of behavioral disorders: From infancy to early adult life. *American Journal of Psychiatry, 141*(1), 1–9.

Thomson, H. (1966). *The successful stepparent.* New York: Harper & Row.

Tierney, C. W. (1983). *Visitation patterns and adjustment of preschool children of divorce.* Unpublished doctoral dissertation, University of Colorado, Boulder.

Toomin, M. K. (1974). The child of divorce. In R. E. Hardy & J. G. Cull (Eds.), *Therapeutic needs of the family* (pp. 56–90). Springfield, IL: C. C. Thomas.

Tschann, J. M., Johnston, J. R., Kline, M., & Wallerstein, J. S. (1989). Family process and children's functioning during divorce. *Journal of Marriage and the Family, 51,* 431–444.

Tulloch, J. D. (1976, May). *Visitation: A view from the couch.* Paper presented at the conference entitled Divorce, Children, Attorneys, and Clinicians, sponsored by the Interdisciplinary Committee on Child Custody and the Continuing Legal Education in Colorado, Inc., Denver, CO.

Turner, J. R. (1984). Divorced fathers who win contested custody of their children: An exploratory study. *American Journal of Orthopsychiatry, 54,* 498–501.

Uniform Marriage and Divorce Act. (1970). Chicago, IL: National Conference of Commissioners on Uniform State Laws.

Vanderkool, L., & Pearson, J. (1983). Mediating divorce disputes: Mediator behaviors, styles and roles. *Family Relations, 32,* 1–10.

Vaughn, B., Gove, F., & Egeland, B. (1980). The relationship between out-of-home care and the quality of infant–mother attachment in an economically deprived population. *Child Development, 51,* 1203–1214.

Vess, J. D., Schwebel, A. I., & Moreland, J. (1983). The effects of early parental divorce on the sex role development of college students. *Journal of Divorce, 7*(1), 83–95.

Viorst, J. (1975a). *Rosie and Michael.* New York: Random.

Viorst, J. (1975b). *The tenth good thing about Barney.* New York: Atheneum.

Visher, E. B., & Visher, J. S. (1978). Common problems of stepparents and their spouses. *American Journal of Orthopsychiatry, 48,* 252–262.

Visher, E. B., & Visher, J. S. (1979). *Step-families: A guide to working with stepparents and stepchildren.* New York: Bruner/Mazel.

Visher, E. B., & Visher, J. S. (1988). *Old loyalties, new ties: Therapeutic strategies with stepfamilies.* New York: Brunner/Mazel.

Visher, E. B., & Visher, J. S. (1989). Parenting coalitions after remarriage: Dynamics and therapeutic guidelines. *Family Relations, 38,* 65–70.

Volgy, S. S., & Everett, C. A. (1985). Joint custody reconsidered: Systemic criteria for mediation. *Journal of Divorce, 8*(3/4), 131–150.

Walker, K. N., Rogers, J., & Messinger, L. (1977). Remarriage after divorce: A review. *Social Casework, 58,* 276–285.

Walker, L., Brown, H., Crohn, H., Rodstein, E., Zeisel, E., & Sager, C. J. (1979). An annotated bibliography of the remarried, the living together, and their children. *Family Process, 18,* 193–212.

Wallerstein, J. S. (1984). Children of divorce: Preliminary report of a ten-year follow-up of young children. *American Journal of Orthopsychiatry, 54,* 444–458.

Wallerstein, J. S. (1985). Children of divorce: Preliminary report of a ten year follow-up of older children and adolescents. *Journal of the American Academy of Child Psychiatry, 24,* 545–553.

Wallerstein, J. S. (1986/1987). Psychodynamic perspectives on family mediation. *Mediation Quarterly, 14/15,* 7–21.

Wallerstein, J. S. (1987). Children of divorce: Report of a ten-year follow-up of early latency-age children. *American Journal of Orthopsychiatry, 57,* 199–211.

Wallerstein, J. S., & Blakeslee, S. (1989). *Second chances: Men, women and children a decade after divorce.* New York: Tichnor & Fields.

Wallerstein, J. S., & Corbin, S. B. (1989). Daughters of divorce: Report of a ten-year follow-up. *American Journal of Orthopsychiatry, 59,* 593–604.

Wallerstein, J. S., Corbin, S. B., & Lewis, J. M. (1988). Children of divorce: A ten-year study. In E. M. Hetherington & J. D. Arasteh (Eds.), *Impact of divorce, single parenting, and stepparenting on children.* Hillsdale, NJ: Erlbaum.

Wallerstein, J. S. & Kelly, J. B. (1974a). The effects of parental divorce: The adolescent experience. In E. J. Anthony & C. Koupernik (Eds.) *The child in his family: Children at psychiatric risk* (479–505). New York: John Wiley.

Wallerstein, J. S., & Kelly, J. B. (1974b). Responses of the preschool child to divorce: Those who cope. In M. F. McMillan & S. Henao (Eds.), *Child psychiatry: Treatment and research.* New York: Brunner/Mazel.

Wallerstein, J. S., & Kelly, J. B. (1975). The effects of parental divorce: Experiences of the pre-school child. *Journal of the American Academy of Child Psychiatry, 14,* 600–616.

Wallerstein, J. S., & Kelly, J. B. (1976a). The effects of parental divorce: Experiences of the child in early latency. *American Journal of Orthopsychiatry, 46,* 20–32.

Wallerstein, J. S., & Kelly, J. B. (1976b). The effects of parental divorce: Experiences of the child in later latency. *American Journal of Orthopsychiatry, 46,* 256–269.

Wallerstein, J. S. & Kelly, J. B. (1977). Divorce counseling: A community service for families in the midst of divorce. *American Journal of Orthopsychiatry, 47,* 4–22.

Wallerstein, J. S., & Kelly, J. B. (1980a). Effects of divorce on the visiting father–child relationship. *American Journal of Psychiatry, 137,* 1534–1539.

Wallerstein, J. S., & Kelly, J. B. (1980b). *Surviving the breakup: How children and parents cope with divorce.* New York: Basic Books.

Walsh, P. E., & Stolberg, A. L. (1988/1989). Parental and environmental determinants of children's behavioral, affective and cognitive adjustment to divorce. *Journal of Divorce, 12*(2/3), 265–282.

Warren, N. J., Ilgen, E. R., Van Bourgondien, M. E., Konanc, J. T., Grew, R. S., & Amara, I. A. (1986). Children of divorce: The question of clinically significant problems. *Journal of Divorce, 10*(1/2), 87–106.

Warshak, R. A. (1987). Father-custody families: Therapeutic goals and strategies. *The Family Therapy Collections, 23,* 101–124.

Warshak, R. A., & Santrock, J. W. (1983a). Children of divorce: Impact of custody disposition on social development. In E. J. Callahan & K. A. McCluskey (Eds.),

Life-span developmental psychology: Nonnormative life events (pp. 241–263). New York: Academic Press.

Warshak, R. A., & Santrock, J. W. (1983b). The impact of divorce in father-custody and mother-custody homes: The child's perspective. In L. A. Kurdek (Ed.), *Children and divorce: New directions for child development* (No. 19) (pp. 29–46). San Francisco: Jossey-Bass.

Waters, B., & Dimock, J. (1983). A review of research relevant to custody and access disputes. *Australian and New Zealand Journal of Psychiatry, 17,* 181–189.

Webster-Stratton, C. (1989). The relationship of marital support, conflict and divorce to parent perceptions, behaviors and childhood conduct problems. *Journal of Marriage and the Family, 51,* 417–430.

Weisfeld, D., & Laser, M. S. (1977). Divorced parents in family therapy in a residential treatment setting. *Family Process, 16,* 229–236.

Weiss, R. S. (1979). Issues in the adjudication of custody when parents separate. In G. Levinger & O. C. Moles (Eds.), *Divorce and separation: Context, causes, and consequences* (pp. 324–336). New York: Basic Books.

Weiss, R. S. (1984). The impact of marital dissolution on income and consumption in single-parent households. *Journal of Marriage and the Family, 46,* 115–127.

Weithorn, L. A. (1987). Psychological consultation in divorce custody litigation: Ethical considerations. In L. A. Weithorn (Ed.), *Psychology and child custody determinations* (pp. 182–209). Lincoln: University of Nebraska Press.

Weithorn, L. A., & Grisso, T. (1987). Psychological evaluations in divorce custody: Problems, principles, and procedures. In L. A. Weithorn (Ed.), *Psychology and child custody determinations* (pp. 157–181). Lincoln: University of Nebraska Press.

Whiteside, M. F., & Auerbach, L. (1978). Can the daughter of my father's new wife be my sister? Families of remarriage in family therapy. *Journal of Divorce, 1,* 271–283.

Wilkinson, G. S., & Bleck, R. T. (1977). Children's divorce groups. *Elementary School Guidance and Counseling, 11,* 205–213.

Wilks, C., & Melville, C. (1990). Grandparents in custody and access disputes. *Journal of Divorce, 13*(3), 1–14.

Wilson, K. L., Zurcher, L., MacAdams, D. C., & Curtis, R. L. (1975). Stepfathers and step-children: An exploratory analysis from two national surveys. *Journal of Marriage and the Family, 37,* 526–536.

Winnicott, D. W. (1971). *Therapeutic consultations in child psychiatry.* New York: Basic Books.

Wolchik, S. A., Braver, S. L., & Sandler, I. N. (1985). Maternal versus joint custody: Children's postseparation experiences and adjustment. *Journal of Clinical Child Psychology, 14*(1), 5–10.

Woody, R. H. (1977). Behavioral science criteria in child custody determinations. *Journal of Marriage and Family Counseling, 3*(1), 11–17.

Wyman, P. A., Cowen, E. L., Hightower, A. D., & Pedro-Carroll, J. L. (1985). Perceived competence, self-esteem, and anxiety in latency-aged children of divorce. *Journal of Clinical Child Psychology, 14*(1), 20–26.

Young, D. M. (1980). A court-mandated workshop for adolescent children of divorcing parents: A program evaluation. *Adolescence, 15,* 763–774.

Zakariya, S. B. (1982). Another look at the children of divorce: Summary report of the study of school needs of one-parent children. *Principal, 62*(1), 34–37.

Zaslow, M. J. (1988). Sex differences in children's response to parental divorce: 1. Research methodology and postdivorce family forms. *American Journal of Orthopsychiatry, 58,* 355–378.

Zaslow, M. J. (1989). Sex differences in children's response to parental divorce: 2. Samples, variables, ages, and sources. *American Journal of Orthopsychiatry, 58,* 118–141.

Zastowny, T. R., & Lewis, J. L. (1989). Family interactional patterns and social support systems in single-parent families. *Journal of Divorce, 13*(2), 1–40.

Author Index

Subject Index